THE ECONOMIC THEORY
OF
'MANAGERIAL' CAPITALISM

BY

ROBIN MARRIS
FELLOW OF KING'S COLLEGE, CAMBRIDGE

THE FREE PRESS OF GLENCOE

658.018
M359

First Published in the United States 1964 by
THE FREE PRESS OF GLENCOE

For Information, address:
THE FREE PRESS OF GLENCOE
A DIVISION OF THE MACMILLAN COMPANY
THE CROWELL-COLLIER PUBLISHING COMPANY
60 FIFTH AVENUE, NEW YORK 11

Library of Congress catalogue number: 64-10371

To
JANE

CONTENTS

CHAPTER   PAGE

INTRODUCTION AND PREFACE   xi

NOTE ON CONCEPTS AND DEFINITIONS   xv

1. THE INSTITUTIONAL FRAMEWORK   1

The Disappearance of the Entrepreneur. The Traditional
Pre-History of a Corporation. The Corporate Collective.
The Influence of the Stock Market. A Theory of Take-
Over. The Concept of Sustainable Growth. Growth which
is both Sustainable and Safe. 'Managerial' Take-Over and
the Constrained Valuation Ratio.

2. MOTIVES AND MORALS   46

Introduction and Survey of the Chapter. Theories of
Motivation. Psychological Motives. Sociological Motives.
A Norm of Professional Competence. Economic Motives.
An Analysis of Bonus Schemes. Stock-Option Plans.
Basic Compensation. The Simon Theory. Policy Implica-
tions of a 'Bureconic' Theory. Generalisation of the Growth
Motive. A Managerial Utility System. Maximising,
Satisficing and Behaviourism.

3. CONCEPTS AND METHODS   110

Characterisation of the Firm. The Internal Restraint on the
Growth-Rate. The Concept of Balanced or Sustainable
Growth. The Role of Diversification. The Role of
Merger. The Economic Environment. Methods of Analysis.
Further Definitions.

4. 'DEMAND'   133

The Consumer and His Brain. The Process of Want
Creation. The Pioneering Consumer. The Chain Reaction.
Socio-Economic Structure. Social Barriers and Social Bars.
Chain Reactions in Intermediate Products. A Mathematical
Model of the Socio-Economic Structure. The Conditions
for Criticality. Growth and Profitability. A Probabilistic
Model. Growth by Imitation. The Bandwaggon Strategy.
Static Markets. General Implications of Imitative Strategy.
Non-Diversifying Growth. Empirical Support. Glossary of
Symbols.

vii

CHAPTER | PAGE

5. 'SUPPLY' — 204

Outline of the Problem. The Basic Equation. Maximising Procedure, First Stage. New Issues, Retentions and Market Valuation. Theories of Asset Holding. Maximising, Second Stage. Effects of a Variable Constraint. Econometric Support.

6. COMPLETED MICRO-MODELS — 224

Model 1: Policy Model for Growth-Rate Maximisation Subject to Minimum Security Constraint. Diagrammatic Analysis. A Mathematical Version. Economic Implications. Model 2: Preliminary Account. The Valuation Curve. Economic Interpretation. Maximising Managerial Utility.

7. BEHAVIOUR AND EVIDENCE — 266

Satisficing and All That. Econometric Support.

8. POSSIBLE MACRO IMPLICATIONS — 289

Working Assumptions. The Aggregate Retention Ratio. Natural and Quasi-Natural Rates of Growth. Inflexible Growth Rate and Fully Restricted Thrift. Inflexible Growth Rate, Thriftiness partly Restricted. A Flexible-Growth Model.

NOTES — 311

LIST OF REFERENCES — 325

INDEX — 331

LIST OF EQUATIONS (other than Chapter 4) — 341

GLOSSARY OF SYMBOLS (other than Chapter 4) — 347

LIST OF ILLUSTRATIONS

DIAGRAMS

PAGE

1.1 Boundary of Safe Policies with Negative Return Discrepancy   38

1.2 Safe and Sustainable Policies   43

2.1 Standard Organisational Pyramid with Constant Span of Control   94

4.1 Primary Groups in a Linear Suburb   152

4.2 Net-Like Structure of Primary Groups   153

4.3 Demand Curve for a Saturated Product   178

6.1 Family of Demand-Growth Curves   238

6.2 Internal-Efficiency Relation   238

6.3 Family of Finance-Supply Curves   240

6.4 Balanced-Growth Curve   240

6.5 Demand Curve and Iso-Valuation Line   252

6.6 Valuation Curve and Managerial Indifference Curve   255

TABLES

6.1 Characteristic Magnitudes of Coefficients in Mathematical Version of Model 1   243

6.2 Summary of Qualitative Relationships in Model 1   245

6.3 Typical Results in Model 1   245

6.4 Values of Variables at Various Positions on Demand Curve and Valuation Curve   257

7.1 Summary of Predictions for Various Disturbance Types   280

7.2 Meyer and Kuh Correlation Patterns   283

7.3 Signs and Magnitudes of Correlation Coefficients in Myron Gordon Data   284

INTRODUCTION AND PREFACE

THIS essay was inspired by a growing sense of frustration at the divorce between the motivational axioms employed in the established micro-economic theories and the type of behaviour most believe to be real. We drill our students in analytical exercises based on these theories. We warn them not to believe the assumptions, but offer only incompletely developed alternatives. By the same token applied research is weakened.

Yet ever since the publication of 'Berle and Means' most of the profession has recognised the existence of some kind of 'managerial' capitalism based on separation of ownership from control. Some have argued that in practice this system behaves little differently from 'traditional' capitalism. Others have asserted the opposite. And recently one or two writers have suggested plausible models based on more appropriate assumptions. So far, however, such models have not been worked out in great detail or integrated into comprehensive theories of the firm.

We therefore feel justified in attempting to carry the development a stage further. We start from the proposition that corporate directors may subject corporate policy decisions to utility functions of their own. We ask after the probable nature of the resulting preference system, given the character of the institutional environment and the nature of the managerial task. We also consider the extent to which the environment will permit such preferences to count. These foundations are then employed in an attempt to reconstruct the 'internal' theory of the firm.

A summary of one of the resulting models appeared in the *Quarterly Journal of Economics* in May 1963, but the reader is warned that the author's ideas have developed considerably since that paper was written. In this book, the first two chapters discuss the inter-relationship between institutional framework and utility system, always against the background of the existence of an organised market for corporate securities. The third chapter relates the results of the first two to the conventional economic environment, defines concepts and explains the analytical methods to be employed later. The next three chapters work out two specific micro-models, which at the end of the sixth are more or less integrated into a single final model. Chapter 7 attempts to apply the models to real behaviour, taking account of known statistical evidence. Finally, Chapter 8 ventures to speculate about possible macro-implications.

On the empirical side we have drawn heavily from existing material, both qualitative and econometric. We also deploy the results of some limited experiments of our own. But the main weight of testing must await the results of a substantial programme of research based on the analysis of ten years of data derived from the accounts of all British quoted companies, which is currently in progress at the Cambridge University Department of Applied Economics. We make no apology whatsoever for publishing the theory in advance.

So many people on both sides of the Atlantic have contributed criticism and advice that it is difficult to guarantee that acknowledgements will be adequately comprehensive. A significant debt is owed at least to all of the following economists and associated institutions:

Kenneth Arrow, A. K. Bagchi, Lee Bawden, William Baumol, Alan Brown, Robert Dorfman, James Duesenberry, Christopher Farrow, Sargent Florence, Gordon Fisher, Aaron Gordon, Frank Hahn, P. E. Hart, Benjamin Higgins, Herschel Kanter, Carl Kaysen, Richard Kahn, Nicholas Kaldor, Harvey Leibenstein, John Lintner, Siro Lombardini, Fritz Machlup, Julius Margolis, John Meyer, Luigi Pasinetti, Michael Posner, Jack Revell, Joan Robinson, Janet Rothenberg, Richard Ruggles, Eugene Rostow, David Snell and Peter Wiles; members of the staff seminar of the Economics Department, University of Texas, fall 1960; members of the author's graduate classes at Berkeley in 1961; seminarists at Harvard, Princeton, Texas A & M, UCLA and Yale in 1960 and 1961; a group of economists in Cambridge, England; The Institute of Business and Economic Research at Berkeley. Mrs. Robinson, however, must be singled out for especial thanks. She has given constant support, encouragement and constructive criticism, and her recent thinking has almost certainly had a considerable influence on the author's.

Another name for special mention is that of Ajit Singh. Acting as the author's assistant, first in Berkeley and later in Cambridge, he not only carried out the econometric work described in Chapter 2, but also read the whole final manuscript, corrected many errors and revised certain passages. The author is greatly in his debt for most efficient and perceptive advice.

Among persons associated with disciplines other than economics, we should mention Noel Annan, John Goldthorpe and Bill Wedderburn. Dr. Goldthorpe's sociological contribution, which resulted from a collaboration between himself and the author in a course of lectures given in Cambridge, was particularly important, as will be apparent to any reader who gets as far as Chapter 2.

Appreciation should also be expressed to the Fulbright Commission and to the Departments of Economics at the Universities of Texas and California (at Berkeley) for facilitating the author's visit to the U.S. in 1960 and thus materially assisting in the research. To the then Chairman of the former Department, Ben Higgins, thanks are due for advice, encouragement and the provision of captive audiences; to the then Chairman of the latter, Aaron Gordon, thanks are due not only for giving the benefit of his very considerable experience in this field, but also for lending his substantial stock of research material connected with the Preface to the 1961 edition of *Business Leadership*.

Finally, if the book is readable, this is entirely the responsibility of the author's wife, who being, unlike himself, literate, has struggled womanfully over a long period to improve the prose. What more could a man ask?

NOTE ON CONCEPTS AND
DEFINITIONS

THE concepts and symbols used in this book are usually defined in the text only once, where they first appear, but a glossary is provided on page 347. Here, by way of introduction, we describe the general method of notation and also name and define some basic accounting conventions. These methods and conventions are not explained in the text and the reader is recommended to study them before starting the first chapter.

Symbols

In general we use upper case English letters for original variables, lower case English letters for ratios. The Greek letters, α, β, γ, etc. are used for coefficients, π, ρ, σ, etc. for special variables and the symbols δ and f for the usual operators. (The letter d, however, is needed for a nominative symbol.) With the exception of coefficients, which may change definition between models, a symbol usually holds its basic meaning throughout the book, subject only to small modifications indicated in context.

An exception to the foregoing is found in the treatment of empirical regression equations: for these we use the standard notation, Y signifying the dependent variable, a the constant, X_1, X_2, etc., the determining variables and b_1, b_2, etc., the corresponding regression coefficients obtained by the method of least-squares; we also adopt the usual procedure of indicating the standard error of a regression coefficient by $\mp$ following the estimate; then t is the ratio of estimate to standard error and R is the multiple correlation coefficient. Outside the context of a regression model these symbols may be used for other purposes (e.g. t may stand for time and R stands for an accounting concept mentioned below).

Another exception is found in the notation of Chapter 4 ('Demand'). This is entirely separate from the rest and symbols used elsewhere may here be used quite differently. A special glossary is provided at the end of the chapter.

As already indicated, a glossary of frequently recurring symbols other than those used in Chapter 4 is provided on the last page, after the index. We also provide a list of equations, in order of occurrence, each equation being restated with an indication of the page on which it first appeared. .

Operators

In addition to those mentioned above, three other operators are employed, one relating to constraints, one to optimum values and one to growth rates, apologies being due for the last which is unconventional.

(i) *Constraints:* a bar placed over a symbol signifies a constrained maximum or minimum value of the corresponding variable according to context.

(ii) *Optimum Values:* an asterisk placed to the side of a symbol signifies the maximum value subject to constraints or other conditions specified; an asterisk so placed when associated with a bracketed suffix, however, signifies the value of this variable required to maximise another variable indicated in the suffix.

(iii) *Growth rates:* A dot placed *above and to the right* of a symbol signifies a *proportional* time rate of change. More precisely,

$$X^{\cdot} = \frac{d \log X}{dt}$$

and hence $X^{*\cdot}$ indicates maximum $X^{\cdot}$ or, loosely, maximum growth rate. The Newtonian operator, with dot placed directly above the symbol, is not employed, and in the rare cases where we have need of dx/dt, this is printed in full.

Numbering

'Equations' (i.e. any formulae containing equalities, inequalities or both), and also diagrams, are numbered by chapters on the Dewey system, footnotes (printed at the end of the book) by chapters in the ordinary manner.

Accounting Conventions

The following conventions and definitions relate to individual joint stock companies whose securities are quoted on a recognised Exchange, in other words to the basic subjects of our enquiry.

Book Value: the original cost of an asset, less the proportion of original value deemed by the firm's accountants to have been lost through depreciation, adjusted for any change in the supply price of assets of this technical description and performance which may have occurred since it was installed. It should be noted that the concept is employed primarily to measure physical capacity.

Gross Assets: Fixed Assets at Book Value (see above), Inventory, Securities at market value, Cash and Net Trade Credit (Symbol: C; the concept is also loosely referred to as 'capital', 'capital employed', 'corporate capital', or simply 'book value').

Debt: Debentures, par value of cumulative non-voting preference shares and net short-term liabilities. (No symbol, but ratio of debt, less liquid assets, to gross assets, called the 'leverage' or 'gearing' ratio, is signified by g.)

Net Assets: Gross Assets less Debt (no symbol).

Liquid Assets: Securities, plus cash in excess of minimum working balance (no symbol).

Productive Assets: Gross Assets less Liquid Assets (no symbol). It should be noted that, as defined, the concept includes not only book value of fixed assets but also other non-fixed assets normally required for trading activity, such as minimum cash, inventory and credit to customers. Hence, given the method of valuation, so long as their technical character and supply price are constant, variations in the magnitude of productive assets may be regarded as synonymous with variations in productive capacity.

Profits: Trading profits net of depreciation and tax, plus non-trading income net of tax (Symbol: P). The appropriate tax deduction depends on the method of taxing companies in the country concerned, but in principle should not include elements of personal income tax being collected at source. In the U.K. the deduction would therefore be income tax on undistributed profits plus Profits Tax, in the U.S. it would be corporate profits tax only.

Internal Rate of Return: the ratio of Profits to Gross Assets (Symbol: p; concept is also referred to as rate of profit or rate of return).

Earnings: Profits less interest on debt and dividends on preference shares included in debt (no symbol).

Retained Earnings: Earnings less Dividends on Ordinary Stock and any other shares not included in debt.

Retention Ratio: Ratio of Retained Earnings to Earnings (Symbol: r).

Net rate of return: ratio of Earnings to Net Assets (Symbol: p').

Par Value: Aggregate par value of all issued securities not included in Debt (Symbol: N).

Market Value: Aggregate of all issued securities not included in debt, valued, except where otherwise indicated, at the current market quotation (no symbol, but ratio of Market Value to Net Assets, called the 'valuation ratio', is signified by v).

CHAPTER ONE

THE INSTITUTIONAL FRAMEWORK

'Two forms of property appear, one above the other, related but
not the same. At the bottom is the physical property itself, still
immobile, still there, still demanding the service of human beings,
managers and operators. Related to this is a set of tokens, passing
from hand to hand, liquid to a degree, requiring little or no human
attention, which attain an actual value in exchange or market price
only in part dependent on the underlying property. . . . A first-rate
manager would not increase the values of the properties were they
to be sold; but he will increase the value of tokens representing
that property. A poor management will have the opposite result.'
— Berle and Means [1]

The Disappearance of the Entrepreneur

'Managerial' capitalism is a name for the economic system of
North America and Western Europe in the mid-twentieth century,
a system in which production is concentrated in the hands of large
joint-stock companies. In many sectors of economic activity the
classical entrepreneur has virtually disappeared. His rôle was essentially active and unitary; once dismembered, no device of collective
abstraction could put him together again. As a result (so a substantial body of writers have suggested), [2] entrepreneurship in the
modern corporation has been taken over by transcendent management, whose functions differ in kind from those of the traditional
subordinate or 'mere manager'. These people, it is argued, can
wield considerable power without necessarily holding equity,
sharing profits or carrying risks.

Of course, there never was a managerial revolution. Like the
industrial revolution, the development from traditional capitalism
to the contemporary form represented the slow replacement of one
type of economic organisation by another, a process which has not
yet ended. The nature of the result is by no means obvious and
indeed puzzles even Marxists. Human societies, however, rarely
arrange their institutions of production with the rules of behaviour,
as seen from the economist's view-point, fully specified. In tradi-

tional capitalism, the decision-taker has private-property rights over his instruments. He has the rights of exclusive use and enjoyment subject only to certain limited restraints on his freedom to damage others. (He may burn the factory, but must ensure that the workers have left, and must not negligently allow the fire to spread to his neighbour's property.) There is also the implicit 'rule' that a capitalist who makes continuing losses will eventually cease to be a capitalist: both financially and morally he is encouraged to aim for profit. But how much profit is not stated.

A similar ambiguity applies to the directors of the modern corporation: in law they owe a duty to the shareholders, but its extent is not defined. Directors who refuse to *maximise* profits because, for example, they pay attention to competing social interests such as those of employees, cannot legally be penalised: indeed they are likely to be popular. And the position is not very different in the socialist forms of managerial society. The manager of an industrial plant under Communism is given specific instructions, usually consisting of quantitative production targets which it may literally cost him his life to ignore, but the rules as a whole, when examined, commonly prove quite inadequate to define the implied system of national resource allocation. The significant difference between managerial capitalism and managerial socialism lies less in the character of the rules of the game than in who sets them. In socialism, the rules are set by political government. In capitalism, they emerge indirectly from a body of law and custom, founded on the concepts of private property and slowly developed.

Because they are so rudimentary, they tell us little about the game. Implicitly, they define a field (the economy), some players (producers and consumers) and some balls (goods and money). Violence to other players (theft) is illegal; certain coalitions (companies) are permitted if approved by the referee, others (combinations in restraint of trade) are not. But as to goals we know strangely little. We may perhaps infer that a player who has no ball under his control for more than a certain period is eliminated (starves), and there are reasons for believing that other things being equal players will prefer more time with the ball than less, but we know little of their views about ball-holding by others. If coalitions are formed, we do not know how these will behave — what goals, if any, they will set themselves, how they will determine the interior distribution of any utility they may acquire. To date, most theories of capitalism have proceeded on particular simplifying assumptions about these questions, many of which now seem doubtful when applied to the special type of coalition represented in the modern corporation. In order to see why this is so, it is necessary to begin by re-examining the traditional system.

The essence of the traditional method of economic organisation is the unification of the functions of risk-carrying, reward-receiving and operational decision-taking in one individual. By combining ownership with management, the person who carries much of the risk also makes most of the decisions determining its extent. As owner he receives the rewards of success, and is therefore motivated to optimise the balance between boldness and prudence. Economic theory has often overlooked this inter-dependence between risk and organisation. Risk is seen as arising mainly from exogenous uncertainty, for example, from uncertainty concerning the future demand for the product of a particular asset. The shape of the resulting probability-distribution of returns is therefore outside the control of any one within the firm. Risk-taking, in this concept, consists only in choosing between lists of projects, with given, unalterable probability-distributions. Real commercial life is much more flexible. If the demand for one product turns out badly, a nimble decision-taker may restore his position by changing the line of production or at least he may minimise losses by timely retrenchment. A slow decision-taker, on the other hand, may fall into a vicious spiral of financial decline; by acting too late he incurs losses inducing actions causing further losses, and so on. Thus the probability-distribution of financial results is not only differently shaped from the exogenous parent distribution (because in the latter, disturbances are independent, in the former not), but also depends intimately on decision-taking skill and will-power. It is difficult for an outsider to assess the ability and integrity of a particular professional manager or team. The assessment itself involves considerable uncertainty and represents perhaps the greater part of the risk of an investment. As such, it must be paid for. By contrast, an individual entrepreneur carrying his own risks considerably reduces this uncertainty, at least subjectively. He believes he knows his own ability and he appreciates a continuous discipline to do his best. Therefore, by combining risk-taking with decision-taking, traditional capitalism reduces the cost of the former while increasing the efficiency of the latter. That is why there is still quite an amount of it about.

The offsetting disadvantage, of course, is that owner-management imposes severe restraints on scale, restraints deriving not only from difficulties of delegation but also from the inevitable emphasis on internal financing and consequent restriction on the firm's rate of growth. Important economies may therefore remain unexploited. It was to overcome these disadvantages that the social architects of the nineteenth century invented the public, joint-stock, limited liability company, and thus invented modern capitalism. In that complex and somewhat peculiar institution, the managerial restraint on scale was overcome by resort to collective ownership and delegated control, while the financial restraint was handled by the issue of marketable shares carrying limited liability.

In England, where the invention occurred, it was greeted by considerable public criticism, so effective for a time that the necessary legislation was delayed for several decades.[3] The critics realised that a major change was involved. They saw the advantages of owner-management being lost; they could not see the advantages to be gained because they did not believe in large-scale organisation.[4] Nevertheless, as everyone knows, the public joint-stock company arrived, prospered and multiplied, until, by the mid-twentieth century, not only was an overwhelming proportion of the national income in Britain and North America produced by companies,[5] but the greater part came from firms of the type in which shareholders were numerous and their holding dispersed.[6]

In effect, then, we now have an economic system in which the traditional and the corporate methods are legally and economically permitted to co-exist, and in which each may predominate where its relative advantages are greatest. But it is by no means necessary that in order to survive both types of firm must adopt the same internal rules of behaviour; either or both, for example, may well dispense with profit maximisation. This is not only because the relative advantages of the one or the other are in some areas so overwhelming that differences in behaviour are easily offset, but also because the competitive environment has been made highly imperfect. Once large-scale organisations appear, they have the capacity to mould the environment in directions convenient to themselves, and whether they are profit maximisers, other maximisers or 'satisficers', [7] they soon find that, rather than competing perfectly in a given environment, it is better to strive to create conditions of monopoly, monopolistic competition or oligopoly. In practice, in the sectors where corporations prevail, the predominant condition is oligopoly.

Economic theory struggled manfully with the 'external' conditions of oligopoly, but persistently refused to attempt to penetrate deeper. Until very recently almost all 'micro' analysis implicitly regarded the corporation as a form of collective entrepreneurship, to be treated in much the same way as the one-man business, and nearly twenty years elapsed between the discovery of the managerial evolution and the appearance of related theories of the firm. [8]

A particularly serious consequence of the refusal of economic analysis to 'go behind' these assumptions has been a failure to consider whether the assumed behaviour of *organisations*, such as companies, could logically be expected to arise from rational behaviour by their members, even when rational behaviour is confined to more or less orthodox utility maximisation. [9] A man's utility system is the result of his social situation, of the society around him and of the way it has moulded his psyche. But his social situation depends in turn on economic organisation. (The conventional separation of economic and social theory was false from birth.) For example, it is by no means obvious that action intended to maximise the utility of a company's stockholders is consistent with maximising the utility of the action-takers, i.e. of the management.

The Traditional Pre-History of a Corporation

Most large companies have grown out of smaller businesses of a more or less traditional type. For the moment, however, let us postulate a situation in which, when new economic activities are to be organised, there is a straight choice between the one or the other form only. Given that a man has noticed an opportunity for profit, how should he decide between a traditional business and floating a company? If he proceeds traditionally, he must have access to initial capital, and he must be prepared to carry a high proportion of the risk. [10] He will receive the whole income from both management and risk-taking, will have absolute right to dispose of that income, and will have absolute and unquestioned control. But the income, the wealth and the empire of power will be constrained by the scale limitations of traditional organisation. If on the other hand a company is floated, some of the constraints are lifted, while the founder is yet able to secure for himself an important position as manager, chairman, or president. This may provide him with prospects of both financial and 'psychological' rewards. But unless he has put up more than half the capital (in which case the organisation can be regarded as effectively more or less traditional) none of these positions is absolutely guaranteed. Each depends on the consent of others and also, in principle, on the service he has to sell, as, for example, special knowledge of the trade. [11] His income will be a salary determined by complex factors by no means entirely under his control. [12] But to the extent that the larger-scale organisation is more efficient, the income prospects may be better than the profit prospects of the traditional organisation; in some ways more risky, in some ways more secure. We might say that, in general, as compared with the pure entrepreneur, the pure manager is safer on capital account, while on balance little less secure on income account. But his total satisfaction will depend also on non-financial considerations, such as his personal evaluation of the relative merits of the two types of rôle. A manager is a different type of person from an entrepreneur, with different ideals and different personal values. A man might prefer flotation then, if he liked a salaried status, if he had little capital to invest, and if the advantages of large-scale organisation were considerable. In other words, taking all things into account, in some circumstances pure flotation might mean greater utility.

But in practice, whatever might be preferred, wherever exploitation of the economic opportunity requires the development of a significant amount of organisation, as is usual, for example, in manufacturing industry, pure flotation is rarely practicable. Investors are not readily induced to subscribe to the shares of an as yet non-existent organisation. The overwhelming proportion of operations involving the formation of new public companies represents re-organisation of traditional enterprises sufficiently successful to command confidence and now attempting to break through their constraints. Let us consider the process of growth which occurred before this point was reached.

Suppose, for the sake of argument, that previous growth has not been limited by demand: either demand exceeds capacity or the entrepreneur knows how to develop new markets when old ones are saturated. His constraints are thus mainly managerial and financial. The management problem has been widely discussed in orthodox literature, and arises essentially from the difficulties of delegation and co-ordination in an organisation originally designed for one-man control. This has usually been regarded as a limit on absolute size rather than on the rate of growth. The financial constraint, on the other hand (which has been less discussed) apparently limits only the rate of growth. For finance to limit ultimate size, special assumptions are required.

If a traditional capitalist firm does not borrow, it can grow no faster than the rate of net profit (after tax, depreciation and 'subsistence' for the entrepreneur) earned on capital employed, and the growth of the owner's wealth and of the firm's assets are synonymous. If, however, borrowing is allowed and is practised, the rate of growth of the size of the firm, measured by capital employed, is no longer necessarily the same as the growth rate of the entrepreneurial property. But provided the profit rate exceeds the interest rate, both can grow faster than the maximum possible when borrowing is not allowed, because the annual difference between profit and interest may be used as a source of capital for further reinvestment. Therefore, whether he derives utility from his own wealth, from the size of the firm or from both, it appears at first sight that rational behaviour requires the traditional capitalist to borrow as much as he can. At second sight, the answer is not so simple.

For if at each round of growth more is borrowed than is re-invested from the previous period's profits, the ratio of borrowed to re-invested money in the capital structure will steadily rise; in effect the firm will become increasingly 'levered', or, in British terminology, 'geared'. Leverage or gearing increases the risks of both lenders and borrower. Lenders know that as the leverage ratio rises the margin of assets covering their loan must be proportionately reduced: there is increasing danger that in the event of an unexpected decline in earning power the value of assets would become less than liabilities. The borrower (the entrepreneur), on the other hand, is more likely to see the problem in terms of the burden of interest charges against his profits: if profits fall, he is liable to default on payments, and may be forced into liquidation in circumstances where, were it not for the leverage, he would have been able to continue in business. Put more generally, the effect of leverage (for both borrower and lender) is to increase the risk of insolvency for any given probability-distribution of earnings.

If, therefore, it is desired to increase the rate of growth nevertheless, 'non-contractual' borrowing will be necessary. But lenders with no contractual rights to interest nor security for their capital inevitably require a share in ownership and control. They otherwise have no protection from wilful withholding of dividends, refusal to earn profits or negligent inefficiency. It follows that a traditional enterprise cannot grow rapidly by means of indefinitely increasing leverage and still remain traditional.

If for convenience we define a maximum-leverage point (i.e. maximum consistent with retaining the traditional organisation) by reference to some ratio of outstanding debt to book value of total assets (see p. xvii above), the financial constraint on the growth rate of a traditional firm can be made precise. Once the maximum-leverage ratio has been reached, growth is constrained by the need to ensure that at each subsequent round of expansion, the proportionate increase in debt does not exceed the proportionate increase in total capital: if debt is permitted to expand faster, the leverage ratio will again begin to rise. Consequently, the maximum growth rate, measured in terms of the book value of capital, becomes:

$$C^{*\cdot} = p \cdot \left(1 - \frac{i}{p} \cdot \bar{g} \right) \Big/ (1 - \bar{g}) \qquad (1.1)$$

where

$C^{*\cdot}$ = maximum financially permitted growth rate,

p = internal rate of return after deducting tax and entrepreneur's subsistence,

i = average interest rate on debt,

$\bar{g}$ = maximum permitted leverage ratio.

Unless there are sons, sons-in-law or other relatives able to succeed the founder and maintain the rate of profit, the maximum financial size can be determined quite easily if we know the initial capital, know the working life of the founder, and can apply these factors to the formula for the maximum growth rate. If the maximum financial size is smaller than the managerial maximum, the typical history of a firm without a successor (in the absence of the possibility of corporate re-organisation) would be to grow to some size no greater than the financial maximum, and then die. If, however, we assume either that the founder's life is very long or that he can always find efficient successors, there is no maximum financial size. The firm will grow until it reaches its managerial limit; finance will merely have determined the length of time taken to get there. This is probably the more typical case.

The limits on size can be penetrated by changing the structure of the firm. By corporate reorganisation the autocratic figure of the founder is replaced by a management team and the financing problem is eased by acquiring shareholders (although, as we shall see, the financial growth rate of a company is by no means without limit). Thus by 'going public' — a British expression for the conversion of a closed corporation into an open one — traditional enterprises can continue to grow in a new form, and this has been the origin of an overwhelming proportion of established public corporations. The advantages to the *firm* are obvious; less obvious are the advantages to the owner-founder. Before the change, the growth of the enterprise was closely associated with the growth of his personal wealth; after the change, the connection is considerably weakened. Why then does he agree? He may be approaching retirement and seeking a convenient method of realising his gains, a motive which is particularly powerful where taxation discriminates against income. Or he may have concluded that the economies of scale he had been losing were so considerable that co-operation with other people and other capital would on balance increase the growth of the value of his own equity, despite the fact that he would no longer be sole owner. Finally, he may in truth be more interested in promoting the continued growth of the organisation he has founded, for its own sake, even though his personal financial position is not to be significantly improved. The organisation may have become an expression of his ego, and its growth as such may provide direct utility. There is nothing in the rules of traditional capitalism to require an owner-manager to exclude all forms of satisfaction other than money. Where the founder can make arrangements which will guarantee him an important continuing rôle until such time as he chooses to retire, this motive of continuity is particularly likely to be effective, but even where he cannot make such arrangements, the founder may nevertheless obtain pleasure from watching the further development of his 'baby' long after he has ceased to direct it.

R. H. Tawney showed how Protestantism released commerce from ethical restraints on money making; Protestantism was thus associated with capitalism in a two-way relation of cause and effect.[13] Max Weber suggested how the Protestant ethic directly provided a drive for accumulation.[14] This originated in a special aspect of the doctrine of Predestination. Society was divided into the elect and the 'rest', the latter being irrevocably damned. The profits earned by a man in his business were to be regarded as manifestations not of a stochastic process but of the hand of God. Business success could be interpreted as a sign of grace (i.e. of membership of the elect), and if, therefore, God showed one of His elect a good investment opportunity, the beneficiary was duty bound to take it.[15] Combined with the Puritan moral injunction against consumption, [16] the resulting morality implied a continual attempt to maximise profits and to re-invest most of the proceeds. The 'Puritan' was thus a man with an almost unlimited appetite for future wealth and could have been interpreted by economic theory as endowed with a negative rate of time discount. His utility function contained only one variable, and this Divine index was the logarithm of net assets. Of course, if one was not of the elect, nothing was of any use anyway, but, fortunately for society, one did not discover the truth until one died.

It might be possible to re-interpret the motives of traditional business in terms of modern analytic psychology, although, as far as the present author is aware, not much has been done on these lines. Evidently the business drive is sublimated libido, and perhaps the business itself represents a castrated son. The position is more complicated, however, when actual (uncastrated) sons are employed in the enterprise, and intended to inherit it. The psychological conflicts set up in these situations are familiar, and it is often unclear what the father really wants. The usual conclusion of observers is that he would rather his son succeeded in an organisational environment of his own — the father's — making, than that he genuinely made his way in the world, thus demonstrating manliness. *En tout cas*, whether as a sign of grace or to satisfy his ego, the father attaches utility to the continuity of the organisation he has founded, as such, irrespective of the direct financial advantage.

As a matter of fact, most organisations have inherent tendencies to attempt to perpetuate themselves. (17) Even though a traditional capitalist would wish his firm to express no more than himself, the firm itself contains individuals who may feel differently. Thus the baby cannot always be prevented from growing and showing signs of independence, whatever the parent may desire. If the baby succeeds, it is almost certain, sooner or later, to be transformed into a modern corporation, an institution of considerable ambiguity, to which we now turn.

The Corporate Collective

Unlike many human institutions, the legal 'constitution' of a joint-stock company is carefully specified. The law, however, is mainly concerned to protect creditors and investors from obvious fraud, and has done little to push these great productive institutions in any particular economic or social direction. Thus company law represents no more than a special aspect of the general protection of property in the ordinary legal framework of capitalism. But however 'non-economic' the purposes of the corporate constitution, it is the framework within which the game is played and must therefore be taken seriously. A joint-stock company is a legal person intended to engage in trade or business, although it is not compelled to trade and may, in practice, undertake almost any known human activity. This person, which is really a specially defined collective, may sue and be sued, prosecute and be prosecuted, employ labour, own assets, incur debts, and be subjected to taxation. Its management is vested in a board of directors who sign documents, bind the company and generally behave as its agents. None of the directors, however, need necessarily hold a significant equity in the company, nor must the directors necessarily be employees of the company in any other capacity. But directors *may* be substantial equity holders and *may* be full-time managerial employees.

The company, then, is a legal institution owning productive assets as if it were an individual. Who then owns the company? The law provides for a body of shareholders, or more precisely for a body of shares. These are the property of individual holders and, like other property, are transferable to other real persons either as gifts or for consideration. They can also be owned by other legal persons. They entitle the owner to a bundle of rights in the company, and generally, but not always, they are originally issued in return for some specific consideration such as the subscription of capital. Usually the resulting rights attaching to the share are *equitable* relatively to the consideration, e.g. if the consideration is capital, capital dividend and voting rights are awarded in proportion to the amount of capital[18] supplied. Thus the *company* issues the shares, but the rights inherent in the shares give real persons some aspects of part-owners of the company. Strictly, however, all that a shareholder owns is his bundle of rights. His shares are his property, the company is not. The shareholders are not the legal owners of the assets of the company, nor even, in many countries, of the current profits before distribution.

The directors, on the other hand, are servants of the company, not apparently, of the shareholders. But do not the rights inherent in the shares provide the holders with virtual *de facto* ownership and control? Many people believe this to be the case (and indeed many believe, erroneously, that shareholders are proprietors *de jure*), and it is certainly true that if a company is not owned by its members, it is owned by no-one. Almost universally, the company meeting appoints the directors; therefore the right to vote at the meeting apparently provides definite indirect collective control. Similarly, the rights to dividend and capital imply a position which, if a long way from that of sole owner, is by no means that of a true *rentier*. This, however, is far from the end of the matter. For it is the directors who determine the dividend, and they have gradually acquired discretion to withhold considerable proportions of current profits, which then, either as fixed or liquid assets, become the property of the company. This capital accumulated from retained profits 'belongs' to the shareholders only to the extent provided by their specific rights. The increased capital behind each share should lead to increased earnings, from which shareholders will benefit provided these are distributed. Shareholders also benefit if the directors decide on a capital distribution or if the business is sold. But the shareholders cannot in general directly initiate a capital distribution except by enforcing total liquidation, i.e. by causing the assets to be sold at break-up value.

In social accounting terms, company law creates concepts of corporate income and corporate capital, distinct from and by no means identical with the more familiar concepts of personal income and personal capital: the value of company assets is not necessarily equal to the market value of corresponding stocks. It has been suggested, in fact, that the existence of corporate income is the essence of managerial capitalism. [19] Through gradual development of the practice of substantial dividend retentions, corporate assets, created from corporate income, have become a partly autonomous factor in the economic system, and the industrial capital of western democracies is no longer divided into two classes, 'public' and 'private', but rather into three, 'public', 'private', and 'corporate'. The corporate sector likes to be described as 'private', but this may represent no more than a desire to conceal, and thus protect, the underlying independence.

Corresponding to the third concept of capital, we may identify a third body of persons, rivalling the shareholders for its control. These are 'the managers' — a term of art which, since Burnham, [20] has been generally applied to people who control and operate, but do not substantially 'own' productive institutions. To Veblen [21] and Burnham they were technicians, and Veblen thought they were not powerful. Berle and Means [22] saw them as neither technicians nor capitalists, but rather as disembodied entrepreneurs enjoying many of the fruits of capitalism without themselves providing much capital or taking proportionate risks. More recent writers, notably R. A. Gordon, [23] have emphasised their rôle as organisers and administrators. This is surely correct. It was by providing virtually a new factor of production—the capacity for large-scale organisation — that the new system broke the restraints on traditional capitalist production. Large-scale production depends uniquely on large-scale organisation. The profits and dividends of large companies are derived from the professional abilities of people who know how to flatten the U-shaped cost curve. This ability gives them considerable influence and bargaining power.

It is sometimes supposed that in the corporate sector boards of directors may be regarded as trustees for shareholders, that they are, in fact, akin to watchdog committees set up to keep management in its place. This view, however, is not supported by legal authorities, [24] and in any case the managers have themselves considerably assimilated the directorial system. Legally the function of the board is to operate the company. For the purpose, it employs executives who may, as we have seen, themselves be directors. But board members who are also full-time employees command the power of organisation and hence must in general dominate: [25] In the U.S. the majority of all directors are in this position. [26] Thus, by combining the functions of employee and employer, the management body is considerably freed from direct external restraints, a condition which is emphasised by the fact that the vast majority of board nominations are proposed by existing directors. In practice, in many firms, the board itself recedes into the background and operations are taken over by committees of senior executives, not all of whom are necessarily directors. [27]

For these reasons, the distinction between 'management' and stockholders is a valid one, and the two groups may properly be regarded as separate elements in the corporate structure. More precisely, we define 'the management' as the particular in-group, consisting of directors and others, which effectively carries out the functions legally vested in the board. This does not mean that shareholders and management are necessarily opposed, or that policy will necessarily differ from that which might be pursued in a system where managers were immanent. All we are saying is that the two groups are sufficiently distinct, and the managers sufficiently autonomous, for the existence of a harmony of interests not to be regarded as axiomatic. Therefore, in order to understand the economic system of the corporations, it is essential to assess the factors determining the relative influence of, or balance of power between, these two forces operating within them.

No empirical investigation is required to assert that the behaviour of an organisation will represent the outcome of the interactions of the desires, ideals, ethics and constraints of the individuals or groups of which it is composed. Individuals may attach utility in varying degrees to what the organisation does for them, to what it does for other members, to what it does for outsiders and to what it does for itself. At one extreme, they may regard the organisation as little more than a vehicle for satisfying personal economic needs, at the other they may identify it with their own egos to such an extent that its collective prosperity takes precedence over all ordinary personal considerations. But whatever the utility function associated with his participation, [28] the individual's influence over policy will depend not only on this, but also on his bargaining position. Neither the most junior office girl nor the owner of a single share is likely to have much influence, unless the one is the managing director's mistress or the other his wife. But even a virtuous office girl will have some influence, because if the organisation does not provide her with sufficient utility to induce her continued participation she will cease to participate. This, of course, is recognised in the orthodox theory of the firm, but only on the assumption that the utility functions of all participants are of the relatively crude kind supposed in the post-classical theory of

B

net advantages.[29] If participants attach utility to other aspects of company policy — for example, if they prefer to work in an organisation which does not aim for large profits — the results, even at the present stage of the argument, could be quite far-reaching. However, it is evident that the influence of individual participants may often exceed many times the inducement minimum, particularly, of course, in the case of high management.

The pull of the management in an individual company greatly exceeds the sum of the values of the individuals' qualifications on the open market. The management is a team which has been built up over a period of time and has acquired unique ability to operate a particular business.[30] The profits earned by the assets depend on the management; they by no means reside entirely in the character of the assets themselves. Indeed, to a considerable extent, the physical assets are notably subordinate to the human assets in the general economic picture of the firm: an investor can far more realistically be said to be buying a share in (i.e. interest in) the organisation than a share in a particular set of physical assets. In truth, he is buying a compound of the assets and the organisation. The organisation has special knowledge and ability in managing the assets and the assets have been built up to match the special talents of the organisation. This is what is meant by a 'going concern'. Hence the value of the team is very much greater than the sum of the salaries the members could earn if disbanded.

Of course, management can always be replaced. But the new team will not be familiar with the firm's particular operation, even if it has considerable experience of the particular trade. A complete change of management is likely to increase the rate of return on the company's capital only if the existing management is very inefficient. This point is of crucial importance because, as we have seen, in cases where a concentration of shareholders is in a position to impose sanctions on the board, their legal weapon essentially resolves into the threat of dismissal. Shareholders cannot legally interfere with any other aspect of management. In order to remove a senior manager not on the board, against the wishes of the existing board, they must at least threaten to replace a majority of the existing directors with their own nominees. Both sides, therefore, possess a 'deterrent' of sorts, and the outcome is uncertain. Therefore, even in a fairly closely-held company, the management has considerable autonomy through economic influence, because its members represent an organisation capable of operating the assets, while the shareholders in general do not. It follows as a corollary that the relative strength of a management's position depends *inter alia* on its relative commercial efficiency.

The factor of commercial efficiency, however, is specific to individual firms. More general factors in the balance of power are the procedural facility with which the directors can be dismissed, the distribution of holdings and the various economic consequences of shares being saleable. The right to elect is of little influence if the procedure for dismissal is cumbersome, and the votes themselves are of little influence if they are statistically dispersed and their holders unorganised. But dispersed votes regain their potency if the firm can be threatened with take-over or if selling activity 'punishes' management in any other way, for example, by affecting future supplies of finance or by damaging managerial prestige.

In England, since World War II, all the directors in any public company can be removed by simple majority at a properly constituted meeting. In the U.S., where the law varies from state to state, the position is sometimes more circumscribed. In both countries there are cases (fewer today perhaps than when Berle and Means were writing[31]) where the majority of shareholders have been disenfranchised by legal devices. In England, shareholders are also restrained by the effect of the law relating to contracts between directors and their companies.[32] And in general, both in the U.K. and the U.S., dismissal of directors is in practice rare, except where an individual or small organised group has acquired a majority holding and is engaged, in fact, in a takeover raid.

As to the statistical distribution of holdings, the familiar facts are that the proportion of British and North American manufacturing output produced by companies of the type where a single person or family holds impregnable control has been small for sometime past; that by the late nineteen-thirties, in two-thirds of large and medium-size English companies and in four-fifths of large U.S.

companies, in each case not even the top twenty shareholders had between them sufficient stock to command an absolute majority; and that since then dispersion has continued to increase, and in England, at least, the trend appears to have been accelerating.[33] It follows that only by organising could shareholders, in the majority of cases, make effective use of their votes. But typical shareholders are unorganised almost by definition. They spread their holdings in order to avoid, among other risks, the risk of finding themselves locked into a firm with whose policies they are dissatisfied, and if in fact dissatisfied, they generally prefer to sell rather than go to the trouble and expense of organising opposition. The directors, on the other hand, have usually a small collective holding sufficient to dominate meetings in the absence of concentrated or resolute opposition. Typically, boards hold from one to two per cent of the total equity,[34] a fact which has often been adduced to demonstrate separation of control from ownership. The reinforcing effect on control has received less emphasis. It is particularly significant that while managements do not usually hold large blocks of shares, their holdings are rarely negligible. They are not owner-managers, because their holdings represent small proportions of their total wealth,[35] and the associated dividends small proportions of their total incomes. Perhaps they could be described as 'controller-managers'. We are forced inevitably to the conclusion that if shareholders in general possess countervailing power, it must be found mainly in the factors we have yet to discuss, i.e. in the transferability of shares and in the existence of an organised stock-market. The subject is so important that we begin a separate section.

The Influence of the Stock-Market (1): A Simple Theory of Valuation

Because shares are bought and sold in an organised market, management policies must affect their prices. But these, in turn, react on management in several ways. Firstly, it is by no means unlikely that the market valuation of a company directly enters the managerial utility function. They may feel prestige associated with healthy prices — a sign of approbation from the investing class —

they may feel loyalty to their shareholders, or they may have a sense of conscience towards the shares as such: under modern conditions, the share *holders*, as a body of persons, are changing every day, but the shares, though abstract, are constant, and their market price well known. The shares may be thought to represent a collective super-ego, enforcing 'good' (i.e. traditional) managerial behaviour as effectively as if Professor Modigliani were sitting in the corner of every board room. This possibility and its implications are discussed in the next chapter. Note, however, that what we are concerned with is the influence of the stock-market as a whole, including potential buyers and actual sellers, i.e. we are not merely concerned with the particular individuals who happen to be holding the company's shares at a particular moment. The price of a company's shares may change substantially without any significant change in membership (turnover of stock), and the membership may change substantially without any significant change in price. We are concerned only with the price, with the way it is affected by management policy and with the way policy may be affected by it. This is the impersonal logic of the corporate system.

Secondly, share prices may also affect supplies of finance, not only new-issue finance but also, by permeation, borrowing-power in the bond market. Here our concern is with new issues alone. There is a double implication. Managers may desire expansion, in which case their utility is affected directly, or, alternatively, if firms pursuing certain policies are unable to expand, in the long run others will predominate: in other words, financial policies inimical to growth do not have survival value.

Thirdly, share prices may favour a radical change in the voting distribution, i.e. a take-over raid. Some policies may depress prices so far that the aggregate market value of the equity becomes significantly less than the value, to a single outsider, of the assets behind the equity. The 'outsider' would be a person or organised group who could value the assets on the assumption that sufficient stock was obtained to guarantee easy dismissal of the present directors and a suitable change of policy. Take-over raids are difficult and risky, but if the prospective gain is large enough, the attempt will seem worth while. Therefore potential raids are, and always have been, a real factor to any management wishing to stay in office. Investors value voting rights [36] not so much because they expect to use them, but because they can be sold to someone who might. The balance of power between investor and manager involves two institutions: on the one hand the stock-market, essentially an exchange for *rentier* paper; on the other, the voting share, something of a pre-managerial phenomenon. Take-overs, as against voluntary mergers, are feared because typically, after a successful raid, the whole top management is dismissed, losing job, prestige and perquisites of office. Thus policies likely to induce raids also lack survival value. [37]

The effects of potential take-over raids and of the long-run supply of finance are intimately connected, because the take-over danger can be affected by dividend policy, and retentions are a source of finance. Both are also affected by investment policy, i.e. by the attempted rate of expansion and profits expected. On orthodox theory, at least, the market's attitude to retentions will depend on how the funds retained are expected to be used. A firm whose investment policy is in some sense attractive may not only be able to raise funds for new issues but also, without risking a raid, enjoy considerable retentions. Conversely, a firm with poor prospective investment returns should neither be able to issue nor safely retain. It is therefore best to divide the analysis into two stages, first investigating theoretical conditions where raids are impossible — in effect, conditions where shares carry all the usual rights except the vote — and then imposing a definite theory of take-over. (As far as is known, no such theory has previously been published.) We also require a theory of stock-market behaviour. We shall use the simplest available theory suitable for the immediate purpose, not one we think realistic. In later chapters we shall go into the subject more thoroughly.

Suppose investors believe they can forecast with complete certainty the internal rate of return to be obtained from every possible policy of every quoted company, and suppose they always think they know what policy each is going to pursue. In general, they also assume that policy, once decided, will not be changed and that the associated asset expansion will yield constant returns. Finally, let them also assume a 'constant' financial policy, i.e. they believe that the proportion of earnings retained, once decided, will be constant, and that a new issue having been made none will ever be made again. (We do not assume policy changes never occur, merely that they are not anticipated; if they happen, they are thought to be once for all.) In such conditions, speculation is impossible and investors are compelled to behave more or less like *rentiers*. In the absence of tax discrimination they are indifferent between income and capital gain, because capital gain being perfectly forecastable, there is no opportunity for gambling. That is to say, they would pay the same price for a security expected to yield an income of $x each year as for a security yielding an income of $(x − y)$ whose market value was expected to appreciate by the equivalent of $y each year. The 'total yield', or *rente*, of any security in any given year is the annual dividend plus the capital gain. Let k be the ratio of this total yield to the demand price, and we obtain the identity:

$$k = y + z \qquad (1.2)$$

where

$y =$ dividend divided by current market price, or 'running dividend yield'.

$z =$ annual proportionate capital gain.

In determining the demand price, the market, believing that earnings and dividends can be forecast perfectly, must assume that the only source of capital gain is rising dividends. If the dividend is expected to grow at a constant proportionate rate, this is the rate of capital gain; the current demand price, ex-dividend, is therefore determined by the next expected dividend and the (constant) expected growth rate. But once the demand price, the next dividend and the growth rate are known, k is known, therefore by redefining y as the expected next-dividend yield (next dividend divided by current demand price), and z as the expected dividend growth rate, the identity becomes a market-behaviour equation, valid, on the assumptions, at all moments of time. k becomes a market rate of discount and the model is equivalent to assuming that the demand price is the present value of all future dividends discounted at k over an infinite time horizon.

With a constant rate of return and constant retention ratio, the expected growth rate of dividend is equivalent to the growth rate of capital per share, which in turn is the product of the rate of return and the retention ratio. Hence:

$$y = k - r \cdot p'$$ (1.3)

where

r = retention ratio.

p' = net rate of return, normally defined.

In real life, k will not be independent of r[38] and will also depend on the extent to which the firm is attempting to borrow or raise money by new issues. In real life, no forecasts are made with certainty and k will be affected by risk. We shall later find these qualifications to be of very considerable theoretical importance, but in the meantime k is to be regarded as an exogenous constant, free of risk premium, largely determined by the total yield available on other securities.

The next-dividend yield (y) is the next-earnings yield multiplied by the pay-out ratio, i.e. by $(1 - r)$, where the next-earnings yield is defined as the next expected earnings per share divided by the current demand price. Expected next earnings are the product of the current book value of capital per share and the expected rate of return. Hence, the expected earnings yield is the product of the rate of return and the ratio of book value of capital per share to demand price, the reciprocal of which latter we shall call the *valuation ratio* (i.e. the valuation ratio is the ratio of the market value of the firm to the book value of its net assets). Then,

$$y = \frac{p'}{v} (1 - r)$$ (1.4)

and

$$p' \cdot \left(\frac{1 - r}{v} + r \right) = k$$ (1.5)

where

v = valuation ratio (see above).

The Influence of the Stock-Market (2): New Issues by New Companies

Suppose a new issue is made by a new company formed either to undertake a new activity or to acquire the business of an established traditional firm. The market must be presumed to know that immediately the transaction is completed the total book value must equal the total amount subscribed, i.e. the average book value of capital per share must equal the average subscription price. Therefore no subscription price implying a valuation ratio other than unity is tenable.

If the valuation ratio is unity, whatever the expected retention ratio, equation (1.5) can be satisfied only if $p = k$, i.e. if the expected rate of return equals the market rate of discount. In effect, if the rate of return is equal to or exceeds the rate of discount, the market will behave in such a way that an unlimited sum can be raised; if the rate of return is less than the rate of discount, the market will subscribe nothing. In these circumstances, then, the market can compel managers to choose, or at least appear to choose, investment policies for which the expected rate of return is at least as great as the rate of discount.

If, later, the expected rate of return unexpectedly declines, for example as a result of a change of policy, the market price of the shares will fall below par, unless the rate of discount has also fallen. Since the book value of assets remains constant, if the share price declines, so will the valuation ratio. Alternatively, if the expected rate of return unexpectedly increases, the valuation ratio rises. The valuation ratio, when not constrained to unity, can be derived from equation (1.5). Hence,

$$v = (1 - r)\bigg/\left(\frac{k}{p'} - r\right) = \frac{1 - r}{1 - r + \pi} \tag{1.6}$$

where

$$\pi = (k - p')/p'$$

Evidently, whatever the value of r, if k exceeds p', v is less than unity; if p' exceeds k, v exceeds unity; and if p' equals k, v equals

B2

unity. We shall call the difference $(p' - k)$ the 'return discrepancy'; expressed as a ratio of p', we shall call it the 'return discrepancy ratio'. The symbol π represents this ratio, defined, for convenience, negatively.

The return discrepancy ratio not only helps determine the valuation ratio, but also affects the way the valuation ratio varies with the retention ratio. If the return discrepancy is positive (i.e. if π is negative), the valuation ratio varies directly with the retention ratio (up to a discontinuity at $r = 1$, when v jumps to zero); if the return discrepancy is negative, this relationship is inverted. When the return discrepancy is zero, the valuation ratio is independent of the retention ratio, being always, as we have seen, unity. This conforms to the orthodox view of retentions, and implies that the market 'welcomes' retentions if they are to be used for 'profitable' projects (i.e. projects able to earn a rate of return at least as great as the rate of discount), and 'disapproves' (by lowering share prices) if they are to be used otherwise. In the former case, the market values the firm at more than the book value of its assets, reflecting supernormal earning prospects; in the latter case, the assets are, as it were, written down on account of having got into the hands of a management intending to 'misuse' them.

(The discontinuity when retentions are raised to 100 per cent and the valuation ratio becomes zero arises because, if the firm is expected to remain in business for ever, and never distribute capital, earnings, though growing fast, are valueless because never distributed. But when the retention ratio, although not unity, is nevertheless very high, the very small current and near-future dividend is supposed to be compensated by the high growth rate, and, provided there is no earnings discrepancy, this offsetting is complete: investors are supposed to apply the same rate of discount however long they have to wait. We have thus the paradox that a firm with zero earnings discrepancy could raise its retention ratio to 99·9 per cent without affecting the valuation ratio, even though this would imply that investors had to wait hundreds of years before receiving an appreciable dividend. Obviously in real life no-one would buy such a share. As we have already hinted, in real life, when retentions reach high levels, the theory breaks down, or at least requires to be modified by making k itself rise with r.)

The Influence of the Stock-Market (3): New Issues by Old Companies

Now consider an established company wanting to make a further issue. Assume for simplicity that the new shares will have exactly the same rights as the old, so that if the aggregate par value of the old stock is x, and of the new issue y, each par-dollar's worth of new stock will always receive the proportion $1/(x+y)$ of any distribution. After the issue, new and old stock must exchange at the same price, and the price at which the market 'accepts' the issue is the new market price for all stock, new and old.

It is no longer the case that the equilibrium valuation ratio is necessarily unity, because the company already has some capital, in the distributed earnings of which the new shares have equitable rights with the old. If the expected earnings on the investment to be financed by the new issue imply a negative return discrepancy on capital employed in the new project, while the expected return on the old capital remains unchanged (together with the market rate of discount), by a suitable adjustment of market price new subscribers can be provided with a 'normal' yield on their investment, i.e. the market rate of discount can be satisfied, and the issue is therefore possible. As a result, the market price falls below the pre-issue level, and old shareholders suffer a capital loss. Conversely, if the 'new' return discrepancy is positive, they enjoy a capital gain.

When the issue causes the share price to fall the process is known as 'dilution'. For reasons discussed below it is not frequently practised, but its theoretical characteristics are nevertheless of some interest. Suppose the pre-existing retention ratio and return discrepancy were both zero and that zero retentions are expected to continue; then the change in market price, as a result of the issue, is:

$$\frac{\Delta\$}{\$} = \frac{\Delta C}{C}\left(\frac{\rho - k}{k}\right) \qquad (1.7)$$

where

$\Delta \$/\$$ = proportionate change in market price.

$\Delta C/C$ = proportionate expansion (ratio of amount to be raised by the issue to book value of old capital).

ρ = expected return on new investment.

The effect therefore depends not only on the value of the marginal return discrepancy, but also on the scale of the proposed expansion. Since the equilibrium market price is the price at which the new issue is sold, if the return discrepancy is negative, the scale of the issue is limited by the condition that the decline in price must not exceed 100 per cent, since stock which is sold for nothing brings in no capital. This limit is

$$\mathrm{Max} \left[\frac{\Delta C}{C} \right] = \frac{k}{k - \rho} \qquad (1.8)$$

But so long as the return discrepancy is not negative, expansion is unlimited. (The case of a new company is a case where the expansion, measured by $\Delta C/C$, has to be unlimited — because, in the absence of old capital, it is the new capital divided by zero — and hence is possible only with a non-negative discrepancy.) When the assumptions of a zero retention ratio and zero 'old' return discrepancy are relaxed, the results are more complicated, but their general import is unchanged. As might be expected, if the new return discrepancy is negative, retentions enhance the decline in market price and reduce the limit of expansion. And a firm with an expected retention ratio of 100 per cent cannot raise any money at all by this method, whatever the return discrepancy.

Expansion by flagrant dilution is relatively rare. In principle it is inhibited by the legal doctrine that old shareholders should have a pre-emptive right to all new issues.[39] In practice, the right is too vaguely defined to offer sure protection, although most firms nevertheless pay attention to it. If the old shareholders are to be fully protected against all possible loss, not only must they be offered the whole of any issue, but any shares they refuse must be suppressed. Alternatively, they must be offered special terms sufficiently favourable for the capital gain obtainable on resale of their allotment of new stock to offset fully the capital loss on their holdings of the old. In either case the result is to put the company in virtually the same position as if dilution were prohibited.

Although the pre-emptive right is no longer legally enforceable either in the U.S. or the U.K., most new issues do in fact take the form of 'rights' issues to old stockholders. For, irrespective of the legal or moral position, the financial potential of dilution is distinctly dubious. Even on the present, static assumptions, there is, as we have seen, a definite limit to the proportionate expansion so long as the (negative) return discrepancy remains unchanged. On more realistic, dynamic assumptions, the limit may be much more severe. When the expansion process occurs in steps, the market has time to learn, and to learn to discount, the fact that the firm is one which is liable to practise dilution. The price will therefore fall more rapidly than would be indicated by simply breaking the static model into successive, but independent *tranches*. Alternatively, if in real life an attempt was made to reach to static limit instantaneously, market imperfections, which we have so far assumed away, would produce the same effect (obviously the process must end well before the equilibrium price has actually become zero).

Continuous growth by dilution is therefore impossible (which is not to say the method is never employed discontinuously). This is true not only in the real world, but also in our imaginary world where all shares are voteless. It is a market discipline which does not depend on threat of take-over.

The Influence of the Stock-Market (4): Retentions

Exactly the opposite is true of growth by retentions: this is a process with which the market is powerless to interfere except by enforcing a change of management or by shaming management through low prices. Suppose a firm which has previously displayed a zero return discrepancy and no retentions (i.e. a firm which was not expanding — we assume no new issues) now finds an opportunity for continuous indefinite expansion at a constant but negative marginal return discrepancy. Instead of attempting a diluting new issue, it decides to obtain capital by means of a permanent increase in the retention ratio to, say, 50 per cent. (I.e. it indicates that from now on only half of any year's earnings will be distributed, the rest will always be ploughed back.) As the expansion proceeds, an increasing proportion of total assets will be engaged in the new venture and the average rate of return, taken over all assets, will gradually decline asymptotically to the marginal rate. With a constant retention ratio, the growth rate of the book value of total assets, which is, at any point of time, the product of the then average rate of return and the retention ratio, will follow a similar pattern. Given this pattern and the various constant ratios, there is a unique time path of all future dividends, which investors, if they understand the problem, will attempt to discount in the usual way and thus determine the time path of the valuation ratio. Since expected dividends are not growing at a constant rate, the effect is complex, but with a negative return discrepancy the valuation ratio must decline discontinuously immediately following the announcement of the new policy. It will then continue to decline (continuously), but at a decreasing rate, until finally more or less stabilising as an increasing proportion of discounted future dividends relates to the period after the average rate of return is expected to have closely approached its asymptote. An approximation to the valuation ratio at this stage is given by equation (1.6). Hence,

$$\lim v = \frac{1-r}{1-r+\pi} \qquad (1.9)$$

It follows that the aggregate market value of the equity (which is the product of book value and valuation ratio) by no means follows the same time-path as the book value. In the short run, market value is reduced, but in the long run, as the valuation ratio is gradually stabilised, the two growth rates become almost identical, and in the very long run, therefore, aggregate market value must regain its original level and continue to grow indefinitely so long as the process is maintained: both aggregates grow together with the one always in excess of the other in proportion to the reciprocal of $\lim v$. Thus if a long enough view is taken, whether the firm is defined in terms of book value or of market value, size and its growth rate are always increased by increased retentions, even with a negative return discrepancy. In the short run, when market value declines, if the shares are voteless, there is nothing for the shareholders to do but suffer in silence and hope that they will not have to suffer too long. Whatever happens, they are bound to lose, because our assumptions imply that had dividends been paid in full, and had been fully reinvested in other securities yielding the full market rate of discount, the compound growth rate of their wealth would have been higher at all future points of time. Thus, where take-over discipline is absent, continuous growth by means of retentions is always possible for a sufficiently determined management, provided only that the marginal rate of return exceeds zero. We therefore pass to the more realistic case, where shares have votes and may be sold to raiders.

A Theory of Take-over

A take-over raider is a person or company aiming for virtual ownership. He or they intend to acquire sufficient stock to be able to dismiss and appoint directors at will, to distribute capital, to amalgamate with other firms controlled, perhaps, by themselves, to appoint executives at salaries of their own choosing — to appoint, perhaps, themselves, their relatives or their friends. They may plan to re-organise the firm, sell the assets, distribute capital and realise quick capital gains. Alternatively, they may intend to continue the business on existing lines, but managed with greater efficiency or with a different pay-out policy. *En tous cas* they require at least fifty-one per cent of the voting stock and probably more; the precise requirement will depend on the existing distribution of holdings, on the terms of the charter and on the laws of the country.

Two methods are typically available. Either the raider may attempt to buy the necessary shares on the open market, or he may publicly announce that he will buy all the existing stock at a stated price provided sufficient acceptances are received to ensure the desired degree of control, — the so-called conditional offer in a procedure known as a take-over 'bid'. The open-market method suffers from the disadvantage that, unless the market is perfect and the operations perfectly secret, the price is almost certain to rise as the purchases develop. The 'bid' method, on the other hand, suffers because, the announcement being public, the offer price will almost certainly have to be higher than the pre-existing market price, and part of the benefits of the raid will necessarily be shared with the old stockholders. Often the announcement will also bring other bidders into the field, as the raider's commercial competitors strive to prevent him increasing his domination of their industry. In practice the cheapest method is usually some combination of the two, but the average price paid for stock will still almost always exceed the price ruling in the market before the operation began or was rumoured.

For the moment, however, let us assume most of these tiresome details away. The raider can acquire all the stock he needs by secret open-market purchases without affecting the price at all: the average price he pays for stock is the price quoted by dealers the day before he began buying. There are no substantial blocks of votes held by persons or groups who value them above the ruling market price, and the raid is not discovered by the existing management until it is too late; they cannot defend themselves by announcing policy changes. The purchase price therefore reflects the market valuation ratio based on the expected results of existing managerial policies.

We then ask how the existing management's policies must be constrained if they desire to avoid creating market conditions in which a raid (on our assumptions, necessarily successful) would be likely to occur. Policies lying within the constraints will be called 'safe'. In real life, because markets are imperfect and raiders unable to maintain secrecy, managements will be fairly secure if they pursue policies considerably more dangerous than the most dangerous of those which are safe on this definition; but we can validly assume that the economic characteristics of 'reasonably' safe policies are determined by and vary with the characteristics of those defined as theoretically safe; therefore by analysing the latter we may also roughly delineate the former (for obvious reasons, the 'limiting case' method is more convenient).

The valuation ratio reflecting market price — the demand price set up by the investing public at large — is, in our present model, the result of two variables within the existing management's control and one which is not. The management controls the retention ratio (r) absolutely, and partly controls the expected rate of return (p). The rate of discount (k) is determined by the market. For a given firm, the ith, let r_{ii} now stand for the retention ratio expected by the market if the existing management continues in office, p_{ii} for the corresponding rate of return and k_{im} for the market rate of discount. A 'policy' of the management is a set of decisions leading to a particular value of r_{ii} and a particular value of p_{ii}. The rate of return, however, depends partly on the investment decisions (character and pace, if any, of expansion) and partly on the organisation's inherent efficiency: in a later chapter we shall see how efficiency in turn also inter-acts with the growth rate. But given the firm's innate efficiency, a 'policy' is characterised by r_{ii} and p_{ii}, and implies a definite growth rate, including the growth rate zero. As r_{ii} is a continuous variable, the number of policies open to a firm is theoretically infinite, but if we regard small changes in r_{ii} as insignificant, so that it is for practical purposes discrete, the set of available policies is finite. We seek to partition these into the subsets 'safe' and 'unsafe'.

The market valuation ratio is determined by the policy of the existing management. The raider, also, has a valuation ratio for firm i, but this is based on the policy he would pursue in i if his raid were successful. His valuation ratio is the maximum price he would pay for a share, divided by the existing book value of assets behind each share. We then assume that firm i is likely to be raided if the valuation ratio of the raider whose ratio for i is higher than that of any other possible raider is also higher than the market valuation ratio for i. Let this 'most dangerous' raider be called j. 'Safe' policies, then, are those which keep the market valuation ratio for i, which we call v_{im}, higher than or equal to j's valuation ratio for i, which we call v_{ij}. All other policies are unsafe.

When one takes over a large company, one acquires a particular set of assets associated with a partly specific labour force and a rather more specific body of middle and junior managers; one also acquires various other ingredients known as 'goodwill'. But whatever or whoever one is, if the assets are to continue to earn, one will have to be able to provide a more or less complete new high management. This is evidently a considerable restriction, for circumstances where the assets can be realised in a quick capital gain involving no continuing management are rare, though lucrative. In this book we are concerned with the large companies which produce the bulk of industrial output, and he who wishes to raid these must be able to provide at least the rudiments of the high management needed for large-scale organisation. Alternatively, he must accept a lower level of efficiency. If 'he' is some kind of traditional capitalist he should not, in principle, be so well-equipped for the purpose as the typical professional managerial team, and must therefore set his organisational disadvantage against the possible benefits of changes of policy; for this reason, in manufacturing industry successful raids by traditional capitalists are almost unknown. [40]

However, the 'pure' traditional capitalist is by no means the only species of wolf in the forest. Some raiders combine traditional characteristics with modern; incorporated, but closely held; concerned mainly with getting rich, but nevertheless capable of considerable organisation. Some with apparently traditional motivation are, in fact, akin to management specialists. Finally, of course, powerful raids are frequently made by other purely managerial organisations. The successful among those represent involuntary mergers imposed by one professional team on another, for motives which at least in principle may differ considerably from the traditional.

One requirement, however, is common to all raiders: they must have the means of payment. They must either possess or be able to borrow large sums in cash, or, if incorporated, they must either have large reserves or mortgageable assets or be able to offer to issue new shares in their own company, in payment for the shares of the raided company at a rate of exchange which is both acceptable to the recipients and does not dilute the raider's own old stock to a greater extent than is considered desirable or safe. This last method is not compatible with our assumption of secrecy, but the fact that it is widely used in conditional offers only serves to emphasise that, unlike us, real raiders assume real stock markets to be highly imperfect. On our assumptions, raiders must have cash.

If the social accounting essence of managerial capitalism lies in the existence of corporate capital, its economico-institutional essence lies in the widespread separation, not so much of ownership from control as of organisation from finance. In the course of the managerial evolution the quantity of organisational talent in society has been vastly increased, but in the process it has become professionalised, bureaucratised and largely separated from finance. The majority of professional top managers spend a large part of their working lives in a single firm, and at any one time only a few are seeking to move. When they do move, their method of transfer is professional rather than capitalistic; that is, they do not take capital with them. In the small business sector, conditions are reversed, and lying between the small and large-scale sectors there is a significant penumbra where traditional and modern methods are mixed. Some of these businesses have large turnovers and yield large profits, but it is noticeable that they are rarely found in industries typically requiring genuine large-scale organisation. It follows that in the modern world take-over raiders, wherever they occur, are scarce, and being scarce, in order to function, must be appropriately rewarded.

But although they are scarce, they exist, and if sufficiently tempted, will pounce. In measuring the temptation represented by a particular firm, a 'traditional' raider can value the assets on the basis of any pay-out ratio he chooses (because, if successful, the choice will be his), on his own, rather than the market's, rate of discount and on the rate of return he expects to obtain with the management he intends to install and the investment policy he intends to pursue. Because he is scarce, his discount rate (reflecting the next most profitable use for his capital) will be high, and because he is traditional we may assume that, although of no great managerial efficiency, he will attempt to pursue the investment policy expected to yield the maximum rate of return, given the nature of the business, the character of the assets and his actual organisational capacity.

Because we are not yet ready to discuss theories of managerial motivation, the case of the 'managerial' raider is rather vaguer. We shall, however, be reasonably consistent with our own later arguments if we assume that he or they apply a rate of discount equivalent to the rate of return obtainable with unchanged policies within 'their' own firm and a rate of return no lower than the rate expected from the highest-yielding policy, in the merged organisation, consistent with a rate of expansion at least as fast as the rate associated with the existing policy in the raider's present organisation. If the managerial raider pays cash, he will also assume a zero retention ratio. (If, violating our assumptions, he uses the exchange-of-share method, he must take account of the fact that any newly created stock will rank equally for dividend with his own old stock, and the result is therefore affected by the terms of the offer and his own expected retention ratio.) We may then say that a successful managerial raid requires that the return in the merged organisation exceed not only the average of the two 'old' rates, but also the rate expected by the market were the unified firm itself to be taken over by the defending management (if not, the defenders could successfully form a company to retake captor and prize). In other words the market must believe, not only that the merger would be profitable, but that the new combine would be better managed by the aggressor management than by the defendant. Here again, however, we are wandering into a world which violates the analytical assumptions, because, on these, the market never has an opportunity of assessing the raider.

Clearly, therefore, a 'managerial' raid is less amenable to formal analysis and, although it is in practice the most common type, we shall attempt first to develop a 'traditional' theory, in the hope that this will throw some light on the other.

The traditional raider's valuation ratio, then, is his expected rate of return divided by his discount rate. But, unlike the case of the market rate of discount, to treat the raider's rate as a constant independent of the amount of finance supplied is not even a convenient working hypothesis, and is certainly unreasonable. To do so would contradict the raider's nature and produce absurd theoretical results. His supply of finance is finite, therefore he is *not* prepared to pay any price for a firm provided only that the expected return is less than some given, constant rate of discount. Raiders, being at least in some degree scarce, must display at least some degree of inelasticity of supply, i.e. their discount rates must increase with the magnitude of the sum to be supplied. Therefore k_{ij}, raider j's discount rate for firm i, is a rising function of T_{ij}, the symbol we shall use for the total cost of acquiring i (the product, that is, of the number of shares to be bought and the average price to be paid). Thus T_{ij} is the product of the book value of the assets of i and the raider's valuation ratio. We have then a model

$$k_{ij} = f_j(T_{ij}) \qquad T_{ij} > 0; \quad f_j' > 0 \text{ for all } T_{ij}; \qquad (1.10)$$

$$v_{ij} = \frac{p_{ij}}{k_{ij}} \qquad\qquad\qquad\qquad\qquad\qquad (1.11)$$

$$v_{ij} = \frac{T_{ij}}{C_i} \qquad C_i > 0; \qquad\qquad\qquad\qquad (1.12)$$

where

C_i = book value of i's net assets,

k_{ij} = j's discount for i,

T_{ij} = sum required to purchase i at the highest price j is prepared to pay,

v_{ij} = valuation ratio reflecting this price,

p_{ij} = rate of return expected by j after taking over i.

Note: it is assumed that j requires 100 per cent control; if he would be able to manage with less, the right-hand side of (1.12) should be divided by the proportion of stock needed (e.g. if only 51 per cent is needed, the equation becomes $v_{ij} = T_{ij}/0 \cdot 51$).

Provided the supply function, f_j, is, as we have assumed, monotonic, there is only one value of v_{ij} satisfying these equations and this, in fact, reflects the highest price the raider is both able and prepared to pay. At that price, the expected yield on the money invested just equals the marginal rate of discount. The solution valuation ratio may be called the raider's 'effective' valuation ratio, signified by v'_{ij}. Depending on the circumstances, the effective ratio, thus defined, may be equal to, greater or less than unity. If high enough profits are expected, the offer price may exceed book value and yet still provide the raider with an expected yield which he regards as satisfactory for an investment of that magnitude, and vice versa.

It is also convenient to define, as the raider's 'standard' rate of discount, the rate he would apply if able to acquire the assets at precisely their book value, i.e.

$$k_{ij}(0)=f_j(C_i) \qquad (1.13)$$

where

$k_{ij}(0) = j$'s standard discount rate for i,

$f_j(C_i) =$ the value of j's supply function when $T_{ij}=C_i$, hence $v_{ij}=1$.

It can then be shown that given the assumptions of the model, the difference between the raider's effective valuation ratio and unity is uniquely related to the difference between his standard rate of discount and his expected rate of return (p_{ij}). If the standard rate of discount exceeds the rate of return, the effective valuation is below unity, and vice versa; if rate of return and standard discount rate are equal, the effective valuation ratio equals unity. We call the excess $(p_{ij} - k_{ij}(0))$ the raider's effective return discrepancy, remembering that it is uniquely related to the discrepancy between his effective valuation ratio and unity, a quantity of some importance.

Any policy of the existing management is 'safe' if it sets:

$$v_{im}>v'_{ij} \qquad (1.14)$$

when

$$v_{im}=\frac{1-r_{ii}}{1-r_{ii}+\pi_{ii}} \qquad (1.15)$$

where

$v_{im} =$ market valuation ratio for firm i under existing management.

$v'_{ij} = j$'s effective valuation ratio for i (see above).

$\pi_{ii} = (k_{im} - p_{ii})/p_{ii}$.

If the raider's effective return discrepancy is positive, safety requires that v_{im} exceed unity. This, we have seen, is possible (whatever the retention ratio) only if p_{ii} exceeds k_m, that is, if the market return discrepancy is positive (π_{ii} negative). To be safe, the existing management must in these circumstances pursue policies which at least provide expected returns greater than the rate of discount. But as the model is at present set out, provided the firm can just do this, the market valuation ratio *increases* with the retention ratio, therefore it must be possible to find a retention ratio to generate any positive valuation ratio (v_{im}). Therefore, given a positive return discrepancy, v_{im} can always be manipulated to exceed any given positive value of v_{ij}. Therefore, any policy involving a positive market return discrepancy is safe. This obviously absurd conclusion would collapse if we dropped our unrealistic assumption that k_{im} and r_{ii} were behaviouristically independent, but for various reasons we are not ready yet to make the necessary modification. We can at least say, however, if $k_{im}(o)$, for instance, is defined as the rate of discount applied by the market to i, when i's retention ratio is zero, then, when the raider's effective return discrepancy is positive, safe policies for i's management will require rates of return at least as great as $k_{im}(o)$, if not greater. Conversely, any policy is safe if it exceeds $k_{im}(o)$ by more than the excess of the raider's effective valuation ratio and unity, i.e. by more than some function of his effective return discrepancy.

When the raider's effective return discrepancy is negative, however, things are very different. His valuation ratio is less than unity (i.e. he rates the assets worth less than their book value) and the market return discrepancy can also safely be negative. But the market valuation ratio now varies *inversely* with the retention ratio and it is necessary to ensure that, given the return discrepancy, an appropriate retention ratio is, in fact, chosen. And since the retention ratio is bounded, very high negative return discrepancies will not be safe in any circumstances, because they would require, in effect, a negative 'safe' retention ratio. There is, therefore, a finite set of safe policies, represented in pairs of values of retention ratio (r_i) and rate of return (p_{ii}), the latter, given k_{im}, determining the market discrepancy, (π_{ii}). These are indicated by an equation defining the maximum safe retention ratio for any given return discrepancy:

$$\text{Max. safe } r_{ii} = \frac{q_j - q_i}{q_j(1 - q_i)} \qquad q_i, q_j > 0 \qquad (1.16)$$

where

$$q_i \equiv \pi_{ii} \cdot p_{ii}/k_{im} \equiv (k_{im} - p_{ii})/k_{im}$$

$$q_j \equiv 1 - v'_{ij}$$

A combination of return discrepancy and retention ratio is unsafe if, when plugged in to this equation, they yield a value of Max. safe r_{ii} lower than the postulated value. Not all discrepancies, however, can be made safe by appropriate choice of retention ratio, because the latter cannot be negative. If a postulated value of q_i plugged in to the equation indicates a negative value of Max. safe r_{ii}, this policy is unsafe under all circumstances. The situation arises, of course, when the negative value of the market discrepancy arithmetically exceeds the negative value of q_j; i.e., loosely, when the management's policy is even more unprofitable than the raider's is likely to be. The position is further explained in Diagram 1.1.

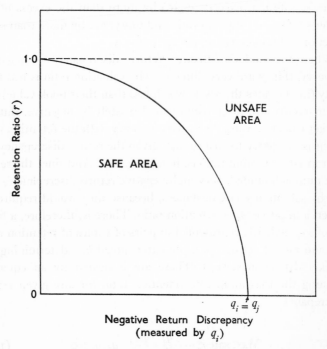

DIAGRAM 1.1. Boundary of Safe Policies with Negative Return Discrepancy

The curve indicates the upper boundary of safe policies when the horizontal axis reads in terms of negative market discrepancy (i.e. as we move to the right, expected return under existing management policy *decreases*), and the vertical axis represents the retention ratio. The reader will remember that the market valuation ratio jumps discontinuously to zero when r_i reaches unity, therefore this upper limit must be thought of as an asymptote. The lower limit, where the curve cuts the horizontal axis, is where Max. safe r_i becomes zero, and is determined therefore by the raider's effective return discrepancy (q_j being a function of this): a decline in his (negatively defined) discrepancy, representing an increase in his potential aggressiveness, pulls the curve leftward and reduces the area of safety. Clearly, the factors determining the raider's discrepancy, and hence extent of the safe area, are of considerable interest.

The factors are, the book value of assets, C_i, the character of the supply function, f_j, and the raider's expected rate of return, p_{ij}. The first measures the size of the firm, the second and third respectively the relative scarcity and relative efficiency of raiders. If raiders were abundant relatively to their efficiency, the most dangerous raider's effective return discrepancy might well be positive. No existing management could then survive unless it had available at least one policy yielding at least the market rate of discount, if not better. Managements with such policies available would be forced to pursue them, and all other managements would eventually be eliminated by raiders. No firm would survive pursuing any policy yielding less than the market discount rate.

Such a world could properly be described as 'neo-classical', an imaginary world, that is, of institutional assumptions appropriate to modern capitalism, behaviour assumptions appropriate to traditional capitalism, and theorems similar to those of the nineteenth century. It is a world, of course, which could never exist; or, more precisely, if created, could never persist, because the assumptions are internally contradictory. The institutions of modern capitalism are impossible to reconcile with the assumption that raiders are not scarce. The truth about neo-classical economics is not so much that it does not apply to the world in which we live as that it could not apply to any viable capitalist system at all. If we repealed the Company Acts, banned large-scale organisation, and/or provided professional managers with almost unlimited supplies of finance at a constant rate of interest, we might conceivably resurrect some kind of traditional capitalism (and thus, no doubt, succeed in making ourselves considerably poorer). But if we did, we should have no need of 'neo'; the results would be 'classical', period. Alternatively, we could pass a series of laws requiring managements to follow decision-rules designed to produce the neo-classical results directly. Then we should have not capitalism but socialism. (It was first pointed out many years ago — by the former Polish Ambassador to the United States[41] — that socialism was virtually the only system theoretically capable of producing classical-type results.) In capitalist countries, for reasons given by Schumpeter,[42] and for others implied below, if an Invisible Hand guides institutional development, it has had the sense to take us in a very different direction. To put the point another way: the productive units of modern capitalism are not only large, but their size distribution is extremely skewed, and the risk of take-over diminishes with the size of the firm: therefore, even in a system in which firms of average size were subject to considerable take-over 'discipline', the giants who produce the bulk of the output would remain relatively immune.

In the real world of modern capitalism, therefore, raiders are generally scarce relative to their efficiency and like other scarce factors, the more efficient they are, the scarcer they are. A raider with a relatively high expected rate of return (p_{ij}) will tend to have a relatively high standard rate of discount, and vice versa. Therefore we can look with renewed interest at the policy constraints facing managements when the most dangerous raider has a significantly negative effective return discrepancy, because this situation is probably typical.

The Concept of Sustainable Growth

Consider such a management facing a situation in which a set of feasible policies possess the property that the rate of expansion is an indirect monotonic function of the rate of return. This might occur, for example, because the rate of growth of demand for the products was in some way related to factors such as price and selling policy which themselves reacted on the rate of return. Then, for every policy there is a rate of growth of demand volume and an associated rate of profit. We then have a model which is subject to an entirely new set of restraints. For no growth rate can be sustained in the long run if associated with a situation in which either the growth rate of assets exceeds that of demand or in which the relation is the other way about. If growth rate of assets exceeds that of demand, either the average utilisation of productive assets must be continually declining or the ratio of non-productive to total assets continually rising: in either case, the overall rate of return must be falling, and any policy which may have been initially safe cannot indefinitely remain so. If the relation is the other way about, the liquidity ratio must be falling, utilisation of productive assets rising, or both. But the liquidity ratio cannot fall below zero and utilisation cannot exceed capacity, so this situation also must end eventually. (For a further discussion, see Chapter 3, p. 118.) Therefore 'sustainable' growth requires that the growth rates of demand and of assets be equal.

If we represent the relationship between demand-growth and rate of return as continuous, inverse and monotonic, and if we assume that the whole capital supply comes from retentions, we may easily generate a set of sustainable growth rates, as follows:

$$D_{ii}^{\cdot} = D(p_{ii}) \qquad (1.17)$$

$$C_{ii}^{\cdot} = r_{ii} \cdot p_{ii} \qquad (1.18)$$

$$C_{ii}^{\cdot} = D_{ii}^{\cdot} \qquad (1.19)$$

$$r_{ii} = \frac{D(p_{ii})}{p_{ii}} \qquad (1.20)$$

where

$D_{ii}^{\cdot} =$ growth rate of demand for i under present management.

Equation (1.20) delineates a set of sustainable combinations of growth rate, retention ratio and profit rate. The right-hand side, however, is a definite function of the profit rate, hence the equation can also be seen as specifying a set of sustainable policies defined in terms of the same two variables (profit rate and retention ratio) as were used in defining safe policies. If we know the market rate of discount (k_{im}), we can transform the equation by substituting a measure of return discrepancy, such as q_i, for p_{ii}, and it can then be shown that the resulting relationship is not unlikely to be approximately linear. (All that is required is that the demand-growth function, $D(p_{ii})$, be negatively sloped throughout and that the negative slope increase arithmetically as the rate of return increases: in later chapters, however, we find good reasons for believing that there will be a range where the slope is positive, and modify the analysis accordingly. In other words, there may be a range of policies over which accelerating growth enhances profitability, rather than the other way about: see, in particular, p. 184, in Chapter 4 and pp. 225–7 in Chapter 6.) We may then represent the set of sustainable policies as a positively sloped line on a diagram which would otherwise be the same as Diagram 1.1. The line cuts the horizontal axis at the value of q_i associated with the rate of return at which the growth rate of demand is zero; this value may therefore be either positive or negative according to whether the corresponding rate of return is greater or less than the market rate of discount. (The reader should remember that q_i is a negatively-defined measure of return discrepancy, its positive movements implying negative movements of the rate of return and hence positive movements of the demand-growth rate.)

Growth which is both Sustainable and Safe

We know that any policy, sustainable or otherwise, yielding a positive return discrepancy will be safe. But we also know that many involving negative discrepancies (i.e. positive q_i) may also be safe, and some (according to the previous section) sustainable. We may therefore combine the two sets of relationships in one diagram, and thus find not only the full set of positions which are both safe and sustainable, but also the policy yielding the maximum safe, sustainable rate of growth. The result is shown in Diagram 1.2. Since movements to the right imply a *declining* rate of return, they imply an increasing rate of growth: therefore the most eastward position

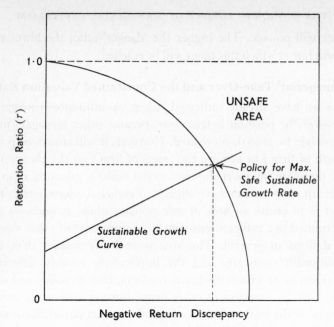

DIAGRAM 1.2. Safe and Sustainable Policies

is the maximum mentioned, and this, evidently, is the position at the intersection of the two curves.

The point at which the safe-growth curve cuts the origin is determined, it will be remembered, by the various factors making up the raider's effective valuation ratio, such as the rate of return expected from the policy he intends to pursue and his standard rate of discount. The more dangerous the raider in these respects, the further is this intersection pulled towards the origin, carrying the whole curve with it. Thus the more dangerous the raider, the lower the maximum, safe, sustainable growth rate. This, then, is how the 'traditional' raider restricts the management's power to grow rapidly by means of retentions. In order to grow rapidly, the rate of return must be permitted to decline in order to encourage the growth of demand. In order to meet this, the combination of declining profit rate and rising capital requirement requires an increased retention ratio. The latter, in association with an increasingly negative return discrepancy, lowers the market valuation ratio and thus brings it nearer to the 'danger' ratio at which the raider will pounce. The higher the 'danger' ratio, the lower the growth rate at which this point will be reached.

'Managerial' Take-Over and the Constrained Valuation Ratio

As we have already indicated, when we introduce managerial take-over the position is less clear, because other managers may themselves be growth-motivated. However, it will always help the growth of firm j to acquire the assets of firm i on the cheap. We may therefore interpret the managerial raider's valuation ratio as made up in the manner we suggested earlier. Unfortunately, the effect is to create an area of safe policies whose boundaries are determined in a rather vague way by the practices of other managerial firms in general. The area is probably smaller than the 'traditionally' safe area and the implications notably different. Managers must within the limits conform, both in policy and efficiency, to the practices of other firms, but not necessarily to the 'desires' of the market. Furthermore, the market rate of discount is likely in turn to be affected by these practices, because management controls the main outlets for high-yielding investment.

But clearly, whether the potential raider is managerial or traditional, the greater the relative innate efficiency of the present management, the weaker the general level of threat and the faster the maximum safe growth rate. For high relative efficiency must tend to place the demand-growth function in a favourable position relatively to the best expectations of the potential raider; that is to say, the relative position of the two curves in Diagram 1.2 will be such as to produce a rather easterly intersection. If the firm had merely had the luck to stumble on a range of good opportunities, as represented in a favourable absolute position of the demand-growth curve (and hence correspondingly favourable position of the safe-growth curve), but was incapable of exploiting these to maximum advantage, the relative positions of the two curves would remain unfavourable and growth be correspondingly retarded. (As a matter of fact, if the technical prospects of the firm were so good that a raider could obtain a positive return discrepancy while the present management could not, the position is hopeless, no safe policy existing anywhere: such paradoxes will in due course be resolved in the more general models of later chapters.) We therefore expect the relatively efficient to grow fast, the less efficient to grow slowly and the very inefficient to be taken over. This is the generalisation of the 'transfer mechanism', first identified in more specific form by J. Downie.[43] Classical models lead to similar conclusions but on far less convincing assumptions.

Evidently, the typical individual firm will in real life be most unsure of the potency of their most dangerous raider. They will not, therefore, be certain of the magnitude of their market valuation ratio at which the probability of take-over becomes unity. Rather they may visualise a functional relationship between the valuation ratio and the subjective risk of take-over. The latter, we shall see, may then enter their utility function. Hence the valuation ratio may itself act as another proxy variate in managerial utility. For the first part of this book, however, (more precisely, up to p. 254), we continue to treat the valuation ratio as a constraint. We suppose that managers set some value of the ratio below which either fear of take-over or the sense of guilt becomes intolerable. But higher ratios yield no gain in satisfaction. The 'safe' policies may then be interpreted as those which meet the constraint, i.e. do not require the firm's market valuation ratio to fall below the constrained minimum.

We thus see how the institutional framework, as specifically represented in an organised market for voting shares, restrains managerial independence in general and, more particularly, the freedom to grow. Unlike the restraints discussed in the earlier part of the chapter, this one is definite and effective, and will be with us for the rest of the book.

CHAPTER TWO

MOTIVES AND MORALS

'The Managerial Revolution is quite fatal to profit maximisation.'
— Peter Wiles[1]

Introduction and Survey of the Chapter

We believe that the arguments of Chapter 1 are sufficient to establish that in the modern system management has considerable freedom of action. Shareholders may impose minimum constraints on, for example, investment policy, but there is no evidence that general equilibrium of the system requires these minima to become maxima. Most of the relevant markets are imperfect, and in one case, that of the capital market, this is a critical factor in the intra-corporate balance of power itself. In some cases, notably those of the markets for manual labour and for products, the resulting problems have been intensively studied by both economists and sociologists, but this work has not been matched by equivalent work in relation to management. Economists have investigated management attitudes to particular problems, such as price determination, and, more recently investment policy, but there exists not one comprehensive or rigorous study of the basic motivational forces determining business decisions in general: a fair literature examines the way the office affects the home[2], little or none the way home and office life affect office decisions.

Whether or not this state of affairs is a cause for surprise it is certainly a considerable hindrance to understanding the working of a modern economic system. The present chapter therefore represents an attempt, albeit tentative, to explore the neglected area in a fuller and more systematic manner. We offer no apology for the fact that in our subsequent analysis manual workers are rarely mentioned: we do not fail to recognise that they, as producers and consumers, are the primary citizens of the system, but we feel they have already been adequately studied elsewhere, whereas, by contrast, quite insufficient attention has been paid to the men who make, rather than merely experience, the contemporary capitalist environment. We are not in a position to offer a major contribution to the study of managerial motivation as such. In the present state of knowledge we can do no more than produce reasoned arguments for hypotheses we believe to be plausible in order to form the basis for a theoretical economic analysis. Ultimately, only the reader himself can decide whether he feels the hypotheses suggested are in fact sufficiently plausible to justify the uses to which they will be put.

We start from the premise, previously discussed, that there are no rigid rules of the game which bind managers to a particular set of policies or to a particular goal in their capacity as organisers and administrators of modern corporations. They have the freedom to chose from a wide range of policies, a number of which affect the rules of the game themselves. Our central problem in this chapter is to discover the policies managers seem most likely to pursue in their conduct of the corporations; what objectives they are supposed, or they set for themselves, to follow and why they do so. In answering this question and in exploring managerial motivation, we shall try to take the problem out of the narrow utilitarian mould of conventional economic analysis and to consider it from a wider perspective. We shall bring to bear on the subject available information from other social sciences and from the behavioural school, and we shall eventually suggest a utility system possessing a number of psychological, sociological and economic elements such as 'dynamic aspiration', 'self-identification', class orientation, and desire for power, status, wealth and personal security. Similarly, we shall find that internal sociology of working in a team, the managerial code of professional competence, the system of rewards for the managers in the form of salary, bonus or stock-option schemes and the objective nature of the organisation of the modern corporation can be made to yield definite behavioural implications. The main concluding theorem is that the various pressures mentioned above lead managers to maximise the rate of growth of the firm they are employed in subject to a constraint imposed by the security motive.

c

Many readers may consider this conclusion to be acceptable on its face value as intuitively obvious or adequately justified by introspection: such may prefer to proceed directly to the next chapter where we use the hypothesis to build our economic models. Thus, for most of the remaining chapters, we postulate a managerial utility function, as finally developed in the present chapter, consisting of two variables, growth and security. We represent the former by the growth rate of gross assets and the latter by the valuation ratio. The former acts as an indicator of the several satisfactions associated with scale (salary, power, prestige) and the latter as a proxy for both security and other utilities, including class orientation, which are discussed below.

Theories of Motivation

There are three main approaches to any problem in human motivation, loosely, the psychological, the sociological and the economic, the last being further divisible into two, which we may call the 'broad' and the 'narrow'. The psychological approach concentrates on the individual's inner wants and drives. The sociological approach modifies psychological drives by systematic reference to the effects of his social situation, of his involvement, that is, with other individuals at work and at play. The two economic approaches are not alternatives; both represent a calculus of rationality founded in utilitarianism; both endow humans with psychological, sociological and material needs, expressed in utility functions which, once specified, serve merely as vehicles for the analysis of consistent behaviour — the latter representing the main problem of interest. The distinction lies in the feature that the 'broad' considers all variates, while the other concentrates on so-called narrowly economic factors such as income, wealth, tangible consumption and saving.

The psychological method may also be subdivided: into that of the 'behaviourist' school on the one hand, and that which for want of a better word might be called the 'purposive' on the other. It is convenient to defer discussion of the behaviourists until later in the chapter: briefly, rather than asking what it is the individual wants or needs, this school asks how, given his neuronic equipment and

informational situation, he appears likely to be induced to behave. [3]
The behaviourist could be said to attempt to consider humans by
analogy to relatively simple machines, rather than as creatively
thinking animals or complex machines. This does not mean that
human complexity is denied, but merely that it is thought that, for
the time being, simple models are most efficient. We do not have to
settle the nature of the mind to appreciate the potential predictive
advantages of analogies with simple machines here, and the method
has, in fact, been used with some effect to criticise the foundations
of economic theories based on maximising assumptions. But in
turn it has its own weaknesses, and, as already mentioned, we
return to the subject later (p. 107 and p. 289).

Psychological Motives

'Purposive' psychological studies of the type required for suggesting ways in which psychology may influence actual business
decisions are as rare as any. Some studies have been made of the
character-types of successful executives, but in no case is it clear
whether the elements discovered may not also be typical of any
successful professional man, or at least of any successful administrator. The work of two writers, however, deserves attention. As
long ago as 1948, W. E. Henry published the results of interviews
with a sample of a hundred successful top managers, concisely
describing his findings as those of a 'study in the psycho-dynamics
of a social role'. [4] He noted that these men tended to be psychologically well-integrated persons who nevertheless possessed strong
drives towards achievement. As might be expected from the fact
that only the successful were selected for interview, these drives
were found to be pressing and continuous; as fast as objectives
were achieved, new aspirations arose. Also unsurprisingly, the
subjects were not merely ambitious but active, not dreamers, but
doers. They were impelled, it seems, to move continually onward
and upward, at least until nearing retirement. The implications for
the theory of the firm would be that whatever it is the executive
wishes to do with his organisation, he is always attempting to repeat
and enlarge the performance; and although the drive is personal,
some of the dynamic effect must surely wash over into the behaviour

of the firm as such. An individual may partly satisfy dynamic aspirations by rising within one firm or by successive inter-firm transfers, but as he approaches the top, unless transfers are easy, he can progress further only by inducing the firm itself to grow. In other words, the motive for collective expansion may be directly founded in personal ambition.

The second psychological contribution to be mentioned is that of George Katona.[5] In a book which is concerned with the psychological aspects of economic behaviour as a whole, this author argues forcefully that the executive is likely to identify his own ego with 'his' own firm. Rather than seeing the firm as a mere apparatus for satisfying personal wants, he sees the prosperity and success of the firm as an actual proxy for his wants. In the extreme, this hypothesis would predict that a man would not mind suffering personal privation provided only that the firm was doing well. Unfortunately, because the relevant criteria of a firm's success are not defined, the policy implications are ambiguous. Katona suggests that business success is defined by profits, but, except to the extent that profits are required to expand other possible indices, such as turnover, this is no more than an induction. William Baumol, for example[6] — one of the only two economists to have previously attempted an overtly managerial theory of the firm — states that in his experience as a business consultant he found a dominant desire for maximum turnover, and suggested that this end was generally pursued, subject to a minimum profit constraint. Baumol's experience is supported by the common observation of anyone with contacts in the business world or who has studied business periodicals. In the periodical literature, for example, 'profits' and 'turnover' seem to be used indiscriminantly as synonyms for 'good'. The real distinction, however, as we shall soon see, lies between indices such as aggregate turnover, aggregate profits or aggregate assets which necessarily vary with the scale of the firm, and others, such as rate of return or profit margin, which do not. If Katona's motive of self-identification is applied to indices which vary with scale, it reinforces our deductions from the findings of Henry, for, if executives tend to identify with the organisations in which they already happen to be employed, they are less likely to seek outlets for ambition by transfer and more likely to choose the method of internal expansion.

With this conclusion we move on to sociology.

Sociological Motives

To apply the sociological method to business motivation it is necessary to characterise the business man's social rôle and his place in the social structure; in particular we need valid descriptions of the class to which he generally belongs and of the norms, if any, to which he is predominantly subject. Is he merely another species of professional man, like a doctor, a teacher or a technician — the ideal type envisaged by the originators of the idea of the managerial revolution? Is he, as A. A. Berle supposes, the possessor of a distinct professional ethic based on a clear perception of duty to society, leading by implication to the concept of a corporate conscience? Is he, as Mr Kenn Rodgers has suggested, [7] governed mainly by unconscious prejudice? Is he the helpless prisoner of William Whyte's conformist organisational ethic? [8] Or is he fundamentally no more than a loyal member of the class identified by C. Wright Mills [9] as the 'corporate rich' — intermarried, interdependent and intermotivated with the small group of families who still own the great proportion of most (non-socialist) nations' private wealth? The answers, of course, are all affirmative. More than any other type, the business executive is many-sided and multi-motivated. He has professional ethics, he feels a sense of public service and is not insensitive to public opinion. He is both a member of the corporate rich and an Organisation Man. But it seems that the nearer he gets to the top, the more he is of the former and the less of the latter (Whyte's account, it will be remembered, related particularly to middle managers, and he noted that chief executives and such appeared rather different [10]). Or, to switch to David Riesman's language, it would seem that top men are still characteristically inner-directed. [11] Neo-Marxists of the Wright-Mills school might argue that these men were of course the ones most closely connected with the propertied class, and that the other-directedness of middle management arose from its relative impotence in face of the power realities in the strata above them. In the present book, however, we are not primarily concerned with the politics or general sociology of contemporary capitalism. We need only the minimum 'non-economic' hypotheses required for the bases of valid models of the system's micro-economics. We are not interested in the way top executives vote, lobby or otherwise pressurise society. We are interested only in the way their norms affect their internal or 'operational' decisions. Thus a good part of the material in debate between those who regard managers as de-institutionalised professional men and those who regard them as institutionalised tycoons can be ignored. The implications of what remain prove tenuous, although not, however, unsuggestive.

The 'professional code' seems particularly elusive. Executives are palpably unlike the idealised medicos so frequently referred to by sociologists in describing normative behaviour. In the first place, as J. H. Goldthorpe has pointed out,[12] if such a code exists it is particularly likely to be afflicted with contradictions: for example, unless one is able to suppress the existence of numerous circumstances where the firm's and society's interests must conflict, it is difficult to reconcile the norm of loyalty to the organisation with the norm of service to society. In the second place, the same sociologist has suggested that there is some reason to believe that managers are in an anomic situation. To quote Mr. Goldthorpe at some length,

'My general conclusion must then be this: that modern corporation managers do not operate within the context of an entirely well-defined normative order. Even supposing that they have a fairly clear idea of what to do to further their own pecuniary gain, what must they do to further those aspects of their self-interest which depend upon their relations and standing with others? In other words, what exactly are the normative expectations of executives which others hold? My suggestion is that there does not exist any consistent set of such expectations; that in modern society there is no generally accepted and clearly represented institutional rôle established for business executives. Thus, on a sociological basis, one would expect that the motivational forces which prompt executive behaviour would tend to be variable, and that they would fluctuate with differing external conditions — e.g. the business situation of the enterprise, the political climate and so on. Also it might be suggested that since there is considerable uncertainty about the institutional rôle of the manager, there will be a greater tendency for him — than, say, for the professional — to concentrate on pecuniary gain; i.e. to concentrate on that aspect of his self-interest which has least direct dependence upon his meeting the expectations implicit in a normative code. It has been frequently argued by sociologists that where the structure of a society is imperfectly integrated, so that essentially incompatible things are expected of the same individual, the common response of the latter to his psychological insecurity is the aggressive pursuit of narrowly defined, material self-interest. This, for example, is what Elton Mayo was getting at when he inverted R. H. Tawney's phrase of the "Sickness of an Acquisitive Society" into "The Acquisitiveness of a Sick Society".

These, then, are some of the general expectations I would have of the findings of sociological research into the motivations of managers, if and when this gets under way. The one more specific probability I would mention is this: that one would expect in the light of the foregoing that managerial motivation would be strongest towards those objectives which satisfy most of the expectations of others and offend the least, and which at the same time are clearly conducive to executives' own material welfare. Of the possibilities here, one it seems to me stands out above all others; that is the objective of growth. The range of satisfactions which this objective has to offer the executive is, I would suggest, significantly greater than any other.'[13]

If Mr. Goldthorpe is right, our enquiry should be concentrated on two problems only: on the determinants of the appropriate 'narrow' economic rewards and on the implications of the motive of growth. That, in effect, is the intent of the later sections of this chapter. (We shall find the two problems to be significantly linked: the corporate world, it appears, has developed financial incentives which, applied in conjunction with certain functional requirements, must tend to stimulate top managers to promote organisational growth.) In the meantime, it is worth seeing whether anything more can be done by means of the orthodox normative approach. In the sections immediately following, therefore, we first further consider the 'external' sociology of the manager's situation, that is to say the effect of influences coming from outside the firm. Then we venture into the virtually unmapped area of 'internal' managerial sociology, with special reference to the possible effects of working in close-knit, professional teams.

The Wright-Mills thesis implies that managers should have a marked sense of loyalty towards the propertied class as a whole, including both those who are themselves managers and those who are not. Being himself relatively rich, the typical manager holds considerably more equity stock than the average citizen, and though the bulk of his portfolio does not typically consist of shares in the corporation which employs him, he may nevertheless feel precisely that sense of 'conscience towards the shares' at which we first hinted in Chapter 1. He may be inhibited from pursuing policies which in his secondary rôle as a man of property he would not like to see pursued by another firm of which he was himself a shareholder. If valid, this would seem a very powerful consideration indeed; as powerful, perhaps, as that represented in the fear of take-over raids.

Ambiguities, however, remain. In the Neo-Marxist conception, the 'corporate rich' are by no means typical investors: they are persons of power with important minority holdings in relatively small numbers of strategically placed companies. Towards more typical shareholders, managers may feel no more and no less a sense of duty than they do towards, say, manual employees or customers. (In nasty old Britain we would say it all depends on whether managers think of themselves as middle-class or as upper-class, the answer being that some *are* middle-class, some upper.) But if we are prepared to ignore this difficulty, we can with reasonable confidence adopt the hypothesis that some kind of stockholder-oriented conscience does usually exist in the managerial breast and that this is best expressed by saying that the current market quotation of the shares may enter the managers' utility function as an independent variate.

A conscience, however, is as much a source of potential conflict as of harmony. Managers, in considering how they would expect other managers to behave, and hence how they themselves should behave, must surely recognise the legitimacy of self-interest,

particularly if, as has been suggested earlier, their world is unusually materialistic. If, for example, policies required to maximise the
market value of the stock would conflict with policies required to
further some other recognized managerial end, moral behaviour
need not insist that the former should always take precedence over
the latter, because managers will expect other managers to sympa-
thise with the position. Consequently, the most likely result is
compromise. This might well take the form of setting a minimum
on the valuation ratio, as suggested at the end of Chapter 1, then,
subject to the constraint, maximising other utilities. If the resulting
policies are criticised for failing to *maximise* the valuation, the
corporate leader may argue that he, and he alone, knows what is
best for the corporation and its shares in the long run. Such an
attitude may be seen as the other face of managerial paternalism.[14]

All ethics conflict with self-interest, and few societies rely on the
effectiveness of conscience alone. Sanctions are universal. But if
moral behaviour depends exclusively on enforcement (as is still the
case in unfortunate countries where the people lack a well-
developed sense of public morality), the outcome is notoriously
inefficient and not infrequently results in social and economic
stagnation. By contrast, in better balanced societies internalised
discipline effectively reinforces external sanction, and the social
mechanism is permitted to function with the minimum of policing.
The analogy must surely be valid for business. In adhering to a
reasonable minimum valuation ratio, the firm not only satisfies
conscience but avoids the sanction of take-over. We have never
intended to argue that managers' attitudes to the stock-market
were governed solely by fear of raiders. We believe their attitudes
in this area to be almost precisely analogous to that of middle-class
children in relation to stealing and the police.

The idea of a conscience reinforced by a discipline can be applied to other aspects of corporate policy, in particular to the double
restraint on excessive leverage which should be imposed by fear of
the personal consequences of financial failure (i.e. of loss of
employment) on the one hand, and by a conscience towards the
equity-holders on the other. These further applications will be
developed in due course. Otherwise, there is little more to be

obtained from 'external' sociological considerations, and we next investigate the internal aspects of the problem; we consider, that is, the policy implications of the office environment itself.

A Norm of Professional Competence

To whatever class he belongs in the context of his home, his club or his general culture, the manager at work is in continuous contact with colleagues from whom he experiences both pressures and stimuli. What form will these take? In attempting an answer, we are faced with an almost complete *lacuna* in established knowledge, and are forced virtually to improvise.

Groups of people collaborating in teams tend to develop what might be described as 'a norm of professional competence' relating to the efficiency of individual performance. When one member is inefficient, the others inevitably suffer, if only because they are often compelled to take on part of his work. Consequently the delinquent may experience contempt and even hatred. Where the interdependence is close, as in football, mountaineering or yachting, such pressures are known to become intense. It is impossible to believe that a similar effect is not felt within business organisations.

The norm, however, has positive as well as negative aspects. Not only are the incompetent despised, but the competent, even when personally unattractive, are admired. And the desire for professional approbation being one of the most powerful features of middle-class masculine psychology, the most competent and aspiring members of any team will tend to favour 'testing' policies, i.e. policies which provide opportunities for demonstrating prowess and by the same token increase the group's relative need for men of ability. In other words, such men will favour the setting of difficult, rather than easy goals, and in business they will press for the adoption of policies which emphasise the least routine aspects of the collective function. Of course, their views will not always prevail: internal social equilibrium (and hence efficiency) will require that attention also be paid to the needs of the weaker vessels. How the balance is struck will vary considerably between organisations, those in which the tear-aways dominate being usually described as 'go-ahead' or 'dynamic'. In all cases, however, because ability to persuade others is in business life fairly well correlated with ability in general (persuasive ability being so much a requirement of the general function), there should be a tendency for the more aggressive policies to push to the front and to be restrained (in a sociological sense) only by the specific 'drag' of the weaker members; apparent exceptions usually turn out to involve firms containing strong residual traditional-capitalist elements.

Unfortunately, to say that executives will be influenced by a norm of professional competence does not provide immediate policy implications, because in the absence of clearly defined goals (unlike the case of football) we have no established criteria by which competence is to be judged or methods by which ability is to be demonstrated. A man may be judged competent by the quality of his decisions, but if we do not know the organisation's goals how do we tell whether a decision is 'good'? The answer perhaps is a criterion based less on the nature of the decisions than on the manner of their taking and execution; alternatively, perhaps, on ability to persuade others of their desirability. In other words, the criterion of competence may be derived mainly from the character of the function.

We have previously argued that the functional essence of management lay in the provision of organisation. Organisation involves not only taking decisions, but also co-ordinating decisions and generally seeing that they are made swiftly, consistently, and apparently in accordance with policy. In principle, the 'pure' organiser is not supposed to make policy but only to carry it out. But the power of management, we have seen, lies in the fact that wherever an organisational task is of a high order — as is necessarily the case in business — persons entrusted with executing policy in practice inevitably acquire considerable influence over its determination. Nevertheless, at the level of operations, managerial society may well perceive its rôle as particularly concerned with the 'executive' function in the literal sense of the term. In other words, in this society, a man's ability and hence his status within the group may well be judged primarily by his ability as an organiser. Today, when one young executive describes another as a 'good businessman', more often than not he does not mean, as in popular parlance, a man with a good nose for profits, but rather a man who keeps his records in order, his staff contented, his contacts active and his pipelines filled; a man who does not make enemies, and is yet sufficiently intelligent to comprehend a complicated brief; not rash, but not suffering from indecision; a good committee man who knows both when to open his mouth and when to keep it shut.

But none of this implies that the system will admire only the humdrum administrator. We said that the norm of professional competence requires outlets for ability to prove competence in a positive sense, to prove not merely that one can jump to a certain height, but that one can jump higher than most of one's colleagues. We must therefore identify those kinds of policies which in particular test the ability to organise.

As we have already emphasised, the testing tasks of business life are those which are the least routine: the development and marketing of new products and of new methods of production, the planning and execution of expansion, the creation of organisation where none previously existed. Business administration differs from other administration in that the unit of organisation, the firm, is autonomous and expandable. A business organisation has the peculiar capacity to promote its own growth, because it can seek its own supplies of factors of production (including those of managerial personnel) and is free to attempt to develop demand for its own products. Unlike a Government department, a business has no 'establishment' laid down by Treasury, Parliament or Congress which can be varied only by negotiation. If sales can be made to expand, the resulting revenue is sufficient justification and means for hiring new personnel, and the necessary capital can be obtained directly or indirectly from the profits of previous successes. But all expansion requires organisation and planning (we discuss further implications in Chapter 6), and if not carefully organised and planned may be halted by various failures expressed economically in reduced profitability. Well-planned and well-executed expansion, on the other hand, is both stimulating and self-sustaining, and may thus represent to the executive a challenge similar to the challenge of difficult climbs in mountaineering. But both in mountaineering and in business there is little sympathy for those who overreach themselves. Here then, perhaps, we have the beginning of a theory. It is difficult to award the accolade of professional ability to a chief executive who competently maintains a constant output, with constant profits, constant product mix, and constant methods of production in a constant market! In order to demonstrate ability he must develop new markets, increase his share of old ones, develop new methods of production, organise a merger or at least do *something*.

There are reasons for supposing that the professional environment will not only favour organisational expansion, but also influence both the quality and direction of expansion and the means employed to achieve it. No-one really believes that real-life traditional capitalists are necessarily interested only in money, albeit with a peculiar rate of time discount. Given imperfect markets and hence an element of transcendence, traditional capitalists are able to choose products because they like them, or at least like producing them. Farmers enjoy farming (and are also heavy eaters); old-style publishers enjoy publishing and publish books they like or admire; small traders and manufacturers discover wants because they feel them in themselves. In general, the social sense of the traditional capitalist, where it exists (and, of course, there are some who lack any), consists in producing goods which he feels he might want to consume himself; alternatively, he may enjoy their vicarious consumption, convinced that at least one major class of consumers will not only buy but need them. Traditional capitalists also derive considerable satisfaction from providing employment; the sense of true paternalism, of having provided new opportunities for earning income, being very noticeable in this type of manufacturer.

The 'bureaucratic' environment of the large corporation, on the other hand, is likely to divert emphasis from the character of the goods and services produced to the skill with which these activities are organised. To the extent that professional competence is tested by expansion, any new product which sells will serve, and turnover, profits and organisational facility may become the exclusive criteria of assessment. Reputations will be built not only on the ability to notice products likely to succeed, but also on the ability to plan development, push sales and control the relation between input and output (witness, for example, the attitudes prevalent within publishing houses that have been modernised). Finally, there may develop a rather cynical attitude to both customers and workers. The concept of consumer-need disappears, and the only question of interest in connection with a proposed new product is whether a sufficient number of consumers, irrespective of 'real need', can be persuaded to buy it. The professional manager may feel less paternalism towards and greater social distance from the manual workers. 'Workers' become analogous to irritating pieces of machinery, always going wrong and interfering with the essential activity of the organisation, whatever that may be: the correct solution to labour troubles is a skilful personnel officer, himself another brand of technician.

In other words, the existence of a 'managerial' norm of competence is a possible explanation for some of the alleged irrationality, purposelessness and soullessness of which modern capitalism is currently accused by many liberal critics. The point should not be overdrawn; purposelessness may be inherent in all conditions of capitalist affluence, whether the institutional form is traditional or managerial. Furthermore, it is by no means certain that organisations of the modern type may not also develop biases for and against particular types of products. Such biases might be mainly unconscious, but none the less effective for that. In principle, if the norm of professional competence works in the way we have suggested above, it leaves no room for the play of 'non-economic' prejudice, but in practice this may well develop through a process of self-selection: variations in the psycho-analytical make-up of individual managers would be associated with both outward personality and internal prejudice: organisations will tend to gather together individuals of similar personality and therefore, perhaps, of similar biases. The theoretical implications would be as follows. Managerial organisations would favour growth, and this, we shall see, usually involves diversification. In principle, given the powers of large-scale organisation, no firm is restricted to any one product group; in principle it is free to roam the economy ever seeking new outlets. In practice, the extent of the search will be limited not only by dynamic restraints, but also, perhaps, by this unconscious bias. Some products will not be considered at all, others will be rejected for economically inadequate reasons and yet others taken up only to fail because feet were dragged in promoting them. Similarly, favoured products will be adopted and made to succeed, from allied causes. Given the very considerable uncertainty involved in assessing the economic prospects of any new product, such suggestions are not implausible. They are reinforced, as we shall see later, by similar factors operating from the side of technology. In the meantime, we suggest the best short description of the motivation induced by social existence in a managerial group is that of a drive towards efficient, well-organised expansion, associated with a persistent search for new opportunities from a set which is perceived as finite, at least at any one moment of time. With these hypotheses, we are ready to enter the supposedly better charted areas of both 'broad' and 'narrow' economic motivation proper.

Economic Motives ('Broad')

Until fairly recently, economists tended to argue that the distinction between the broad and the narrow economic approaches, as we have defined them, represented mainly a question of convenience: because the effects of the narrower variates in the utility function, such as income and wealth, were more easily analysed, the profession felt justified in concentrating on them alone, and in assuming that the introduction of others would be unlikely seriously to modify the qualitative, if not the quantitative, character of conclusions. In the field of consumer behaviour, the dangers of this approach have now been appreciated for some little time, and it is known, for example, that the introduction of sociologically interdependent preferences[15] may seriously affect important theorems in both normative and positive economics. On the side of production, however, discussion of the implications of 'broad' behaviour is still more or less rudimentary. Apart from the work of the behaviorist school, such discussion as there has been of economic motivation among salaried executives has been vitiated by the influence of a utilitarian tradition which grossly over-simplifies the character of the pleasures and pains associated with 'work'. In classical economics, there were virtually two sorts of people: entrepreneurs concerned exclusively with profits, and workers concerned only to maximise the difference between the pleasures derived from income and the pains derived from labouring. Work was always unpleasant, always axiomatically a source of purely negative utility. We now know that even for manual employees this simplification can lead to serious errors, especially when applied, for example, to incentive schemes. [16] When applied to the kind of 'worker' supposedly represented in management, the errors are even greater and their economic implication more far-reaching. The orthodox approach regarded both the modern manager and the traditional entrepreneur as, like the manual worker, little more than crude machines, delivering output in one-for-one direct relation to the associated monetary reward. The possibility of deriving considerable positive satisfaction from the function was thus ignored. Several writers, including Norman Buchanan and Chester Barnard, [17] began questioning the orthodox view as long ago as the late nineteen-thirties, but few of their pertinent observations were absorbed into the main stream of economic theory. The first comprehensive survey of the problem was undertaken by R. A. Gordon in 1945 as part of his classic study *Business Leadership in the Large Corporation.* [18]

Gordon first summarised the position as follows:

'The most important spurs to action by the businessman, other than the desire for goods for direct want-satisfaction, are probably the following: the urge for power, the desire for prestige and the related impulse of emulation, the creative urge, the propensity to identify oneself with a group and the related feeling of group loyalty, the desire for security, the urge for adventure and for "playing the game" for its own sake, and the desire to serve others. . . . These motives can be satisfied more or less through monetary rewards. They can also be satisfied in good part by other attractions which the large corporation offers its business leaders.' [19]

He then went on to discuss the various motivational elements identified above at greater length. For example, of the desire for power, he said:

'One of the most important of the non-financial incentives offered by the large corporation is the opportunity to satisfy the urge for personal power. The corporation executive possesses power by virtue of his position of authority in a firm which is itself powerful. His power is a product of his position rather than of personal wealth. Power in this case means authority over subordinates, control of the disposal of vast resources, and great influence over persons and affairs outside the firm. The corporation is a vehicle through which power comes to be held and exercised. . . . Power thus secured increases with the size of the firm. Here lies an important explanation of the tendency of many firms to become larger, even if sometimes the profitability of such expansion is open to serious question.'[20]

And of the desire for security,

'As we have seen, the large corporation caters effectively to this desire for security. The executive's compensation is relatively stable, and he is likely to have a high degree of security of tenure. Wholesale purges of executive ranks are rare, and top management, usually securely in control of the proxy machinery, seldom has to worry about retaining its position'[21]

Gordon's conclusions have since become widely accepted, although it has to be admitted that none of the hypotheses have been tested by methods which sociologists would regard as rigorous. The author was relying considerably on secondary material and did not clearly indicate to what extent the conclusions were directly supported in the case studies on which his book as a whole was based. Nevertheless, it can hardly be denied that the arguments are persuasive, and many would no doubt accept them as self-evident or adequately supported by introspection. In what follows we shall accept them as broadly correct.

We take as working assumptions, then, that in addition to 'narrow' economic rewards, such as salary, bonus, stock options, expense allowances, call girls[22] and the like, executives desire power, status, opportunity for creative satisfaction, opportunity for group-belonging and security. What are the policy implications? In attempting an answer, it is essential to distinguish between the collective and the individual aspects of the problem. Some policy decisions affect overall managerial utility in a Paretian sense, others do not. Some factors entering individual utility do not affect collective utility and vice versa. As a matter of fact, the individual executive rarely has the opportunity to trade off between power, salary, security, etc., because these are usually offered him in rather fixed proportions. For a number of reasons, some obvious, some further discussed later in the present chapter (p. 105), a man's advance in the executive hierarchy is almost always associated with commensurate gains in salary, 'perks', power, status (both internal and external) and security (the last through the medium of service contracts and pension arrangements). Thus this package of utilities, seen from the viewpoint of the individual, is no more than a general measure of personal success, and tells us little directly about decision-taking. With the possible exception of departmental empire-building, there is no obvious way in which an individual's policy decisions affect his relative chances of promotion. Furthermore, it is not until he has already reached a high position that he has much influence over policy anyway. It follows that the key to our problem is to be found, if anywhere, in the factors affecting collective utility alone.

There are clearly wide areas where policy choices affect the capacity of an organisation to provide utility for its members as a whole, and for its top executives in particular. In some cases the results come in combination, as for instance when expansion increases the number of high-level posts available to be filled by internal promotion, and thus enhances the prospects of both power and salary for existing members — but in others they do not. The effect of expansion on security, for example, depends on the associated effect on the likelihood of collective dismissal, which depends in turn on the danger of take-over or financial failure. Unlike the civil servant, the industrialist's immediate livelihood depends intimately on the continuity of his own organisation; if the organisation is disbanded there is no residual institution available to guarantee him employment. And if a top executive is thrown on the market because his previous firm has failed, he himself will be tainted with the failure and the demand for his services correspondingly affected.

A large firm is more difficult to take over than a small firm, but a firm attempting to grow too fast may, as we have seen, incur serious risks. Thus if two firms growing at different rates happen to reach the same absolute size at a given moment, the faster grower may be less secure, although, if it survives it will eventually, of course, overtake the slower grower not only in size but also in security.

Similar arguments apply to security from financial failure. J. Downie argued[23] that a large firm in crisis is more easily able to find temporary assistance than a small firm, but we must observe that the likelihood of crisis is itself considerably affected by leverage, which in turn, as we saw in Chapter 1, reacts on both size and growth. For example, consider two firms in the same industry at the same moment of time. Both are the same size in terms of book value of gross assets, earn the same rate of return, retain the same proportion of profits and display the same market valuation ratio. Neither, however, has any gearing and in both the common valuation ratio is already at the constrained minimum: neither could increase retentions or make a new issue without causing an impermissible decline in their stock prices. Both are growing at the same pace (measured in book value) and in both the growth rates of demand and of capacity are in balance.

Now suppose that the market conditions for their product change in such a way that the growth rate of demand increases, but the prospective rate of return does not (e.g. they are selling in a perfect market). Firm A decides to exploit the opportunity by issuing bonds; Firm B does nothing. With the proceeds of the bonds Firm A is not only able to expand discontinuously, but its maximum safe growth rate is also enhanced (see equation 1.1). If we then anticipate later argument by assuming that the growth rates of salary, power and prestige of the present senior members of A will increase *pari passu* with that of capacity, we can say that these men will steadily gain in utility relatively to their opposite numbers in firm B. But firm A is now more highly geared, more vulnerable to trade fluctuations and hence on this account less secure. At modest levels of gearing the effect may be small, but if growth by gearing were carried to extreme lengths the dangers would be real and serious. It is therefore significant that the great majority of firms practise only moderate gearing: in the U.K. for example, it has been found that over half the quoted companies pay out less than ten per cent of their net profits in interest, while, at the other extreme, only an insignificant fraction pay out more than 50 per cent:[24] in the U.S. the value of g (ratio of debt to gross assets) has been typically found to be less than twenty per cent.[25]

So when expressed in terms of effects on collective utility, the policy implications of the 'R. A. Gordon motives'[26] prove both analysable and important. They imply that power, salary, status, etc. come as joint products on one dimension of a transformation function, while security from take-over and financial failure is a competing product on another. The rate of transformation between them depends on accounting practices and stock-market behaviour, a relationship which must be a fundamental feature of any well-developed theory of the managerial enterprise.

So far, however, the existence of a further link between power-salary-status and organisational growth is no more than a working hypothesis. Our next task, therefore, is to show convincing argument why decisions leading to the expansion of a firm are likely to increase satisfaction for the men who make them.

For this purpose we propose to concentrate attention on the narrowest of all economic rewards, i.e. the various financial elements incorporated in salary, bonus and stock-option profits. If it is accepted that these almost always come jointly with power, status, etc., propositions established in relation to the one group of utilities will tend also to be valid for the other.

Economic Motives (Narrow)

The empirical study of managers' incomes is largely confined to the United States; even there, until fairly recently the amount of material hardly did justice to the importance of the subject. In contrast to the volumes that have been published about the wages of manual workers, probably less than half a million words have been devoted to the factors determining the rewards of the small group of men who, at the heads of large corporations, determine the economic destinies of nations.[27] In the present and following sections we rely considerably on the excellent work of David R. Roberts, supplementing his results with additional regression analyses, based on largely the same data, undertaken by ourselves for specific purposes according to the requirements of the argument. (Professor Roberts, of course, can in no way be held responsible for the uses we have made of his figures.)

First, a few basic facts. In a typical firm, the total compensation of all corporate offices (Presidents, Vice-Presidents, Treasurers and Secretaries) represents about two per cent of value added and about five per cent of profits, the inter-quartile ranges of these ratios running from one per cent to three per cent and from one per cent to ten per cent respectively.[30] Among corporate officers as a whole, current bonuses (excluding stock-option profits) account for thirty per cent of the total remuneration, but for chief executives of giant corporations this figure may reach as high as 60 per cent, while for middle managers, not corporate officers, it is typically around 20 per cent.[31] As to stock-option plans, it is thought that at the time of writing about three-quarters of all U.S. quoted companies operate some form of plan, the great majority of these having been instituted since 1950, when capital gains from the exercise of options became liable to tax at the capital-gains rate and no longer, as previously, at the more severe earned-income rate.[32] Finally, because compensation is intimately bound up with mobility, we note that although the extent of statistical inter-firm mobility among middle and junior executives is a matter of dispute, there is no doubt at all that mobility among senior men is very low indeed: Roberts[33] found that in a sample of 500 corporate officers only one in seven had changed firms since becoming an officer, and on average each had had only two and a half employers since the beginning of his career. It thus appears that while there is a fair amount of movement in the early stages of a managerial career, once a man has succeeded in reaching a high position in a firm he usually stays with it.

Against this general background, we may now consider the analytical implications of the various forms of financial reward in more detail. For convenience, we discuss first bonus, then stock options and finally basic compensation. Basic compensation or 'salary' is the most 'managerial' form, bonus schemes and stock-option plans being regarded in many quarters, of course, as positive devices for inducing traditional motivation among the salariat, or at least for bringing the interests of managers and stockholders into closer accord.

An Analysis of Bonus Schemes

'Current' bonuses may be related to the firm's aggregate gross profits, to aggregate net profits, or to net or gross profits after deducting a sum intended to provide a 'normal' return for share-holders. They may also be related, at least in principle, to the actual rate of return or to dividends. This multiplicity of possibilities may be described in a series of formulae, each expressing the total amount distributed in bonus as a function of the appropriate variables. The formulae, in effect, are algebraical representations of the rules for determining bonus laid down in the relevant documents. (For this reason we do not treat them as equations.)

Formula No.

$$(1) \quad B = \alpha \cdot p \cdot C$$

$$(2) \quad B = \alpha \cdot C \cdot (p - i \cdot g)$$

$$(3) \quad B = \alpha \cdot C \cdot (p - i \cdot g - k')$$

$$(4) \quad B = \alpha \cdot p$$

$$(5) \quad B = \alpha \cdot (p - i \cdot g)/(1 - g)$$

$$(6) \quad B = \alpha \cdot C \cdot (1 - r)(p - i \cdot g)$$

$$(7) \quad B = \alpha \cdot (1 - r)(p - i \cdot g)/(1 - g)$$

where

B = total amount distributed in bonus,

α = constant implied in the contract (this coefficient is not, of course, constant as between formulae or, with given formulae, between firms.),

k' = assumed 'normal' rate of return (not necessarily equal to market k).

On examination, these schemes can be seen to divide into two groups: on the one hand those in which aggregate bonus is made to vary with both profitability and scale, and on the other those where the amount depends on profitability alone, and is therefore independent of scale. In the first group, bonus may be increased by an expansion of the size of the firm (measured by C) with a constant rate of return; in the second group an increase in size will have no effect unless accompanied by a disproportionate increase in profits. The policy implications evidently differ considerably. We therefore analyse the two groups separately, calling the first, which includes formulae numbers (1), (2), (3) and (6), 'scale dependent', the second, comprising the remainder, 'scale independent'.

Managers subject to a scale-dependent formula are provided with an incentive to expand the size of the firm relatively to the number of people with whom the total amount of bonus must be shared. In practice this is just what happens when a firm grows: in the U.S., for example, a ten-per-cent increase in size is typically associated with a two-per-cent increase in the number of corporate officers.[34] Therefore all these formulae do in fact provide a considerable growth incentive, although some may appear to restrain the methods employed. Formula (1), however, favours any method, including high retentions, leverage and new issues, and is, in fact, likely to induce in management a considerable distaste for paying dividends.[35]

Formula (2) might superficially appear to provide a restraint on leverage, but this proves fallacious: provided the profit rate exceeds the interest rate, as leverage enhances net profit-earning capacity so it enhances bonus. Both the first two schemes, therefore, enhance rather than inhibit any managerial predisposition to expansion. (3) does so only if the expected return exceeds the chosen k', and (6) puts management into the same position as the stockholder: increased retentions lower immediate bonus, but accelerate the growth rate of bonus. Under (6), therefore, rational managers will favour growth by retentions only so long as the expected return exceeds their own rate of time discount, unless of course other utilities (such as increased basic salary) provide a sufficient offset. Significantly, (3) is less widely used than (1) and (2), and (6) is used hardly at all. It follows that under most typical scale-dependent schemes, even managers receiving more than half their remuneration in bonus could be behaving rationally if they permitted quite substantial downward variations in rate of return in exchange for the possibility of accelerated growth, provided only that significant other utility were associated with expansion as such.

The implications of the scale-independent formulae (4, 5 and 7) are obviously rather different. Although (5) encourages leverage, each favours maximisation of the net rate of return, and this, in some circumstances (see Chapter 6), might definitely inhibit expansion. (All the formulae, of course, encourage 'efficiency' in the sense of attempting to obtain profitability relatively to growth rate.) It is therefore of considerable significance that while some of the scale-dependent formulae are adopted widely, none of these are. No direct case of (7) is known, although a scheme having similar effects was recently ruled illegal by an American court![36] The author has heard of one example of (5): it arose in a management contract between a U.S. parent firm and the directors of their wholly owned British subsidiary — since the British directors would have no control over capital supplies, the only effect was that of an incentive to general efficiency.

Why are scale-dependent schemes so popular and the others not? Dare we suggest that it is because managers rather than share-holders devise them? Perhaps, therefore, we should not be surprised that Roberts[37] found little evidence of statistical association between form of compensation and rate of return: firms with above-average rates of return proved just as likely to be relying entirely on salary as firms making considerable use of bonuses, and similarly in the case of firms with below-average rates of return. Some writers, indeed, (e.g. Mrs. Penrose[38]) have gone so far as to imply that the true function of bonuses lies mainly in offering respectability for high levels of compensation which might otherwise be questioned by public opinion!

Stock-Option Plans

Stock-option plans are another matter. In the typical arrangement, the recipient is awarded by the company a right to buy, at a fixed price, a limited quantity of ordinary stock, which then becomes his absolute property to hold or sell as he pleases. Although he does not have to exercise the right immediately, the price is usually fixed at a small discount on the open-market quotation for the company's regular shares on the day of issue. He is therefore placed in a good position to realise a speculative profit.

The tax regulations, however, require that if the profits are to attract tax at the capital-gains rate alone, the option must be taken up within a relatively short time from the date of issue and the stock must be held for at least two years before selling. In other words, any capital profits must perforce be of the long-run kind, and the beneficiary is precluded from realising large net gains on a 'quick turn'. But provided the shares do not enter a period of secular decline after the option has been taken up, once the two years have elapsed it should not normally be difficult for senior executives aided by inside information to choose a good moment for selling, if that is what they want.

Provided the profits are not offered in lieu of regular salary, the arrangements are obviously most attractive to the recipients. Professional people, however well paid, find that because their incomes rise gradually, rather than in jumps, socio-dynamic factors inevitably cause expenditure to rise continuously in parallel; they therefore experience peculiar difficulty in saving and thus in accumulating those free assets so desirable for independence, security and a sense of belonging to the propertied class. Discontinuous increases in wealth, as provided in windfall capital gains, are therefore even more welcome than a comparison with the equivalent increase in time-discounted future salary would indicate. Furthermore, the benefit does not appear as a 'cost' in the company's accounts: the option discount (ratio of option price to market price on day of issue) is paid at the expense of regular shareholders in the form of dilution, and the effect, though certain, is difficult to observe. By contrast, if similar sums were paid as orthodox bonuses, they would appear in the accounts as profit-reducing expenses, and would not only attract tax at the full rate, but also, in all likelihood, public comment as well: they would be seen as profit-reducing, dividend-reducing or both. The stock-option method, therefore, represents a way of paying gratuities to managements which has the double advantage of ensuring that the whole cost falls on shareholders, while at the same time reducing the chance that the effect will be noticed. If shareholders, rather than managers, controlled methods of remuneration, they would serve their own interests better by providing incentives of the types offered in scale-independent bonus formulae. But, like bonus schemes, stock-option plans are devised, of course, by managers themselves, and in view of their real nature it is hardly surprising they are popular.

The implications are considerable. Whether the recipient finances the transaction from his own resources or employs a loan, he is immediately put in a 'bull' position in relation to his company, a position which, if he wants to avoid income tax, he must maintain for a substantial period. It is also likely that when the statutory period expires, even though a rational *rentier* arrangement of his portfolio would suggest selling at least part of the issue, both inertia and internal pressure to avoid becoming known as a man who sells his company short may lead him to hold on. It seems inevitable, therefore, that whatever the original intention behind the schemes, they will ultimately lead to a significant statistical increase in the proportion of his own company's stock held by the average manager. Actually, statistics relating to the stock proportions held by full-time directors do not yet show any marked trend, although nothing is known, of course, about holdings of managers who are not directors. The holdings of the full-time members of a typical board still represent no more than one per cent of total stock,[39] and it is possible that these men have been balancing their portfolios by selling old holdings to the equivalent of the amounts of the options taken up. If so, the effects of the movement would be largely confined to middle and upper-middle management and the policy implications correspondingly reduced. None of these arguments, however, provides sufficient grounds for dismissing the quantitative implications of stock options as trivial. The legislation must have been intended to encourage 'neo-classical' behaviour, and there can be little doubt that in the United States, somewhat in contrast to the other Western countries, the ideological yearning to legitimise the modern system by restoring classical-type motivation is powerful. Business-school texts increasingly emphasise profit and shareholder-welfare maximisation as normative axioms, and any tendency to increase managerial stockholding is bound to strengthen the incentive to obey. Do these stock-option schemes, together with the associated developments in the ideological climate, represent an institutional change which might gradually remove some of the contradictions otherwise inherent in the neo-classical conception of capitalism?

To answer the question we need to undertake a fairly precise analysis to attempt to determine whether, in fact, the qualitative effect of option schemes is likely to do any more than merely reinforce the pressures we have already identified as favouring a constraint on the valuation ratio. This done, we must attempt to quantify the relevant variables. A complete analysis involves some rather complex algebra, but we may obtain reasonably general results by concentrating on one or two simplified cases. We first consider the effect of an option scheme on policy towards the retention ratio in a firm which has unlimited investment prospects at a given, constant, and negative return discrepancy. This done, we consider the case where, the rate of return being an adjustable variable related to growth, a wide range of policies is consistent with both a constrained valuation ratio and balanced growth, and then ask how the option scheme may affect the choices made from among them. In the course of the analysis we anticipate later findings by assuming that any increase in growth rate of capacity leads directly to increased growth rate of expected salaries.

The most convenient approach is to define first an aggregate called the 'total imputed wealth' of the manager, i.e. the sum of the present value of his discounted stream of expected future salary payments and the market value of his holdings of company stock. We ignore holdings of other assets, and for the moment assume that the manager is a typical investor in relation to his company, applying the same discount rate to the expected total return from his shares as is applied by the market as a whole. Also — a rather bolder and more drastic assumption — we suppose that he applies this same rate of discount to his salary expectations (both salary and dividends are in practice uncertain, but differently so and the relevant time horizons are also very different): we do not think a more realistic assumption would seriously affect our conclusions, and, in any case, we do not know which way the effect would go. Then we define the following symbols:

W_1 = market value of management holdings,
W_2 = present value of salary expectation,
W = total imputed wealth,
f = proportion of company's stock in management hands,
s = ratio of total current salary and bonus (excluding dividends on stock) to current profits,
β = a structural coefficient quantified later in the chapter (pp. 83–4).

Assume no leverage, no new issues, and no liquid assets. The company has sufficient demand to match any growth rate of capacity, therefore the growth rate of dividends, of book value and of productive capacity is given uniquely as the product of the rate of return (p) and the retention ratio (r). As in Chapter 1 we assume a perfect capital market, and value management holdings exactly in accordance with the simple theory described there (pp. 18–22). The market value of management holdings then becomes

$$W_1 = \frac{C \cdot f \cdot (1 - r)}{1 - r + \pi} \qquad (2.1)$$

The present value of future salary is the current salary discounted at k minus the expected salary growth rate. The expected salary growth rate is a function of the expected growth rate of capacity, whose form (implied by later findings) is

$$S^{\cdot} = \beta \cdot C^{\cdot} = \beta \cdot r \cdot p \qquad (2.1a)$$

The co-efficient β is later found to be a number lying between 0·5 and 0·2: aggregate salaries of corporate officers appear to increase by five per cent for every ten per cent increase in capacity, but a ten per cent increase in size is associated with a two per cent increase in the number of officers, therefore *per capita* salaries increase by about three per cent. It can then be shown that the discounted value of expected salaries is given by

$$W_2 = \frac{C \cdot s}{1 - \beta r + \pi} \qquad (2.2)$$

The most important difference between (2.1) and (2.2) lies, of course, in the fact that in the former retentions have a two-way effect on value (reducing dividends but increasing growth), whereas in the latter, because neither salary nor bonus is affected by the dividends (see above), the effect is positive only.

Total imputed wealth is

$$W = W_1 + W_2 \tag{2.3}$$

— where π, as defined in Chapter 1, continues to signify the negative return discrepancy ratio. Both W_1 and W_2 vary with retentions, therefore by differentiating W with respect to r, we may discover the qualitative effects of retentions on wealth.

Suppose a firm at present retaining nothing ($r=0$), and therefore on the assumptions not growing at all, discovers a method by which rapid growth could in fact be achieved by policies involving a significantly negative return discrepancy, that is to say, in order to achieve the necessary growth rate of demand the rate of return would have to be allowed to fall significantly below the market rate of discount. Suppose there is a range of such policies all consistent with balanced growth, and that for some reason the management has neither conscience nor fear of raiders, so that the only possible motive for not adopting one of these policies would derive from the effect, if any, on their imputed wealth. In their capacity as stockholders they necessarily dislike all such policies and would prefer zero retentions, but in their capacity as employees they appreciate that the policies may enhance their salaries.

The policies require that the retention ratio be raised from zero to some appropriate positive value, and it follows that unless, when r is zero, $\delta W/\delta r$ is positive, none of the policies can be 'profitable' to management, unless the derivative itself increases with r. Conversely, if, when r is zero, $\delta W/\delta r$ *is* positive, there is a *prima facie* case that at least one of the policies will be favoured. It is possible to show that $\delta W/\delta r$ cannot, in fact, increase with r, and that the critical condition favouring increased retentions, starting from the position where retentions are zero, is given by

$$\frac{s}{f} < \frac{\beta}{\pi} \tag{2.4}$$

— this being the condition for the derivative to be positive.

If the discount rate were 0·10 and the rate of return were 0·05, π would be 1·0. With these values, and the value of β at 0·30, the right-hand side of the inequality would be a fraction of the order of one third. The left-hand side is the ratio of two ratios, that of aggregate salary to current profits in the initial position and the managerial stockholding ratio. It represents, in a dimensionally standardised form, the extent to which management wealth is derived from two alternative sources. We have already seen (p. 67 above) that in a U.S. corporation of average size the salary bill for all corporate officers averages five per cent of profits, and we know from other sources [40] that the total stockholdings of directors who are full-time officers are about one per cent. We have no record of the stockholdings of other managers, however, and, as already indicated, it is possible that through the spread of option schemes these are becoming quite substantial; but we are concerned, of course, only with the holdings of those who are genuine members of the top decision-taking in-group. If the suggested values for s and β are accepted it will be seen that, in order completely to deter a discrepancy ratio of unity, management stockholdings would have to reach about $1\frac{3}{4}$ per cent. If the rate of discount remained at ten per cent and policy were modified in such a way as to increase the rate of return to seven per cent f would have to reach about $3\frac{1}{2}$ per cent, a state of affairs which, we suspect, would probably represent a doubling of the present true figure. In short, in order completely to deter all investments at significant negative return discrepancies, the extent of management stockholding would probably have to increase dramatically.

What happens when the expected return discrepancy is positive rather than negative? More precisely, suppose that a firm pursuing a given policy (implying a specific rate of expansion, rate of return and retention ratio) observes that not only does this policy yield a positive discrepancy, but that there exist alternative policies implying faster rates of expansion with little or no reduction in the rate of return. As we saw in Chapter 1, such situations are difficult to analyse without a more sophisticated theory of stock-market values than we have been able to describe so far. However, if the reader will accept as a working hypothesis that we can validly modify the simple model by assuming that, instead of being independent, the market discount rate varies directly with the retention ratio while the rate at which managerial salaries are discounted does not, the problem can be put in the following way: Policy A, let us say, consists in staying put; the return discrepancy on existing assets is positive, the market valuation exceeds the safe minimum and no growth is attempted: the management's total imputed wealth consists in their stock, valued above par, and their salary, valued on the assumption that this is static. Regular shareholders, and managers in their stockholding capacity, benefit from the super-valuation in the market; managers in their capacity as salary-earners suffer from the absence of growth. Policy B consists in raising retentions and accelerating expansion until the valuation ratio is reduced to the safe minimum; the firm obtains maximum growth consistent with the constraint. As compared with Policy A *shareholders* are less well off. But *managers* now benefit from the prospect of rising salary due to positive growth, and whether, from their point of view, Policy A or Policy B is best will depend on the general algebra of the problem and also, as in the previous example, on the ratio between their initial holdings of stock and their initial salaries.

Is it likely that the position will be such that on the basis of narrow managerial self-interest only, Policy A will be favoured? The answer appears negative. We do not give a detailed proof here, but the reader will find that if he applies the stock-market-behaviour equations (5.4) and (5.5), as set out in Chapter 5 below, only in rather unlikely cases would Policy A be managerially 'profitable'. The explanation of this result is that the magnitude of the initial return discrepancy enters both sides of the calculation: the higher it is, the more the stockholder has to lose if it is eliminated, but so also the salary-earner if it is not, because the larger the discrepancy the greater the acceleration of growth required to eliminate it.

Thus, up to this point we may conclude that managerial stockholding on either the present or even a substantially enhanced scale, while significantly reinforcing the incentive to maintain a reasonable valuation ratio, is unlikely to do much more than that, is unlikely, for example, to enforce profit maximisation in the ordinarily understood sense. We are now ready, therefore, to consider the most important narrowly economic incentive of all, that is, basic salary. What determines it and why have we been so confident that it increases with the size of the firm?

Basic Compensation: a Neo-Classical Model

Basic salary is the largest single source of income for all but the heads of corporate giants. A modern business is inevitably partly 'bureaucratic', and reward in the form of regular salary is an essential element in any general characterisation of bureaucracy. Increased salary often leads to increased bonus and almost always leads to increased status. Salary, therefore, remains by far the best single indicator of overall managerial ophelimity.

Who or what determines executives' salaries? The general answer, it appears, is 'other executives'.[41] This almost unique feature of corporate life creates obvious problems of analysis, problems which, rather than being solved, are merely suppressed by assuming that salaries are determined by some person or body attempting to maximise the welfare of shareholders. Nevertheless, it is possible that a form of 'neo-classical' approach may provide a convenient stalking-horse with which to begin an attack on the question. In Chapter 1 we suggested that the essence of managerial capitalism lay in the separation of organisational talent from supplies of finance: a neo-classical system, we argued, would require that although large-scale organisation was widely exploited this separation did not occur. Organisers (managers) would need to be held to genuinely subordinate rôles and virtually deprived of all influence on policy except in a purely advisory capacity. Company policy would have to be determined by a quasi-entrepreneurial body, for example a committee or board specifically charged and powerfully motivated to act for the shareholders alone. This body, among other functions, would control salaries and ensure that all concerned had the incentives necessary to induce desirable behaviour. Let our stalking-horse, then, be a theory of the firm in which just such an arrangement actually existed.

Instead of electing a Board of Directors as we now know it, the Company Meeting would elect a committee of shareholders which would in turn appoint a subsidiary body to carry out the more detailed 'operational' functions now vested in boards. The superior committee would lay down the general lines of policy and keep control of all senior executive appointments and salaries, including all appointments to the subsidiary committee. The subsidiary committee would consist largely of full-time managers, none of whom would sit on the superior committee, and in fact no member of either committee could legally be a member of the other. Managers, therefore, would attend meetings of the policy-determining committee in the capacity of expert witnesses, and it would not be the practice for even the chief executive to be present throughout deliberations. Things would somehow be arranged so that membership of the shareholders' committee was not unduly onerous and need be only nominally remunerated. Whether, in real life, such a genuinely 'part-time' committee could succeed in its objects is doubtful, but we assume here that it does.

To add artistic verisimilitude to an otherwise unconvincing picture we might additionally assume that the committee had the right to employ outside consultants whose fees would be paid from company funds, the consultants being allowed to require from the management on the committee's behalf any information they desired, and being generally permitted to snoop around the office. They would owe loyalty exclusively to the shareholders and no ideas for 'the good of the company as a whole' should be supposed to colour their thinking.

Apart from these changes — the picture, surely, of an executive nightmare — the legal structure of the company would remain unchanged! The resulting institution would conform relatively closely to the corporate image projected in undergraduate schools of business. How then should the shareholders' committee determine salaries if the overriding criterion for all decisions were maximisation of the current market value of the equity?

The quantity to be determined is the salary-bill of the whole top-management team, i.e. the aggregate salaries of those persons who effectively make the high-level decisions still left to management under the new arrangements. (The decisions could be 'big' but genuinely executive alone.) By definition no firm has more than one such team. In large firms the number of members may be greater

D

than in small firms, but however large the firm the central group cannot exceed the maximum number of persons who can maintain regular intimate contact, safely share secrets and quickly make collective decisions. In the U.S., where it is the practice to designate substantial numbers of senior executives as Vice-Presidents (who are then recorded as company officers), the total number of corporate officers is probably a fair indicator of the size of this team, at least in manufacturing. Even though the two sets are not necessarily identical, the size of the in-group is certainly unlikely to exceed the number of officers, and the ratio between in-group and officers is likely to diminish with the size of the firm. In the Roberts sample (p. 69 above), it will be remembered that a ten-per-cent increase in size, measured by turnover, was statistically associated with about a two-per-cent increase in the number of officers, suggesting that the elasticity of the size of the in-group with respect to the size of the firm may well be less than a fifth.

Because, in our conception, the management team is basically unitary and indivisible, unlike other inputs, management cannot be subjected to ordinary quantitative variation. True, as the evidence mentioned above suggests, the optimum number of members may be a little greater in larger companies, but the team's capacity to earn profits cannot properly be thought of as a dependent function of its size. Instead we may imagine the variation as being qualitative, quality being defined by reference to some convenient standard, such as that of the ability of a team of optimum size to earn profits from a standard set of assets under standard conditions, a concept which should in principle be capable of measurement by the consultants. In effect, 'quality' would be analogous to intelligence in the individual, in the sense that whatever the method of measurement, the results were known to be highly correlated with specified types of performance, in this case with ability to earn profits from assets. Indeed, we might even conceive of each team as possessing an 'Ability Quotient', a number up to a linear transformation measurable by some method which did not involve observation of performance in the particular firm in which the subjects were now employed.

Given the concept of AQ, for good neo-classical results we

further require that teams and individuals are perfectly inter-
changeable in the sense that in a given firm — defined as a set of
physical assets, an established labour force and 'goodwill' — any
team of given AQ will with given policies obtain the same expected
profits. There is no special relationship between teams and their
firms, no tendency for a team's profit-earning capacity to be greater
in the firm in which it grew up than in others. We also assume there
is a unique market-determined supply price (total salary-bill) for
each ability level, and that to individual firms there is a perfectly
elastic supply of teams of given abilities. In other words, although
the firm will have to pay higher prices for superior teams, it can
always instantly obtain at least one team of given ability at the
appropriate price. The supply prices are determined entirely by
factors external to the managerial market: managers of all ability
levels face well-defined alternative occupations providing comparable Pigovian net advantages, and the market is always in overall
equilibrium; at any hint of disequilibrium large numbers of managers immediately convert themselves into teachers, doctors,
farmers, labour leaders and even politicians, or alternatively
teachers, farmers, labour leaders and even a few doctors successfully offer themselves as managers, as the case may be. The task of
the shareholders' committee, then, is to decide the optimum ability-
level for the team that is to manage their firm. In so doing, given
the assumptions, they determine the salary-bill. In other words
they are deciding the optimum salary.

Since there is a one-for-one relation between salary and AQ, we
may treat salary as a regular input in the production function, and
AQ need not feature directly at all. Given large-scale organisation,
the appropriate production function should display constant returns to scale: provided a team of appropriate ability is employed,
we assume the firm has no optimum size: if, when the scale of output is doubled, salary and all other inputs are doubled, the rate of
return is constant. Management then becomes a factor of production behaving exactly like manual labour in a Cobb-Douglas
function and we may in fact ignore manual labour, together with all
other inputs bar capital, and replace output with profits as the dependent variable. Then we have a model:

$$P = \alpha \cdot S^{\kappa} \cdot C^{1-\kappa} - S \quad 0 < \kappa < 1 \tag{2.5}$$

$$S^{*}_{(p)} = C \cdot \sigma_1 \tag{2.6}$$

$$p^{*} = \sigma_1 \cdot \sigma_2 \tag{2.7}$$

$$S^{*}_{(p)} = \frac{C \cdot p^{*}}{\sigma_2}, \text{ or, } \frac{S^{*}_{(p)}}{C \cdot p^{*}} = 1/\sigma_2 \tag{2.8}$$

where

P = profits,

S = management salary,

$S^{*}_{(p)}$ = optimum salary for maximum rate of return,

p^{*} = maximum rate of return,

σ_1 $= (\alpha \cdot \kappa)^{\left(\frac{1}{1-\kappa}\right)}$

σ_2 $= (1 - \kappa)/\kappa$

These results are obtained by differentiating P with respect to S.

Equation (2.5) represents the production function, or more correctly, the 'profit function', the production function proper being represented by the part to the left of the minus sign. Equation (2.6) shows the optimum salary level, obtained by differentiating equation (2.5) for maximum P and hence, given C, for maximum rate of return. The maximum rate of return, p^{*}, is shown in equation (2.7), and is constant and independent of C. Equation (2.8) is an alternative formulation of the optimum-salary relation, showing firstly how the salary is related to both size and (maximum) rate of return, and secondly the optimum ratio of salaries to profits: on the assumption that firms in the Roberts sample were modally optimising, the empirical value of this ratio is, as we have seen, typically of the order of 0·05.

In equation (2.6), the optimum salary is determined by size and the compound constant σ_1. This constant, however, also enters the equation determining the maximum rate of return. If it is low, perhaps on account of a low value of one of its components such as the coefficient α, the firm has qualitatively 'inefficient' assets or is pursuing policies tending to depress the rate of return even when factor combinations are optimal. In consequence the 'maximum' rate of return is itself depressed and the effect may be seen in equation (2.8).

Thus innate profitability of assets or policy or both, in affecting p^* also affects optimum salary. If something happened to depress α and hence p^* (for example, a secular decline in the relative prices at which the output could be sold), the existing management should be fired and replaced with a less expensive team of inferior ability. The model therefore predicts that if firms are optimising, both the observed rate of return and a measure of size will enter homogeneously into a valid estimating equation, or alternatively, that salaries will vary in strict proportion to total profits. So we employ an estimating equation of the form

$$\log S = a + b_1 \log C + b_2 \log p \qquad (2.9)$$

According to the present theory, b_1 and b_2 should not differ significantly either from each other or from unity, a prediction which may easily be tested on the Roberts data.

The Roberts sample is drawn from manufacturing corporations in a wide variety of industries, and it would be expected, therefore, that the constant α would vary considerably between them. The observed rate of return does in fact display substantial variance, and although it is directly associated with size to an extent which is statistically significant $(r = +0.3)$, this cross-correlation is not sufficiently strong to affect the validity of the estimates. For various statistical reasons, however,[42] it is desirable to substitute observed sales (turnover) in place of capital as the measure of size (given the Cobb-Douglas assumption, the capital output ratio must be independent). We also substitute total compensation including bonus (but excluding stock-option profits) in place of salary, because we have found that bonus is paid largely in lieu of salary (it would certainly be absurd to relate management ability to basic salary alone). We therefore computed the regression

$$\log Y = a + b_1 \log X_1 + b_2 \log X_2 \qquad (2.10)$$

where

Y = average total compensation of corporate officers (including salary and bonus) before tax, in the Roberts sample, 1948–50, $000's,

X_1 = average annual gross sales, 1948–50, $000,000's,

X_2 = average ratio of net profits to tangible net worth, 1948–50;

and obtained the following results:

$$b_1 = 0.55 \mp 0.04$$
$$b_2 = 0.19 \mp 0.11$$

$$R = 0.8$$

We also computed results for other forms of the same basic model, substituting other measures of size, such as employment and value added, and as an alternative measure of profitability, the ratio of profits to turnover. None of these variants improved the fit or yielded significantly different results; mostly they did not even improve the fit when included in multiple regressions along with the original variables.[43]

It will be seen that the estimates of b_1 and b_2 both differ very significantly from unity. They also differ significantly from each other, and b_2 is barely significantly different from zero ($t = 1.7$). The theory thus fails spectacularly, the more so as a highly significant result, but of quite the wrong magnitude, is obtained in relation to one of the variables, size, while in the case of the other, profitability, there is little evidence of any association at all.

It was Professor Roberts, of course, who first discovered that profitability had no apparent effect on salaries, and in his book he discussed the econometric ramifications of the problem at some length: the reader unconvinced by our account should read the original. It is possible that despite the fact that the data are averaged over three years, the explanatory failure of the rate of return is due to disturbance of profits by transitory factors which should be ignored in determining compensation, but this would not get round the fact that although b_2 is not significantly different from zero, it *is* significantly different from the value predicted by the theory. To rescue the theory, therefore, it would be necessary to find some convincing source of bias in the method of estimation. But as we do not believe the theory anyway, we leave that labour to others; we are quite satisfied with the plain man's conclusion that the theory is disproved. We need, then, either a different production function, different behaviour assumptions or both.

One apparent possibility is that the managerial production

function is usually non-homogeneous in the sense that the exponents of C and S do not sum to unity. If that were the case, the coefficients b_1 and b_2 in the predicted regression equation could take on almost any (positive) values and either, for example, could be greater or less than unity. However, it can be shown that if b_1 is substantially less than unity, as is found in the Roberts data, the great majority of firms in the sample must by implication be working under conditions of management-induced diminishing returns to scale, i.e. must have expanded beyond the conventional static optimum size. Since the sample displays a positive correlation between size and rate of return, this is not very convincing (although it would be conceivable that other economies of scale were overwhelming the managerial diseconomies). Non-homogeneity of the production function is, therefore, not a solution, and evidently the hypotheses need to be more radically changed.

A Revised Production Function

Suppose the production function is different altogether. For example, suppose capital and 'management' are required in unique proportions. In post-classical, static micro-economics, the U-shaped cost curve of the individual firm was usually explained by some intrinsic non-expandability of the function of co-ordination; the concept of an 'optimum size' of the firm was derived almost exclusively from a belief that beyond a certain point, however many managers were employed or however highly they were paid, inefficiency through co-ordination failure would be inevitable. The modern view (see Chapter 3 below), based on the observation that many firms appear able to grow continuously and apparently indefinitely, suggests that, provided the technical production function itself displays constant returns, profitability can be maintained given only that the firm is appropriately organised. In other words, rather than an 'optimum' management, there is a 'necessary' or 'appropriate' management. Management, instead of being represented as a variable factor of production, behaves more like oil: without minimum lubrication the machine breaks down, but more lubrication has little or no positive effect and is sometimes even harmful. In terms of the concept of AQ this would mean that, given the scale of the firm, a management of minimum ability was required in order to earn any profits at all, but that ability in excess of the minimum had no further effect. The larger the firm the more high-powered would be the team required, and by adjusting the team appropriately a firm could always obtain constant returns in expansion. The constant returns, however, would be profits before deducting compensation; consequently, the employment of 'excessive' management would depress true profitability, the additional salaries yielding no return. If so, we have a model:

$$P = \alpha . C . \mu - S \qquad \begin{array}{l} S < \bar{S}, \mu = 0 \\ S \geqslant \bar{S}, \mu = 1 \end{array} \qquad (2.11)$$

$$\bar{S} = \gamma . C^\beta \qquad (2.12)$$

if β is small,
$$p^* = \alpha - \gamma . C^{\beta-1} \qquad (2.13)$$

$$\delta p^* / \delta C \eqsim \gamma / C^2 \qquad (2.14)$$

where

$\bar{S} = $ 'required' compensation,

$\mu = $ binary variable.

These results are not obtained by differentiation. Both equations (2.11) and (2.12) represent original features of the production function, equation (2.13) stating that unless the salary $\bar{S}$ is paid, the capital earns no profits, while if S equals or exceeds $\bar{S}$ it earns constant returns, and equation (2.12) states that $\bar{S}$ is a function of C. Thus, provided a management of the AQ level indicated by the salary $\bar{S}$ is hired, the rate of return p^* is obtained, as given in equation (2.13). If an inferior management is hired, profits before salary are zero and profits after salary negative — if a team of ability $\bar{S}$ or better is unavailable, losses are minimised by closing down. If a superior management is hired, profits before salary, with given assets, remain constant and profits after salary decline; therefore maximum return is obtained with $S = \bar{S}$ only.

It will be seen that provided management is optimally adjusted as a firm expands, if the β coefficient is substantially less than unity there will be modestly increasing returns to scale, owing to managerial economies, and a reasonable approximation to the effect is given by equation (2.14); the returns increase at a diminishing rate according to an inverse square law. The model therefore predicts as follows:

(i) significant exponential relationship between compensation and size;

(ii) coefficient unrestricted, but if observed less than unity, there should also be positive association between size and rate of return, and if observed greater than unity, there should be corresponding negative association;

(iii) when size held constant, no significant association between compensation and rate of return;

(iv) logarithmic error distribution around predicted compensation should be positively skewed.

Predictions (i), (ii) and (iii) were tested, and confirmed, by the results already described. Prediction (iv) flows from the implicit assumption that the penalty for paying less than the required minimum salary is, in theory, disappearance, while firms paying more merely experience a relatively modest reduction in rate of return. This, too, is confirmed, the coefficient of skewness in the logarithmic deviations working out at about $+0.25$,[44] a result which is highly suggestive because particularly difficult to reconcile with the previous theory, or indeed with any theory implying a smooth transformation function between management input and profits. It has also the implication that compensation levels predicted from an estimating equation obtained by least-squares will significantly exceed the true minima, a point which should be borne in mind when interpreting the actual figures (in effect, the coefficient γ is over-estimated). Thus the model performs well predictively, and powerfully discriminates against other models. But it should be noted that it does not discriminate between the validity of alternative assumptions as to who or what actually determines salaries. According to the model, any viable firm must conform to the minimum payment, and even in the presence of a shareholders' committee the restraint on 'excess' payments is weak, particularly if we add a small dose of realism in the form of uncertainty. In other words, although the results strongly support the model's hypothesis as to the character of the managerial production function, it tells us little, so far, of implications for motivation. The observed results, and especially the error distribution, are consistent *both* with the hypothesis that the assumed production function is associated with salary determination by shareholders *and* with the hypothesis that it is associated with some other method.

There are further difficulties. Although the model performs well predictively it is not intuitively convincing from a conventional economic point of view. In the previous model, management is paid the value of its net marginal product, which in turn varies with the aggregate profit-earning capacity of the assets; in the present model management has no marginal product and is paid in unique proportion to the scale of the assets alone. To say that the optimum 'quantity' of management will vary closely with the scale of the job to be done is one thing, but to add that once a necessary minimum of this input is applied nothing will be gained by further increases is another. It is difficult to be convinced that, if a firm of given size and asset character fires a 'satisfactory' management and hires a more highly-paid 'superior' management, it can experience no gain at all in gross profits before salary. However, once we suggest that management does have a marginal product, we come up against the econometric contradictions: if management has a marginal product, this must vary, *inter alia*, with the profitability of the co-operant factors, therefore observed profitability should correlate; but, as we have seen, it does not.

The solution would seem to be to abandon orthodox economics. Perhaps there is no close relation between compensation and 'ability'; perhaps managerial ability is a spurious concept altogether? If so, we should have to look for another mechanism linking compensation with size, and generating the apparent 'production function'. It need not be 'non-economic'; it might merely result from types of relationships not normally considered by economic theorists. On one such theory, the original brain-child of Herbert Simon, [45] we shall build extensively below. In the meantime let us complete our neo-classical stalking-horse by applying the old assumption of the existence of a shareholders' committee, but to the new assumption concerning the production function.

Provided the committee employed the principle of profit

maximisation the altered production-function hypothesis would not, in fact, lead to greatly altered implications for managerial motivation. A management team which somehow succeeded in biasing policy in such a way that their firm expanded would still be signing their own dismissal notice, for if, as the assumptions require, the team's measured ability is independent of both policy and the size of the firm in which they are currently employed, expansion must require that a new team of superior ability be brought in from outside. Conversely, if a team's AQ increased but the size of their firm did not, they should immediately seek, and would easily find, better-paid employment elsewhere. Finally, if both size and AQ happened to increase simultaneously and in the correct proportions, strictly speaking the incumbent team would merely compete on equal terms with other candidates for meeting the new requirement. Thus the manager has no incentive to attempt to bias policy in any direction; true, if the firm's size changes he must change employers, but he can always find other positions at the same wage, and costs of movement are ignored. He can advance in life only by improving his AQ rating, and this, it will be remembered, is unaffected by historical events in his firm.

Here, then, is the finally revised neo-classical model. It is consistent with certain econometric facts, although not, of course, with other well-known facts of real life. What happens when we come down to earth?

The Simon Theory

Down on earth there are no shareholders' committees, at least in our sense. Managers determine one another's salaries and are far from elastic in supply. They represent a non-competing group in relation to the rest of the population and are typically paid considerably more than would be necessary in the long run to discourage them from turning to alternative occupations. They are not good substitutes for one another, and when combined in teams are normally much more 'productive' in the firm where the team was developed than in any other firm of comparable size and character. (If this were not the case we should expect to observe considerably more statistical mobility among corporate officers.)

All these realisms have far-reaching implications for methods of compensation, for motivation and for the behaviour of the system at large. But to say that managers, as a class, determine their own remuneration does not necessarily imply that they can take any sums they care to name. They are not acting collectively or conspiratorially and not necessarily even monopolistically. They are probably working within a system of rules developed from their own functional needs and based on their own norms. A managerially evolved system of executive compensation will be the socio-economic outcome of the whole office environment and not in any crude sense a mere conspiracy against the public. We are therefore presented with a considerable chicken-and-egg problem. The system of compensation is the result of the function, but must also, through motivation, affect the way the function is performed, i.e. must affect policy. Of course we shall never be able to say which came first. Rather we shall assume that managers have developed a system of incentives reflecting their own perceptions of their rôle, and so, by observing the results, we shall hope to gain insight into the ultimate origins of their motives.

All societies tend to develop economic incentives matched to sociological intent, and there is nothing very special about management in this respect. But in other walks of life the implications have already been analysed; so far, unlike traditional capitalism, where the 'profit motive' clearly matches a social ideal, managerial capitalism has escaped. (This is almost certainly the reason why the true implications of typical bonus schemes, for example, have been overlooked, for, as we have already suggested, these only begin to make sense when it is appreciated that instead of being designed by capitalists to induce managers to behave as capitalists think they ought, they are rather designed by managers as a self-inducement to what they believe their behaviour should be.) We seek, then, a reward system meeting the functional and social needs of a class of persons whose role is to provide the large-scale organisation necessary for economic activity on the scale of modern industry.

As a starting point we observe that all large organisations are compelled to adopt many of the characteristics of ideal-type bureaucracy in the sense originally described and employed by Max Weber.[46] In order to function efficiently they must be to some extent hierarchical, must to some extent define offices independently of persons, and must to some extent employ well-defined chains of command. In practice, particularly in business, it is difficult to avoid some semblance of the conventional pyramidal structure in which members are arranged in ascending levels of authority, the number of occupants declining as the level itself rises. This stems from the needs of co-ordination. To co-ordinate is to resolve disputes and inconsistencies, and if two or more persons occupy a given level of authority there must be at least one above them to perform this function. In practice, few business organisations are compelled to adhere to the principle rigidly: 'line and staff' methods cut across vertical boundaries and disputes can be resolved by committees. Nevertheless, a pyramid of sorts inevitably underlies almost all administrative structures, and can hardly be avoided if essential delegation is to be achieved without anarchy. In fact, the greater the degree of delegation the greater the need for authority. Committees may be, and are, widely employed as a partial substitute, but when these, as they must, fail to agree, some superior authority is compelled to act. (Informal committees such as exist widely in modern business firms are observed to achieve remarkably consistent apparent unanimity, a result which is almost certainly due in part to collective appreciation of the dangers of disunity, but also in part to the presence of chairmen who are senior to most of the other members and whose view is usually deferred to in the last resort: the committee system works precisely because it is backed up by the hierarchy.) When an organisation is described as 'flexible', what is usually meant is that it is not as rigidly hierarchical as some. Outside such relatively cloistered areas as intra-departmental administration in Universities, probably the only viable 'democratic' organisations operating anywhere in the world today are the co-operative settlements in Israel, and there, significantly, because the output is mainly agricultural, the administrative task, though not insignificant, is relatively small. Partly democratic institutions have been tried in agriculture by both Russia and China, but all have more or less failed. In manufacturing, democracy in the sense of government by all is unknown. The only alternative to government by all is government by pyramid, and it has everywhere prevailed.

Once it is accepted that pyramids are inevitable, it is difficult to escape a corresponding salary structure. For it has been forcibly argued (and this is the starting point of the Simon theory)[47] that the belief that a man must be paid more than his subordinates is virtually universal — a social law which has no conventional economic rationalisation, because, since middle-class males typically enjoy the psychic satisfactions of responsibility, the 'net advantages' approach would suggest that higher posts be paid less than lower posts, rather than the other way about. There are, of course, dozens of reasons why this does not happen, of which we need mention only three, each sufficient in itself to produce the familiar result. First, in any society where income and status are closely associated (which means almost any modern society where incomes are unequal) it is difficult, if not impossible, for authority either to be exercised or accepted in reverse order to income, or, more precisely, this is impossible wherever the persons concerned are in close contact. Authority may be accepted (up to a point) from a lower-paid policeman or other public official, but not from a lower-paid 'boss'; and where, as occasionally happens, such inversion is attempted, pathological tensions and suspicions almost inevitably arise. Secondly, position in bureaucratic hierarchies tends to be closely associated with age and experience, and, unlike the working classes, the middle classes 'expect' their incomes to rise over the life cycle, a distinction which remains as valid in the U.S., where there are supposed to be no classes, as anywhere else. Thirdly, in a system where the salaries of individual managers are decided by other managers, the salaries of subordinates are naturally decided by seniors, and are unlikely to be settled in such a way that determinors are paid less than determinees.

Therefore, the world over, Presidents are paid more than Vice-Presidents, Commissars more than Deputy-Commissars, Admirals more than Rear-Admirals, Peoples' Chiefs of Police more than Deputy Peoples' Chiefs of Police, and middle managers more than junior managers. This law, however, is internal to organisations and applies to whole societies only by aggregation. There is little apparent similarity in either the salaries paid at given levels in organisations of different types, or in the scale of gradation. In the U.S.S.R., top 'intellectuals' (academics, writers and the like) receive more than non-top intellectuals, but both, it seems, do better than corresponding administrators or industrial organisers, a position which, unfortunately for Western intellectuals, is elsewhere precisely reversed.

Once established sociologically, the law or convention spreads. Individuals may feel compelled to refuse high positions unless the salary is commensurate, even though on 'narrow' economic grounds they would have been happy to accept a lower figure. So we have an economic supply-relationship. Firms will see salaries as organisational status symbols, and within organisations of similar types both seniors and subordinates will come to expect and accept a conventional rate of gradation; if this is not obeyed, authority may break down. Thus observance becomes a functional necessity.

It is also worth noting how exceptions are typically dealt with. When, as indeed often happens, middle or junior managers supported by better offers from other employers succeed in negotiating increased personal salaries, the change is often legitimised by some real or simulated increase in responsibility. Indeed, in Western countries, 'responsibility' seems to be the key ideolog. In these countries the law in question may be stated as a widespread belief in one-for-one relationship between income and responsibility, an essentially aristocratic convention of possibly feudal origin. This may explain the relative downgrading of otherwise worthy persons who are notably free of responsibility. In Communist countries, on the other hand, there is some evidence that power and responsibility are regarded as their own rewards, while artists and such are provided with relatively high incomes in the hope of keeping them out of politics. Be that as it may, if we can find an appropriate measure of relative responsibility under managerial capitalism, we may have a considerable clue to the salary system.

If the basic idea of the pyramid is accepted, we may stylise the consequences as in Diagram 2.1. Each dot represents one manager, every individual has one boss — indicated by the apex of the

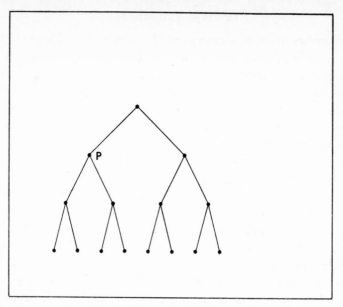

DIAGRAM 2.1. Standard Pyramid with Constant Span of Control

subsidiary pyramid of which he is a member — and the span of control— ratio of members at a level to members in the level below — is vertically constant. The last feature, however, is not essential. For the 'responsibility' of an individual may be measured by the number of people at the bottom level who, directly or indirectly, report through him. Thus the responsibility of the member at P is four, and the responsibility of the chief executive is all the occupants of the bottom level, i.e. eight. If then there is to be a behaviour relation between responsibility and salary, there must be a corresponding relation between span of control and rate of gradation. That is to say, if the span of control is not constant, the proportionate increase in salary between any given level and the level below must be a function of the span of control at that level; the more men you control, the greater the proportionate excess of your salary over theirs. If so, as Simon noticed, the algebra comes out rather nicely.

Assumptions:

let there be 0, 1, 2 ... L ... T levels of authority;

let o signify the lowest level, T the highest level, and L any given level;

there is only one occupant of the highest level.

Then if

$$h_L = x_L^\beta \qquad (2.15)$$

it can be shown that

$$Y_T = Y_0 . E_0^\beta \qquad (2.16)$$

and

$$Y_L = Y_0 . R_L^\beta \qquad (2.17)$$

where

h_L = ratio between salary at level L and salary at level $L - 1$,

x_L = span of control at level L (ratio of occupants of L to occupants of $L - 1$),

Y_L = salary at level L,

Y_0 = salary at level o (exogenous),

E_0 = number of executives at level o,

R_L = responsibility at level L (as defined in text),

β = gradation coefficient.

The size of the organisation is measured by the number of occupants of the bottom level. The salary at the bottom level is a market — or conventionally-determined — price paid to new entrants in general, and the *Beta* coefficient measures the sociologically determined rate of gradation. In the final result, however, span of control disappears (variations in span being matched by variations in salaries) and an individual's salary can be shown to depend ultimately on his responsibility alone. In other words, if two organisations of the same size differ in span of control, and hence in the number of levels required to complete the pyramid, the effect on salaries will be offset by opposing variations in the differentials: occupants of level L in the organisation with wider spans of control and fewer levels will be paid more than occupants of level L in the other. An individual's salary is thus independent of the number of subordinates interposed between him and the bottom level (unrealistic perhaps, but the likely effect of a more realistic assumption is by no means obvious) and consequently, although personal salaries are in a sense independent of organisational structure, the total salary-bill is not; given the gradation coefficient, the wider the average span of control in a firm of given size, the lower the bill.

This does not mean, however, that the salary-bill for the top-management team, as we have been using the term, is much affected by structure. Whatever the arrangement of levels in an organisation, each level corresponds to a level of responsibility. If, as seems appropriate in the present context, the 'management' is defined as all those persons occupying the highest n levels numbered *down from the top*, the salary-bill of this group depends only on the organisation's size measured by E_0, and is independent of inter-mediate structure. (For example, draw two organisations of size 16, A with four levels above the lowest and span of control 2 throughout, B with only two levels above the lowest and span of control 4 throughout. Let salary at the bottom level be 100 *per capita* and the gradation coefficient unity. Define 'management' as all those persons occupying the two highest levels — the chief executive and two subordinates in firm A, the chief executive and four subordinates in firm B — and it will be found that the total bill for both is 3200.) But provided the number n, which defines the limits of the management, is held constant, the wider the average span of control the greater the management membership, and hence the lower, other things being equal, the *per capita* management salary. It is not unlikely that large organisations tend on average to adopt wider spans of control than smaller ones, an effect which we will call 'hierarchical compression'; evidence of its operation is found in the tendency for the number of corporate officers to in-crease slightly, in the U.S., with size. [48] For convenience, however, in the discussion below we shall ignore compression and argue as if the span of control was given and constant over all firms of all sizes; it can be shown that the main theorems are easily re-expressed algebraically (if not verbally) in terms of responsibility.

This then is the 'bureaucratic' theory of salaries. As already explained, it is not to be regarded as a rival to the economic theory, but rather as an (unconventional) explanation of it. The number of persons at a given level, say the lowest, can be taken to vary closely with productive capacity, and the theory states that the greater the desired productive capacity the greater the number required of administrators of given responsibility or the greater the average responsibility of a given number of administrators. The 'required' salary-bill for the top management varies directly and uniquely with size, according to the *Beta* coefficient. The 'bureaucratic' Beta coefficient *is* the economic Beta coefficient, because if these salaries were not paid the firm would fail through socio-organisational misfunctioning: if for sociological reasons the task of production cannot be carried out without a particular income-distribution, the social law becomes an economic one. Rather than 'bureaucratic', therefore, we might give the theory some name which combines both origins, and for want of a better we try 'bureconic'.

It has further characteristics we have not yet mentioned. From its bureaucratic parent it inherits the character that individuals' salaries represent less their personal qualities than their offices; true, to reach high office one should display ability, but the system as such merely lays down a set of relativities, and there is no indication that the absolute income of a person of given ability must take on any particular value. Consequently, the general level of corporate salaries, like that of most other incomes, is left indeterminate. If all executive salaries were halved tomorrow, although some effects might be felt at the lowest levels, neither in the short nor the long run would any effects be felt at the top, i.e. if the average corporate officer in the U.S. were brought down to a gross compensation of $30,000 per annum, he would continue to function efficiently and no special difficulty would be experienced in finding his successors. If, as may well be the case, there is genuine competition between business and other professions at the new-entrant level, so that the absolute starting salary had to be held constant, the change would imply, of course, a reduction of Beta. But we have seen that Beta varies considerably between countries and professions. Thus the theory is saying no more than that once a conventional level of the 'business' Beta is somehow established, within limits, functional efficiency is in the long run independent of its magnitude.

This leads to a point of more immediate importance. In the 'neoclassical' economic model, payment of salaries in excess of the minimum was prevented, or at least restrained, by the imaginary shareholders' committee attempting to maximise profits. In the present theory, no such restraint is obvious. We have seen that the frequency distribution of salaries predicted by size is positively skewed; but in the absence of upper restraint, why should it not be rectangular? What in fact prevents compensation in individual firms from taking on any value above the minimum? We have already hinted at one answer: subordinates may become discontented and hence function badly, if they observe that their immediate seniors are paid an unconventional differential. This factor is likely to be important wherever subordinates and seniors are in close daily contact and can observe both each others' work and each others' standard of living. There is more than fear of internal misfunction, however, to deter senior executives from awarding each other grossly excessive salaries. The prevailing gradation coefficient is as much a valid social norm as any other. If they offend, others may accuse them of 'milking' the business and they in turn may feel their own 'Wright-Mills' loyalties coming into play. However, unlike the case of investment and financial policy, these factors are not reinforced by any very powerful external agency, for, with the magnitudes currently prevailing, the effect of salary variation on rate of return is relatively slight; characteristically an average excess payment of the order of one hundred per cent reduces the rate of return by no more than one-twentieth (i.e. a ten-per-cent rate of return would be reduced by half a point only). Hence, on a cynical view, we should not expect these supposed restraints to be as strong as they might be. Again, and finally, the facts fit. Although the salary distribution is not rectangular, and although the correlation coefficient of the regression which originally tested the relation between salaries and corporate size was high, these results were nevertheless consistent with some remarkable positive deviations. Since (if the model is valid) it is certain that least-squares estimates overstate the predicted minimum salary, we cannot easily quantify the point, but at a rough guess there appear to have been as many as a dozen cases (in the sample of 77) where actual compensation was at least double the theoretical minimum for firms of the size in question, [49] a result, incidentally, which would be difficult to reconcile even with the modified version of the neo-classical model. All in all, therefore, we feel justified in basing our main motivational analysis on the assumption that the bureconic theory, as we have described it, is reasonably valid.

Policy Implications of a 'Bureconic' Theory

The organisation of modern business combines features which the man in the street would describe as 'bureaucratic', in the sense of 'like Civil Service', with features he would describe as 'commercial', in a sense somehow implying more flexibility. Now armed with the bureconic theory of salaries, we shall continue the analysis by attempting to isolate these two sorts of feature, beginning with a model representing an extreme form of bureaucracy, and gradually relaxing or modifying the assumptions until we have something more like a real-life, profit-making corporation. By this means we hope to be able to establish motivational theorems which are both more rigorous and less dependent on intuitive reasoning than has been possible so far. In particular, we shall hope to provide a solider logical basis for the motive of growth, a motive whose existence the reader has so far been asked to accept as only a working hypothesis.

Imagine a Weberian and socialistic nightmare in which all production was organised on strict Civil Service lines, 'firms' representing no more than subordinate departments with carefully defined and limited spheres of activity, no freedom as to internal organisation and no control over salaries or appointments. Some central body (e.g. Treasury) would lay down internal structures, set (constant) spans of control, determine salaries of new entrants and, more important, fix the gradation coefficient. Departments could differ in size (measured by occupants of the bottom level), but this would be decided by the central body alone and could not be influenced by members. The heads of the larger departments would therefore be paid more than the heads of the smaller, because the larger would represent taller pyramids. Promotion would be based partly on merit and partly on seniority, and inter-firm transfers at all levels would be freely encouraged. Indeed, whenever any vacancy occurred, the central appointments board would consider candidates from throughout the system and would try to avoid any bias in favour of internal promotion. Thus the average rate of promotion would be independent of size, and a man with high ambitions could in principle as well start in a small department as in a large one. In fact, the system would be not dissimilar to that adopted by government bureaucracies the world over. In such systems personal advancement is supposed to depend exclusively on merit; the organisations being static and transfers easy there should be little room for any form of built-in policy bias and none whatsoever for the growth motive.

But now suppose that with otherwise unchanged arrangements the policy on transfers is reversed: unless they are hopelessly incompetent, 'inside' candidates are always given absolute priority. Since vacancies arise from natural wastage alone, the rate of promotion and 'prospects' generally will then be inferior in small departments to those in large, and a man reaching the head of a small department would have little chance of moving to a better post in a large department and would have to sit out his position until retirement.

If initial appointments were made by centrally decided postings over which the subject had no influence, and if the total supply of new entrants to the system as a whole was normally equal to requirements, the main effect of a prohibition on transfers would be discontent in the small departments. A man's prospects in life would depend on the accident of his initial posting, a type of situation which, while acceptable to working-class fatalism, violates almost every principle of middle-class individualism. Some malfunctioning would be almost inevitable; the smaller departments would tend to lose their best men to employers outside the system and to become inefficient, strings would be pulled to influence postings, and so on. If the central body, aware of the dangers, sought remedies other than a change in transfer policy, it could adjust either starting salary or Beta coefficient in the smaller organisations, so that, in partial compensation for their bad luck, the members would be paid higher salaries at level L than their opposite numbers in large organisations. (Socio-economic tensions might well continue, however, because so long as society continued to expect income to be closely matched to responsibility, the relative positions of the heads of small and large organisations might be regarded as anomalous.) Little is changed if we assume a free market in new entrants. If new entrants could choose their own initial postings, the same adjustments would be necessary to avoid chronic imbalance between supplies and requirements in departments of different sizes. Motivation would remain unaffected.

At last we are ready for Hamlet. He is brought on by removing the assumption that the departments are static. We know that the most fundamental difference between business firms and government departments lies in the formers' capacity for autonomous growth. Once an otherwise bureaucratic organisation is permitted to grow, while high-level mobility continues to be inhibited (as is empirically the case in firms), the policy implications are considerable. In the bureconic model, if initial salary and rate of gradation are the same for all organisations, persons occupying given levels, numbered from the bottom, are everywhere paid the same salaries, the essential difference between large and small firms being that the former are 'taller' and therefore provide *more* posts at any given salary; in the large organisations there are high posts which in the small do not exist at all. In other words, the large firms provide better 'opportunities' for personal advancement. If transfers were not restricted, this, we have seen, would represent a purely abstract state of affairs devoid of personal implications, but with transfers restricted (and expansion permitted) it provides a powerful motive for senior officials to attempt to induce expansion and thus create higher vacancies into which they themselves are surely most likely to be appointed. There can be no doubt at all that this fundamental characteristic of the interaction between salary system, organisational structure and poor transfer market provides a real and powerful motive for inducing internal expansion in every modern business. As a managing director who held not a penny of stock in his firm once told the author, 'the reason, quite frankly, why I want growth is so that I and my colleagues can all have more money' (meaning higher salaries).

Generalisation of the Growth Motive

Here, then, is how the typical manager has the power to affect himself by affecting his environment. The effect is reinforced when we also drop the assumption that ability is judged independently of performance *in situ*. When a man takes decisions leading to successful expansion, he not only creates new openings but also recommends himself and his colleagues as particularly suitable candidates to fill them (and the colleagues, recognising this, will be glad to allow him a generous share of the utility-proceeds). He has demonstrated his powers as a manager and deserves his reward. So personal ability also becomes judged by achieved growth, and the encouragement of growth becomes a motive for not only collective but also individual advancement, thus reinforcing the basic connection. True, if personal promotion were in fact decided by shareholders' committees, ability (in the absence of AQ tests) might be judged by achieved profits, but when, as is in fact the case, an individual manager's rate of advance is determined exclusively by peers and superiors, it is more likely to be governed by criteria derived from the collective situation of the managerial class, which, we have now seen, means favouring expansion. This does not mean that a man's profit-earning ability will necessarily be ignored, for profits are required for growth and minimum profit is necessary for a minimum valuation ratio. But it does mean that a man is unlikely to be judged by his ability as a profit *maximiser*. By contrast he may well be judged by his ability to maximise, or at least promote, organisational growth.

The association between personal responsibility and achieved expansion resolves the disequilibrium in the supply of recruits to organisations with different prospects. Without this association, recruits would still be faced with a nice problem in assessing relative prospects in large, relatively static firms as compared with smaller, faster-growing firms. On occasion, in real life such choices do have to be made, but the effect is damped by the probability that unless an individual has had some responsibility for expansion he is not necessarily so much favoured over outsiders of comparable ability for the new resulting middle-level vacancies, a conclusion which is confirmed by the observation that among middle and junior managers mobility is relatively high.[50] We are chiefly concerned with conditions at the tops of pyramids; and by this we mean conditions among given levels numbered down from the highest, i.e. the levels in or adjacent to those defined as 'the management'. If the reader will visualise the population of firms as a set of disembodied pyramid tops, then he will see that, with transfers inhibited, management members can improve their position only by expansion, which, as it were, pushes them up from below: the summit rests on a structure of middle and junior managers whose 'lift' increases whenever organisation expands, an effect which is quite independent of where the new subordinates are recruited.

In fact, most of our theorems can be obtained from a single assumption about recruitment, to wit that whenever and wherever a vacancy occurs, the *probability* of its being filled by internal promotion increases with the *level* at which it occurs. With this assumption, which we know to be empirically valid, policy theorems become independent of the level chosen for defining the management. For example, we can say that both an individual's policy influence and his motive for promoting expansion will increase with his level, and thus the theorem that the system must produce bias in favour of growth is made general. The same applies to other collective policy motives, for example that of security. The policy bias of an organisation as a whole can be thought of as resulting from the preferences of its individual members weighted by their relative influence position. Wherever there is a reason to expect correlation between a particular type of individual bias and his relative weight in the collective decision-making function, we shall expect a corresponding bias in collective policy. We have now discovered a general source of such correlations, i.e. the association of both bias and influence with a 'third factor' — hierarchical level. Obviously the correlation between level and influence must always be strong, therefore, wherever there is a further correlation between level and some particular type of policy bias, that type of bias will become collective. In the case of security, it is clear that the personal consequences of financial failure or take-over will be more serious for senior executives than for junior, not only because mobility in general is less free among senior executives (implying a shortage of comparable alternative employments), but also because they are more likely to be personally associated, in the minds of outsiders, with the causes of the failure. The same may apply to many of the psychological and sociological motives we discussed in the opening sections of this chapter, where Katona-like self-identification with the firm occurs; for example, the strength of the sensation will necessarily increase with responsibility, while Wright-Mills-like class identification with the 'corporate rich' will vary with proximity, in other words increase with position and income. In short, unlike the problems treated in Welfare Economics, inside the corporate sphere there is no great difficulty in deriving conclusions about collective behaviour from assumptions about individual preferences, a state of affairs which is due, of course, to the fact that we are not attempting, and do not intend to attempt, to give our theory any normative (economic) content.

Perhaps a dozen other writers have previously asserted that size or growth will be a major factor in managerial motivation,[51] although nowhere, we would think, has the case been presented in detail. There are many who would accept this case as intuitively obvious, but we offer no apology for the length of the foregoing discussion, because in elucidating the detailed mechanism of the motive we may expect to reduce the danger of falling into error from inappropriate applications. There also are many non-believers. These include not only persons residing in such places as Chicago, Los Angeles and London (England), who are driven by an ideological thirst for neo-classical assumptions, but also many other analysts who feel that no case has been established for supposing corporations to have any dominating motives at all. Thus P. E. Hart, in a letter to the author, suggested there was no more reason to believe in growth maximisation than there ever had been for believing in profit maximisation. Leaving aside for the moment the question of whether growth, or anything else, is maximised, we would now reply that given corporate enterprise, there are indeed very good reasons for so believing, just as, given traditional capitalism, there were at least some good reasons for believing in profit maximisation. Another distinguished contributor, Robert Dorfman, wrote, 'Typically a business firm watches manifold consequences of its operations including rate of profit, value of its shares, sales volume, share of market, *et hoc genus omne,* and is not willing to increase its performance in any one of these respects at unlimited sacrifice in the others'.[52] Here, we would argue, there is no real conflict. Dorfman, in our view of things, lists a number of proximate objectives, which we would say were derived from 'deeper' motives, such as growth and financial security. The latter in turn result from a more basic managerial utility system, incorporating a number of psychological, sociological and economic variates, such as dynamic aspiration, self-identification, class orientation, and desire for power, status, wealth and personal security. Indeed, we do not care whether the growth and security motives are regarded as primary, intermediate, 'fundamental' or, for that matter, proximate. All we ask the reader to accept is that, given the facts of corporate life, they dominate.

It is important to appreciate that unlike some bolder spirits we are not implying a whole new system of social relationships. With characteristic *elan*, J. K. Galbraith once wrote:

> 'The income of a business-man is no longer a measure of his achievement: it has become a datum of secondary interest. Business prestige, as a moment's reflection will suggest, is overwhelmingly associated with the size of the concern which the individual heads. American business has evolved a system of precedence hardly less rigid than that of Victorian England. It is based almost exclusively on corporate assets.'[53]

In England, if only because the easiest path to the peerage lies by way of contributions to the funds of political parties, the ultimate basis of precedence always was, and is, hard cash. Therefore it matters little that in Dwightian America corporate presidencies may have come to look like Earldoms, because, just as most British aristocrats are also plutocrats, so executive compensation is closely correlated with corporate assets. Of course, if the correlation were somehow destroyed, personal status within the corporate society would continue to be associated with responsibility (and in the public arena the relative status of the Presidents of General Motors and Harvard would continue to depend on the character of the Administration in Washington), but economic theory would now be presented with a distinct new problem in handling cases where income and status had to be treated as trade-offs. All we are trying to establish is that with things as they are this problem rarely arises. Nor is there much evidence of tendencies to change; belief in the propriety of the income-status correlation is probably spreading rather than receding, so much so in fact that a young American economics professor recently asserted that a particular analytical method must be 'right' because one of its practitioners was very highly paid![54]

The Galbraithian picture, as quoted above, leads, however, to a final point of central importance. If he and the reader will forgive us, his picture could be likened to one of a range of corporate mountains, log-normally distributed as to height, the summits inhabited by gods who battle *inter se* by hurling thunderbolts, called countervailing powers, across the intervening valleys. These gods have a status order based exclusively on altitude: in order to acquire kudos it is necessary to struggle to the top of, and then sit firmly upon, one of the higher peaks; a game, in other words, which is played in a largely static environment. Now this is probably a fair indication of the best approach for anyone with ambitions to become Secretary of State for Defence, but it is not the picture which emerges from our analysis of the internal mechanics of managerial motivation in general. For how, knowing that inter-peak transfer is difficult if not impossible, would one explain the absence of battles at the *feet* of the larger mountains? In other words, although it is true that in general more utility is obtained from *being* at the head of a large firm than of a small one, in practice the most effective means of obtaining this pleasure is by inducing one's own firm to grow. Furthermore, to the extent that transfers are possible, personal ability is likely to be judged by actual growth performance in previous firms, and internal prestige is similarly generated. In short, we argue, this motivation is inescapably dynamic, and the relevant variate in the actual or proximate utility function is not size but change in size, i.e. rate of growth.

A Managerial Utility System

A consumer attaches utility to the growth of his income because it implies potentially rising consumption; as he has normally to pay for this by current abstinence we conventionally apply a rate of time discount to the problem. A manager, on the other hand, is not usually required to sacrifice personal consumption to induce his firm to grow; 'his' saving is here done by others. But there are important possibilities for trading off between the firm's growth rate and variables on other dimensions of managerial utility. Growth may be traded for security and a similar though not identical effect arises if direct utility is obtained from the stock-market quotation as such.

For most of the rest of the work we shall concentrate on the two managerial utility dimensions, growth and security, representing the former by the growth rate of gross assets and the latter by the market valuation ratio. The former then acts as an indicator of the several satisfactions associated with scale (salary, power and prestige), and the latter as a proxy for both security and the more positive utilities connected with the market quotation. Throughout Chapters 3, 5 and the first part of 6 we shall treat 'security' measured by the valuation ratio as a minimum constraint, and assume that, subject to this, the growth rate is maximised. Then in the second part of 6 we suggest a more sophisticated formulation in which there is supposed to exist a managerial utility function permitting continuous trading-off between the two dimensions: in effect, we postulate the existence of a set of indifference curves between growth rate and valuation ratio. Throughout all, however, we also assume a separate security-motivated constraint on leverage, represented in some maximum on the corresponding ratio, the symbol for this being $\bar{g}$.

Maximising, Satisficing and Behaviourism

In the next chapter we shall provide mensurable definitions of some of these concepts. For the present there remains one last question. Are we justified in assuming that anything is *maximised* at all?

We have already mentioned the 'behaviouristic' approach to economic analysis. As all American and some British readers will be aware, this school has mainly developed under the influence of Professor Herbert Simon, and is associated in most people's minds with the concept of 'satisficing', that is a form of behaviour in which the subject, faced with a difficult problem to solve, prefers to sacrifice some of the rewards of the optimum solution in order to reduce the pains incurred in searching for it. Rather than maximise, he chooses to 'satisfice', i.e. to accept some solution which is 'good enough' in relation to various criteria such as survival, aspiration or avoidance of shame. The significance of the approach lies in the possibility that the satisfactory or 'satisficing' levels of reward may be determined by dynamic processes which have no particular relation to the optimum solution. The subject is endowed with various adjustment reactions (for example, a rate at which aspiration increases over time relatively to the time rate of growth of achievement) which yield a system of differential equations whose solution, if stable, represents an equilibrium from which he has no necessary tendency to depart and to which the optimum solution relates only coincidentally.

Closely allied to these concepts is the concept of 'organisational slack', [55] representing a belief that the decision-making and general efficiency of most organisations is often for long periods well below potential, particularly if no new talent is imported. All organisations, it is argued, being prone to slack, socks will be pulled up only in response to definite stimuli, such as the stimulus of observed bad performance. Firms which in some sense have recently 'done badly' may be expected now to do better, while firms which have done well may be expected to become slack. Such behaviour may set up an oscillatory process difficult to reconcile with the orthodox concept of maximising.

These ideas are clearly suggestive. They seem particularly likely to be useful where the corresponding maximising problem is already well-defined and the analyst is now mainly concerned with empirical testing. Where, however, the task in hand is that of defining some problem afresh, 'satisficing' qualifications may import more complexity than understanding. It is of little use to consider the implications of satisficing behaviour if one does not know what is to be satisficed — if one has not yet decided, for example, what is meant by 'doing badly'. Thus, in a well-known article by Professors Cyert and March the supposed underlying motivation is never clearly stated: we infer that the objective is some measure of profitability, but if the inference is correct the postulated set of stimulus and reaction relationships is not easy to rationalise.[56]

The procedure we adopt in the present work is therefore as follows. In the first five chapters, wherever the question arises we shall write as if we were considering only a maximising problem. We also continue in this manner through Chapter 6, where the completed maximising models are assembled. Then, having delineated what we believe to be the essential characteristics of the optimum solution, in Chapter 7 we specifically consider the possible effects if, with the same basic structure of the problem, managers were to engage in appropriate satisficing behaviour. Only after that do we attempt econometric predictions.

CHAPTER THREE

CONCEPTS AND METHODS

HAVING, as we hope, set our stage, we now attempt to characterise the players. We must also explain the language they are to speak and the meanings of some of their clothes. We have discussed at length the economico-institutional environment of the modern corporation and the possible motives of the managers. Both now require to be dressed for operationality. We have suggested that managers may derive utility from growth, but what does this mean in measurable economic terms? And if 'the firm' is no longer to be regarded as a chattel of proprietors, how is it to be regarded?

The present chapter, therefore, represents a bridge-passage intended to lead the reader from ideas expressed in the first two chapters towards the models developed in those which follow. We consider first the character of the firm and nature of the processes of growth. We then sketch in our view of the general economic environment. Finally we discuss definitions, concepts and methods of analysis.

Characterisation of the Firm

In orthodox economic theory, the firm was either no more than an abstraction hypothesised for a particular role in theories of price formation and resource allocation, or, where recognised as a living institution, the form assumed was essentially traditional. One can hardly blame Alfred Marshall for ignoring the implications of the joint-stock company in his otherwise realistic and homely descriptions;[1] one can be more censorious, however, of subsequent theorists. Until the relatively recent contributions of Downie[2] and Baumol[3] the firm continued to be regarded mainly as an organ for maximising profits and allocating resources, or, where it was admitted that, in the presence of oligopoly, maximising procedures might become impossible or even meaningless, the alternative behaviour-hypotheses were almost exclusively formulated in terms of price theory. [4]

About twenty years ago, however, there began to be developed in the United States the new academic discipline which came to be known as Organisation Theory. Largely resulting, one suspects, from a desire for academic legitimacy among the staff of business schools, the new subject at first seemed likely to have an immediate impact on economics, for it indicated numerous ways in which productive organisations may develop independent *raisons d'être* merely by virtue of their internal functional character and requirements. [5] In the event, although a number of interesting developments occurred, things did not work out quite as might have been hoped. It was soon widely recognised that firms should be seen as administrative organisations, that as such they were of considerable intrinsic interest and that their behaviour might well deviate from consistency with so-called 'higher' objectives. Significant normative studies of optimal administrative structures also appeared in due course. [6] But from the point of view of economic theory, 'the organisation' remained the tool — albeit unreliable — of those for whom the higher objectives had been set, and the objectives themselves were almost always traditional or neo-classical. Nor was the position changed fundamentally in this respect by the development of satisficing theory. [7] The potential impact of organisation theory on economic theory was thus considerably weakened. No doubt university departmental structure was partly responsible: in the U.K., it should be noted, there being no business schools, there was no Organisation Theory.

To all the foregoing, there are two major exceptions, two works by economists who have specifically considered the relation between their subject and the other. We refer to *The Theory of the Growth of the Firm* by Mrs. Edith Penrose, [8] and to *Economic Theory and Organisational Analysis* by Harvey Leibenstein. [9] The second work is concerned with the general interaction of the two approaches and, although it has influenced the present author considerably, is not of the same specific relevance as the first, which is concerned with precisely our own problem, or in other words with the ways in which corporate organisations may develop quasi-higher

E

objectives of their own, and the means by which they pursue them. Mrs. Penrose, as the title of her book implies, is essentially concerned with the motives and means associated with growth. The present chapter is based considerably on her work, although in places the interpretation may perhaps be rather free.

In the language of Organisation Theory, the previous chapters of this book were attempting to reconstruct Higher Objectives. In the usual conception, the organisation is set up to achieve certain definable ends. These it is intended to serve faithfully, but the results may be otherwise; such deviations, however, are rarely thought of as purposive. Yet we have seen that in the corporate system far-reaching, high-level purposive objectives may be pursued by persons who are organisation members, i.e. are other than those whose interests the organisation was formally set up to serve. Organisation is required to exploit the advantages of large scale, and persons capable of providing this acquire considerable bargaining power. In the resulting balance, it is impossible to confine the senior executives to a purely immanent rôle, and, indeed, it might almost seem as if the institutions of managerial capitalism were developed to serve this class, as much as any other. Managers are persons with ability to organise. In order to exploit their talents they require appropriate instruments and institutions, in other words they require organisations. The joint-stock company might well be regarded as *their* creation, and its shareholders as merely one of several co-operating elements (of which, another, for example, would be the non-managerial labour force). On such an interpretation it is not clear that even a normative approach would not recognise valid 'higher' objectives in managerial motivation.

So the productive function in a modern economy is carried on by autonomous administrative organisations with minds and capacities of their own. On an extreme view, the 'higher' arrangements become details, and any economic system — Capitalist, Socialist or *Dirigiste* — may be seen as a collection of competing and co-operating organisations. Consistently with this, economists have also defined 'the firm' in relation to the specifically technical function of operating transformation processes. The firm is thus the ultimate allocator of resources, or the ultimate cell of the input-output system. For this type of usage it is necessary to specify the relevant activity-set with some precision; the firm is thus usually supposed to exist to select from limited lists the commodities it will produce, the techniques to be used and the prices and scales of output. Once the data have been specified, together with some appropriate objective function, little remains but to solve the mathematical problem. This, in essence, is the approach of activity analysis. As soon, however, as we recognise the firm as a transcendent organisation with a will of its own (still analogous to a computer, perhaps, but one now capable of programming itself), the concept of the limited specification, except in a purely proximate sense, becomes rather fuzzy. The firm has the power to mould the environment, and to add new possibilities to its own information; we must then consider the limits on its power to change its limits.

It is here that the influence of Mrs. Penrose becomes so important. She sees the firm as an administrative and social organisation, capable, in principle, of entering almost any field of material activity. The firm is not necessarily limited to particular markets, industries or countries; indeed, there is no theoretical reason why firms should not venture anywhere in the universe. In practice, of course, they find advantages in specialisation, but this represents a deliberate choice whose direction and degree may be varied at will. Every firm, at any one moment, inherits a degree and direction of specialisation from its own past, and this is represented in the knowledge and talents of the existing members and the sphere of technical and commercial activity with which they are familiar (as well as, of course, in the nature of the physical assets). But new members and new assets can always be recruited; the firm is a changeable bundle of human and professional resources, linked through the corporate constitution to a corresponding bundle of material and financial assets. The matching between the humans, *inter se*, and between the humans on the one hand and the machines on the other is a unique result of the historical process by which all have been built up. The result may be far from ideal, but in non-pathological cases is at least viable.

Thus individual firms are not only unique, but possess the capacity for biological growth. In the traditional theory, the size or growth of one firm was no more than the indirect result of the performance of the profit-maximising function. And size could be determinate only in the presence of diseconomies of scale. (Rates of growth were rarely discussed.) Significantly, these diseconomies were usually attributed to problems of organisation. If the administrative problem could be solved, it was usually admitted that growth was in principle ultimately unlimited.

But the managerial-capitalist corporation possesses the unique capacity to initiate its own growth: members may be recruited, demand induced to expand and suppliers of capital persuaded to provide the wherewithal. Unlike organisations subject to the pathology of Parkinson's Law,[10] however, such growth must be based on past success, and the rate is therefore subject to considerable dynamic restraint. The restraints, in effect, are the subject of this book, those arising from 'Demand' being investigated in Chapter 4, those arising from the need for finance in Chapter 5, and the whole brought together in Chapter 6. All are derived from those rules of the game which prohibit the incurring of continuing financial losses, rules which did not apply, of course, to the examples given by Parkinson.[11] However, the growth rates of administrative organisations are also limited by factors which are not directly economic, and these we now discuss.

The Internal Restraint on the Growth Rate

Almost by definition the planning and execution of expansion is the least routine of administrative acts: organisation must be created where none existed before, recruits must be found, new tasks undertaken and new delegation-patterns developed. It is axiomatic that such planning can only be undertaken by existing members. If an organisation is to remain efficient, it cannot possibly expand at an indefinitely rapid rate merely by infinitely rapid recruitment.

This proposition we have elsewhere called the 'Penrose theorem'.[12] But why, in fact, should not a firm at time t recruit large numbers of highly qualified managers (representing, say, a doubling of the size of the relevant echelons) and then expect to be able to employ these men to bring about a very large increase in activity between $t+1$ and $t+2$? The answer is as follows. The new member of an existing going concern, however highly qualified, can almost never become fully efficient as a non-routine decision-maker on the instant he is recruited. He may have been fully efficient in his previous post, but he now requires time to learn his new colleagues' ways and they to learn his. He also requires time to acquire the experience necessary for the exercise of good judgment in the new context. Whether he be an imported President, Vice-President, Chairman, Managing Director or relatively junior sub-ordinate, he has to be 'trained' in his new position, and the process inevitably requires time. The length of the period may vary considerably according to the circumstances, but is never insignificant.

The need for 'training', however, is not itself sufficient to set up a dynamic restraint on growth. There is still no reason apparently why the firm should not recruit large numbers of recruits at time t, await the completion of their training through $t+1, ..., t+n$, then expand rapidly. Provided n, the training-period, is independent, the average growth rate could always be stepped up merely by raising the numbers hired at t. Everyone knows that this is not realistic, but, as far as the author is aware, formal explanations have so far been lacking. They must arise from the nature of the training process; n is not, evidently, independent of the attempted expansion rate. The average time required to train one new member must vary with the numbers recruited.

The existence of such a 'saturation' effect seems extremely plausible, and is confirmed, of course, by everyday administrative experience. The recruits are 'taught' by peers, superiors and subordinates. At high level, they must find out the nature of the human and material jig-saw puzzle represented in the organisation, and in particular must find out the shapes into which new pieces will have to be fitted if further expansion is contemplated. They cannot learn these things from one another. They must learn them on the job by personal contact with old members, and the capacity of these 'teachers' is necessarily limited. For example, if the teacher is a superior, the necessity to keep things going will limit the amount he can delegate to inexperienced persons requiring close supervision: if provided with too many such, he will probably concentrate his attention on a limited number, leaving the others with only trivial responsibilities until he has more time for them. If the 'teacher' is a subordinate, similar effects are produced by processes which may be less obvious, but none the less real. And once they are admitted, the theorem is as good as established.

For suppose we represent the average decision-taking efficiency of a management team at any one time as composed of two ratios, the ratio of the efficiency of the average recruit to that of the average old hand and the ratio of the total number of recruits to total membership. Then, if the former varies with the latter, average efficiency varies with the attempted expansion rate as indicated by the latter. If efficiency declines with the attempted expansion rate, and actual expansion depends on efficiency, expansion is dynamically restricted.

The foregoing could be generalised by assuming that the efficiency or usefulness of individual members varied directly and continuously with length of service. Average length of service evidently varies with the rate of growth of the number of members, therefore average efficiency would vary continuously and indirectly with the growth rate of the firm.

But in so gaining generality we would almost certainly over-simplify. It is most unlikely that efficiency — especially efficiency in relation to the planning of further expansion — varies with length of service in quite so crude a fashion. For the length of service is likely to be strongly correlated with age, and it is probable that for any given managerial task there is an optimum age: if the average age passes the average optimum, a counter-effect on efficiency sets in. And apart from the question of age, there is also that of staleness. Outside recruits may import new ideas which transcend mere expertise, and their freshness may be vital to expansion. In other words, there is a sense in which attempts by an organisation to expand breed the capacity to expand. What recent recruits lack in immediate ability to co-ordinate, they may partly make up in drive and vision.

In other words, it may well be the case that, at low rates of growth, acceleration, rather than affecting efficiency adversely, has precisely the opposite effect. This does more than merely demonstrate the organisation's efficiency by its ability to accelerate. It means that accelerations of the recruitment rate — as indicated by permanent decreases in average length of service — may well have beneficial effects on the quality of a wide range of decisions which are connected with expansion only indirectly. Resource allocation, sales management and production costs, for example, may all be affected. The economic consequences are worked out in Chapter 6. In the meantime we note that if the effect exists, its range must be limited. As growth is increasingly accelerated, the adverse effects previously described must, eventually, take over. Otherwise we would in the limit reach the absurdity of an organisation attempting to expand at an infinite rate, whose members, their average length of service being infinitesimal, would not even know each others' names. So the continuous relationship between some measure of the attempted growth rate and some measure of decision-taking efficiency may well be non-monotonic: with efficiency the dependent variable, at low growth rates the relation may be direct but at high growth rates it is always inverse. Once the peak is passed, the organisation must become liable to suffer in the way described by a corporation President who told Professor Mason Haire,

> 'We just got too big *too soon* and began to lose money. We had to trim back to a reasonable size' (italics my own). [14]

Although the working-out of the economic implications of these assumptions is reserved for later chapters, the reader should appreciate that they underlie our whole argument. They are not strictly vital — without them the models would by no means entirely collapse — but they are of great importance. They may be thought of as representing a dynamisation of the old conception of diseconomies of scale. A non-growing firm may be subject to positive economies of scale in the sense that it would be more efficient at a larger (constant) absolute size than at a smaller. But once these static economies are exhausted, the existence of corporate organisation creates the presumption that returns to scale are thereafter constant. The ultimate size of the firm is therefore unlimited. We say, however, that the ultimate size is then meaningless, and turn our attention to the rate of change. In place of a relationship between efficiency and absolute size we substitute a relationship between efficiency and growth rate. The 'optimum' managerial growth rate is then that rate which maximises efficiency. There is no reason, however, why managerial utility-maximisation will require that this particular rate be chosen, because the losses of efficiency associated with other rates may be more than offset by their other advantages, especially, of course, if the growth rate itself, rather than efficiency as such, is the object of desire.

The Concept of Balanced or Sustainable Growth

Throughout all that has gone so far we have spoken recurrently of growth, of motives to grow and of restraints on growth rates, as if 'growth' was, in the context, a concept both universally understood and clearly defined. We have made little attempt to provide a precise definition of growth; nor have we much discussed the means by which growth is to be achieved. If size is to be measured by output, for example, growth requires sales-expansion. If size is to be defined by gross assets, capital must be absorbed. Which of these and many other possible definitions should be used?

There is no real problem here. We are concerned, of course, mainly with what we have described as 'sustainable' growth, that is to say with growth which is consistent with the firm's continuing on a financial basis such that the same rate can be maintained indefinitely or at least until there is some change in the data. In this condition, most of the alternative measures of size are required to expand in balance. For example, if capacity in terms of gross assets were to expand more rapidly than the volume of saleable output, average capacity utilisation must gradually decline and with it the rate of return. But a steadily declining rate of return cannot normally be reconciled with a constant growth rate; hence 'unbalanced' growth in this sense cannot be sustainable.

We therefore confine the analysis largely to conditions where growth is balanced in the sense that the long-run growth rates of demand and of capacity are equal, and we shall frequently use the adjectives 'balanced' and 'sustainable' synonymously. Furthermore, we shall typically consider situations in which constant, balanced growth rates are associated not only with constant rates of return, but also with constant overall profit margins and capital-output ratios. In such conditions almost all measures of size, including, for example, aggregate profits (*vide* Penrose[15]) and aggregate turnover (*vide* Baumol[16]) march together; then to maximise the growth rate of one is to maximise that of most of the others.

In general, for dimensional convenience, we shall most generally define size and growth by gross assets, using, as previously, the symbol C^*. But in analysing the effects of the balance condition we shall need also a symbol for the 'demand' aspect of size, and for this we use D^*. D^*, then, is defined as the growth rate of gross assets which would be required to maintain some constant utilisation rate, while never refusing an order. C^* is the growth rate of assets as actually recorded in the balance-sheet. For growth to be sustainable it is generally required that C^* and D^* be equal, but they are by no means identical. When, however, they are in fact equal, the growth rate measured by C^* is said to be balanced. The C^* aspect is loosely referred to as 'Supply' and the D^* aspect as 'Demand'.

The Role of Diversification

So much for definitions of growth; what of the means? We have already indicated, in Chapter 1, something of our view of the process of obtaining capital, and we shall expand this into a definite model in Chapter 5. But how may a firm *cause* deliberate variation of demand-growth, i.e. how may the magnitude of D^* be made subject to policy? In earlier theory, the firm faced a statically conceived demand-curve, whose trend — or rate of bodily shift over time — if any, was entirely exogenous. In the Marshallian arrangement, price was then the only decision-variable capable of influencing quantity sold; post-classical writers added others, such as advertising expenditure or quality variation, but none such could conceivably be employed for sustainable growth. If demand were to be continuously increased by price reduction, rising unit selling expenditure, or both, profitability would be continuously declining and the growth, therefore, inevitably non-sustainable. Continuous sustainable volume increase could result only from residual trend in the demand-curve, and this, as already indicated, was by definition something incapable of influence by policy.

These conclusions, which seemed so inconsistent with the evident fact that most business executives appeared to believe that, on the contrary, the influencing of demand was one of their most important functions, arose because the orthodox analysis presupposed that before the demand-curve was drawn up, a large number of important policy decisions had already been taken. We refer, of course, to decisions determining what goods should be produced—what demand-curves, in effect, should be created. Even for a firm which is going to produce only a single product, this decision is likely to be far more important to its destinies than the subsequent price and volume decisions, and one sometimes wonders why economic theory has previously taken so little interest in the subject. Be that as it may, we know that, ever since the industrial revolution, firms have been able to grow by successively marketing products they had not previously offered, thus enabling themselves to progress by successive 'jumps' to appropriate positions among an ever-growing family of otherwise static demand-curves. That business-men have become increasingly aware of this over the past thirty years is apparent from only a cursory glance at the literature. [17]

It is Mrs. Penrose again who appears as the leading contemporary writer to emphasise the role of continuous diversification in the normal process of growth. She points out that by this means many firms have continued to grow over very long periods, such as fifty or even seventy-five years, although there is, apparently, some evidence of a tendency for the rates of growth themselves to decline over time. [18] The planning of diversification is *par excellence* a typical function of high management. Characteristically, it has been found, these decisions are taken at higher levels within the management hierarchy than are, for example, pricing decisions, and they rarely, of course, originate among small shareholders. [19] We may therefore define a distinct decision-variable, to be known as *the rate of diversification*, intended to summarise the implications of the series of individual decisions which lead up to the marketing of new products. Many new products, of course, fail to succeed in the sense that their sales prove so small that their contribution to overall growth is insubstantial (one might say in these cases that the static demand-curve proves to be unfavourably located). The rate of diversification, however, is to be taken as referring to both successes and failures: it may be defined either as the ratio of the number of new items added to the catalogue during a given period to the number already catalogued at the beginning of the period, or, more precisely, but less evocatively, as the value of D' which would be experienced if all new products in fact succeeded. We realise that this still leaves the definition 'fuzzy', in the sense that we do not know how to distinguish strictly between new products and minor variants of old ones, but we believe that it should not in practice be difficult to develop appropriate conventions for converting the diversification rate into an observable variable. Further clarification, we hope, will be found in Chapter 4. For the time being the reader can best visualise the concept as measuring the rate at which the firm is attempting to increase the number of independent demand-curves relating to products it is actually producing.

Clearly, if a 'new' product is expected and intended largely to kill the demand for a product the firm is already selling, as in the case of new fashions in clothes and road vehicles, it does not represent meaningful diversification, although, evidently, deliberately induced increases in the rate of obsolescence may offer a method of fostering growth in an otherwise saturated market for consumer durables. But as the U.S. automobile industry has recently learned, this is yet another method which cannot easily be made continuous. Diversification may involve marketing products which are close substitutes for those of other firms, but they must not be substitutes for products already marketed by the diversifying firm. In Chapter 4, where the new products are predominantly competitive with existing products of other firms, we say the diversification is 'imitative'; where they are not we call it 'differentiated'.

Diversification, as usually understood, is not of course the only method of fostering demand-growth. There may be occasions where substantial increases in the sales of an existing line can be induced without necessarily involving a severe reduction in profitability. A technical improvement in consumer-appeal, for example, may permit the achievement of a major increase in the firm's share of an old-established market, perhaps at the expense of an old-established rival. These events, however, must also be regarded as discontinuous. In any one product, for example, the growth potential is exhausted when all rivals have been eliminated. Continuous growth requires such actions to be successive, i.e. to be taken in relation to first one product, then another, and so on. At each successful attempt a discontinuous increase in demand is achieved; when this is completed, attention must at least temporarily be turned elsewhere. Where a major increase in market share is achieved without any apparent change in price or quality whatsoever (for example, by costless improvement in marketing technique), we have the limiting case of 'imitative' diversification. In Chapter 4, therefore, we subsume this case within the general theory of imitative growth, and suppose it to be subject to similar dynamic restraints (see p. 200).

The Role of Merger

There is another important method of growth to be considered, namely the 'growth' involved in mergers. This does not fit into the conceptual scheme very easily. In Chapter 1 we investigated 'take-overs'; these, although often leading to the union of two organisations, are in one sense clearly distinguishable from 'voluntary' mergers, i.e. unions welcomed by both managements. But although the take-over raid performs a mainly punitive or restraining function from the point of view of the raided firm, the act remains 'voluntary' from the point of view of the raider, and can thus be regarded as a means of his growth. This is particularly relevant, of course, in the case of the inter-managerial raid (see p. 32). So all forms of merger, from one point of view, are part of a growth process. In practice, successful take-overs which are opposed by one party represent only a small proportion of the very large number of unions which actually occur. Whether a tiddler is absorbed by a giant, or whether the merging firms are of comparable size, in most cases the arrangement is not unsatisfactory to the managers of both. According to Mrs. Penrose, many of these cases represent acts of diversification.[20]

With mergers as an aspect of monopolistic concentration we are not in this book directly concerned. Their causes and effects have attracted attention from economists from Adam Smith onwards,[21] and their implications being as it were static, the type of analysis we are employing has little to contribute in the area. But we are of course much concerned with mergers as a means of diversification, i.e. means of furthering sustainable growth in an identifiable continuing firm. Mrs. Penrose believes that it is in fact possible in a great many cases for a firm to preserve its original identity despite a long series of absorptions.[22] Evidently the method is adopted because it permits faster growth than would be permitted by others.[23] But like others, it is also subject to dynamic restraints, and cannot be made to yield growth at unlimited rates.

When a firm is diversifying by internal expansion only, demand, capital and administrative capacity must all be extended in balance. But the expansion rates on each dimension are variously restricted and constrained. By taking over a going concern, on the other hand, it is possible that some of these restrictions may be considerably weakened. True, the merger itself requires organisation and presents new problems in co-ordination, but these are evidently often less serious than the corresponding difficulties which arise in internal expansion. The firm taken over may be modified or improved, and may, indeed, eventually be so absorbed as to lose all vestige of identity. Alternatively, much of the original identity may be deliberately preserved, and the process be seen as part of a programme of growth by decentralisation in the central firm. In either case the result is from our point of view the same; growth can occur at a faster rate for given efficiency and the administrative restraint is weakened.

Like all other methods, however, this one in turn must be subject to dynamic limits. The digestive capacity of the absorber is limited,[24] so also the number of suitable 'victims' available at any one time. There have been numerous cases of predators experiencing substantial reductions in efficiency through having attempted to eat too fast. Thus the potentialities of merger do not eliminate the administrative restraint on growth, but rather they modify it: the effect is quantitative rather than qualitative. For this reason, through most of what follows we shall write as if internal expansion were the only method of growth; the administrative restraint will be assumed to operate in the manner described in the previous section, and merger possibilities are to be regarded as subsumed in specifying the functional forms. Alternatively, the reader may prefer to regard our theory as representing an account of the limits on growth rates among firms which do not merge, and, as such, as an explanation of why the method of merger is so often attractive.

The Economic Environment

We have now characterised the firm as an autonomous organisation capable of growth (subject to rules of the game) at a limited rate in a pliable environment. This growth may occur mainly at the expense of other firms in general, or of a small handful of other firms in particular, or alternatively it may mainly reflect expansion of the economic system as a whole. Where growth occurs through diversification which is innovatory in the full Schumpeterian[25] sense, developments in consumption tastes and production methods go hand in hand. A firm marketing a product which is new both to itself and the economy may soon be required to create a significant amount of new technology. In other cases most of the technology may be absorbed from the national stock of knowledge, and, if necessary, suitably qualified specialists may be recruited (another common explanation of merger — to acquire a going team of specialists). Evidently, then, for our theory to have any bite, the firms must be living in an environment where these things are possible.

They must be living in an environment where both consumer and producer techniques are capable of responding to continuous development and change. Both consumption and production functions must be capable of organic extension, and in the sociological sense the society must be neither primitive nor traditional. In other words, our theory applies to typical modern developed economies, such as those of the U.S.A., U.S.S.R. or Europe, and does not apply to the Trobriand Islands. Modern developed economies are known to be pliable, are known to progress both by increasing production and consumption of 'necessities' and by the constant development of new wants and new products. Although, strictly speaking, the theory which follows could be formally applied in a static economy, it would not be of much interest there. Firms could grow only by 'imitative' diversification and this would always be at the expense of others. In the absence of diseconomies of scale, production should eventually be concentrated in a giant monopoly or, alternatively, an extremely rigid oligopolistic stability might develop. In either case, comparative statics, possibly modified by a stochastic model of perturbations, would be the most appropriate method of analysis. Indeed, as Schumpeter first pointed out,[25] although technical dynamism is intimately associated with industrial concentration, it may also be partly responsible for the fact that concentration does not go further. The reader may take it, therefore, that we are assuming a dynamic economy.

Typically, then, we envisage an environment with continual change and new product creation, and in which new products, both final and intermediate, are responsible for the lion's share of incremental output and demand. In Chapter 4 we distinguish between 'exploding' and 'saturated' products, the former being relatively new products for which demand is still growing rapidly — for example, at 10 or 15 per cent per annum — and the latter the relatively old products for which demand is growing, if at all, only slowly — for example, at one or two per cent per annum. In an ideal simplification, at the macro-level the trend in demand for saturated products would be zero, and new products would be responsible for all marginal expenditure. (Such a picture is not so very fantastic: if exploding products grew at 15 per cent per annum and accounted for 15 per cent of total expenditure, the overall growth rate would be two and a quarter per cent per annum, a figure which compares favourably with recent experience, for example, in the U.S.) It might even be possible to envisage a situation in which demand for old products on balance always declined by precisely the amount necessary to make way for the new, and the appropriate chain-index of real output would display no trend: the economy could still be described as dynamic. But, more typically, real product *per capita* is supposed to be rising, and technical progress to be positive.

Technical progress, however, although an essential ingredient of the macro-picture, requires little analysis at the micro-level. As firms grow, their orthodox production functions change with the process of diversification, and we may presume that the firms at all times attempt to find the most efficient choices from the kaleidoscope of technical possibilities ever unfolding before them. But the effects on profitability, on efficient factor ratios and on optimal prices will depend also on the external development of the macro-wage-price relationship. Consequently, the total effects of progress on the dynamic-equilibrium conditions for the individual firm appear capable of qualitative analysis only in specific cases. (A possible exception is discussed in the section following.) Generally, therefore, until we reach Chapter 8, we shall assume that whatever happens to production functions in the course of diversification, things somehow turn out so that the implied technical progress (in association with the implied macro-wage-price developments) leaves the conditions of dynamic equilibrium for the individual firm unchanged. The various functions which will eventually determine the conditions of equilibrium are therefore assumed stable over time. When we do reach Chapter 8, however, these assumptions are relaxed and some not uninteresting theorems emerge.

Methods of Analysis

Methodological differences are increasingly dividing the profession of economics, no less among mathematicians than between mathematicians and others. Techniques are becoming increasingly specific to training and general formation, and all tend to believe that the methods with which they are familiar are best. The author very much hopes therefore that the ideas he is trying to sell in this book can be objectively evaluated even by persons who find the analytical methods distasteful. One can only use the methods in which one has been trained, and it is simply not true that any one style of analysis has so far proved overwhelmingly more effective in economics than all others.

In the present work we employ the approach which has been described as that of 'comparative dynamics', a method which is particularly suited to persons (such as the author) who wish to discuss moving equilibria but are untrained in classical mathematical dynamics. It is also a useful instrument for distinguishing woods from trees. In classical dynamics, the analyst specifies a system or systems of differential equations, solves them, notes the resulting time-profiles of the variables in which he is interested, and investigates the possibilities of stable equilibria. A dynamic equilibrium usually implies that the rate of change of all variables is either constant or zero and that the system tends to recover stably from disturbance. In comparative dynamics, the equilibrium, whether stable or unstable, is approached more directly. The analyst first defines the characteristics of the solution and then deduces the implicit economic conditions. He then conceptually varies some exogenous variable or variables, and notes the effect on these conditions, ignoring almost completely the process by which the movement from one equilibrium to another may be achieved. He may then subsequently consider stability. Practitioners of both methods frequently deny the opposing school the right to employ the adjective 'dynamic', the classicists saying that if there is no stability problem there is no dynamical problem, their critics retorting that the classicists are frequently mesmerised by trivial adjustment problems in what are basically static situations. As a matter of fact, there is a sense in which the theory below could be translated into comparative statics, although one might reasonably think that where at least one of the main objective variables is a rate of change, to do so would be stretching the language unduly.

The danger of misrepresentation in using comparative dynamics depends partly on the extent of feed-back in the behaviour system under analysis. In most macro-systems, feed-back is inevitable; it plays an essential role, for example, in almost all post-Keynesian trade-cycle models. In the micro-theory of the individual firm, however, the position is less clear. If the firm is thought of as a rational, centralised, decision-taking unit, the management should usually experience little difficulty in directly proceeding to desired equilibrium states, and thereafter maintaining stability by methods analogous to those used by a person driving a car at a constant speed along a straight road. Just as the driver can expect reasonable stability characteristics in his steering gear, so the high management of a firm should be able to arrange similar stability in the operation of its instrumental variables. For example, if it is desired to achieve and maintain a certain leverage ratio, and the present ratio is lower, it is only necessary to set up a financial policy in which debt grows faster than assets so that the ratio rises until the desired level is reached. Nor, within one firm, should there be any dichotomy between savings and investment decisions.

If, however, the firm's behaviour is less rational and unitary, if for organisational reasons instrumental variables cannot be made to behave stably, or if 'satisficing' behaviour occurs, things are rather different. The analytical implications of satisficing are in fact non-trivial only when some classically dynamic effect is present, for it is essentially by such means that 'irrational' satisficing levels find stability. When, therefore, we come in Chapter 6 to consider non-maximising forms of behaviour, we shall adapt our analysis accordingly. We are then able to show that a plausible adjustment process may indeed lead to stability at non-optimal (i.e. non-maximising) equilibrium positions.

Another possible source of serious error in comparative dynamics would be found if some factor we had taken as an exogenous variable turned out in reality to be endogenous to the equilibrium conditions themselves. If it were the case, for example, that technical progress experienced by an individual firm was partly affected by a variable such as the growth rate itself, then the growth rate is feeding back into one of its own determinants in a manner over which the firm has no control. A firm so placed that its initial equilibrium growth rate was rapid might find itself experiencing above-average technical progress, causing productivities to rise faster than the macro-wage-price ratio. Constant policies would therefore produce a rising growth rate, and, in the absence of an opposing effect, no 'equilibrium' rate could be stable. Initially fortunate firms would grow faster and faster, the less fortunate slower and slower, and concentration would continue unless and until stochastic disturbance in the data came to the rescue. Since it is almost certain that effects of this kind exist, it would be of some interest to consider them, but this task, unfortunately, must be reserved for a later publication. In the micro-analysis, we adhere rigidly to the assumption, already mentioned, that technical progress does not disturb equilibria, and in the macro-analysis, where technical progress is specifically considered, we evade the difficulty by assuming that all firms are identical.

Our general method, then, is as follows. We first consider some vector of decision-variables which is capable of being shown to be consistent with some stable, sustainable condition of growth, in the sense that once the growth rate is established, neither it, the decision-variables nor any other endogenous variables will change so long as the exogenous data remain constant. (All such conditions, of course, require that the growth be balanced.) Then we consider alternative equilibrium vectors against the same exogenous data, or alternative data values against the original vector, and compare the characteristics of the various equilibrium states. If the fact of changing the vector would in reality induce disturbances, our gaze is averted until such time as things have settled down again, and we assume, of course, that the firm is in a position to ensure that things always will settle down, eventually. This implies that whenever any particular position is analysed it is implicitly assumed that all relevant variables have been constant for some time past and will be constant for some time into the future. For example, only if the diversification rate and 'success' ratio have been constant for some time is it necessarily true that the growth rate of demand is precisely equal to the product of the two. Similarly, only if the gearing ratio has been for some time constant is it true that marginal and average gearing are the same, a condition which is also required for steady equilibrium. The reader will therefore appreciate that the concept of balanced growth, explained earlier, is closely associated with this methodology. The method also carries the implication that choices between fast growth in the immediate future and slower growth later, and the antithesis of this, have never to be made. We consider only equilibrium states in which the growth rate is constant over the whole theoretical future. Since the firm is a continuing organisation with a changing management, the approach seems not unreasonable. But we do not deny, of course, that the history of many firms has much of the appearance of a growth-curve: our assumptions are merely intended to represent a convenient analytical simplification.

Finally, we conclude the section by reminding the reader that up to the end of Chapter 6, the whole operation represents an exercise in partial-equilibrium analysis. This means that in general, when policies and conditions vary within the single firm which is being analysed, all relevant aspects of the environment are assumed to remain constant. 'All relevant aspects' will usually include general economic variables, such as factor supply prices (although high management itself has no supply-price in the ordinary sense — see Chapter 2, pp. 85–101 above — we do assume 'given' supply prices for junior and middle managers) and the general level of product prices; they will also include the magnitudes of the policy variables, such as diversification rate, set by other firms. Other individual prices, however, will not always be constant, because in the theory of demand we do take account of anticipated oligopolistic reactions. The significance of the 'partial' assumptions becomes clearer when, in Chapter 7, they are finally relaxed.

Further Definitions

At the end of Chapter 2 we promised operational definitions of certain variables such as size and leverage. We finally provide them, together with certain others.

The *size* of a firm is measured by the book value of gross assets according to the usual accounting conventions (see p. xvii above). The *growth rate* is the compound-interest rate of increase of size in a rather long-period sense, i.e. should best be measured as an average over a period of, say, five years. When movements of the general price level are occurring, some reasonable adjustment should be made in order to hold the concepts of size and growth to (in some sense or other) 'real' terms. The symbol for the growth rate is C^*. Inasmuch as the variable also measures the growth rate of the firm's capital supply, this aspect of the analysis is loosely referred to as 'supply'.

Demand is defined by reference to the book value of assets required to meet the total volume of demand for all the firm's products at a standard rate of utilisation. The *growth rate of demand* is the growth rate in book value which would be required if all orders were always met in full, and the average level of utilisation, taking one year with another, were constant. The symbol for the compound growth rate of demand is D^*.

Diversification represents the act of marketing a product new to the firm's catalogue with the intention of increasing demand. New variants expected to kill the demand for an existing line are therefore excluded. Diversification need not, however, be necessarily successful: new products may fail to achieve substantial sales and thus fail to contribute to growth as hoped. The *diversification rate* is loosely described as a measure of the rate at which diversification is *attempted*, and loosely defined as the ratio of attempts per period to the number of items already catalogued. A more rigorous definition states that the diversification rate is that value of D^* which would be expected if (a) the trend for saturated demand was zero, and (b) all new products were successful. It follows that in the long run D^* is approximately equal to the diversification rate multiplied by the average proportion of successes. The symbol for the diversification rate is d.

Leverage or Gearing was defined in Chapter 1 as the ratio of liabilities to gross assets. Many firms with significant leverage, however, also maintain substantial proportions of liquid assets. These, from our point of view, are virtually antipodean: liquid assets in excess of minimum working balances reduce the insecurity associated with a given degree of leverage because they could always, in principle, be applied to debt reduction. Liquid assets also reduce the overall return relatively to the productive return, offsetting the opposite effect in gearing. Some liquid assets are cash, others easily marketable securities. In the case of the former, a firm with both leverage and liquidity is borrowing long to 'lend' short; in the latter, it is borrowing long to lend long, i.e. the proceeds of its own bonds are partly invested in securities issued by other institutions. The numerous technical factors favouring such practices are not, to us, of great interest, and we therefore adopt the simplification of treating liquidity as negative gearing. The gearing or leverage ratio (symbol g) is then defined as the ratio of liabilities, *less* liquid assets, to gross assets. Evidently, it is not necessarily required to be positive.

The reader is also reminded of the definitions given in the Note on Concepts in the preliminary material (p. xv) and of the glossary of frequently recurring symbols provided on the back page.

CHAPTER FOUR

'DEMAND'

Note: the reader is reminded that the notation in this chapter stands apart from the rest. It is summarised on pp. 202–3 below.

We have seen that in order to sustain growth a firm must either create new products, enter existing markets which it has previously ignored, or merge. The first two methods are called 'growth by diversification', the second 'growth by merger'. These, as we have seen, are related, 'growth by merger' often representing no more than a means of overcoming dynamic organisational restraints on growth by diversification. In this chapter we are concerned with the dynamics of growth by diversification. We are concerned, that is, with the relationship between the rate of growth of the productive capacity required if there is to be no trend (in either direction) in the level of capacity utilisation. In essence, the problem is one of policy; we are asking how certain variables within the control of the firm, such as price policy, diversification policy, research and development expenditure and selling expenditure, react on the endogenous variables which feature in the conditions for maximum (sustainable) growth. How do the policy variables affect the growth rate of the quantum of demand for the firm's products; how do they react on such factors as rate of return, which govern the growth rate of the firm's supply of capital?

In micro-economics, we may consider 'demand' either from the point of view of the firm or from the point of view of the consumer. In the latter case the theory should relate to items of consumers' needs — to such entities as 'potatoes', 'private motoring' or 'refrigerators'. But a *firm* may sell in a number of such classes; for example, a firm may produce both cars and refrigerators. A theory of the growth of demand for the products of a firm as a whole will stem from, but must go beyond, the ordinary theory of consumer-demand and, as we shall see, it is certainly wrong to treat the forces controlling 'demand for the firm' as nothing more than some simple compound of the forces controlling consumers' demand for the products the firm happens to manufacture. In what follows we develop a theory we believe to be appropriate to the problem of the individual firm; to be appropriate to the conditions of a dynamic managerial economy (or, if preferred, of an 'affluent society'); and, going beyond the analytical convenience, to represent a considerable advance in realism.

As already indicated, growth by diversification may be 'differentiated' in character, 'imitative' or both. In either case the products marketed are 'new' to the firm, in the sense that it has not produced or marketed products of this type before, but in the 'differentiated' case, they are also largely new to the public. More precisely, the effects of the diversion of consumer expenditure involved in the growth of demand for a successful differentiated product are, by definition, spread thinly over demand for products in the economy at large, and are not perceptible to the producers of any one existing product or narrowly defined group of products. By contrast, the growth of sales of a product which is 'new' to one firm, in the sense defined above, but nevertheless 'imitative', is only at the expense of the sales of the product or products of a relatively small number of other firms, and, if the imitation is successful, these other firms will experience a noticeable reduction of demand in relation to the sales they could have expected had the imitation not been marketed. Many products, of course, will contain both imitative and differentiated elements; for example, suppose the growth rate of demand in the economy as a whole is two per cent per annum, and this rate precisely is being experienced by a group of producers of a product, X. A firm under analysis then markets a product X'. During the period immediately after it is first marketed, sales of X' grow at ten per cent per annum, in consequence of which, sales of X, instead of growing at two per cent, grow more slowly or even decline. When X' has ceased its rapid phase of growth, both it and X resume the two per cent rate, but the absolute level of sales of X, of course, will now be lower at all future points of time than would have been the case had X' never appeared. Then we say that X' is only 'partly' imitative if X experienced only part of the total divertive effect, the growth rate of demand for all other products in the economy at large having also been slightly (but imperceptibly) reduced during the same period; the potential sales of X' are 'large' in relation to those of X, but small in relation to the economy at large. Had the whole effect been spread over the economy at large, X' would have been defined as fully differentiated; had none been so spread, as fully imitative.

In the first part of the present chapter we concentrate analysis first on the case where the firm diversifies through the medium of products all of which are as 'differentiated' as the definition allows, and then on the case where all are fully imitative, and finally we attempt to combine the results in a model which not only takes account of partly imitative products but also of the need for policy decisions between them.

The Consumer and his Brain

Economists are notorious for bias in favour of behaviouristic inductions which fit conveniently with favoured analytical methods. Thus the 'Marshallian' static demand-curve was the convenient concept for the method of comparative statics. This, one often suspects, at least partly explains why the associated static theories of utility and consumer preference — essentially philosophical and axiomatic — have gripped the subject for so long.

By a static demand-curve we mean a stable, reversible and, in general, monotonic and fully differentiable functional relationship in which quantity demanded depends on prices, income, etc. This conception remains 'static' as much when the function is allowed to 'drift' over time as when it is not. [1] To accept that quantity demanded can exhibit residual variation which may be treated as a statistical trend does no more than introduce slow change into a set of basically statically-conceived relationships; reversible dependence on price and income remains the dominant feature of the system. The practical weaknesses of the conception stem from two implicit assumptions. The first is the assumption that the consumer's brain incorporates a relatively stable and comprehensive preference system analogous in character to a computing machine governed by a definite exogenous programme. The second is the assumption that the preference systems of individuals are independent; more precisely, that the effects of the decisions of individual brains on the decision-taking functions of others are, in this field, sufficiently unimportant to be ignored.

In affluent societies, neither assumption is plausible. Both were first identified and attacked by James Duesenberry. In *Income, Saving and the Theory of Consumer Behaviour*,[2] published in 1949, Duesenberry outflanked the stable reversible preference system and destroyed the assumption of independence. But at that time his main concern was to construct a new macro-economic theory of the relation between income, consumption and saving, rather than to develop the micro-economic implications; consequently the third section of the sixth chapter of the book, which provided an original model of the growth of demand for individual new products, remained somewhat isolated from the rest; the macro-theory did not depend on this particular piece of micro-theory. In the present work, although we do not adopt his particular theory, the influence of Duesenberry will be obvious. Once the standard of living has bettered 'subsistence', the static reversible preference system becomes particularly implausible. The brain probably possesses a virtually infinite capacity for recording experiences, and its state — an electro-chemical condition — is the product of everything that it has felt and done during the whole of its history. Each experience, however trivial, makes a permanent alteration. But although the present state of the brain is the product of all that has gone before, it is also the sole determinant of how it will react to stimuli received now. Hence although the act of consuming a certain quantity of a certain commodity (a consequence of a decision of the brain) may represent response to current stimuli such as price, income, advertising and the behaviour of other consumers, it is also an act which permanently alters the actor. Therefore there is no presumption whatsoever that repetition of a particular constellation of prices and income will induce approximately the same consumption decisions as before; one price movement may be needed to induce a man to consume a new product, another to make him give it up, yet another to revert, and so on. The preference 'system' existing in the mind of a single consumer at a particular instant of time is the product of past experience, and is therefore continually developing. This fact, which no one seriously denies, invalidates both the assumptions of stability and of reversibility in the demand curve. It has also incidentally interesting implications in welfare economics. For the primary biological goal of the organism (the brain) is as likely to be development as the achievement of static equilibrium. 'Maximisation of consumer welfare' might be better defined as consisting in the maximisation of the rate of refinement of preferences than in the achievement of a stable state within a given system. [3] In other words, as we often say that the general goals of human endeavour lie primarily in the development of new capacities rather than in the exploitation of existing ones, so we might define the primary economic goal as the refinement of new wants rather than the satisfaction of existing wants. The last argument, however, is superfluous to the immediate purpose, for which we need consider only objective behaviour.

The Process of Want Creation [4]

It is not difficult to identify primary elements in the mental processes leading up to a consumption decision. In the first place, the brain contains a store of memories of previous consumption experiences, and these form the framework against which current decisions are taken. The most common reason for purchasing a product is the fact of having consumed it before and found it satisfactory or (to use more dangerous language) 'satisfying'. More precisely, the previous experience, whether repeated or isolated, has in some sense gratified a psychological motive — has provided pleasurable sensations, prevented pain or met a social requirement. 'Wants' therefore are largely the product of experience. But the relevant experience need not always be direct; wants can also result from vicarious experience, such as is provided by the reports of other consumers or the blandishments of advertising. Furthermore, it is clear that in addition to this apparatus (which can very loosely be described as 'habit') most human brains are also constantly scanning for possible new experiences. In many people the scanning mechanism may be so weak as to be practically non-existent, but the achievements of the human race as a whole bear witness to its strength in others. It is clearly of vital importance in the struggle between new products and old. Finally, there remains the fact that the same mental forces which encourage the consumption of one commodity also encourage the consumption of others, and the results do not automatically harmonise. The force of the scanning effect, for example, encouraging a decision to sample a new product, a, has to battle with a similar force encouraging the choice of new product b, or, alternatively with the force of habit asking for old product c. By some means a decision is taken, and, with limited income, the decision-taking process must involve some weighing of relative sacrifices, and hence consideration of prices.

How does a typical consumer come to decide to buy a product he has never bought before? He evidently requires stimulation, he requires in fact to be made for the first time strongly aware of the potentialities of the product. Advertisements can provide this stimulus, but their obvious bias makes many people at least resist them to some extent. There is considerable sociological evidence that[5] the most effective stimulus remains that of contact with other existing consumers — more conversions are made by previous converts than by priests. We can illustrate this argument with two examples, one a new consumer 'durable', the other a traditional perishable. Suppose, for the first time, an effective dishwashing machine is put on the market. No one believes the advertiser's claims that the machine eliminates practically all the labour of washing dishes; most, however, will accept that the labour is probably reduced in volume or at least favourably changed in character. But, for the average family, these potentialities must seem very uncertain. How many woman-hours of work will in fact be eliminated? How far will the change in the nature of the task lighten the psychological burden? Will a new machine in the kitchen encourage the males to help more often? Will they, in their turn, feel a worth-while reduction of guilt? These questions can only be answered after extended practical experience of using the machine. Alternatively, if the members of another family who have already bought one are consulted, their views will be of value only if, as a family, they are sociologically similar. And in practice, of course, it is usually contact with a sociologically similar family already using the machine that puts the idea of buying into the first family's collective head.

Our second example relates to meat. Suppose a family with a specified income has been in the habit of buying only low-quality beef. Their real income rises. Among other things on which they might spend the increment is beef of better quality. But at first, never having tasted anything better, they do not believe the commodity could yield them any 'utility'; they continue to regard such things as pointless luxuries and in consequence a large proportion of their marginal income is saved. Then, one day, they eat with friends who for one reason or another are already consuming good meat. The gastronomic experience is a revelation to them; from now on they will find it difficult to eat cheap beef again. This is not a process of emulation, but of stimulation. The behaviour is not simple conformism, but the acquisition of acquired tastes. The habit-forming commodity is not the exception: it is, and always has been, the rule. [6]

Once, therefore, a person has been stimulated to buy a new commodity, he possesses a 'want' or 'need' where he had none before; stimulation, in this sense, is a process of want creation.

In fact we may distinguish between needs and wants. A product meets a need if it provides the consumer with sensible advantages in the achievement of specific socio-economic aims. But consumers cannot 'want' the product until they have experienced it in action, until in fact it has been created and is in use. When they do come to want it, they also need it. Before this, the need can be described as latent. There is a latent need for a product if, were it created, it would become wanted. The commercial process consists of sensing the existence of latent needs and exploiting them, i.e. converting them into conscious wants by marketing and advertising appropriate products. It is sometimes argued that wants can be created from nothing, without the existence of objective latent needs. If this were generally true, nothing would limit the rate of growth of capacity required by the individual firm, and relative growth among firms would depend on factors other than demand. But it is not true. Consider two case histories, neither of them relating to 'durables'.

After World War II, American manufacturers of 'Cola' type drinks made a considerable attempt to expand further into world markets. Among the countries they attacked was Great Britain. 'Cola' drinks are to some extent habit-forming in the ordinary sense of the term, but, although they are consumed in both winter and summer, the 'craving' can only be effectively sustained in continental climates with regular long dry summers and winters sufficiently cold that interior space heating significantly dries the domestic atmosphere. In the U.K. these conditions are absent and the drinks have not really caught on; although they have achieved a modest steady sale their position in the consumption pattern cannot be compared with their corresponding position in the U.S. and many other countries. Notice a difficulty in separating cause and effect: one might well argue that the relative failure of these drinks in the U.K. stemmed from failure to develop distribution methods in the characteristic American manner. But this only leaves the basic question unanswered; we must still explain the explanation. Cola drinks must be served cold: in the U.K. they rarely are. Once bottled they are bulky. Hence success depends on a wide distribution of large-capacity refrigerating plant in retail outlets. But despite all attempts to induce them to behave otherwise, potential British retailers of this type of commodity have by and large refused to invest in the necessary machinery, although no difficulty was experienced in persuading food retailers to invest in deep freezes. The answer, surely, lies in the mildness of a climate which makes the cold drink, though often desirable, rarely essential. The retailer, therefore, invests elsewhere.

Consider the now famous British product 'Babycham'. This is an alcoholic beverage made from pears and possessing some of the more superficial characteristics of champagne: it is fizzy and straw-coloured, and capable of inducing a fairly 'light' or 'gay' variety of intoxication. It is also rather sweet and in general not very attractive to the sophisticated palate. For the unsophisticated, who like it, it is not overwhelmingly improved by chilling and is generally served at room temperature. This drink was marketed with spectacular success in British inns in the 1950's, following a large-scale advertising campaign. The success flew in the face of the virtual failure of all earlier attempts to create a mass market for products derived from the cider and perry family, and was due to a new, sociologically created latent need, acutely observed by the manufacturers. British pubs had been becoming more respectable, more bourgeois and more feminine. But the new female customers found a deficiency in the products traditionally offered: they did not drink often, they wanted to get intoxicated without appearing so to want, they disliked beer and were more than dubious about hard liquor. Gin, the traditional drink of women, had severe drawbacks, and the American cocktail was impossible to serve properly in the average pub because there was never enough ice (and there was never enough ice for the reasons given above). To cut a long story short, Babycham proved the answer to the maiden's prayer.

The first point of this second story is that before the product's introduction, the maidens' prayers were quite inaudible. A latent need is latent, and the consumer himself is hardly aware of it. Ordinary processes of questioning would have been unlikely to have revealed the potential market for *Babycham*; 'market research', with samples, operates after a product has been invented. The second point is to draw attention to genuine objective conditions favouring the product, without which it could not have succeeded. And as a postscript it might be added that the invention also represented a considerable technical achievement. The drink is less cloying than anything of this type made before, and, in particular, provides a major improvement in the character of the intoxication produced by beverages fermented from pears or apples. Thus not only is it the case that wants cannot be created without latent needs, but one cannot normally exploit a newly discovered latent need without technical innovation — more precisely, given the technology of time t, even should there exist an unlimited number of latent needs awaiting exploitation, only a limited number could be exploited by any one innovator during δt; and in general a firm is likely to find that the greater the number of new products it markets in a period, the lower the technical efficiency of production.

The Pioneering Consumer

In the dynamic theory of demand, then, instead of adjustment to price-changes among established commodities, we emphasise the process of inter-personal stimulation and want creation. How does it originate? If no consumer ever bought a new product until stimulated by an existing consumer, new products would never get started. There must be some 'pioneers' among consumers — individuals or families who decide on new purchases without benefit of stimulus from others. We must therefore make a formal distinction between these pioneers and the general run of consumers, or 'sheep'. Pioneers may, but not necessarily, represent a distinct psychological type, and different people may at different times pioneer different products. For our purposes, therefore, the concept of the pioneer need only be defined in relation to a 'given' product. But this does not mean we can get away with assuming nothing about pioneers beyond that they exist. For one thing, we must assume that each pioneer is sufficiently in touch with the rest of the community that, although himself able to act without stimulus, he can stimulate others; otherwise his behaviour is of little interest. But the biological machine in the skull of the pioneer is basically the same as in the skull of the sheep. Just as with the sheep, so the pioneer's new consumption experience can create want where none existed before; and as a result of the experience, his brain is permanently altered. The only essential difference is that, unlike the sheep, the pioneer for one reason or another chooses to undergo the experience without social stimulus. One might say that in both pioneers and sheep wants are established by consumption experience, but with sheep they must first be planted in the mind by another person. Unusual ability to perceive one's own latent needs, unusual adventurousness or unusual susceptibility to advertising might all explain pioneering decisions. Alternatively, as we shall more generally assume, in relation to any given new product they are stochastic events distributed among the whole population of 'sheep'[7]

The total number of new pioneers acquired by a product in a given period will therefore be a function of its intrinsic qualities, of the money and skill devoted to advertising and other forms of sales promotion, of its price, and of the social and economic characteristics of the population. In general we assume that, unless special steps are taken to arrange things otherwise, a given number of pioneers will be randomly distributed in a given population, in the sense that in the absence of special knowledge about a consumer (such as that he has a special disposition to pioneering) he has the same probability of being a pioneer as every other consumer. The act of becoming a pioneer, however, represents merely a decision to become a buyer, it does not determine the quantity bought except in the case of commodities where only one unit is taken. We can well assume that, having decided to become a pioneer, a consumer then behaves according to a perfectly orthodox demand function, but, and it is a very important but, the behaviour-function controlling the total number of pioneers cannot normally be derived directly from the characteristics of the post-pioneering demand functions of the individuals. The 'pioneering function' is inherently 'macro' in character, derives from 'macro' social and economic variates, and cannot, in general, be obtained by mere aggregation. For example, many firms believe this function to be rather insensitive to price,[8] and there is some evidence that they are right, but this does not necessarily imply that the 'pioneer's' function which determines the quantity actually bought by a person who has already decided to pioneer will also be inelastic. For example, a product might be marketed at a high price and acquire N_p pioneers, each of whom, on account of the price, took only a small quantity. A reduction in price might significantly increase their *per capita* consumption but not greatly influence their number, and vice versa. Or the situation might be reversed. When firms say that the demand for new products is inelastic, they sometimes mean the one thing, sometimes the other, sometimes both; we shall find the distinction important. The case most easily analysed is, needless to say, the one where both the pioneering and the pioneer's functions are inelastic.

Evidently, the foregoing ideas *could* be expressed in orthodox terms, for example by assuming suitably peculiarly shaped individual demand-curves, and building by aggregation a model

F

based on an analysis of the elasticities around the points where these curves cut their origins, but the result would not be convincing. The act of becoming a pioneer is different in kind from that of moving along an established demand-curve. Pioneering consists of becoming aware of the product, of incorporating it into the preference system—the very act, in fact, of establishing the demand-curve itself. Pioneering is thus irreversible: before the act no curve exists, consumption is zero at all prices and incomes; after the act, zero consumption happens only if prices are above a definite (positive) level.

Precisely the same applies to 'sheep'. When a 'sheep' is stimulated to become a consumer as a result of contact with other existing consumers, a process we call *activation*, he is irreversibly changed. Before, he had no demand-curve; now he has. Its form, however, may be of many varieties, and indeed we need not necessarily assume that he actually buys any positive quantities. Activation might be defined as a change of state indicating merely that now, if the price were low enough, the consumer would buy some positive quantity, whereas before he would have bought none at any price. Many firms say that, as compared with the pioneering phase in a product's development, it may often prove rather sensitive to price [9] in the rapidly expanding or saturated stage, although we do not know whether by this is meant that in such circumstances it has usually acquired competitors or that 'sheep' are naturally more price-sensitive bodies than pioneers.

The point is important because it is vitally involved in the mechanism by which the demand for new products grows. We have described the process of activation as that of receiving stimulus from other consumers with whom one is in socio-economic contact. In the 'Opinion Leader' concept of the process, [10] certain particular members of the population are endowed with the quality of being able to activate other members of their primary groups, but not the other way about. For demand to grow, therefore, it is necessary that pioneers be concentrated among these people, and the resulting process, involving carefully planned selective selling, is not properly cumulative. In our view, any active consumer should be regarded as in principle potentially capable of stimulating others, irrespective of whether he was himself originally a pioneer or an 'activated' sheep. By this means (and we believe the picture to be more generally realistic), chain reactions are obtained. It therefore becomes important to know whether or not a 'sheep', having been activated in the sense of now possessing a demand-curve for the product, finds himself so placed on this curve as to indicate some significant positive consumption; for, if he does not, he cannot pass on the effect to others. In order to ease the analysis, therefore, we shall assume that pioneers' demand functions, once established, are in general of some form implying significant positive consumption even at high prices; in effect this is a part of the definition of a pioneer. In the case of sheep, we define the concept of a *market population*, this being the population of all consumers who, if activated (or if pioneers), would at a given price consume sufficient positive quantities to be capable of stimulating others. The size of market population is therefore a function of price, of other characteristics of the product and, of course, of characteristics of the population. It follows that if the activated sheep's demand function is linear throughout and also elastic, both the size of the market population and their aggregate consumption in the event of total activation are price-sensitive. A manufacturer appreciating this would therefore behave differently in face of an activated population than he would if faced with a population in which all the buyers, if any, were pioneers. Essentially the point is that although pioneer's and sheep-like demand functions may contain similar variates, the respective elasticities may well be different.

The Chain Reaction

The characteristic early history of a new commodity in a society where the standard of living of a large number of people is well above subsistence is therefore as follows. When it is introduced, the number of immediate consumers is small, because pioneering is a minority activity. As time passes, pioneering purchases increase, but in the absence of other influences would probably eventually flatten out. If the pioneers give their contacts a good account of the product, they may stimulate them into purchasing it, and these sheep may in turn stimulate others. In this way a chain reaction may spread consumption far beyond the pioneering frontier. The idea would be trivial unless the beginning of the reaction could be shown to depend on the number of pioneers reaching some definite critical size: to put the point another way — if the 'critical' number were no greater than one consumer — the first — we might just as well ignore the chain reaction and concentrate attention, as in orthodox analysis, on the situation existing after it is finished. The evidence, however, is otherwise.

The process of stimulation and penetration is inevitably stochastic in character, because the chances of life determine who stimulates whom, or (to parody the words of an unprintable limerick) who does what, when and to whom. *Criticality*, therefore, is defined as a condition where the probability of a continuing chain reaction tends to unity. In a limiting case, where a product is so appealing that almost the whole market population can be activated with the minimum of stimulation, criticality in this sense occurs almost the instant the product appears and after only a very small number of pioneers has been obtained. We shall later be able to define this case with some mathematical precision. In the meantime, we concentrate on the conditions for criticality in the more general case where the number of pioneers required represents a significant proportion of the (market) population as a whole.

In order to stimulate one another consumers must be in a state we shall define as socio-economic contact. One is stimulated by one's friends, and sometimes by one's neighbours. But not everyone with whom one is in social contact, in the sense of 'knowing', living next door to, meeting at work, meeting at play, is a socio-economic contact. The tautological definition of a socio-economic contact is a contact with a person who is capable of inducing one to consume a new commodity, and to this end it is necessary that one shares at least some of the contact's tastes and values. Evidently, therefore, socio-economic contacts will tend to be concentrated among social contacts within one's own social class. Reports of a new commodity from a person whose values in general one does not share are unlikely to have much effect. This may be a matter of snobbery, but may also represent a quite reasonable appreciation that his pattern of living is so different from one's own that a commodity which discovers a genuine latent need in his life may be valueless to oneself. If one belongs to a social class where a mother-in-law spends much of her time in the daughter's home and gives substantial help with the housework, a dishwashing machine may be more trouble than use, but with an upper-middle-class mother-in-law who merely creates work, the same machine may be a godsend. To someone belonging to a social class in which wine is drunk regularly, nothing can make *Babycham* acceptable. In other words, as Katz and Lazarsfeld more soberly put it, 'Seeking out a woman of like status for advice means seeking out a woman with similar budgetary problems and limitations.'[11]

The correlation between social class and socio-economic contact is, of course, reinforced by the correlation of the two with income. The theory we are propounding by no means purports to eliminate the hard reality of income from consumption decisions. Many new commodities are quite out of the range of certain income groups, and no amount of social stimulation can alter the fact. 'Not being able to afford it' remains the most important reason for not consuming most things. Nevertheless, 'affording' is a relative term, and becomes increasingly so as affluence increases. Suppose, after meeting his so-called 'subsistence' needs, a manual worker has half of his income left over for so-called 'luxuries'. There is nothing in principle to prevent him from devoting the whole of the margin to one item normally regarded as a preserve of the much better off; but normally he is dissuaded from so doing by competing temptations from other 'luxuries'. Many working-class families in the U.K. in the late nineteen-forties spent little less on drink and tobacco than the cost of running a small automobile: now that the standard of living has risen still further, cars are becoming the vogue: if tobacco had never been invented, and was not habit-forming, or had been invented after the car, the car might perfectly well have come in first in the Engel-curve hierarchy. In short, over a wide range of consumption, what people can afford is what they choose to afford, and what they choose to afford is the product of both normative behaviour and socio-economic stimulation.

We cannot say for certain that either shared social class or shared income class is an exclusive ingredient in a socio-economic contact.

The lady who comes to help with the cleaning in the author's house belongs to a family with a net income after tax of about a third of her employer's. Some of the things she sees consumed in her employer's house are ruled out in her own on the 'cannot afford' argument, others by virtue of an entirely different set of social values. But some of the things she sees in her employer's house, she persuades her husband to buy for her. Conversely, some of the ideas about new types of 'do it yourself' equipment gleaned from her husband's workshop are effectively communicated to her employer. So we are driven back on the tautological definition of social contact; we can however lay down the required conditions more precisely. A socio-economic contact is a person with whom one has a relationship such that his consumption behaviour is capable of influencing one's own. The socio-economic contacts of an individual are therefore limited to those persons with whom he is in general contact (sees and speaks to fairly regularly), and, among them, to those with whom he shares enough relevant values for the contact to be economic as well as social.

We define a single stimulus as the automatic consequence of a socio-economic contact with one existing consumer of a product during a given period of time. Thus if, during δt, I am in contact with one existing consumer, I have experienced one stimulus. If during a second δt I am in contact with another existing consumer, or my contact with the first is repeated, I have experienced two stimuli. Thus the number of my stimuli in any given finite time period is the product of the number of separate sources of contact with separate individual existing consumers, and the average number of times I have been in contact with each during the period. It is probable that in order to be induced to consume a commodity which is new to them, most people need more than one stimulus. It is also likely that they usually need stimuli from more than one source. We tend to distrust the evidence of any single individual or family, however many times the fact of their consumption of the new commodity is brought home to us. And in any case, the forces of emulation and conformism, though not the only factors in the chain, are by no means negligible, and, evidently, to any extent that conformism is in fact important, the greater the number of separate sources of stimulus the greater the chance of activation. Indeed, in cases where conformism is really the dominant factor, evidence from a single contact only, unless subsequently reinforced by evidence from others, may lead to the suspicion that the original individual was a crank; it is known, for example, that the Organisation Man who buys an automobile one grade more expensive than that of his neighbours, far from inducing them to follow suit, may instead find himself ostracised.[12]

Socio-Economic Structure

A society of consumers thus consists of a large number of individual units, each of whom is in socio-economic contact with a limited number of others. Some of these contacts will represent relationships with consumers who are themselves inter-connected, others not. Within any large population, therefore, we can also identify a (large) number of *primary groups*, i.e. groups of consumers all of whom are in socio-economic contact *inter se*. Such groups may, and in general probably will, intersect, in the sense that an individual may belong to more than one: for example A may be in contact with B and C, who are in contact with one another, and also with B' and C', who are similarly related, but neither B' nor C' need be in contact with either B or C. *A pair of groups whose intersection contains at least one element can be said to be 'linked' and if the intersection contains at least n elements we shall describe them as 'linked in degree n'.*

This conception of a primary group is of considerable importance. If within one group there exists the minimum number of active consumers required to activate one sheep, because every member is in contact with every other member, every member must in due course become active. Furthermore, if the 'threshold' number of separate contacts is m, then any other group with which the first group is m-degree linked will also, eventually, be saturated (i.e. all its members become active), and in turn these will activate and saturate all other groups with whom they are similarly linked, and so on. The reaction, in fact, will continue until every group which is linked either directly or indirectly with the original group is saturated. It follows that the chance of obtaining a chain reaction depends intimately on the structure of the system of groups and links.

To assist the analysis, let us clear the decks by eliminating 'redundant' primary groups, i.e. all those which are subsets of others. If A, B, C, and D form a primary group, there is little point in separately identifying the subsets A, B, and C, D, since anything of significance that can be said about the one can also be said about the other — a condition which by no means applies to pairs of groups which though linked are not inclusive. For example, if m is the threshold and A, B, C and D form a primary group with subsets A, B, and C, D, in order to saturate both A, B, and C, D it is necessary only that there occur m pioneers located in any arrangement among the group A, B, C, D; e.g. if m were 2, one pioneer could be A and another D. By contrast, if two groups, although intersecting, are not inclusive (i.e. one is not a subset of the other), then in order to saturate both it is necessary to obtain m active consumers located either entirely within the one or entirely within the other. Redundant groups, therefore, are of little interest and we may 'rationalise' our structure by ignoring them. A 'rationalised population' is then defined as the set of all possible primary groups derivable from a given market population other than those which, if included, would prove to be proper subsets of others. In what follows, unless otherwise indicated, all populations considered are implicitly assumed to be rationalised. Consequently, every consumer in the market population is included in at least one of the elements of the rationalised population, but not every element in the rationalised population necessarily contains more than one consumer.

What determines the size, shape and linkage of typical primary groups? Socio-economic structure is often conditioned by such economically trivial factors as housing lay-out, but in other cases, particularly those of older societies, the arrangement of contacts in geographical space is more the result than the cause of sociological phenomena. Alternatively, among classes able to afford the custom of frequent distant visiting, contact systems may represent spacial networks which are both many-dimensional and non-geographical. In the crudest example of patterns caused or at least occasioned by elementary geographical factors, the linear suburb, it is often customary to maintain contact with both immediate neighbours to right and left, with the family immediately opposite and with their immediate neighbours, but not with any of the families beyond the backyard fence. In some types of older British semi-slums, almost the opposite situation was sometimes found. In 'ribbon' developments along congested highways, contacts may literally be confined to immediate neighbours only. In high-class, non-linear suburbs, the network may prove almost identical with the system of blocks and courts. Thus, writing of his famous subject, the Chicago suburb of Park Forest, William Whyte said,

> 'It is the group that determines when a luxury becomes a necessity. This takes place when there comes together a sort of critical mass. In the early stages, when only a few of the house-wives have, say, an automatic dryer, the word-of-mouth praise of its indispensability is restricted. But then as time goes on and the adjacent housewives follow suit, in mounting ratio others are exposed to more and more talk about its benefits.'[13]

Whyte was discussing a new and mobile society. It must be emphasised that in older societies, if families are established long enough to develop contacts on deeper anthropological, psycho-logical and sociological bases, these geographical analogies of socio-economic structure become less valid. In such societies definite structures exist, of course, but they require a more sophisticated mathematical representation.

Geography must nevertheless always remain important. A well-defined system of primary groups requires more than that people merely have contacts; it requires the existence of some factor tending to encourage the probability that among all those with whom a typical consumer is in contact a certain number will also be inter-contacted. If I am in contact with only B, C, D and E, and if I am to belong to a reasonable-sized primary group, there must be some factor tending to make the probability of occurrence of contacts between these persons considerably greater than chance; if not, either primary groups will be very small or the average number of contacts per person must be unrealistically large. Many non-geographical social and economic phenomena may help perform this role; in old rural societies the village, in urban societies the family, and in modern suburban societies the club and the Church. But in all societies, new or old, until the day when travel becomes free, effortless and infinitely convenient, geography will remain the predominant de-randomiser among all but the richest or most sophisticated classes. Simple geographical examples of socio-economic structure, though inaccurate, are therefore unlikely to be grossly misleading.

The simplest example of all, as previously mentioned, is the linear suburb depicted below in Diagram 4.1. Each dot represents a porch, the space between the row of dots is a drive, the broken lines yard fences. Each family, without exception, is supposed to be in contact only with neighbours to the left and right and the three nearest families opposite. Each has therefore five contacts and belongs to two primary groups, but the primary groups themselves (indicated by circles) contain each only four elements. Each, however, has two 2-unit intersections with adjacent groups and the

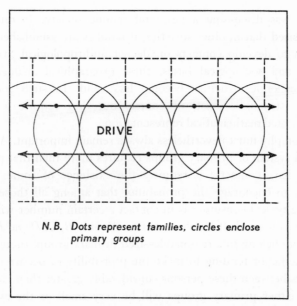

N.B. Dots represent families, circles enclose primary groups

DIAGRAM 4.1. Primary Groups in a Linear Suburb

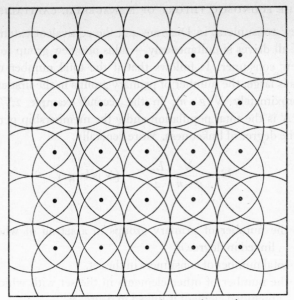

N.B. *Dots represent families, circles enclose primary groups*

DIAGRAM 4.2. Net-Like System of Primary Groups

population of the drive as a whole forms a set of groups all of which are linked in the second degree. The author experienced almost precisely such a situation in the Fall of 1961, on Mullen Drive, Austin, Texas.

What happens when there are also contacts over backyard fences? In Diagram 4.2, we indicate a system of such contacts, assuming that the contacts permitted in Diagram 4.1 are also maintained. Each family now has three additional contacts, making eight in all, and each primary group acquires two more 2-unit intersections (we are assuming the system extends indefinitely). The size of the groups, however, remains the same.

The change of pattern is of considerable significance, for although the size of the primary groups is unchanged, the increase in the degree of 'compactness' alters the size of the rationalised population relative to that of the market population. In other words, in the more 'compact' pattern, more non-redundant primary groups are derivable from a population of given size. In Diagram 4.1, as the drive is extended, one new primary group is added for each

two new consumers; in Diagram 4.2, the equivalent extension —
that of all drives simultaneously — adds one new group for every
one new consumer. It follows that if the total number of consumers is large, the number of primary groups in the first example
is approximately $N/(g-n)$, in the second example $2N/(g-n)$,
where N is the total population and g the membership per group
and n the degree of linkedness. More generally,

$$G_n \eqsim \frac{N}{g-n} \cdot \frac{L_n}{2} \qquad (N \text{ is large}) \qquad (4.1)$$

where

    G_n = the number of primary groups in a set all of whom are
           linked in degree n,

    N = total number of consumers in the set,

    L_n = the number of other elements in the set with which each
           included element is linked in degree n,

    g = number of consumers per primary group.

The above formula applies to a regular structure in which L_n and g
are constant over all groups, and all intersections contain precisely
n consumers; it may, however, be used as an approximation in
irregular cases also. Evidently, the 'chainlike' arrangement of the
linear suburb described in Diagram 4.1, where L_n is 2, represents
the minimum degree of compactness consistent with a chain of any
length, the maximum membership of a set in which L_n is 1 being
two, and in which L_n is 0 being one. Thus $L_n = 2$ also represents
the minimum condition for a significant chain reaction; in fact the
very definition of a chain, of course, requires that each element is
linked to at least two others.

It will also be seen that the number of consumers with whom
each consumer is in contact is related to both g, the size of the
primary groups, and to L_n, the number of links per group. The
character of this relationship depends however on the pattern of
the structure; all we can say is that contacts *per capita* must tend to
vary directly with both g and L_n, an increase in either with the
other held constant necessarily increasing the contacts, and vice-
versa.

Social Barriers and Social Bars

So far we have been arguing as if patterns were not only regular but unbroken. If a pattern permits a family to be in contact with their neighbours, then, we have assumed, every consumer is in neighbourly contact. Obviously this is unrealistic. If Mrs. A does not like her neighbour, or if they merely belong to different age-groups, she may refuse to contact her; she may find other friends outside the prescribed pattern, or may simply have fewer than the specified number of contacts. More generally, if we redefine the concept of a pattern as a system of *possible* contacts, actual contacts will be fewer and quasi-randomly distributed among the possible. The 'missing' connections could be described as social bars. If social bars are present in significant numbers, actual primary groups will be irregularly shaped and variable in size, and the chains of linked groups extensively interrupted. Some of these interruptions will be of little economic importance, because, being relatively trivial, they will usually be consistent with the presence of other routes by which chain reactions starting from given sources can pass through the population. Others will be more significant. In a very crude example, a housing location is bounded by congested highways which discourage the inhabitants from venturing further afield. This does not mean that they may not have numbers of contacts all over town whom they regularly visit by car, but it does mean that these 'out' contacts are less likely to represent elements of intersections of primary groups. In other words, even in a relatively homogeneous population it is extremely unlikely that the largest set of linked groups will contain a substantial proportion of a total market population, except in the case of products where the market population is small and in some appropriate sense highly localised. In consequence of both random and non-random interruptions in the chains of contacts, any given rationalised market population will be divided into a considerable number of distinct linked sets which we may conveniently describe as 'secondary' groups. More precisely, we call any unbroken chain of n-degree linked primary groups '*a secondary group of degree n*', and we refer to the consumers contained in such a group as a 'secondary population'. And when a rationalised population has been arranged in the minimum number of secondary groups of degree n permitted by its structure, we shall say it has been 'stratified in degree n'.

Highways, random interruptions and other similar factors are, of course, far from being the only causes of stratification. In all but the most classless societies there will be important areas in social space where the bars are both non-random and dense. For although, as we have seen, for some products, cross-class contacts are possible, income and class barriers are inevitably powerful inhibitors. In the words of Katz and Lazarsfeld[14] — using the contemporary American euphemism for class — socio-economic contacts are necessarily to some extent 'status bound'.

'Barriers' operate on a different plane from the more trivial 'bars'. In new development areas barriers may be superimposed on, but consistent with, a basically geographical system, in the sense that in such areas most neighbourhoods are, for familiar reasons, rather homogeneous as to class. In old urban centres, on the other hand, large populations of different classes can live in close proximity without ever exchanging a word, let alone a contact. In effect, then, for a product of given type marketed at a given price, these broader social strata define the market populations: a manufacturer can in theory activate any homogeneous population, however much stratified, provided only that he can achieve a chain reaction in each of its secondary groups, but when he has exhausted these, he cannot necessarily repeat the process by moving in on another homogeneous population unless that population, also, has sufficient income to belong to the product's market population. For example, if he has saturated all the secondary groups of a primary population whose members have incomes greater than Y, where Y is the minimum income required for positive consumption in the sheeplike demand function, he can expand sales no further until either the income of the non-saturated groups rises, or he is able to lower his price. But notice that where a product is within the means of all but the poorest members of the population, so that the market population contains several socio-economic strata, the presence of these less economically significant barriers to contact has no more significance than the interruptions that occur for other reasons already described within a homogeneous population. From the manufacturer's point of view, both phenomena present him with more or less the same problem, that he must get a chain reaction going on each side of the break if he is to achieve total saturation. We need only take special note of 'barriers', therefore, where they delineate the bounds of a market population; otherwise they represent no more than an additional cause of quasi-random stratification phenomena.

Clearly, the number of secondary groups into which a population is divided depends not only on the causal factors responsible for interruptions, but also on the specified degree of stratification, i.e. on the value of n — the number of elements required for the specified intersections: obviously a particular intersection is less likely to be 'missing' if it is only required to contain one consumer, say, than if it is required to contain two; for example, in Diagram 4.1, the groups are linked up to degree 2, but if one Mrs. A breaks contact with one immediate neighbour, at this degree the whole chain is broken. At degree 1, however, the chain remains intact.

It is therefore convenient to represent the underlying stratification by means of some index simplifying the relationships between the various aspects of stratification, i.e. in some index defined in such a way as to combine the effect of degree and of division into secondary groups. Since we should expect the n-sensitivity of the number of secondary groups to be considerable (for example, in both Diagrams 4.1 and 4.2, as soon as n exceeds 2, the number of secondary groups in the stratified population becomes equal to the total number of primary groups (in fact the sets representing rationalised population and secondary groups become identical), we may reasonably write

$$\lambda = \sqrt[n]{S_n} \qquad (4.2)$$

where

λ = index of stratification (definition),
S_n = number of secondary groups.

Given this definition, we suppose that, other things being equal, the lower the index the easier it is to saturate a given market population with a given new product. Strictly, since pairs of consumers may be in contact in respect of some products but not of others, the appropriate socio-economic structure is partly specific to products, and the value of λ in relation to a population of given social and economic specification may vary from product to product. In what follows we shall ignore this point, and assume that if λ_i is the index of stratification in relation to the market population for product i, λ_i is independent of i and can therefore be written without suffix. (We make this assumption not because we believe it to be realistic, but because, until products are specifically described, no allowance can be made for differences.)

Chain Reactions in Intermediate Products

So far we have only considered final consumer goods, largely of the manufactured variety. A similar theory clearly applies to producers' goods also. If technology were fixed, in the sense that the economy was governed by a never-changing matrix of Leontief coefficients, changes in the demand for producers' goods would depend entirely on the effects of explosions occurring among consumers' goods. But technology is not fixed; new methods of production are invented, new intermediate products are substituted for old, new machinery is introduced. Inevitably there is inertia. The effect of inertia is greatest in the production of saturated products, where, since output is not expanding, new equipment need not so often be considered, and control is probably in the hands of the more routine-minded among the average firm's salariat. Planning the production and marketing of new products will usually be concentrated among the more enterprising members of the staff; they not only 'invent' the product but also, to some extent, the methods of production to go with it. Even here, however, there is room for conservatism. The methods employed to produce something which has never been made before inevitably borrow much from existing technology, and a firm contemplating the introduction of a specified new product will often be faced with a choice between several distinct manufacturing processes. If, for simplicity, we imagine the alternatives are only two, one in which the basic operation is done by the prevailing technique for operations of that type and the other involving a new and as yet untried technique, then the cautious will adopt the one, the adventurous the other.

It is well known that the rate at which machinery is scrapped is very variable. If equipment is scrapped before it wears out or becomes uneconomic to repair, the reason must be a desire to substitute new machinery of an improved type. We may suppose that management requires stimulus to introduce new machinery in the similar sense that the consumer requires stimulus to undertake new wants. What is the character of the stimulus here? Managers may be stimulated to innovate in two ways: by personal contact with other managers who have already innovated, or by feeling the effects of others' innovations through competition in the product market.

In the first case, each manager will have a limited number of contacts with managers in other firms specialising in the same field of technology, and the process of stimulation, activation and propagation is directly analogous to the process described among final consumers, the only major difference being, perhaps, that it has greater economic rationality. Social space becomes managerial social space; the society of the lunch club replaces the society of the parlour. In the second case, in the characteristic 'competitive' situation, each firm faces a relatively small circle of close competitors and is largely insensitive to the actions of firms outside it. As among consumers, the circles are not exclusive; they form an interlocking network, interrupted by various kinds of barriers and bars, spreading through the whole of industry. The type of system we employed in the consumer example is, therefore, equally appropriate to describe this network of competition, or 'commercial space'. When, say, three out of a firm's close competitors have adopted an innovation, the quantitative effect on the firm's trade is likely to be such as to force it to follow suit. And once this firm has made the change, it may in turn contribute to creating a similar situation for a rival who is also a rival of some, but not all, of the original three innovators; so the chain reaction spreads. The starting point of the process, as with consumer goods, is the appearance of a sufficiently large number of pioneers (who innovate without the stimulus of managerial social contact or commercial competition) to create criticality; and the end comes when the innovation has spread through all firms for whom it is appropriate, i.e. when the reaction is halted by an industrial barrier.

A Mathematical Model of the Socio-Economic Structure

We may now express the foregoing ideas in a more clearly defined form, beginning with a recapitulation of definitions:

Primary Population: all the consumer units of a market population (symbol, N; for definition of market population, see end of section).

Socio-Economic Contact: a relationship between a pair of consumers such that, in appropriate circumstances, one is able to activate the other and vice versa, where 'to activate' means to bring into operation a sheeplike demand function (see below).

Primary Group: any set of consumers having the property that all elements are in socio-economic contact with all other elements.

Rationalised Population: the set of all possible primary groups derivable from a primary population of given size and structure, except those which are subsets of others. (It follows that every consumer in the primary population is included in at least one of the primary groups of the rationalised population.)

Linked Groups: a pair of primary groups is said to be 'linked' in 'degree n' if their intersection contains at least n elements.

Secondary Group: a set of primary groups is said to form a 'secondary group of degree n' if each element is n-degree linked to at least one other element; hence 'secondary population' (N_s), the consumers contained in a secondary group (symbol for number of elements, G_n).

Stratified Population: a primary population is said to be 'stratified in degree n' when its rationalised population is arranged in the smallest number of secondary groups permitted by the structure (symbol for number of secondary groups, S_n).

Variables:

(i) *'Gregariousness':* average number of elements in primary groups (symbol g),

(ii) *'Compactness'* : average number of groups with which each primary group is linked (symbol, L_n, signifying number of links of degree n),

(iii) *'Stratification'* : the index of stratification is λ, where,

$$\lambda = \sqrt[n]{S_n} \qquad (4.3)$$

Number of primary groups : it can be shown that,

$$G_n \simeq \frac{\frac{1}{2}L_n \cdot N}{S_n(g-n)} \qquad (4.4)$$

Demand Functions :

(i) *Pioneer's*

$$q_{ij} = \phi_p(\tilde{x}_i \tilde{x}_j) \cdot \mu_{ij} \qquad (4.5)$$

where,

q_{ij} = the quantity of product i bought by consumer j,

$\tilde{x}_i$ = a vector of characteristics of i (such as price),

$\tilde{x}_j$ = a vector of characteristics of j (such as income),

μ_{ij} = a binary variable randomly distributed among consumers in the following sense:

Let G_n be the number of primary groups in a secondary group, and let N_p be the total number of cases where $\mu_{ij} = 1$, then let the probability that a particular primary group will contain one consumer with $\mu_{ij} = 1$ is the same for all groups and equal to $1/G_n$; hence the probability that a group will contain n such consumers is $(1/G_n)^n$. Consumers with $\mu_{ij} = 1$ are called 'pioneers' in respect of i.

(ii) *Sheeplike* (ϕ_s)

As pioneers, except that:

(a) For the binary variable, μ_{ij}, is substituted another, v_{ij}, taking unity when and only when j has received 'threshold stimulus', that is when j has been in socio-economic contact with a specified number of pioneers or other active consumers. (A consumer in the state $v_{ij} = 1$ is said to be 'active' and the change to this state from the state $\nu_{ij} = 0$ is called activation.)

(b) The derivatives of ϕ with respect to $\tilde{x}_i$ and $\tilde{x}_j$ are not necessarily the same in the two functions.

(iii) *Combined*

Every j has both a pioneer's and a sheeplike function. In the event that he becomes a pioneer, by chance, before he has been activated, he consumes according to the pioneer function. In the event that before becoming a pioneer, he is activated, he consumes according to the sheeplike function. But if, after becoming a pioneer, he receives threshold stimulus, he throws away his pioneer's function and consumes according to the other. Once his sheeplike function is activated, however, the change is irreversible. Hence, to (i) and (ii) above we add the additional statement, if $\nu_{ij} = 1$, $\mu_{ij} = 0$.

Aggregate Demand

Consider a secondary group in which, on account of close association between secondary groupings and socio-economic characteristics, consumers are homogeneous as to all the elements of $\tilde{x}_j$. Then the total demand for i, say Q_i, is

$$Q_i = N_p \cdot \phi_p + N_a \cdot \phi_s \qquad (4.6)$$

where

N_p = the number of pioneers,
N_a = the number of active consumers.

The number of pioneers, N_p, is assumed to be governed by another function, known as 'pioneering' function, which is not directly derivable from the pioneer's function and contains as variates such factors as intrinsic merit of product, advertising expenditure, and the income, age, family structure and class distributions of the population.

If a population has been stratified in degree m_i, where m_i is the threshold stimulus for product i, once m_i consumers have been obtained in some one primary group of a secondary group, all the consumers in the corresponding secondary population will be activated by chain reaction. Therefore aggregate demand in the group must be in one of three states:

(i) 'Gestation'; $N_a = 0$ (all $\nu_{ij} = 0$), $\quad Q_i = N_p . \phi_p$,

(ii) 'Saturation'; $N_a = N_s$ (all $\nu_{ij} = 1$), $\quad Q_i = N_s . \phi_s$,

(iii) 'Explosion'; unstable process of change from gestation to saturation.

We then say that when the probability of explosion tends to unity the group has become *critical*.

Hence we now define *market population* as the total number of consumers for whom ϕ_s exceeds zero. The 'saturated demand' for a product is $\phi_s . N$, when N is the market population. Hence the saturated demand is the total demand when all the secondary groups in a market population have been saturated.

Clearly, it is of considerable importance to know how a market becomes critical.

The Conditions for Criticality

We have already seen that if some product, i, has threshold stimulus of say, m_i, and m_i pioneers are obtained in any one primary group of a secondary group of degree m_i, then the whole of this group must explode and eventually saturate. 'Criticality' is defined as a condition where the probability of such an occurrence tends to unity. We now attempt to specify the conditions for this more precisely.

Evidently, we are faced with a by no means trivial problem in probability theory. Conventional 'epidemic' models cannot guide us, because they are generally based on the assumption that infection spreads through carriers who move about among the uninfected population at random and are equally likely to infect any member, a state of affairs which is palpably inconsistent with our view of the relevant consumer behaviour. Instead we offer below a development which is flagrantly unrigorous and based on a number of rather drastic logical short cuts. Of these, the most important is that we shall regard the probability of any one member of the secondary population being a pioneer (for a given product) as exogeneous to the probability model, and equal, in fact, to the probability of his being selected in a random sample, from that population, of size equal to the total number of pioneers found in that population as a whole. This assumption enables us to adopt a rather simple application of the binomial formula.

A more rigorous treatment will be attempted in a future publication. For the present our main concern is to indicate the broad lines of a solution and to suggest qualitative implications.

Let p_i, then, represent the ratio of the total number of pioneers obtained in a secondary group to the total number of consumers in that group (i.e. to the secondary population) and let $\bar{p}_i$ represent the corresponding ratio taken over the whole market population. Let $\hat{p}_i$ represent the value of p_i required, if pioneers are randomly distributed between primary groups, in order that $P(E_i)$, the probability of explosion, be approximately unity. Then $\hat{p}_i$ is called the 'critical ratio'. It follows that if, unlike the distribution within secondary groups, the distribution of pioneers between secondary groups is non-random and perfectly even, i.e. if by some method of selective selling the manufacturer ensures that whatever the value of $\bar{p}_i$, every secondary group has just this value, then by obtaining a value of $\bar{p}_i$ equal to $\hat{p}_i$, saturation of the whole market population can be assured. If the distribution between secondary groups is also random, the problem is more complex. Conversely if it is non-random within groups, e.g. because by highly sophisticated methods of selective selling (such as the 'Tupperware party'[15]) non-random pioneering concentrations are achieved within specific primary groups, it is, mathematically speaking, relatively simple; the manufacturer, however, is faced with the non-simple problem of locating and conquering the groups. We deal first with the case where the distribution of pioneers is random within secondary groups, although perfectly even between them, and then with the case where it is random between groups (of the case where it is non-random within groups, there is little to be said).

We seek a general formula for finding the value of $P(E_i)$ in a market population stratified in degree m_i, where m_i is the threshold stimulus of the product under analysis. This problem is evidently one of some complexity, possibly involving delicate areas in probability theory; a more thorough investigation must await a later publication. In the meantime we believe that by relying on the fact that, whatever formula is used, the critical ratio will in general turn out to be small (i.e. in a population already containing just the critical number of pioneers, the discovery of a pioneer in a given household will remain a rare event), we can obtain an approximation which at least is valid for qualitative analysis and is probably adequate for quantitative application in a fairly wide range of cases. To reach it, we ignore all the probabilities of obtaining more than one saturated group (because these will all be of a smaller order of magnitude than the probability of obtaining one); we treat $(1 - p)$ as if equivalent to unity throughout; and we also ride somewhat cavalierly through the complications caused by the overlapping of primary groups. The result is as follows:

$$P(E_i) \simeq \binom{g}{m_i} \cdot p^{m_i} \cdot G_{m_i} \tag{4.7}$$

— the bracketed expression representing the binomial coefficient for m_i successes in g trials.

We have defined $\hat{p}_i$ as that value of p_i for which $P(E_i) \to 1$, hence,

$$\hat{p}_i = \sqrt[m_i]{\left[2 \cdot S_m \cdot (g - m_i) \middle/ N \cdot \binom{g}{m_i} \cdot L_{m_i} \right]} \tag{4.8}$$

where

m_i = threshold stimulus for product i,
$\hat{p}_i$ = critical ratio for product i.

It must be emphasised that these results are valid only when the indicated value of $\hat{p}$ is small: if it were more than say ten per cent, the ignored terms in the binomial formula could begin to become significant, and the result itself might be so inaccurate as to be virtually meaningless.

This formula, it will be seen, presents the answer in terms of one characteristic of the product in relation to the population, m_i, and three characteristics supposedly relating to the population alone (but see pp. 158–9 above), g (gregariousness), and S_m and L_m, aspects of stratification. All four variables are in principle measurable. The formula, however, although having the advantage of laying out the primary elements of the solution in terms of quantifiable variables, is nevertheless none too easy of economic interpretation. Apart from its complexity, it suffers also from the presence of independent functional relations between several of the variables. Not only are S_m, L_m and m related in a manner already described, but it is also possible that there is a further connection between m and g. An increase in gregariousness implies an increase in the number of contacts maintained by the average consumer. This in turn might be expected to increase m_i for given i, because, sociologically speaking, it might well be that the most potent factor leading to activation would be less the absolute number of active contacts than the proportion of such contacts among the total maintained. In other words, if I am in contact with only two persons, and one of these becomes active, these persons being my only source of marketing advice and 50 per cent of them having now given me the green light, I am likely to be activated. But if I maintain ten contacts, the effect of activation of one of them may be considerably less compelling. The more conformist the society the more likely this is likely to be so. Thus William Whyte, in a continuation of the passage already quoted, said,

'Soon non-possession of the product becomes almost an anti-social act — an unspoken aspersion of the others' judgement or taste. At this point only the most resolute individualists can hold out, for just as the group punishes its members for buying prematurely, so it punishes them for not buying.'[16]

Of course, not all societies are as other-directed as this. To the extent that the process of stimulation and activation represents mainly the exchange of 'rational' economic information, as in our first account of it, 'threshold' may remain as an absolute rather than a proportional effect, and we shall below present models in both forms. As a matter of fact, the appropriate definition of 'conformism' is by no means obvious. If activation occurs when only a small *proportion* of contacts are active, the society can be said to be 'sensitive', but as the final sentence in the above quotation suggests, it is not exactly conformist. Nor on the other hand can it be said to be conformist if the average individual does not conform until, say, three-quarters of his contacts have already done so, i.e. when m_i is a number equivalent to 75 per cent of the total contacts. Conformism, in effect, represents a desire to follow the majority, and should be so defined. It is a condition therefore where the *proportionate* threshold lies close to 0·5. If we approximate the ratio of threshold to contacts by that of m_i to g, and call the result $1/\alpha_i$ (i.e. $\alpha_i = g/m_i$), then an 'index of conformism' could be defined as one minus the square root of $(0·5 - \alpha_i)^2$. We do not develop this idea further, as the applications lie outside the scope of our present work, but it is relevant to note that if the basic *modus operandi* of the threshold effect is absolute rather than proportionate, or more precisely if m tends to be independent of g, the society cannot meaningfully be described as conformist even if the above-defined index happened by chance to turn out to be large, for the index derives its meaning from the assumption that m and g are functionally related, albeit in varying forms. Perhaps we should better say that a society should always be described as loosely 'conformist' (in an economic sense) if g and m are related, while reserving the index for measuring the *intensity* of the phenomenon. A society where m and g are independent is then described not so much as non-conformist as different in kind — inner-directed or individualistic.

A further difficulty is that in measuring sensitivity by the relation between m_i and g we present only a very rough approximation to the behaviour of the relation between threshold and total contacts, because, depending both on the value of L_m and the character of the structure, total contacts will exceed primary group membership in varying degrees.

About this, however, we can do nothing; we merely warn the reader that the value of α_i, as defined above, will depend not only on the character of product and on the inherent sensitivity of the consumers, but also, and to an unknown extent, on underlying stratification and the pattern in which the system of contacts is arranged. To the extent that the society is individualistic, of course, the problem is less serious.

Fortunately, in other ways the mathematical gods are benevolent. It happens that the binomial coefficients have the property that the element $2(g - m)\Big/\binom{g}{m}$ can within a wide range of realistic values of the variables be reasonably approximated by $\alpha_i^{-1/3}$. For example, provided α_i lies between 2 and 4, the error involved in this approximation does not exceed 10 per cent in one predictable direction. Even with α_i as low as 1 or as high as 5, errors are little more than 20 per cent, and for reasons which will shortly be apparent, errors of such magnitude are unlikely to be of great economic significance in the final application. We may further simplify by substituting the index of underlying stratification for its various components appearing in equation (4.8), and finally obtain two alternative formulae for $\hat{p}_i$, the first appropriate if the society is believed loosely to be conformist (at least in respect of the product analysed), and the second more appropriate if the society is believed to be individualistic.

$$\hat{p}_i = \frac{\lambda}{{}^{(g/\alpha_i)}\sqrt{(N \cdot L_n)} \cdot \sqrt[3]{\alpha_i}} \tag{4.9}$$

or,

$$\hat{p}_i = \frac{\lambda}{{}^{m_i}\sqrt{(N \cdot L_n)} \cdot \sqrt[3]{(g/m_i)}} \tag{4.10}$$

These formulae, then, represent the goal to which in this and the immediately preceding sections we have been working. They state in a precise and reasonably accurate way the manner in which the critical ratio for a product — the conditions for criticality — depends on basic socio-economic characteristics of the primary market population. An increase in underlying stratification makes the task of obtaining criticality more difficult (because more pioneers are required to ensure a high probability of explosion). Increase in sensitivity, with given gregariousness, has the opposite effect and vice versa (because increased gregariousness with given sensitivity implies increased m_i). A less obviously expected result is that relating to population size: other things being considered, a larger market population is relatively easier to saturate than a smaller one, or, more precisely (multiply both sides by N), the required number of pioneers rises considerably less than in proportion to the size of the market to be attacked. Clearly, this is a result of some significance.

Results produced by examples are reasonable. Thus if the structure pattern were that of Diagram 4.2 ($g=4$, $L_{m_i}=4$, $m_i=2$, hence $\alpha_i=2$), the market population were large, i.e. 1 million, and λ were 10 (implying a stratified population of 400 secondary groups of 2500 consumers each), the critical ratio, $\hat{p}_i$, works out at about one per cent (precisely 0·008). If α_i is raised to 3·3, implying that activation occurs when one-third of a sheep's contacts have become active, the critical ratio is reduced to one-third of one per cent, and so on. The effect of stratification is proportional; if the index of underlying stratification is doubled, so also the critical ratio. On the whole, these figures, which were chosen for convenience of exposition, probably understate the typical result; one would usually expect stratification to be greater and the market population smaller; it should be remembered that the market population relates only to a particular product.

Special cases work out as follows. Suppose λ were 1, representing the existence of a perfect unbroken chain stretching right through the market population. Suppose m_i were also 1 and g were 2, representing the minimum meaningful threshold and the smallest degree of gregariousness consistent with the existence of any sort of chain, then

$$\hat{p} = \frac{1}{N \cdot \sqrt[3]{\alpha_i}} \simeq \frac{1}{N} \tag{4.11}$$

Hence,

$$N \cdot \hat{p} \simeq 1$$

$N \cdot \hat{p}$ represents the absolute number of pioneers 'required' for criticality and is in this case unity: under these conditions, like a row of toy soldiers, when one goes all go. With the same assumption about λ_i, α_i may be raised to its meaningful maximum by setting it equal to g, i.e. a sheep is never activated until all his contacts are already so. Then,

$$N \cdot \hat{p}_i = N^{(1-1/g)} \tag{4.12}$$

If g is reasonably large, the right-hand side approaches N, and the result states that under these conditions a significant chain reaction is impossible, the only way for the great majority of the market population to become consumers being for them to become pioneers. Finally, what would be meant if $m_i = 0$? This would be a mathematical statement that the product was one in which consumers are obtained without any stimulation through socio-economic contact at all, in other words a product for which the whole process we have described is inappropriate. If m_i is zero, equation (4.12) implies, so is the required number of pioneers.

The Economic Significance of the Critical Ratio

On the assumption that selective selling ensures that the proportion of pioneers obtained is the same in all secondary groups, $\hat{p}_i$ is the ratio of the number of pioneers required to saturate a market of given size to the population of that market. In effect, therefore, it is a measure of the relative cost of obtaining the market in terms of pioneers, and as such is of considerable economic significance. For if, as seems likely, a considerable part of the development costs of a new product are those associated with the process of obtaining pioneers, or if, to put the point another way, the value of $\bar{p}_i$ actually obtained depends, via the pioneering function, on the amount of money spent on research, development advertising and other selling efforts, then our theory indicates that the cost per unit of ultimate sales is governed by a precise formula in which this unit cost declines with scale. If development costs are thought of as an overhead to be recovered from the profits of ultimate sales, [17] then a firm whose process of diversification consists in attacking a succession of large markets will, other things being equal, experience a higher long-run rate of return than a firm which only attacks small markets. *Consequently, in this area of decision, no conflict between profit maximisation and volume maximisation arises.*

Consider two alternative paths of growth. In path a the firm attacks a new market of size N_0, obtaining saturation for a certain development cost according to the argument above; this done, it attacks another market of size N_0 and repeats the process at regular intervals thus causing capacity required to grow at a constant rate.

In path b everything is the same except that the markets attacked are all sized 2 N_0, and the relative cost of development is correspondingly lower. In the long run, the proportionate growth rates on the two paths are the same, but on path b (as compared with a) not only is the absolute level of sales higher at all future points of time, but so also the maintainable rate of return. Consequently, no matter whether the utility system governing the decision is traditional or managerial, if path b is possible it will always be preferable.

The Case of Random Distribution Between Secondary Groups

Much the same result is obtained when we abandon the assumption of selective selling. If the total number of pioneers actually obtained is normally distributed between secondary groups, the distribution of the proportions obtained is governed by the formula for the standard error of a proportion, i.e. by $\sqrt{[p(1-p)]}/\sqrt{N_s}$. The problem then becomes one of statistical inference. Suppose $\hat{p}_0$ is the critical ratio derived from equation (4.8) for a particular product in relation to a given, homogeneous, market population. Suppose the firm spends enough on development to obtain a certain value of $\bar{p}$, say $\bar{p}_1$. In what proportion of secondary groups will the actual value of p be $\hat{p}_0$ or better? If the answer is defined as q, then,

$$q \simeq F(z) \qquad (4.13)$$
$$z \simeq \mp(\bar{p}_1 - \hat{p}_0) \cdot \sqrt{N_s}/\sqrt{\bar{p}_1}$$

where $F(z)$ is the appropriate segment of area under the normal curve for given z (again, because p is small, we ignore $1-p$); q, in effect, is the proportion of the total market population which can be expected to be saturated with given $\bar{p}$ and *thus indicates the probable number of ultimate consumers to be expected for each successfully obtained pioneer*. However, because $\hat{p}$ is typically small, it turns out this pioneer/ultimate-consumer ratio not only falls rapidly as $\bar{p}$ rises from zero, but does not decline again until q is high. In other words, we again find that at this level of decision-making profits and volume do not conflict. Consequently, we may without deception work generally with the case where a given number of pioneers is always spread evenly between secondary groups.

Effects of Heterogeneity among Sheeplike Functions

All the foregoing results, of course, depend on the assumption that there is a close relation between market populations and social populations, or social status. In effect, in assuming that the population analysed was identical with a market population we have been assuming that the social networks under analysis contained no consumers who were not members of the market population, an assumption which is valid only if the propensity to be in socio-economic contact is highly correlated with the variates of the sheeplike demand function. In other words, in a diagram such as Diagram 4.1, we have assumed that the Drive is inhabited by no families who if appropriately stimulated would not consume the minimum quantity required for activation of a further neighbour. In fact, this assumption applies to every member of a secondary population.

On Riesman-William-Whyte-Katz-and-Lazarsfeld type[18] sociology, the assumption is reasonable; with more 'rational', but not necessarily more realistic, economic behaviour it is less so. Although Mrs. A. may be in some sense in socio-economic contact with Mrs. B., and share with her many characteristics such as income and social class, unlike Mrs. B. she may just happen to have a sheeplike function which, given price and other factors, does not induce her to consume the product. In an orthodox sense, she has less 'taste' for it. If so, and if she happens to be a vital member of an intersection, she will fail to pass on essential stimulations. The effect is similar to that of social bars, and with a given degree of heterogeneity in a given real population network, may be assumed to be randomly distributed (it continues to be binary, because Mrs. A, on activation, either consumes the requisite amount or she does not), but is of rather different economic significance. For an increase in the number of these 'economic bars', although having much the same effect on the critical ratio as an increase in the number of social bars, is differently caused; that is to say, it is caused by factors such as price, product merit and population income distribution in the 'body' of the sheeplike function.

If there is an increase in the number of randomly distributed bars, whether social or economic in origin, the underlying stratification of the population is raised and so also therefore the critical ratio. The critical ratio thus becomes itself subject to such factors as price and income. The extent of the effect depends on the degree of non-homogeneity of the population in respect of the sheeplike function, that is to say on the extent to which our assumption that the quantity demanded of product i by (activated) consumer j was independent of j was invalid.

We may appropriately take account of the point by supposing that the index of underlying 'social' stratification is multiplied by a further factor called 'inhibition'. 'Inhibition' is then defined as the number by which the value of λ would need to be multiplied in order to take account of 'economic' bars in the determination of the critical ratio. The factor depends in turn on the underlying non-homogeneity of the population in respect of their sheeplike demand functions, on the values of the relevant variates (such as price of product), and also, of course, on the required degree of stratification, i.e. in effect, on the product's threshold stimulus, m_i. Then we should say that inhibition, thus defined, and signified by I, is a function,

$$I = I(\tilde{x}_i, \tilde{\bar{x}}_j, \tilde{\sigma}_j, m_i) \qquad (4.14)$$

where,

$\tilde{x}_i$ represents the vector of product characteristics as originally defined in relation to equation (4.5),

$\tilde{\bar{x}}_j$ represents a vector of population means of values of consumer characteristics, including 'tastes',

$\tilde{\sigma}_j$ represents the vector of standard deviations of the consumer characteristics (a measure of heterogeneity among the population).

The shape of the function depends on the nature of the distribution, among the population, of the relevant consumer characteristics. The concept may be better understood with the aid of a simple example. Suppose only one x_i is considered, i.e. price, and that the sheeplike function reduces to a simple linear form such as,

$$q_{ij} = a_j - b_j \pi_i \qquad (4.15)$$

where q_{ij} is the quantity of i demanded by consumer j (who is an activated sheep), π_i is the price of i, and a_j and b_j are behaviour coefficients. Suppose, however, that although a_j varies between consumers, b_j does not, so that the latter may be treated as a constant. Let q' represent the minimum consumption required of an activated sheep for him to be able to activate others. Then the jth sheep may act as an economic bar if

$$a_j < q' + b\pi_i \qquad (4.16)$$

Evidently, the magnitude of inhibition varies with the number of such sheep.

Suppose the inter-consumer distribution of a_j is normal. Then if

$$z = \mp (b\pi_i - \bar{a}_j)/\sigma_a \qquad (4.17)$$

we may suppose

$$I = [1/F(z)]^{m_i} \qquad (4.18)$$

where

$\bar{a}_j$ = mean of a_j over all consumers,

σ_a = standard deviation of a,

$F(z)$ = the appropriate segment of the normal curve.

More generally, we may write,

$$I = (\xi_i)^{m_i}$$

where ξ_i is an index of inhibition, recognised to be a function of the product and consumer characteristics, having the property of becoming unity when the variances of the several consumer characteristics are all zero. (For example, in the case described above, when the variance of a_j is zero, z tends to infinity, and the appropriate proportion of the area under the normal curve tends to a hundred per cent.) The suffix indicates that the index applies to a specific product in relation to a given population.

Hence we may revise the formula for the critical ratio as follows:

$$\hat{p}_i = \frac{\lambda \cdot \xi_i}{\sqrt[1/\alpha_i]{N} \cdot \sqrt[3]{\alpha_i}} \qquad (4.19)$$

Note that N continues to signify only the market population (itself, of course, usually a function of price), and does not include 'inhibiting' consumers. We are still concerned essentially with members of the market population, but we now take account of the fact that entwined in the network of contacts among them are also non-members who inhibit the chain reaction in a similar manner to social bars. The main differences between ξ_i and λ are that the former is a function of, *inter alia*, characteristics of the product, such as price, while the latter (we assume) is not, and that the former, unlike the latter, is affected by the nature of the inter-consumer distribution of behaviour coefficients in the sheeplike functions. It follows that variates in the sheeplike functions now also affect the critical ratio; an upward variation in prices, for example, may, by affecting the size of market population, not only affect the ultimate 'saturation' level of demand, but will also, through inhibition, increase the relative cost (in terms of pioneers) of saturating that population — a conclusion, evidently, of some importance.

Growth and Profitability: (1) Pricing after Saturation

We have now seen how a new differentiated product becomes critical. The growth of demand for products of a firm practising differentiated diversification depends, then, on policy decisions governing the development and launching of new products, and on the measures taken to obtain their success. Growth is provided by successful explosions. A firm whose catalogue contains none but saturated products will experience growth only from secular trends, if any, in the sheeplike demand functions, and in our conception such trends are generally slow and by definition incapable of influence from policy. By contrast, a firm listing a high proportion of exploding products is a firm whose product-mix contains a high proportion of rapidly growing products and therefore a firm with a relatively high average growth rate of required capacity. Thus, by varying the product-mix in this sense, i.e. by varying the rate of diversification, the firm acquires positive influence over its expansionary destiny and hence over the utility of its own decision makers.

The time profile of required capacity will depend, of course, not only on the rate of diversification but also on the ultimate size of the saturated market. As we have already noticed, if two firms market new products at the same rate, in the sense that both increase the number of catalogue items by x per cent per annum (in other words they adopt the same rate of diversification), but one aims successfully for large ultimate markets while the other aims at small, although the proportionate growth rate of the two may be the same, the former is at all times absolutely larger than the latter. And although, for reasons discussed in Chapter 2, managerial utility will depend mainly on proportionate rate of change of size, rather than on size itself, at any instant of time immediate growth is maximised by aiming for the largest immediate prospects; hence we are compelled to ask whether at each instant of time the firm may not on this account be faced with conflicts between volume and profitability.

We have seen that the cost in terms of pioneers for obtaining a given ultimate market tends to fall, *ceteris paribus*, relatively to the size of the market as size itself increases. Here, therefore, there is no conflict. But the possibility remains that the sheeplike demand function is so formed that after the saturation of an individual product the firm will be presented with an orthodox choice between low price, high volume and modest profitability on the one hand, and a profit-maximising policy involving higher prices and profits and lower volume on the other.

We have already noted that it is widely believed that demand price-elasticity for new products tends to begin low and then rise. We may interpret these statements as saying that elasticity is low during gestation, [19] intermediate during explosion and gradually rises after saturation. The rise may be due to greater elasticity in the sheeplike function as compared with the pioneer's function, to increased competition or to both. We also know that during the latter part of the explosion phase many imitations are likely to appear, a large proportion of which are later eliminated, leaving a relatively small number of producers to consolidate their positions, reap economies of scale and permanently discourage new entry.[20] Once this has happened, the price structure becomes oligopolistic and market shares rather inflexible. The individual firm, whether originator or imitator, has then relatively little influence over either volume or profitability, and if an originator, its reward for development now materialises as a reasonable dose of growth with reasonable profits and reasonable security. (Not infrequently, of course, the originator is one of those driven out, an inevitable risk of the whole operation.)

In the intermediate phases, however, there is a wide range of possibilities, and it is by no means unlikely that even if numerous imitations do eventually appear an originator will go through a period when he can safely enjoy the profits of quasi-monopolistic pricing. Until demand becomes price-elastic or the market oligopolistic he may be able to obtain high profits without significantly affecting volume, and in this way realise a better average rate of return than would be available from typical saturated products. Alternatively, even if an oligopolistic situation does not develop, the sheeplike demand function, although elastic, is unlikely to be indefinitely so. More probably it is 'elastic' mainly in the sense that small price changes may significantly affect sales among consumers within a particular socio-economic stratum, while outside the bounds of the market delineated by this stratum only large changes would have noticeable effects. In other words, even in the absence of competition, the 'saturated' demand-curve may well appear as in Diagram 4.3.

Demand-curves of this shape are frequently incorporated in the programmes of business games played on computers. We may reasonably assume therefore that, in considering their saturated price policies for individual products, firms will rarely experience significant conflicts between profits and volume; for example, if profits were maximised at a point such as A in Diagram 4.3, a downward variation of price from this point would very greatly reduce profitability in return for only a small gain in volume, and a similar situation exists, of course, if the demand-curve is kinked by

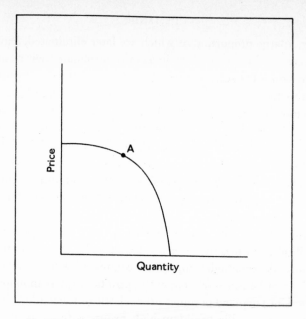

DIAGRAM 4.3. Demand-Curve for a Saturated Product

oligopoly. We shall assume, therefore, that saturated price policies for given products are determined in such a way as to maximise as nearly as possible the product's contribution to the firm's average rate of return, and that, with such policies, saturated sales volumes are little smaller than the maxima consistent with earning any profit at all. Alternatively, we assume both price and volume to be controlled by oligopoly.

Growth and Profitability: (2) The Optimum Order of Marketing

The foregoing applies to individual products only. For reasons we shall shortly discuss, most firms will find that they cannot diversify at an indefinitely rapid rate; therefore at any given moment of time they may be forced to choose between alternative candidates for development. Evidently, although all products on saturation might be priced according to the same principles, as above, they would by no means necessarily produce the same results. A firm may be faced with a set of candidates, each offering in the event of success a specific prospective increase in capacity required and associated expected contribution to profits. If the ordering in terms of volume (measured in capital cost of capacity required) is directly correlated with the ordering in terms of profitability, the most profitable and most growth-inducing candidates will presumably be taken first. But if the correlation should happen to be inverse, or even merely imperfect, the order required to maximise managerial utility is by no means obvious. For we saw in Chapter 1 that a growth-maximising policy by no means ignores profit, and in the present context we can describe the problem by saying that the profits earned on saturation by products developed early are partly required to finance capacity expansion for products developed later; hence it may turn out that the maximum sustainable growth rate is obtained from a development order in which some low-volume products come relatively early. In effect, there will be an 'optimum order', about which, in the absence of details relating to specific cases, little more can be said than that if volume and profitability are directly and perfectly correlated, optimum order is identical with volume order (the trivial case) and that this may also prove the case when they are not; for low-volume products to tend to come first not only must the correlation between volume and profitability be negative but the regression coefficient must exceed a certain magnitude. The point is reinforced when we remember that products for which the intended market population is small tend also to prove relatively more costly to develop, on account of higher critical pioneering ratios. Indeed, the last-mentioned factor should also, strictly, be taken into account when optimum order is assessed. Since optimum order cannot be more generally specified, for the rest of the book we assume that firms always attempt to develop in optimum order, which does not mean they necessarily succeed. In truth, the analysis would be little affected if we assumed marketing order was arbitrary.

Growth and Profitability: (3) The Costs of Criticality

With the working assumptions described, we are now ready to

investigate the relationship between rate of diversification, rate of growth and rate of return; to investigate, that is to say, the whole structure of policy problems involved in a programme of growth by differentiated diversification. If all new products succeeded in exploding and there were no trend in the size of ultimate markets, the long-run rate of growth would be the same as the average rate of diversification, the latter being here defined as the ratio of new products put into the catalogue, per period, to the number of (saturated) items already included at the beginning of the period. But if some products prove 'failures' in the sense that no amount of effort whatsoever could make them become critical, the identity breaks down. In a realistic model the success/failure relationship should therefore be treated probabilistically. For the moment, however, we assume that all products do, in fact, succeed, reserving the uncertainty case for a later section. In effect, we assume that a manufacturer in marketing a product spends as much, and no more, on research, development and advertising as is necessary to obtain precisely the critical number of pioneers. (Many firms actually attempt this policy and others are increasingly encouraged to do so by articles in business periodicals. In other cases, however, the failure rate among products actually marketed may be as high as 50 per cent.[21])

Given the policy of 'no failures', as each successive new product in a programme of differentiated diversification is marketed, a wide variety of development costs is compulsorily incurred, these ranging from the costs of fundamental research at one extreme to the expenses of high-pressure advertising at the other. On the production side there are also the 'abnormal' expenses attributable to diseconomies of small-scale production during gestation, to once-and-for-all tooling-up costs and to the costs of teething troubles of all kinds. If we call the minimum total of all these costs required to obtain criticality the 'critical marketing expenses' of a product, we may define for each an 'index of profitability', as follows:

$$T_i = \frac{P_s}{E_i - P_g} \qquad (4.20)$$

T_i = index of profitability of new product, i,

P_s = annual average gross profits earned by product i after saturation,

E_i = critical marketing expenses,

P_g = total profits earned during gestation, gross of marketing expenses.

(Note: the i-suffix also applies to P_s and P_g but is for simplicity omitted.)

The bottom line taken as a whole may be thought of as 'net' marketing expenses. It will be seen that they are defined so as to be independent of time, i.e. to represent the total net expenditure attributable to the product from the moment research on it begins to the moment it 'goes critical'; they may according to circumstances either be spread thinly over a long period or concentrated in a relatively short one. In addition, there should also be included (in E_i) some appropriately pro-rated share of the overheads of the research, development and sales departments. We may then reasonably assert that the lower the average value of the index of profitability — taking one new product with another — the lower will be the average internal rate of return associated with a given rate of diversification, and vice versa. What then determines the behaviour of this index?

Average annual saturated profits are the product of the size of the market population and profits per product per head of that population. The latter, if the firm is following the optimum order and pricing rules described above, may be taken as 'given'. Profits during gestation may similarly be expressed as the product of the critical number of pioneers and the total gross profits earned, per pioneer, over the whole gestation period; the critical expenses likewise. The index then becomes,

$$T_i = \frac{N_i \cdot \bar{P}_s}{\hat{p}_i \cdot N_i(e_i - \bar{P}_g)} = \frac{\bar{P}_s}{\hat{p}_i(e_i - \bar{P}_g)} \qquad (4.21)$$

where

N_i = market population of product i,

$\bar{P}_s$ = saturated profits *per capita*, for product i,

$\bar{P}_g$ = gestation profits per pioneer,

e_i = critical expenditure per pioneer.

The critical ratio, $\hat{p}_i$, and the average gestation profits per pioneer ($\bar{P}_g$), are both functions of the product's gestation-period selling price, the former through the effects of inhibition and the latter through the pioneer's demand function; in effect, $\bar{P}_g$ may be thought of as governed by the ordinary procedure of monopolistic pricing, modified for scale by dividing maximum profits by number of customers. It follows that it must in principle be possible to find for each product a price which specifically maximises the index. This optimum gestation price will not normally be the same as the optimum saturation price and according to empirical observation is usually somewhat higher. If then we assume that firms always attempt to set this price on all new products, the index of profitability for each new product is uniquely determined by the pioneer's demand function, and by e_i, marketing expenses per pioneer. What are the main factors influencing the result?

Growth and Profitability: (4) Diversification and the Consumer

The answer, of course, lies in the consumer appeal, or intrinsic utility, of the product itself. If it discovers a latent need which proves strong, i.e. one for which pioneers are relatively easy to obtain and/or for which they are prepared to pay high prices for given quantities, then e_i is likely to be small and $\bar{P}_g$, under optimum gestation-price conditions, large. More precisely, e_i is small relatively to optimum $\bar{P}_g$. Conversely, if the product is unattractive, not very useful or both, the opposite situation is to be expected. It follows that the higher the average intrinsic merit of the products included in a given programme of diversification, the higher their average index of profitability and vice versa.

If average intrinsic utility were God-given (as economic theory has previously implicitly assumed), there would be little more to be said. In mathematical terms, 'God-given' means independent of the policy variables. Under these conditions, firms could grow by diversification at indefinitely rapid rates without any apparent reaction on the rate of return, a state of affairs which, to say the least, is highly implausible. The stock of exploitable needs latent among consumers at any one time cannot but be limited and so also must be the capacity of any one managerial organisation to perceive them. More precisely, capacity to innovate is limited relatively to the size of the organisation, and so also, therefore, is the *proportionate* growth rate. Perception and exploitation of latent needs requires imaginative thought, research and planning. The further the inventive resources of a firm are stretched within a given period, the less useful are likely to be the results. In other words, we must postulate that the new products launched by a given firm in a given period are subject to declining intrinsic utility. Of course, as time passes, social and economic conditions change, latent needs multiply and a firm of given talents has the time to develop better ideas. But in the meantime, if diversification is accelerated, declining market populations cause critical ratios to rise, and critical marketing expenses per pioneer to behave likewise, while average profits per pioneer fall. Inasmuch as there may exist economies of scale in the research, development and selling departments, at low rates of diversification the effects may not be fully felt, and perhaps felt not at all, but, beyond some point, if diversification is further accelerated a declining index of profitability must become inevitable. Thus the average index of profitability among new products is itself a function of the rate of diversification, at first rather insensitive perhaps, then falling away rapidly until a point is reached where marginal products are so devoid of merit that the expenditure required for success becomes virtually infinite.

Growth and Profitability: (5) The Final Relationship

The relationship between diversification and index of profitability does not, of course, indicate directly the relationship between diversification and overall rate of return, because the latter includes not only new products but also 'old' or saturated products. If the firm does not diversify, all its products are old, and the profits they earn are determined by the economic conditions of the later stages of a typical product's life. As we have already hinted, these are more than likely to be less favourable than during the early stages, because as time passes competition hardens, the consumer becomes more experienced and a wide variety of possibilities for general decay of the product's relative utility arises. In fact we may reasonably view the profitability of a product over the whole history through gestation, explosion and saturation as consisting of an early rise followed by flattening, then gradual, possibly asymptotic, decline. If this assumption is correct (and it has been recommended to the author by many qualified observers), the average profit contribution of young or youngish products must always exceed that of old products, and the higher the proportion of moderately young products in the catalogue at any given time, the higher, other things being equal, the average rate of return. This effect, which is positively associated with the diversification rate, must be set against the negative effect of declining intrinsic utility. We may then suppose that at moderate rates of diversification, the average rate of return *increases* with the rate of diversification, then, as declining intrinsic utility sets in and becomes increasingly severe, the position is reversed. This is probably what is implied when business men say that diversification may sometimes enhance profitability. (Of course growth always increases aggregate profits; what is being said here is that faster growth leads to increased profits relatively to absolute size.)

So we may now see rate of growth and rate of return as associated with a third variable, the diversification rate, the choice of which represents a basic policy decision; the elements determining associated profitability are then contingent decisions required to ensure that the chosen rate is fully expressed in demand-growth actually experienced.

A Probabilistic Model

The model presented above is evidently of considerable analytical convenience. Unfortunately, however, in assuming that all products succeed it is not only unrealistic but inaccurate, for we can show that an optimum growth-maximisation strategy may well involve deliberately permitting a certain proportion of products to fail; by this means a given rate of growth may be achieved with less cost than if the full critical expenses were incurred in every case. We know that many products do fail, and we know that many manufacturers regard a proportion of failures as inevitable. It is difficult enough to calculate critical ratios, and even were this not so, there remains the problem that the marketing expenses required to obtain a given number of pioneers depend on intrinsic utility or 'consumer appeal' — a property which, however much is spent on consumer research, can never be estimated precisely.

When a manufacturer markets a given new product, therefore, he may be assumed to have only a rough idea of the critical expenses required, and, having decided to lay out a given sum, he is forced into the role of awaiting events and hoping for the best. If after a certain time the product shows no sign of exploding, he knows that his estimate was wrong, which means by implication that the product was wrongly placed in the estimate of optimum order: either it should have been developed later or not at all. He then has to choose between abandoning the product altogether and increasing expenditure in the hope that his underestimate of the critical requirements was sufficiently modest for the policy of 'throwing good money after bad' to prove best. If this policy is chosen and still fails, it may well be repeated, but we can safely assume that if success is not achieved within a finite period, eventual withdrawal is inevitable. We may therefore picture the growth process as consisting in the successive marketing of new products, all of which are kept on the market for a given length of time, and some of which, during this time, explode to eventually saturate while the remainder fail to explode and at the end of the period are withdrawn. The rate of diversification is then the ratio of new products 'tried' per period to the number of (successful) products listed at the beginning of the period, while the rate of growth, provided the rate of diversification is steady, becomes the rate of diversification multiplied by the average proportion of products which succeed in the sense of not being withdrawn. As previously, these relations assume that there is no trend in the magnitude of the ultimate markets of successful products.

An index of profitability for individual products is no longer a very useful concept, since we do not know the critical marketing expenses, and the critical expenses are not, in fact, necessarily incurred. We might employ an index based on the expenses required to obtain a given probability of criticality (a given probability, that is to say, that the amount spent is enough to achieve the critical number of pioneers, the latter itself being a probabilistic conception), but the concept would be awkward. Instead we may conveniently pool the net amounts spent on marketing all products, and recognise that the greater this sum, relatively to the size of the firm, the higher will be the *average* probability of success among all new products, at any given rate of diversification. The larger the scale of research and development expenditure relatively to the number of products under development, the greater the relative size of the total advertising budget and the lower the prices charged for representative gestating products, the more likely it is that the representative product will attract its critical number of pioneers within the regulation period. (We may of course assume that in allocating expenditure between products the firm does its best to take account of their different characteristics, but we treat this as a tactical question outside the rather general scope of the present analysis.) Then it follows that the more the firm does spend, in relative terms, on research, development and advertising, the greater the proportion of successes, but the lower, other things being equal, the average overall rate of return. The theoretical implications are worked out in Chapter 6.

Growth by Imitation

We have now completed our account of the demand-growth function for a firm expanding by means of differentiated strategy. The reader will recognise that the analysis has involved a considerable excursion to the frontiers of economic theory, most previous writers having for good reason regarded the area as one where angels should fear to tread. Imitative activity, on the other hand, looks much more like familiar stuff. An imitative product is a 'competitive' product, whose vendors perforce must play games which have been the subject of economic study for more than a century past. Admittedly, except on the implausible and often inconsistent assumptions of 'perfect' competition, the results have to date been somewhat inconclusive, but this has been due mainly to the difficulty of the problem rather than faults of the investigators; it may well be the case that the reason why the earliest discoveries in the field (such as those of Cournot) have held their positions for so long is that there are few others to be made. However, it is now clear that the approach by way of game-theory, or at least by kinds of arguments which, if not strictly game-theoretic according to an acceptable mathematical definition, nevertheless owe much to this source, is at last beginning to bear fruit. 'Competition', variously defined, is now widely recognised as a special case of oligopoly, and oligopoly is clearly a game of conflict; the only problem is to find useful and solvable formulations. The latter task, however, reminds one of the man on a long-distance bus ride who, for the sake of conversation, asked a lady sitting by him whether she would accept a hypothetical million dollars in exchange for her virtue. When she replied that she supposed that if actually faced with such an offer she would probably accept, he said, 'Well, then, how about fifty cents?'; she expostulated, 'Of course not, what do you think I am?' 'Madam', he retorted, 'we have settled what you are, all we are now discussing is the price.' All we are now discussing is the ultimate mystery of price theory.

There is one case, however, of considerable importance (to us, at least), which has received almost no analytical attention whatsoever: the case of oligopolistic entry into a market which is in the process of exploding. The advantages are virtually self-evident: the job of starting the chain reaction is already done, much of the uncertainty of the outcome removed and no act of innovation required. As compared with the situation in a static market, the tension between competitors is likely to be less severe, and co-operative, not necessarily collusive, solutions are therefore especially plausible. Consequently it is not surprising that the tactic appears empirically to be one of the most popular methods of growth. We shall call it 'bandwaggoning'.

'Bandwaggoning' is particularly appropriate for a loose, game-descriptive, but not strictly game-theoretic type of analysis. The other types of imitative growth are not. In static markets the conflict situation is necessarily intense, and the whole gamut of oligopoly theory (and for that matter of competition theory) may well have to be run in dealing with them. The most suggestive contribution, at least since the appearance of *The Theory of Games and Economic Behaviour*,[22] comes from Martin Shubik, whose book *Strategy and Market Structure*,[23] first published in 1960, is now, at the time of writing, gradually but surely beginning to make itself felt. Below, after dealing with bandwaggoning, we do little more than attempt to derive from Shubik's work a few generalisations appropriate for consideration of restraints and constraints on policies involving successive entry into static markets, or in deliberate, discontinuous, increases in shares held in static markets already entered earlier.

The Bandwaggon Strategy

If there were no such thing as commercial retaliation, dynamic, fully imitative strategies would correspond to static perfect competition: if the price of any of the imitations were set slightly below that of the corresponding rival, sales would grow rapidly until the rival had been driven out altogether; after that, if the market were still exploding, sales would grow at the market explosion rate, or, if the market were saturated, they would stagnate. The larger the proportion of successful unsaturated imitations in a firm's catalogue, the faster would be the rate of growth in terms of capacity required. But the larger this proportion, the lower on average would have to be its prices and so also, of course, the rate of return.

In reality, if firm i grows noticeably at the expense of firm j, j is likely to retaliate. Retaliation may consist in either price reduction or intensified selling effort; in what follows, for simplicity, we assume that the former method predominates. An imitator must, therefore, assume he will meet retaliatory price reduction, and should take account of this in his calculations; in such a set-up, the effective sensitivity of growth rate with respect to rate of return must usually be smaller than might at first appear.

A firm contemplating an imitative attack on a particular existing product must attempt to assess the lowest possible level to which its opponents could, in the process of retaliation and counter-retaliation, reduce their prices. It may treat this estimated enemy 'sticking price' as a datum. Presumably it will declare war only if it can see its way to cutting its own price at least to that level. If it believes it can undercut the enemy sticking price, it can start a war to the death, and an overall strategy for a number of products could, in principle, be constructed of a series of such wars. But in practice total war is not common. Rivals' sticking prices are uncertain; the strategy is risky, unpopular and psychologically unrewarding. Business communities, like many animal societies, develop many ethical restraints against fighting to the death, transgression of which may invite the costs of commercial ostracism.

In an exploding market, however, close imitation is not synonymous with war to the death. Suppose i imitates the explod-ing product of j, charging a price noticeably lower than j's. i's share of the market will begin to rise, j's to fall. But in contrast to the assumptions of competitive statics, we do not assume that adjust-ment occurs instantaneously. We assume that it takes time; more precisely we assume that the greater the difference in the prices charged by the two firms, the faster the rate of change of their respective shares in total sales. With a given price differential, therefore, so long as the market is exploding, j's sales are subject to opposing tendencies: they represent a falling proportion of a rising total. In the early stages when i's sales (representing a rising proportion of the rising total) are still of little weight, the un-favourable tendency for j will be more than offset by the favourable. Later the position will be reversed. From the moment of i's entry, therefore, j's sales curve will flatten, i.e. continue to rise but at a diminishing rate. Eventually, if the price differential continues, the curve will reach a peak and go into decline.

For example suppose, as a result of a price differential, i in each period gains x per cent of the total customers of j in the previous period. In addition, i's entry into the market means that an increasing proportion of the new consumers of the product recruited in any period will have been stimulated by existing customers of i, rather than of j, and hence will themselves be likely to buy from i. Even in the absence of customers who shift from j to i, therefore, i's sales are likely to grow at least at the same rate as the explosion rate of the market as a whole: i experiences a 'normal' chain reaction of growth, whose speed is determined by the same factors as those governing the explosion rate for the whole market; but i obtains his 'pioneer' customers by piracy from j rather than by the normal method. The growth of demand experienced by i, there-fore, for any given price differential over any given short time-period, will consist of the sum of direct gains from j, plus the effect of i's share in the explosion. Thus, let j start with 100 customers, exploding at 10 per cent per period, and let i enter when j has reached 110, and then make direct gains of 5 per cent of j's existing customers per period; this, plus the fact that i must be assumed to acquire customers who are new to the product altogether, at the rate of 10 per cent of his own existing customers in each period, will create conditions in which j's rate of growth will be reduced to zero in ten periods from the starting point. At that point i will have 40 per cent of the total number of actual customers.

During the early phases of the process j will not be strongly stimulated to retaliate; he may well be uncertain as to how fast the total market is expanding, and his own sales charts will not tell him how his *proportionate* share is behaving. But he knows for certain his absolute sales are still expanding and at a price he finds profitable. He may be concerned about the competitive activities of i, but before reaching for his gun he has to consider the possibility that i's price policy may soon get i into financial difficulties, difficulties which he, j, would also meet if he copied the policy. In other words, the problem of competition from i may solve itself, either by i's raising his price or by his retiring altogether. j is therefore very likely to pursue a policy of wait and see. Only if i maintains his position and j's sales curve begins to look seriously unhealthy is j forced to take action. If he retaliates with a price cut, open war breaks out and retaliation will be followed by counter retaliation. i is now established in the market and j's most likely, if limited, objective will be to prevent any further change in their relative shares. Depending on how aggres-sive i still feels (which in turn will depend on the volume of sales he has already achieved), the war may be long and severe or short and mild. It will normally end in the establishment of a 'peace' in which the proportionate shares are, in fact, stabilised. For con-

venience we shall define the whole period from the entry of the
imitator to the establishment of peace as a period of 'war', and
divide the latter into two subsidiary periods — the period of
incipient war, when retaliation is not occurring, and the period of
open war, when it is. Peace requires peaceful prices, or, for short,
'peace prices'. These may or may not be collusively arrived at in
the sense of resulting from direct parleys, and they need not be the
same for each firm. Each firm's peace price is the price which,
taken in relation to the price charged by the other, will keep market
shares constant; when both are charging peace prices the proportionate rate of growth of each firm's sales is identical with that of
the market as a whole. Evidently, in the case of close imitations, the
two peace prices are unlikely to differ more than slightly, on account
of the high cross-elasticities. Thus a peace price for a single
product contains two elements — a differential against the price
charged by the rival, and an absolute level. The differential depends
on the character and closeness of the imitation, and is, therefore,
'given' in this context. The absolute level depends on the absolute
level of the price being charged by the rival. Hence, although the
required differential can be defined independently, the absolute
level cannot. The absolute levels of peace prices can only be
determined in conjunction with one another; they can only be
defined in pairs, and established jointly. A single firm's peace price
is thus an aspect of a pair.

Before the peace is established, the precise moment at which
retaliation occurs will depend on the character of, and the information available to, the defenders. In some cases retaliation may never
be necessary. The imitator, once he has established a reasonable
share in the market, may anticipate retaliation and raise his price
before it happens: peace breaks out before incipient war becomes
open. Before saturation is reached, therefore, any highly imitative
product has a determinate prospect of growth at virtually one price
— the ultimate peace price for that product. At a significantly
higher price, the probable growth of demand is very small if not
zero, but, because of retaliation, a lower price makes little difference.
A more accurate way of describing the position is to say that there
is a determinate path of growth for the product, together with an

associated path of prices. The paths contain two phases; in the first, price is any price markedly below the enemy price and sales are growing very rapidly; in the second phase, price is the peace price and sales grow at the explosion rate of the market as a whole; eventually they saturate when the market saturates. In circumstances where the first phase is short relatively to the second, the rate of growth in the second (i.e. market explosion rate) can be regarded as characteristic of bandwaggon growth; otherwise it is necessary to consider some average of the rates experienced in the two phases together. *En tous cas*, a strategy relating to a group of successive imitations of exploding products offers a firm a determinate prospect of average overall growth (of demand) at a specifiable constellation of prices. Given the strategy, there is at any moment a narrowly limited range of 'right' prices for each of the close imitations it comprises; in this sense the firm does not have much freedom of action in respect to prices. But, of course, it can vary average profitability by varying the strategy, since profitability will depend, *inter alia*, on the proportion of very imitative products in the catalogue as a whole, for with less imitative products the prices consistent with growth are evidently less circumscribed.

Static Markets

Any firm attempting to enter a static market already dominated by a relatively small number of established producers faces considerable problems. If the product-type is one which is inherently 'differentiable' (in the subjective consumer sense), there may in principle be room for a new partial imitation, but, as Professor Bain has shown in his classic study,[24] the very same conditions are likely to present particularly high barriers to entry on account of consumer loyalty to established brands: the greater the extent to which consumers can be persuaded to see differences in brands, the greater the tendency to brand loyalty. The reason for this phenomenon, familiar to hidden persuaders, is that the greater the consumer's uncertainty and misinformation about a product, the more likely is he or she to hold desperately to brands known to perform reasonably satisfactorily. Thus the housewife, unable to conduct controlled experiments, has not the faintest idea whether one brand of washing powder is better than another, and so this particular market is notoriously susceptible to the blandishments of advertisements or the opinion leaders of the Katz-and-Lazarsfeld type (i.e. of persons whose opinions are followed less on account of their rationality than of some quality in the holder).[25] At the other extreme, among producers' goods, not only is non-informative advertising less effective, but (irrational) brand loyalty less prevalent. Where brand loyalty prevails, the potential entrant must face the prospect of having to accept for a substantial period a significantly lower rate of return than that enjoyed by incumbents, even though his product is by any objective test quite as good as theirs. The resulting loss of profit would be analogous to the marketing expenses in non-imitative diversification.

Alternatively, if the product-type is one which is easy to imitate, in the sense that brand loyalty is weak, the potential entrant faces all the problems of retaliation, for the more easily he is able to damage incumbents by conventional methods, the greater their incentive to fight him off. In other words, the better his chances of success with the customers, the greater the likelihood of 'trouble' from the producers. In fact, since the potentialities of retaliation are also closely related to concentration,[26] easy prospects from this strategy are likely to be generally confined to areas where for some reason concentration is still relatively moderate.

The problem may be characterised by an actual or potential game of 'economic survival'.[27] In this type of game the players make a series of moves, representing combinations of product quality, price and advertising policies set and adhered to for short tactical planning periods, the outcomes of which are uncertain. That is to say, at the beginning of each period, all players decide their tactics for the period according to hunches as to how both consumers and the opponents are likely to act, and at the end of the period each experiences various outcomes in terms of profits, volume, etc. Some find they have gained in one or both dimensions, others lost, and the objective observer can do no more than specify the probabilities of any particular result. If an individual player finds he has not done well, he may decide to try again, hoping next time to do better. If he succeeds, well and good; if he fails he may yet try again. The process continues until either he or one or all of his opponents have experienced such losses that they are forced or prefer to retire, leaving the victor(s) in sole possession of the market. In other words, if a potential entrant desires to establish a reasonable share of a static market, he may be compelled to fight a war in which one (or more) producer is driven out to make room for him, and this means entering a game of chance which may result not only in failure to achieve the objective, but also substantial financial losses through wasted investment in specific equipment and non-recoverable development expenditure. To lose such a game is equivalent to a failure to explode in differentiated diversification.

The most conveniently analysed models of games of economic survival are two-person zero-sum gambling games, such as 'gambler's ruin'. The results can then be shown to depend intimately not only on the chances-in-play (probability of either player winning at each round), which may be thought of as analogous to relative commercial advantage, but also on the maximum amounts each player is able or prepared to lose before retiring; the latter, called 'initial resources', may be considered as analogous to financial strength. Thus in 'gambler's ruin' the players successively match pennies, the loser at each round paying the winner one unit. The chances-in-play, with unbiassed pennies, are 0.5. Each player starts with a limited stock of pennies, and the game ends with an ultimate win for one when the coffers of the other are exhausted. If the initial resources are equal, the chances of ultimate victory are, of course, also equal, i.e. 0.5. But if the initial resources are unequal, the chance of ultimate win for a given player is $1/(1 + r)$, where r is the ratio of opponent's initial resources to his own. When the game is played against a Casino, r tends to infinity, and the probability of breaking the bank is virtually zero. Shubik has shown how this type of game may well be adapted to correspond to the characteristic conditions of economic conflict, including those of entry.[28]

We should add that, in economic applications, initial resources are appropriately defined as the total resources available to the firm — e.g. the total amount it is prepared to lose on all projects — and need not be confined to sums supposedly earmarked to support particular attacks. If a policy of earmarking is adopted (as is evidently the case in some real-life firms), significant advantages are thrown away. For imagine a gambler entering a Casino where in contrast to the usual situation he is faced with a number of tables each of which has a bank equal to his own resources, but none being allowed to borrow or lend funds to others. Suppose he is then permitted to play gambler's ruin against each table simultaneously, transferring resources at will: in effect, the usual roles of Casino and gambler are reversed. He plays until either his own funds are exhausted, or those of all his opponents; if one opponent is defeated in the course of play, he continues to the death against the survivors. It can then be shown that his monopoly of the power to switch resources from tables where he is doing well to tables where he is doing badly gives him considerable actuarial advantages. For example, if he plays two opponents in a game in which chances-in-play are even, the probability of ultimate victory is precisely the same, i.e. 0·5, as if he had played one table only. But since in playing two opponents the value of an ultimate win is doubled (because he then takes the total resources of two players), while the cost of losing is the same, the mathematical expectation of profit or 'value of the game' is doubled. The author once heard the owner of a famous Las Vegas establishment tell a television interviewer that, rather than bias chances-in-play, this phenomenon (in reverse of course) was the source of the greater part of a typical Casino's profits.

We could suggest as a loose economic generalisation that a firm prepared to diversify by taking on a number of games of economic survival simultaneously will be in a stronger position than its opponents, even if their average resources are equal to its own, provided, of course, that they themselves are wedded to single-product strategies only. If its typical opponents are similar to itself, however, the presumption vanishes. We may therefore suppose that at any moment of time a firm under analysis will perhaps be presented with a *limited* number of opportunities where, even though its commercial strength does not greatly exceed that of incumbents (i.e. chances-in-play may be even), its initial-resource position is such that if it attacks all simultaneously, it may expect a reasonable proportion of successes associated with a reasonable level of financial return. That is to say, if it plays a limited number of survival games simultaneously, it may expect to drive out opponents and achieve a good market share in a sufficient proportion of cases, so that the losses suffered on the failures do not depress average profitability by more than is tolerable. Its 'marketing expenses' are the failures' losses, and its gains are the increases in volume and relatively assured future profit streams resulting from successes. Then, because the opportunities are limited in time, the usual dynamic restraints must come into operation, and we can assume that if it attempts further to accelerate growth by this means, at least beyond a certain point, despite the advantages of resource switching, it will increasingly encounter cases where the initial-resource position is less favourable, and the failure rate will correspondingly rise. The rate of return will decline, and the rate of growth fail to increase in proportion to rate of diversification.

Another type of market suitable for attack by warlike methods is that in which, although the initial-resource position is more or less the same as the opponent's, the chances-in-play are not. Obviously, if gambler's ruin is played with loaded dice, the players' chances of ultimate victory are affected irrespective of resource position. The inventive resources of the attacking firm have been successfully deployed in the development of a product which is *likely*, but not certain, to prove more attractive to consumers than the existing variants, so that at each round of play, however skilfully the defender chooses his strategies, he has less than a 50-per-cent chance of winning (unless, of course, he can in turn imitate the new variant, which is what, in fact, he usually does try to do). Even when the chances-in-play are only equal, a firm may be prepared to attempt a set of attacks simultaneously, hoping that the losses on the failures will be worth the gains in both volume and profit on the successes. More precisely, maximum sustainable growth might be obtained with a policy of moderately rapid diversification into market situations with only even chances of success, because the net overall profits at each round would still on average be sufficient to support the capital expansion required for the next round. Again, of course, the policy is restricted by the dynamic limits on the number of cases with at least reasonable odds discoverable at any one time.

However, it is of course by no means certain that the game of survival will actually have to be played. An alternative approach to the problem of entry is by way of the concept of 'threat'. 'Threat', in game theory, is the capacity to inflict damage on one's opponent even at the cost of damaging oneself (nuclear deterrents being a case in point). For example, a defender may have to incur considerable losses in warding off an attack, even when he is ultimately successful. And inasmuch as he has also to face the possibility that in the event the effort will prove to have been of no avail, the mere advent of an attack implies for the defender the certainty of definite loss (in the sense that profits will be less than would otherwise have been the case). Rather than face this, he may prefer to seek a co-operative solution, that is, in the manner of the bandwaggon case, seek a 'peace' in which the interloper is conceded a definite, but limited market. The defender then takes a certainty of some loss of volume (and, probably, of profits as well), instead of an uncertainty of more serious penalties. He may well in fact adopt this course even in cases where successful defence would be costless, because his Neuman-Morgenstern utility of a certainty of keeping a reduced share may exceed that of a risk of losing all.

Various methods of reaching co-operative solutions have been studied in the literature, and are mostly analogous to the gestures exchanged by animals preparing to fight over territory: each participant is trying to tell the other how vicious he is able and willing to be, and thus build up the mutual information necessary for both sides to realise that a co-operative solution along given lines will maximise utility for each. In situations of this type, the equilibrium division of spoils will probably be related to relative strengths of threats,[29] these, strictly defined, being measured by the relation between the utility losses likely to be suffered by each side if one threat is enforced.

With some temerity, we may stretch the concept by suggesting that the threat in many cases is, in fact, the threat of playing a sub-game of survival. For it is in the essence of that game that provided resources on both sides are limited, any one player can always force the opponent to participate. If a player persistently enforces his most vicious strategy, and ignores all co-operative gestures, the opponent is willy-nilly involved in a game of survival whether he likes it or not. That is to say, co-operative solutions require co-operation. Then we may suggest that the likelihood of a prospective entrant being co-operatively permitted to absorb a given market share after appropriate signalling depends on the probability of his winning, in the event that he had enforced war to the death. Thus the general conditions governing growth through actual games of survival also govern the cases where the eventual outcome is more peaceful, and the features of the potential game of survival have similar policy implications to those of actual games of survival. Growth by successive efforts intended to end in co-operative outcomes is therefore restricted as to pace for almost precisely the same reasons: the number of cases where the potential threat position is adequately powerful will be limited in time, and excessive acceleration of a diversification programme designed on these lines will therefore encounter the usual penalties. In particular, as acceleration involves declining average threat-strength, the average size of market share obtained in actual solutions will also be declining, so that attempted and actual growth will separate in a manner similar to that obtaining from a rising failure rate in differentiated diversification. The only way growth by threat of war would appear to differ significantly from growth by actual war is that in the former the costs of battle are avoided and the main analytical effect is felt in a declining success rate (as diversification rate increases) for given average profitability. But this is not a very realistic qualification. As already mentioned, in order to make a threat appear convincing it is almost always necessary to offer at least some hostile gestures (e.g. at least get a product variant into production); only rarely will defenders concede a reasonable share merely on receiving a threatening letter. These gestures, evidently, cost money and the outcomes remain uncertain. It is always possible that, as a result of the information exchanged during the display period, the defenders will decide to play for survival and the entrant eventually lose.

Hence the cases of growth by actual war and growth by threat of war are not really distinct, and a characteristic programme wil contain an uncertain mixture of both results. Therefore, as in the case of differentiated growth, we may set up two alternative models, one in which it is assumed that the firm always expends sufficient resources on research and development, and that in the cases where imitative entry is actually attempted, a reasonably successful outcome (either warlike or co-operative) is virtually certain, the other in which it is accepted that it might be a better policy to admit a certain proportion of failures. In the first case, the rate of growth remains equal (in stable conditions) to the rate of diversification, but as diversification and growth are accelerated, the increasing cost of ensuring success leads to declining rate of return. In the second case the same general conditions are complicated by the added effect of declining success rate, leading rate of growth, for given rate of return, not to increase in proportion to rate of diversification.

General Implications of Imitative Strategy

It should now be apparent that, taking the whole range of imitative strategies, including bandwaggoning, the implications for the form of the demand-growth function are similar to those of differentiated strategies. We have already seen, in the immediately preceding section, how similar relations between diversification rate, growth rate and profitability arise, and how both 'no-failure' and probabilistic policy models are available. We then observe that again, as in the differentiated model, it is by no means unlikely that at moderate rates of imitative diversification the overall rate of return may well exceed the results which would be expected if no attempt was made to grow at all. The functional structure of the policy problem is therefore unchanged, although, of course, for any individual firm in any given situation the positions and detailed shapes of the functions in the two types of strategy may well differ significantly. It follows that the firm is faced not only with policy decisions within the types of two strategies, but also with a decision as to how much emphasis to place on each. For example, a firm which for historical reasons is relatively weak in imagination, but clever in production, would find comparative advantage (in terms of sustainable growth) by emphasising imitation, and vice versa. Except where otherwise stated, we shall henceforth assume that firms under analysis always attempt to make this decision in such a way that the growth rate actually experienced is maximised for all given rates of return.

Non-Diversifying Growth

In Chapter 3 (p. 122) we suggested that the ultimate limiting example of 'imitative' growth was represented in the case where the firm achieved a discontinuous increase in its share of a market for a product it was already producing. Such developments, evidently, could not generate sustainable growth unless successively repeated over a number of such markets. Now, in the light of the more recent discussion, we can describe the process better. The share held of an existing market will depend, we have seen, on the various elements, such as threat strength, which characterise the particular game-situation in question. If one of these elements is quantitatively changed, the quantitative characteristics of the 'peaceful' solution are likely to change also. For example, an increase in relative threat strength may lead, after a short outbreak of demonstrative hostilities, to a permanent revision of market shares in favour of the gainer. If, therefore, a firm can successively improve its threat-competitive position in market after existing market, it can achieve by this means a form of continuous growth.

Such improvements must require definite innovation. Costs of production may be reduced, or consumer appeal increased, in such a way that, whether prices are actually reduced or not, competitors realise that the chances of this firm's winning a war of survival are increased and/or its probable relative losses in total attrition reduced. But the capacity for making innovations of this kind is evidently limited in much the same way as the capacity to differentiate or imitate. Hence the whole process is subject to precisely analogous dynamic restraints, and requires no special analysis. We assume that, in optimising the balance between imitation and differentiation, the firm also makes optimal decisions in relation to the balance between this limiting case of imitation and the more general case. (Empirically, the limiting case is obviously quite important.)

Empirical Support

To a considerable extent the whole of the foregoing 'theory of demand' may be regarded as an explanation of a body of facts which have been known for some time: we know that new products follow growth-curves, we know that oligopolistic imitation accompanied by price-stability is a general phenomenon. The reader will also remember that we have supported our arguments with references to a considerable body of existing material relating to the way price and diversification decisions are taken within firms. In the notes he will also find references to numerous articles in business periodicals which lend support to the view that our concepts and assumptions are well represented in the language of the business world; indeed, we would claim that the theory presented above is better related to the relevant problems of real concern to business-men in this area than any predecessor.

Since most of the foregoing was written, however, there has appeared one piece of econometric evidence which seems both to support the specific socio-economic explanation of the growth-curve given in the above theory, and to discriminate it from earlier models (such as that of Duesenberry for example),[30] which implicitly assumed that all consumers in a market population were in contact with all others. This evidence comes in a study of the growth of sales of television sets in the U.K. recently completed by Andrew Bain.[31] He finds that the curve which best fits the data is one whose mathematical characteristics would be difficult to explain other than on the hypothesis that consumers are arranged in groups, more or less as in our model, and are not, in other words, much subject to 'demonstration effect' from people whom they do not know. Of course, the general theoretical framework we are attempting to build depends only on the relatively general hypothesis that sales of new products follow growth-curves of some kind (i.e. that they saturate), but since we have built a rather specific policy-conditioning theory, including prescriptions concerning price policy, it is satisfying that the previous qualitative supporting evidence is now, apparently, receiving more rigorous backing. It is intended to pursue the matter further in a future publication.

GLOSSARY OF SYMBOLS FOR CHAPTER 4

N.B. Bracketed references indicate page where first defined.

(i) *English Letters*

e_i = critical marketing expenditure per pioneer (p. 181)

g = 'gregariousness', number of consumers per primary group (p. 154)

G_n = number of primary groups in a set, all of whom are linked in degree n (p. 154)

L_n = the number of other elements in a set of primary groups linked in degree n, with which each individual group is linked in degree n (p. 154)

m_i = threshold number of contacts for product i (p. 163)

N = primary population = number of consumer units in a primary population (p. 154)

N_a = number of active consumers (p. 162)

N_p = number of pioneers (p. 162)

N_s = number of consumers in a secondary population (p. 160)

p_i = (see p. 164)

$\bar{p}_i$ = (see p. 164)

$\hat{p}_i$ = critical ratio for product i (p. 164)

P_g = gestation profits per pioneer, for product i (p. 181)

P_s = saturated profits *per capita*, for product i (p. 181)

q_{ij} = quantity taken of ith commodity by jth consumer

r = ratio of opponent's initial financial resources to own (in a game of survival, see p. 194)

S_n = number of secondary groups in a population stratified in degree n (p. 157)

T_i = index of profitability for product i (p. 181)
$\tilde{x}_i$ = (see p. 161)
$\tilde{x}_j$ = (see p. 161)

(ii) *Greek Letters*

a_i = (see p. 167)
v_{ij} = (see p. 161)
μ_{ij} = (see p. 161)
σ_a = (see p. 174)
$\tilde{\sigma}_j$ = (see p. 173)
π_i = price of product i (p. 174)
λ = index of stratification (p. 157)
ξ_i = index of inhibition (p. 174), for product i.

CHAPTER FIVE

'SUPPLY'

'Durand . . . would seem to be concerned with the cost of capital
to management, whatever that might be' — Franco Modigliani[1]

Outline of the Problem

Capital has a 'cost' to management because it is needed for
growth, and because management has only limited resources in
profits for obtaining it. In this chapter, therefore, we consider
more carefully the relationship between maximum growth rate of
capacity — as limited in time by the supply of finance — and the
internal rate of return. On the severest type of neo-classical assumptions, no such relationship exists, or, more precisely, exists only in
the sense that where the internal rate of return exceeds some
exogenously given value, the supply of capital is infinite, but otherwise is zero. We have repeatedly indicated that, along with many
other reasonable persons, we find this particular neo-classical
position hopelessly unrealistic. We believe that in varying degree
all economic institutions face partly inelastic capital-supply curves,
a fact of life from Adam and Eve to the present day. The expected
return to the investor required to call forth a given supply to a given
institution within a given period is in general some rising function
of the amount required, and since we are mainly studying the
growth *rate* of the institution, if the elasticity increases with the
length of the period, we are little concerned.

If the supply of capital to the individual firm is inelastic, the
'market rate of discount' becomes a measure of supply price, and is
no longer exogenous to the policy model. In taking decisions about
growth, the management takes decisions about capital required
which, if they are to be implemented, imply a determinate price.
k is no longer a constant, but an endogenous variable, a consequence of, rather than a fixed constraint on policy, and the role of
restraint is transferred to the factors determining the shape and
position of the supply-curve as a whole.

Corporate finance, and the related topics of investor behaviour and stock-market values, unlike many other questions of importance to the study of managerial capitalism, have by no means been neglected by economic science, and there is a considerable literature of both empirical and inductive analysis. [2] Even here, however, much of the most important work is quite recent and the results at the time of writing still controversial. With some of the controversies we are not directly concerned, and, indeed, since our main purpose is to establish no more than a general presumption that provided the firm is subject to some behaviour restraints of the types discussed in Chapters 1 and 2, its total new-capital supply, expressed as a ratio of existing assets, is in some way limited in time yet also a function of the rate of return, [3] a case could be made for avoiding the subject altogether: the number of readers who would agree with the general presumption would be likely to exceed the number who would accept any particular formulation of it. But to take this course would make our theory vague at a point where it should be precise, and also savour of evasion. We therefore adopt the compromise of spelling out a specific model of the corporate capital-supply curve which may in some places contradict rival theories, while not extensively entering the business of defence and counter-attack. Thus the reader will appreciate that the analyses carried out in other parts of this book do not stand or fall on our particular financial model; as already indicated, they depend ultimately on the assumption that the supply of finance is limited in time in *some* way only.

More specifically, we shall attempt here to find a relationship between the maximum growth rate of capacity (for given internal rate of return) consistent with a constrained valuation ratio, and thus hope to uncover a plausible causation for the curve of maximum safe or moral sustainable growth first outlined in Chapter 1 (p. 42). For the purpose we shall employ particular assumptions about investor behaviour, including assumptions relating to asset-holding in general. (One of the weaknesses of contemporary studies to date lies in failing to attempt to integrate theories of asset-holding with theories relating to the demand for particular securities: the prices of individual shares are generally seen either as the result of non-disaggregable assumptions about the behaviour of the stock-market as a whole, or as of 'partial' models relating only to the individual investor and the individual share. Consequently, to the author's knowledge there is no extant econometric study of share prices based on a model of investor behaviour which takes any specific account of hedging and risk-spreading.)

The Basic Equation

Let us recapitulate the problem. We wish to discover the determinants of the ratio of the amount of new capital on which a firm can lay hands in a given period to the aggregate book value of its gross assets at the beginning of the period, this ratio representing in effect the maximum growth rate of its productive capacity. We assume that whatever gearing or leverage ratio is associated with the process, it is held constant over time, so that the growth rate of debt, of gross assets and of net assets must all be equal. We call the growth rate of gross capital $C^{\cdot}$, and when it has been maximised subject to constraints will write it $C^{\cdot\ast}$. The gearing ratio (debt to gross assets) is g and is believed to be subject to a financial-security (maximum) constraint $\bar{g}$ (see Chapter 1, p. 9). The growth rate of gross capital is then composed as follows:

$$\frac{\text{Retained Earnings} + \text{Net Borrowing} + \text{Proceeds of New Share Issues}}{\text{Gross Capital at Beginning of Period}}$$

With gearing constant, because the growth rates of gross and net capital are the same, this leads to an equation,

$$C^{\cdot} = r \cdot \frac{(p - i \cdot g)}{1 - g} + N^{\cdot} \cdot v \qquad (5.1)$$

The problem, then, is to maximise $C^{\cdot}$, as above composed, subject to various functional interdependencies and constraints. The constraints arise from management's concern with both security for itself and normative treatment of shareholders. Thus leverage is restrained to a maximum, $\bar{g}$, in order to avoid undue risk of financial failure and hence loss of employment and prestige — loosely, in other words, to avoid excessive borrower's risk — and the valuation ratio, v, is constrained to a minimum, $\bar{v}$, to provide adequate freedom from fear of take-over and/or pangs of conscience towards shareholders.

Maximising Procedure, First Stage

If the interest rate, i, is lower than the rate of return, p (which we may generally assume to be the case), C^* increases with gearing *provided* gearing has no effect on the valuation ratio. The likelihood of the latter effect is a matter of controversy: leverage increases lenders' risk but also increases the net rate of return, and there is at first sight no presumption that the one influence will necessarily outweigh the other. Furthermore, there is at least one school where it is vehemently argued that the rational investor should in a sense be indifferent to gearing, because he should be able to offset or enhance the 'personal' gearing involved in holding any particular share by appropriate borrowing or lending transactions in other differently geared assets.[4]

If, in fact, investors are indifferent to the risks of gearing, a theory of share valuation such as outlined in Chapter 1 (to be recapitulated below) would predict that provided the net rate of internal return is held equal to the market rate of discount appropriate to an unlevered stream of dividends of otherwise comparable risk, the market valuation ratio and the gearing ratio should be independent. The valuation ratio has as numerator the market price of a share, as denominator the book value of *net* assets per share. Given gross assets per share, as gearing is increased net assets per share decline, and the theorem implies that the associated decline in market price is due to this factor and no other, hence both numerator and denominator of the valuation ratio always vary with gearing in precisely the same proportions. Professor Myron Gordon, however,[5] has shown that even on its own assumptions the theorem is strictly valid only when the retention ratio is zero: in the presence of growth by retentions it is no longer true that personal gearing and corporate gearing maintain the supposed relationship. But the required modification is apparently complex, may go in either direction, and we are here forced to ignore it. More specifically, we shall assume that when gearing is held below the relatively moderate levels required for the security constraint (i.e.

H

when $g \leqslant \bar{g}$), any effects of gearing variations on the valuation ratio are of such character that in ignoring them we shall not be led into significant qualitative errors. We shall also assume that the rate of interest is independent of gearing, i.e. is exogenous. In real life, growth-by-borrowing is limited in a variety of ways: through borrower's risk, through imperfections in the supply of loan capital and through possible investor reactions to the implications of gearing for their own probability-distributions of returns. But having noted that most firms do in fact hold gearing down to moderate levels, and having formed the view that borrowers' risk (in the broad sense implied in Chapter 1) is a particularly powerful factor in this situation, we feel justified in treating the other possible limits somewhat cavalierly.

If the interest rate is exogenous and smaller than the gross internal return rate, and if gearing does not affect the valuation ratio, it will always 'pay' in terms of growth to set the gearing ratio at its security-constrained maximum. When this is done, given the gross rate of return, the net rate of return is also given and constrained. Let us then write,

$$\bar{p} = \frac{p - i \cdot \bar{g}}{1 - \bar{g}} \tag{5.2}$$

where

$\bar{p}$ = net internal rate of return, given p, when $g = \bar{g}$.

Then (remembering that with constant gearing the growth rate of gross and net capital are equal) we can write,

$$C^{\cdot} = r\bar{p} + v \cdot N^{\cdot} \tag{5.3}$$

This completes the first stage of maximisation.

New Issues, Retentions and Market Valuation

We are now faced with two policy variables, the retention ratio, r, and the new-issue rate, $N^{\cdot}$, and a market-behaviour variable, v, which latter may be a function of either or both policy variables and is itself subject to a policy constraint. In no circumstances is any combination of values of r and $N^{\cdot}$ inconsistent with $v \geqslant \bar{v}$ permissible. The possible functional relationships between these variables are therefore of first-order importance.

Let us now recapitulate the theory of market valuation first outlined in Chapter 1. In that theory there was assumed to exist a market rate of discount, k_i, applied by investors to the 'total return' expected from the shares of firm i in order to evaluate the worth to them of an equity in the book value of the particular collection of net assets owned and controlled by i. The concept of total return incorporated both the expected next dividend and the expected long-run growth rate of dividend, the latter corresponding to expected growth rate of market value or capital gain. The growth rate was assumed to be equal to the growth rate of book value of net assets per share, which was in turn the product of expected retention ratio and internal rate of return. Thus we obtained the formula,

$$v = (1 - r) \Big/ \left(\frac{k}{\bar{p}} - r \right) \qquad (5.4)$$

In effect, this formula ignored new issues. For it will be seen that in assuming that the growth rate of assets, earnings and dividends per share was expected to be equal to rp, the investor was supposed to expect that retentions would be the only source of expansion. More precisely, he was supposed to assume that new issues would have no influence on earnings per share: increased earnings due to increased capital would be precisely proportionate to the increased number of shares over which the earnings would have to be spread. The assumption is logical only if there is no return discrepancy. If expected $\bar{p}$ exceeds k, each new share expected to be issued brings in proportionately more capital than the associated increase in expected earnings (assuming that the latter is given by the product of capital subscribed and $\bar{p}$), and hence, because all shares rank equally for dividend, the resulting surplus is partly available to the holders of 'old' shares. It follows that an investor who anticipates both that the return discrepancy will be positive, and that some new issues will be made, will expect the growth rate of dividend to exceed the growth attributable to expected retentions by a determinate amount, and the greater either the return discrepancy or the expected new-issue rate, the greater the adjustment to be made. [6] As the theory stands, therefore, so long as the return discrepancy is positive, the valuation ratio varies positively not only with the expected retention ratio (as we said in Chapter 1), but also with the expected new-issue rate. When the return discrepancy is negative, the entire position is reversed and any upward variation of either r or N^* will affect the valuation ratio adversely. If the return discrepancy is zero, the valuation is independent of both retention ratio and new-issue rate, and is, in fact, always unity. In other words, provided the market rate of discount is equal to the net internal rate of return, not only is our policy constraint on the return discrepancy satisfied, but we do not have to worry about the possible effects on the maximum solution of interdependence between the variables. So far, therefore, the picture is entirely neo-classical: so long as the return discrepancy remains zero or positive, increases in retention ratio or new-issue rate have no adverse effect on the valuation ratio and the capital supply is unlimited. But, as we saw in Chapter 1, this result depends on the assumption that, in varying the retention ratio or new-issue rate, the firm in no way affects the discount rate. Once it is admitted that k may itself depend on these policy variables, the model collapses.

Theories of Asset-Holding

We do not need to deploy any particular theory of asset-holding to support the assertion that at any moment of time an individual investor faced with a set of imperfectly perceived probability-distributions of expected total returns from a wide range of securities will spread his holdings in some non-random manner by a mental process which may be described as maximising Von Neuman-Morgenstern utility in conditions of partial information. [7] That is to say, the investor considers a limited number of possible portfolios, each representing, in effect, a gamble. To each gamble he attaches utility, which in these circumstances is a number up to a linear transformation. He then chooses the portfolio of maximum utility. The number of alternatives considered is limited, because the act of consideration involves costs in both obtaining and evaluating information, and these costs themselves imply disutility (consequently the behaviour could also be described as satisficing). In practice most individual investors restrict their decision horizon by considering a limited list of specific shares; not necessarily homogeneous as to industrial classification, risk and expected return; not necessarily constant; not necessarily invariant to economic events. The larger the investor, or the more resources available to him for obtaining and evaluating information, the longer the list, but it is doubtful if even the very largest institutional investors are genuinely thinking about every quoted security at every instant of time. We therefore assume that, in order to induce an investor to add to or substitute in his list a security he had not previously considered, it must be brought to his attention by some definite event, of which the most significant type of course would be a discontinuous improvement in the security's attractions. This does not mean that once a share is on the consideration list, some positive quantity of it is always held, but rather that once it is on the list the chosen holding becomes a *continuous* function of its (probabilistic) properties. We then assume that the quantities held among the considered securities are determined by a utility function which reflects a mixture of both gambling and precautionary motives.

A. D. Roy has shown[8] that only the most reckless gambling behaviour will lead to concentration in one security which happens to offer a particular combination of expected return and risk. The 'normal' investor will always hedge at least to some extent. We may therefore assume that with a given set of subjective probability-distributions for total returns of securities on his considered list, there is for each investor a determinate desired distribution of holdings. Then let x_{ij} represent the proportion of the total value of his portfolio which the ith investor desires to hold in the jth security, and let $\tilde{x}_i$ represent his vector of such proportions. Given the prices of all securities, the consideration lists and subjective probability-distributions of all investors, there will then be a corresponding vector $\tilde{X}_j$, representing the proportions of the total current value of all quoted securities represented by the total market value of each separate security (i.e. the X_j's are proportions aggregated over all i). If then we specified a vector of relative prices of all securities, given $\tilde{X}_j$, we should specify the total quantity (par value) of each and every security in public hands. Behind this structure there then lies a structure of book values of assets, indicating for each security the par value plus the capital surplus due to previous reinvestment or windfall capital gain. Let us call the structure of book values the 'equity structure' of the situation. More precisely, ignoring debt (so that C_j can stand for the net assets of firm j), let c_j be the ratio of C_j to ΣC_j (summation over all quoted corporations), then the 'equity structure' is represented by $\tilde{c}_j$, the vector of c_j's. Clearly both for the market and for the individual it is this equity structure which comes closest to representing the quantitative aspect of the asset distribution, for, with given internal rates of return and retention ratios, it is the equity structure which mainly determines the whole pattern of total returns. Then any firm attempting to grow faster than the average is attempting to disturb the equity structure, a development which requires either a change in the asset distribution ($\tilde{X}_j$) or in relative prices.

Roy showed[9] that where 'safety first' is the dominant motive (in the sense that the investor is concerned only to minimise the probability that his actual returns will be less than a specified 'disaster level'), in a simple case the optimum distribution of holdings is such that the ratio between any pair of holdings, x_{ij}/x_{ik} should precisely equal the ratio of expected return from security j to that from k. This result assumes that the variances of all the subjective probability-distributions are the same; if, as in real life, they differ, less money should be put in those securities offering higher variance for given return, and vice versa. More generally, if, as is usually the case,[10] there is among securities a positive association between expected return and risk, the optimal asset distribution will be 'damped' in the sense of containing smaller relative values of holdings of high-yielding shares than in the case where all variances are equal. But whatever the pattern of variances, and with all but the most incautious utility functions, given the whole set of all investors' probability-distributions there is one unique determinate overall asset distribution, i.e. one unique $\tilde{X}_j$. This implies either a unique equity structure or a unique price structure. Therefore, in order to alter the equity structure it is necessary to alter either the price structure or the probability-distributions of returns.

If firms made no new issues, a constant equity structure would imply that the value of rp (product of retention ratio and rate of return, i.e. growth rate) of every firm be the same, leading to the somewhat paradoxical result that the firms with the highest rates of return should have the lowest retention ratios, and vice versa. If a firm desired to adopt a higher retention ratio (and hence growth rate), it would have to suffer reduced share prices in order that the continuous disturbance to the equity structure be accommodated. (The fact that an internal rate of return was above average in relation to risk would not of itself justify the disturbance, because, once static equilibrium is reached, the desired equity structure already reflects all the probability-distributions.) Clearly, precisely the same argument applies to new issues. It then follows that, both for growth by new issues and growth by retentions, there is for every firm some point at which attempted acceleration must disturb the market, depress share prices and thus, in effect, raise the firm's 'market rate of discount'.

The above is an extreme statement, depending on a rigidly static approach and leading in some cases to rather incredible conclusions. Evidently, the real-life market is never in equilibrium, and a more thorough investigation would require a dynamic analysis involving, *inter alia*, consideration of important 'frictions' affecting the time rates at which investors react to changed information. Nevertheless, the underlying argument gives powerful support to the intuitive belief (which — see below — is well supported by econometric evidence) that other things being equal there is for almost all firms some restraint on capital supply attributable to (possibly non-linear) interactions between retention ratio and new-issue rate on the one hand, and market rate of discount on the other.

If the equilibrium equity structure were the only factor in the situation, it would be convenient to frame a model in which the valuation ratio of a firm with given $\bar{p}$ was affected only by its overall growth rate, i.e. was not affected by the distribution of financing as

between retentions and new issues. Two types of further consideration, however, suggest that to do so would represent over-simpli-
fication. In the first place, there is another and quite separate
reason for expecting investors to react directly to the retention
ratio, as such. This is that another neo-classical assumption which
in our discussion so far has passed unquestioned is also implausible, namely the assumption that the rate of time discount
applied by an investor to an expected future dividend is independent of the date in time the dividend is to be declared. Thus a
person is assumed to apply the same rate of time discount to a dividend to be declared after he would be 100 years old as to one to be
declared next year, and so on. To the extent that the population of
investors contains many persons of widely different ages, and that
banks and other financial intermediaries provide facilities for persons to trade off *inter se* between differently dated annuities, it is
likely that no significant effect from this error will be felt until the
annuities in question become rather long dated, but at some point,
in any society of mortals, some such effect is inevitable.

Perhaps an even more powerful reason for expecting the market
rate of discount to be endogenous to the financial policy itself is
found in the fact that, as well as time preference, subjective risk
almost certainly increases with the length of futurity; since the
market rate necessarily includes an element of risk discount, this
implies that any factor, such as the retention ratio, tending to increase futurity must have a like effect. As far as the author is aware,
the first comprehensive and rigorous development of this point was
given as recently as 1962, by Myron Gordon, to whose work[11]
the reader is referred for its further elaboration.[12]

If the rate of discount applied to future annuities differs among
them according to date, the rate employed in evaluating a share
must represent some form of weighted average of the whole series
of rates, the appropriate weights being the annuities themselves.
Then if there is, after some point, a general tendency for the discount rates to increase with futurity, the weighted mean will vary
directly with the retention ratio, because a rise in the ratio increases the relative weight of the more long-dated dividends. The
supposed non-linear relationship between retention ratio and

discount rate is thus reinforced from a quite independent source. It is also worth noting that when the retention ratio is varied upward from an initial low level, there may be an effect on subjective risk working in the opposite direction from that suggested for the case where the initial level is high: an unduly low retention ratio may reduce confidence in the near-future expected dividends, because in the absence of 'earnings cover' the firm would be less well able to absorb adverse fluctuations in earnings without reducing the dividend below the expected level. This argument provides a further source of possible non-linearity. Examination of the financial press of almost any country suggests that it is an important one.

In the second place, there is also a separate factor operating in the new-issue area. We have seen that investment behaviour is manifestly affected by restraints on information, and we suggested that in practice individual investors restrict their consideration to limited lists of specific securities. To expand the market's holdings, measured in par value, of any security will generally require that at least some new individual shareholders be acquired, that is to say, an expansion of a company's issued capital will generally require some expansion in the number of members, it being unusual that the optimal reaction of old members to a new issue involves taking up their whole pre-emptive right in full. If so, a new issue means that some investors must be induced to add a new company to their consideration list. This in turn will require a significant improvement in expected total yield. It follows that any new issue is likely to have some adverse influence on the market price of the shares, in the sense that, given the appropriate probability distribution, the price will be lower than had the new issue not been made (this is assuming, of course, that no positive return discrepancy is expected, either before or as a result of the issue). The effect may be regarded as linear, and directly related to the new-issue *rate*, because, the shares of a large company being more widely known and easily traded than those of a small, a company in making a new issue creates conditions leading to an increase in the absolute size of any subsequent issue consistent with a given effect on market price.

The upshot of the arguments is that if k is to be represented as a function of r and $N^{\bullet}$, the partial derivatives must be assumed to differ significantly. The effect of r is the result of several factors, all suggesting non-linearity, all suggesting in fact that $\delta k/\delta r$ would be small and probably insignificant at low values of r, but increasing with r in such a way as to become important when it began to exceed, say, about 50 per cent. The effect of $N^{\bullet}$ is also the result of at least two factors, but in this case it can be shown that little of importance is lost if we adopt a linear approximation. A convenient formulation, therefore, is one such as the following:

$$k = \alpha_1 + \alpha_2 \cdot N^{\bullet} + \alpha_3 \cdot r^2 \tag{5.5}$$

A typical value for α_1 might be 0·05, representing the market rate of discount for a firm making no new issues and retaining no profits; for α_2, perhaps 0·5 (there is no reason, however, why this should not be considerably higher or lower: for econometric evidence, see below); for α_3 perhaps 0·1. The effect of r would then become significant when, as already suggested, r reaches 50 per cent.

Maximising, Second Stage

The 'market' rate of discount thus becomes contingent on the policy decisions concerning retentions and new issues. It thus becomes itself an indirect policy variable, the subject of deliberate choice. In effect, therefore, our task is now to manipulate the market rate of discount in such a way that, for any given rate of return, the growth rate, $C^{\bullet}$, is at maximum subject to the constraint on the valuation ratio. The assumptions to date imply that the constraint will always be effective, i.e. that by increasing the retention ratio, new-issue rate, or both, the growth rate of finance supply can always be made to increase at the expense of a decline in the valuation ratio. For example, suppose the retention ratio were held constant at some arbitrary value, such as zero, and expansion improbably confined to new issues. Then every increase in the new-issue rate would raise the rate of discount and lower the valuation ratio, but on the assumptions above, this effect would always be insufficient for the associated change in the growth rate to be negative. The relationship is in fact asymptotic, with the first derivative of growth rate with respect to new-issue rate tending to zero as new-issue rate becomes large. This conclusion is almost certainly unrealistic; there is almost sure to come a point where the marginal yield of new issues becomes negative. (Realism could be restored by the introduction of some appropriate non-linearity in connection with the new-issue rate in equation (5.5), but we have deliberately omitted this step because we believe the restraint on managerial behaviour implicit in the valuation ratio is of much greater interest than the possible restraints associated with non-linearity in the supply of new-issue finance. If both restraints were admitted to the analysis, we should introduce evident mathematical complexities without adding commensurately to our insight into the system.)

If the constraint on the level of the valuation ratio is set, for the time being, at unity, and if, as we have now seen, the constraint is always effective, we know that in the optimum conditions things will have been so arranged that the market rate of discount equals the rate of return, this being necessary for $v = 1$). This implies,

$$k = \bar{p} \tag{5.6}$$

hence,

$$\alpha_1 + \alpha_2 \cdot N^* + \alpha_3 \cdot r^2 = \bar{p} \tag{5.7}$$

and, (since when $k = \bar{p}$, $v = 1$),

$$C^* = r \cdot \bar{p} + N^* \tag{5.8}$$

The problem, therefore, is to maximise (5.8) subject to (5.7) and the result (obtained by combining the two equations and differentiating for a maximum, there being no positive minimum), is as follows:

$$r^*_{(0')} = \frac{\bar{p}}{2} \cdot \frac{\alpha_2}{\alpha_3} \tag{5.9}$$

$$N^*_{(0')} = \frac{\bar{p} - \alpha_1}{\alpha_2} - \frac{\bar{p}}{2} \cdot r^*_{(0')} \tag{5.10}$$

$$C^{*} = N^*_{(0')} + \bar{p} \cdot r^*_{(0')} \tag{5.11}$$

— equation 5.11 representing the insertion of optimum values in 5.3, with $v = 1$.

It should be emphasised, of course, that these represent results for long-run values for long-run maximisation only: i.e. if a firm were maximising in precisely the manner we suppose, $r^*_{(c\cdot)}$ would then correspond to John Lintner's 'target' ratio.[13]

Substituting (5.9) and (5.10) into (5.11), we obtain

$$C^{*\cdot} = \frac{\bar{p} - \alpha_1}{\alpha_2} + \frac{\bar{p}^2}{4} \cdot \frac{\alpha_2}{\alpha_3} \qquad (5.12)$$

Here then is the relation between growth rate and internal rate of return towards which we have been working. It is apparently non-linear, but unless $\bar{p}$ is large, given our assumptions, (which imply *inter alia* that the overall coefficient of $\bar{p}^2$ is unlikely greatly to exceed unity) the second-order term can reasonably be ignored. This is equivalent to assuming that the firm ignores the possibility of growth by retentions, and concentrates all energy on new-issue finance, setting the new-issue rate at the highest level consistent with a non-negative return discrepancy. With the orders of magni-tudes of coefficients suggested, such a policy would provide a fairly close approximation to the true maximisation policy. We know, of course, that this approximation is rarely employed in practice, and a similar or better result could be obtained by setting the retention ratio at some arbitrarily chosen or 'reasonable' value, then appro-priately adjusting new issues. Because the problem has the pro-perty that what is gained on the roundabouts of retentions is lost on the swings of new issues ('gain' meaning here variation in valuation ratio), this type of approximation may do very well indeed, and there is considerable evidence, both from the existence of substan-tial and otherwise difficult-to-explain inter-firm variations in retention ratios, and from the conversations of company directors, that it may well be used widely.

If we then write,

$$C^{*\cdot} \simeq \frac{\bar{p} - \alpha_1}{\alpha_2} \qquad (5.13)$$

we have

$$C^{*\cdot} \simeq \frac{p - i \cdot \bar{g}}{\alpha_2(1 - \bar{g})} - \frac{\alpha_1}{\alpha_2} \qquad (5.14)$$

Given i, $\bar{g}$, α_1 and α_2, this suggests,

$$C^{**} = \alpha \cdot p - \beta \qquad (5.15)$$

where α and β, without suffix, represent corresponding derived constants, that is to say,

$$\alpha \equiv \frac{1}{\alpha_2 \cdot (1 - \bar{g})} \qquad (5.16)$$

and,

$$\beta \equiv \frac{1}{\alpha_2}\left(\frac{\bar{g}}{1 - \bar{g}} + \alpha_1\right) \qquad (5.17)$$

(5.15) is the fundamental equation for maximum, safe sustainable growth. Typical values for α and β are 2·0 and 0·10 respectively.

Effects of a Variable Constraint

Given our assumptions, the proposition that the constraint on the valuation ratio is always effective is valid for all levels of the constraint itself. Having found the maximum growth rate when the constraint is set at unity, we may now, therefore, generalise. Let $\bar{v}$ stand for any given level of constraint. Then it can be shown that,

$$C^{**} = \frac{\bar{p} - \alpha_1 \cdot \bar{v}}{\alpha_2} + \frac{\bar{p}^2}{4} \cdot \frac{\alpha_2}{\alpha_3} \cdot Q^2 \qquad (5.18)$$

where

$$Q \equiv 1 + \frac{\bar{v} - 1}{\alpha_2} \qquad (5.19)$$

When $\bar{v} = 1$, $Q = 1$, and the formula is identical to equation 5.12. It is worth noting that when $\bar{v} = 0$ (management would not mind if the shares became worthless), the maximum growth rate tends to infinity, this not very meaningful result being due to our having included no non-linear effect in the relationship between market rate of discount and new-issue rate (see equation (5.5)). The other extreme case, where the valuation ratio is very large, deserves more attention, because it is a well-known weakness in the theory of stock-market values which we are employing (equation (5.4)) that under certain circumstances it appears to imply that the value of a corporation could become infinite. This result is equally meaningless, and, if obtained, shows the theory has broken down. In the present formulation, it turns out that the growth rate itself tends to plus or minus infinity according to the sign of Z, where

$$Z = \frac{\bar{p}^2}{4} - \frac{\alpha_1}{\alpha_2} \qquad (5.20)$$

From this it follows that in order to avoid the nonsense implication of an infinite positive valuation ratio associated with an infinite positive growth rate, we require only that,

$$\bar{p} < 2 \cdot \sqrt{(\alpha_1 \cdot \alpha_2)} \qquad (5.21)$$

We therefore recognise that the model breaks down if at any time it is possible to exceed this value. But characteristically the break-down value of $\bar{p}$ would be well over 50 per cent.

As in the previous section we find there is a good case for ignoring the second-order term in the final equation. Unless $\bar{v}$ differs very substantially from unity, the coefficient of $\bar{p}^2$ is much the same as in equation (5.12). We may therefore conclude with an appropriately modified version of that equation, i.e.

$$C^{*\cdot} \simeq \alpha \cdot p - \beta \bar{v} \qquad (5.22)$$

the coefficients α and β being virtually identical with the coefficients signified by these symbols in (5.12); they depend, of course, on both stock-market conditions and gearing (now that p has been substituted for $\bar{p}$). The maximum growth rate now appears, interestingly, as a function of two variables, the rate of return *and* the minimum valuation ratio. Thus, variation of the minimum ratio has the effect of shifting the supply curve bodily, leaving the slope approximately unchanged, a result which will later prove of very great assistance in developing the promised 'trade-off' model between growth and security. Indeed, in the theory of managerial capitalism, (5.22) is a fundamental equation.

Econometric Support

The theory outlined above has two limbs. The first is a theory of stock-market behaviour, the second a theory of corporate reaction to this behaviour. The question of empirical testing of the second limb must be deferred until it has been fitted into a completed model (see the chapter following), because until that has been done we cannot safely derive testable predictions from it. The first limb, however, represents an essentially empirical sub-theory, and should be considered as such.

Its most important prediction is that the price of a stock is affected by both the expected rate of return and the retention ratio, or, alternatively, by the retention ratio and the current dividend. There is a very considerable econometric literature on the sub-ject,[14] and all writers bar Professor Modigliani believe that the retention ratio plays a definite independent role in any empirically supported theory. Modigliani believes that the retention ratio figures only by virtue of its role as an indicator of growth, and that, in consequence, in the absence of an expected return discrepancy, shareholders should be indifferent to it. He ignores the possibility that it may affect the rate of discount.[15]

Every known econometric result, bar two, states or implies that the retention ratio has an effect on share prices which is indepen-dent of dividend, but the real issue, of course, is whether the effect is 'non-linear' in the sense that, while raising valuation through the implied effect on growth rate, increased retentions have also the opposing effect of raising the discount rate. This issue, however, has only recently been subjected to positive test, and the results are not yet conclusive, but Professor Gordon, using a model similar to our own, has succeeded in providing at least reasonable support, on both the theoretical and statistical fronts.[16] We feel that his evi-dence, together with the very strong intuitive plausibility of the hypothesis, justifies us in relying on it.

As to negative tests, there are, as mentioned above, two results which might seem to work against us, and there is also Professor Modigliani's forceful argument that most of the previous models had not eliminated the possibility that investors paid independent attention to dividends because, owing to the considerable short-run instability of profits, they believed current dividends represented a better guide to future earnings than current earnings themselves. We take these points in turn.

In a paper read at the 1960 (St. Louis) meeting of the Econometric Association, but at the time of writing published only in summary form, [17] Professors Modigliani and Miller gave the results of three separate annual cross-section regression analyses on a sample of electricity supply concerns. In these models, the market valuation ratio was made to depend on earnings, leverage, current growth rate of assets and the current dividend. The growth rate was included on the assumption that the market expected a positive return discrepancy, and the dividend was included separately from earnings in the hope of establishing that it had no independent significance. In two years (1957 and 1956) this result was, in fact, obtained; in another (1954) the separate coefficient on dividends came out with a t-value of 3·3; the inference is clearly ambiguous. If, however, Modigliani's two favourable results were more generally confirmed, they might appear to cast serious doubt on the hypothesis that the retention ratio affects the rate of discount, because, it will be seen, the growth element in retentions had, in this model, already been taken out. But the model in fact does not test the hypothesis at all. In it, dividends figure twice, first as part of earnings and second as themselves. (Retained earnings are likewise doubled in effect, appearing first as part of earnings, then as implicit in the growth rate.) A moment's thought will show that the implications for the significance of the retention *ratio* depend on the characteristics of the co-variances in the error terms; these do not necessarily cancel, and therefore a non-significant result in the Modigliani model might be quite consistent with a real situation such as we and Professor Gordon hypothesise. This adds to our confidence in supporting Professor Gordon.

On the second point, the obvious method of resolution would seem to be that of setting up a model based on five-year averages of the relevant variables; there are, however, a number of statistical-theoretical snags involved, and the interpretation of results is not so straightforward as might be supposed. But the problems have now been thoroughly gone into by Gordon Fisher, and in a careful paper based on U.K. averaged data he has again concluded that the retention ratio is, indeed, significant. [18]

We therefore conclude by asserting that the econometric evidence supports us well, but again remind the reader that all we are fundamentally asking him to believe is that for any firm which pays attention to its valuation ratio the supply of capital from all sources is limited in time, yet varies directly with aggregate profits. No more than this is required for basic support of the 'supply' conditions built into the models now to be assembled below.

CHAPTER SIX

COMPLETED MICRO-MODELS

IN Chapter 3 we gave a general account of the methodological and analytical problems involved in our conception of the managerial firm, and of the methods we proposed for handling them. The main tasks involved in constructing the basic functional relationships accomplished, we now attempt to assemble the results in complete micro-models.

To recapitulate briefly, the position appears as follows. A firm may influence the growth rate of required capacity (demand) by various policy decisions relating to diversification, prices and marketing expenditure, all of which, given the production techniques employed and the general level of internal efficiency, have contingent effects on profitability (Chapter 4). But internal efficiency is itself also affected by these decisions, because the rate of efficient managerial expansion is limited by 'Penrose' restraint (Chapter 3). In turn, profitability is a vital element in the final solution because (Chapters 1 and 5), if management is to feel reasonably secure and be reasonably fair to shareholders, there is a close relation between the rate of return and the maximum sustainable growth rate of capacity. Thus the decisions relating to the growth of demand also affect the growth of 'supply', and the set of possible growth rates of demand is confronted with a set of safe growth rates of capacity. Since no path involving a continuing discrepancy between the trends of demand and of capacity is sustainable, we are thus able to identify the set of growth rates and associated policy decisions which are both sustainable and safe. From among these it may be possible to identify those with special economic characteristics, such as that of maximising the rate of return or maximising the rate of growth, the latter, of course, being the case in which we are particularly interested.

It will readily be seen that models built from this basic structure may be as complicated as the analyst desires to make them. Reasonable clarity requires some simplification, and this we propose to achieve by dividing the work into two stages. In the first stage we concentrate on obtaining results in terms of the direct decision variables; we ask, that is, how diversification rate, price policy and other variables affecting demand, together with retention ratio, new-issue rate and gearing ratio, should be set if the firm desires to behave according to our original working hypothesis (i.e. the hypothesis that growth rate is maximised subject to a minimum valuation-ratio constraint). At this stage we also make certain other simplifying assumptions, later to be dropped (see next paragraph), designed to sharpen the immediate focus. This model, called model 1, is therefore chiefly concerned with the problems of management. In the second stage, we rearrange things to emphasise matters of greater concern to the economist. The economist, for example, is concerned with the relation between growth rate and rate of return, although the latter is not, in our conception of the management problem, a direct decision variable (but see p. 257 below). Model 2 is therefore set up to produce results almost exclusively in terms of growth rate, profit rate and valuation ratio. It also restores some complications assumed away in model 1. To these we now turn.

If the structure in relationships developed in the previous chapters is accepted, there emerge two analytical difficulties, both of which arise from the role of the rate of return. The first results from the assumed duality of the connection with the growth rate, and the second from specific complexities involved in one arm of that connection, that is to say in the demand-growth theory. The internal managerial restraint implies that, on account of declining decision-taking efficiency, costs rise if growth is accelerated beyond a certain point, while the 'external' model implies that in order to accelerate the growth rate of demand it is usually necessary to incur relatively heavier development and marketing expenses and/or to adopt more liberal price policies. Thus the internal restraint states that with given marketing expenditures and prices, the rate of return is affected from the cost side, while the external restraint implies that, with given production costs and decision-taking efficiency, it is affected by the needs of the demand side. Both effects militate in the same direction, but it is inconvenient to analyse them in combination because neither can properly be depicted in operation by the usual device of holding the other absent. If the difficulty could not be overcome, we should not be unlikely to end up in a position where all that could be said was that growth rate and profitability were in some way related. The second difficulty is that both effects are not only non-linear but also non-monotonic: at low rates of growth, we believe, managerial efficiency may well vary directly with growth rate, and, similarly, there is a range of diversification rates over which acceleration enhances profitability (because, it will be remembered, it is likely that the average rate of return on recently saturated products exceeds that on 'older' products). For obvious mathematical reasons, a model which attempted to combine these last-mentioned features with all the other assumptions required would be embarrassingly complex.

In model 1, we employ the more complex probabilistic model of the demand relation, but assume a relatively simple pricing situation, which has the effect of eliminating the non-monotonic aspect of the relation between growth rate and profitability. We are then able to introduce an explicit form of the internal managerial efficiency effect, again, however, ignoring non-monotonicity. In model 2, the non-monotonic effects are restored, but some of the decision variables (for example the diversification rate) can no longer be directly presented in the equations: instead, as already indicated, we provide relationships between growth rate, rate of return and (standing as a proxy for security) valuation ratio. The second model thus in effect represents a development of Diagram 1.2 in Chapter 1: consequently, a growth-rate-maximising financial policy is no longer *assumed*, and its effects are compared with those of other policies.

Model 1. Policy Model for Growth Rate Maximisation Subject to Minimum Security Constraint

In the previous chapters we identified three main groups of relationships which, taken together, can now be seen to form the basic structure of the policy problem facing a 'growth maximising' management. These were: the relationships connecting the growth of demand with the associated policy variables and with profitability; the relationships connecting profitability with the maximum safe growth rate of capacity; and the relationship between the attempted growth rate and managerial efficiency. If techniques of production were given, we could (as was done at the end of Chapter 4) conveniently represent the demand relation as a family of curves linking rate of return, rate of diversification and growth of demand, the latter representing the growth rate capacity required. A given rate of return would then be taken as implying some restrained combination of pricing policies and relative development and marketing expenditures; therefore if the rate of return were analytically held constant, upward variations of the rate of diversification would imply that an increasing proportion of attempts would fail, so that the process became subject to 'diminishing returns' in terms of growth actually achieved. With a given rate of return, therefore, the growth rate of the firm is a dependent function of a specific policy variable, namely the diversification rate, this function taking the form of a rising but flattening curve which, because the success ratio in diversification cannot exceed 100 per cent, never passes the 45° line. More specifically, we may conveniently assume that, in the absence of autonomous trends in the demands for saturated products, the field of the demand function is restricted to positive values of both variables, that it begins at the origin and that the flattening effect is asymptotic. The last-mentioned assumption implies that, as diversification is accelerated, the increase in the absolute number of failures per period never exceeds the increase in the number of trials; the worst that can happen is that all the 'marginal' trials fail. (This seems reasonable, although it might happen, of course, that the diversion of inventive resources to marginal trials, all of which were doomed to fail anyway, also affected the success ratio among intra-marginal trials, but the analytical results would be little affected.) Then, when the assumption of a fixed rate of return is relaxed, we have a non intersecting family of such curves ordered in inverse relation to the rate of return: the greater the relative expenditure on research, development and advertising and the more liberal the typical price policy, the higher the success ratio for all given diversification rates; consequently, for all given diversification rates, the lower the rate of return, the higher the growth rate of capacity actually required.

If, however, we wish to combine the demand relation with other relations which include the internal managerial restraint, the above-described presentation is unsuitable, because the rate of return cannot, in fact, be held constant. We shall therefore employ a most convenient modification which was first suggested to the author by Professor Fritz Machlup.[1] If managerial efficiency and technique of production *were* given, this would imply a specific overall ratio of capital to output. More precisely, the quantity of capital (assuming given utilisation) required to be associated with any growth state of the firm is on these assumptions unique: if we know the specification of each gestating, exploding and saturated product in the catalogue, and know the technique chosen for the production of each, there is one complete outfit of equipment which will most efficiently meet all the requirements. The book value of the required outfit is the measure of the 'quantity' of capital required. The associated capital-output ratio is the ratio of this measure to some suitably weighted measure of the quantum of total output. Then, with a given capital-output ratio, thus defined, a given rate of return implies a given ratio of output to *profits*. The latter, in turn, is the reciprocal of the gross profit margin, which for convenience we define as the ratio of gross profits to the quantum of output as measured by whatever convention is used for the purpose in defining the capital-output ratio: ideally the quantum measure for an individual firm should be net output valued at fixed selling prices, but for new products these prices would have to be chosen arbitrarily. With these definitions, we may validly transform the family of demand curves ordered by rates of return into a family ordered by profit margins.

Apart from analytical convenience, the step also represents a realistic description of the relevant decision-making procedure. The demand relationship involves two main elements, price policy and marketing-expense policy. For reasons given in Chapter 4, the lower the average prices set at various stages in the early history of any given product and/or the larger the relative scale of the sums devoted to research, development and advertising of new products in general, the greater the average proportion of successes expected to be obtained from any given programme of diversification (whether differentiated, imitative or mixed). We may envisage a corresponding division in decision-making. Price policy may be represented in a decision as to some 'normal' or 'target' mark-up to be charged during various phases of a typical product's history, [2] deviations from which are only sanctioned for well-specified, pre-arranged types of reasons. This indicator might be defined as, say, the expected ratio of profits mainly attributable to the product to the value of its sales, 'profits' being defined for the purpose as gross not only of capital charges but also of a wide variety of general overheads, including a major proportion of costs incurred in marketing. Then a decision to vary the indicator would represent a decision to charge lower prices on new products in general, including products yet to be marketed. Conversely, if the indicator is fixed, a decision to increase the overall budget for marketing expenditure (relatively to the size of the firm) has comparable implications. Both types of decision affect the realised overall gross-profit margin. From the analysis of Chapter 4 we have seen that an optimal combination of price policy, marketing expense and, for that matter, of the balance between differentiation and imitation, involves complex problems which, in a growth context, are difficult to solve with generality. [3] We are here forced to assume that the firm takes the best decisions in these respects of which it is capable; we then treat the profit margin as a proxy for the consequences. For any given gross margin, we assume, the firm has attempted to adopt a combination of subsidiary decisions such that, given the margin and given the diversification rate, the success ratio is as high as possible. A variation in the 'given' margin, therefore, represents the results of a series of decisions deliberately intended to vary this ratio. Profit margin variations can thus be thought of as representing both the act and the result of decisions tending to vary the growth rate of actual demand associated with any given diversification rate.

The realism of the approach lies in the empirical fact that it has been found that top managers rarely concern themselves with individual price decisions, and frequently delegate many decisions

relating to individual marketing expenses also. Instead they usually prefer to lay down general operating rules designed to maintain
consistency and rationality, and to protect certain overall requirements. The application of the rules to individual cases is then left
to subordinates. In the case of price policy, still the most popular
method of defining rules implies, in effect, the use of some kind of
ratio such as a 'normal' or 'target' mark-up suggested above. This,
surely, is the basic conclusion of the whole large literature about
'full-cost' pricing. [4] Much the same result is obtained when a board
of directors decides to set up and maintain a research department,
new-product division or advertising budget of a given relative size:
although expenses attributable to individual products are frequently discussed at high level, in the sense that proposals made by
subordinates are subjected to consideration and possible rejection, [5]
the decisions made are also usually governed by the constraints of a
global budgeting procedure, more money for one project usually
(but not always) implying less for some other.

A firm's overall rate of return is the ratio of its overall gross-
profit margin to the capital-output ratio. If, therefore, having
concentrated the effects on the demand side into movements of the
margin, we could for analytical purposes similarly concentrate the
internal effects into movements of the capital-output ratio, we
should be able to represent both effects conveniently and simultaneously. We saw in Chapter 3 that the internal restraint arose
mainly from the inability of a management team to expand at an
indefinitely rapid rate without endangering efficiency. Following
Mrs. Penrose, [6] we agreed that the managerial function was specially related to expansion because, being concerned with non-
routine decisions, it was especially concerned with organisational
development and planning. Not only, therefore, does the restraint
arise from the unique role of the existing team in relation to the
organisation and planning of its own expansion, but it implies that
the inefficiencies likely to result from attempting to buck the effect
will be particularly sensitive to the rate of expansion attempted.
Some of the consequences have already been incorporated in our
assumption that the marginal probability of success in diversification declines as the rate accelerates, but we are here concerned with

other consequences, and particularly with those affecting internal efficiency in the use of productive resources. The co-ordinating function of high management in relation to internal resources is essentially the function of allocation, especially of 'dynamic' allocation, that is to say the function of deciding when resources should be diverted from one activity to another. If, through over-strain, such decisions are taken badly ('too little and too late'), the overall ratio between output and input will deteriorate even when maximum efficiency is still maintained in all individual activities. Where a major programme of uncertain diversification is under way, the point is of very considerable importance indeed: inevitably, in these conditions, it is necessary continually to reallocate resources as events unfold, and it is not unlikely that speed and efficiency of reaction will prove to be of greater survival value than forecasting ability. The most probable result of over-extending a management will be inadequate supervision of all operations. But this effect will inevitably be more serious where the operations are new rather than old-established: routine operations almost by definition require less attention from high management. In effect, therefore, it is the operations that are themselves the consequences of growth that will suffer most from the over-extensions which may result from attempting to grow too fast. Unfamiliar products are likely to involve unfamiliar methods both in production and marketing; a new differentiated product may involve developing production techniques that are new to all firms, while an imitative product may present equally severe problems that are new to this firm: imitation is not necessarily 'easier' from the individual firm's point of view, because standards already set by the originating firm may be difficult to match.[7] Every item in the programme of diversification, therefore, requires the development of new 'know-how'; the more extended the management, the less easily will this be acquired.

A consequence which particularly concerns us here is the likelihood of an all-round reduction in the speed and judgement displayed in the reaction of the control to the development of events: if speed is maintained, judgement will probably deteriorate or prove maintainable only at the cost of delay. A firm launching several products at time t may be quite unable to envisage which is most likely to succeed. If all succeeded, the management would be not so much surprised as pleased; if all failed, rather than surprised they would be disappointed. Unlike the girl under the mistletoe the business executive must always expect to be surprised, and must learn to behave accordingly. In practice it appears he aims to minimise uncertainty, to minimise the consequences of uncertainty, or both. By the use of planning and research, he tries to give new products at least reasonable chances of success, and by careful internal control he tries to arrange things so that, whatever the outcome in fact may be, the firm can make the best of it. A good firm is organised so that if things are 'going wrong', not only is the fact discovered at the earliest possible moment, but there is also enough flexibility to escape with minimum loss. The large majority of major business losses are attributable not so much to wrong forecasting, but to insufficiently quick reaction to the manifestations of wrong forecasts. Many are due to plain lack of adequate financial control. Similarly, the failures of short-run government economic policy in the United Kingdom during recent decades were not 'caused' by wrong forecasts, because wrong forecasts of economic fluctuations are inevitable: they were caused instead by the fact that political and administrative machinery associated with economic planning was inherently Dinosaurian in its reaction time. It is fairly certain that the less carefully a new operation is supervised, the slower the speed at which the control will learn of new developments connected with it. Furthermore, if the control itself is over-extended, it will be slow to decide what to do about developments, even when informed of them.

This is particularly obvious where the operation is the production and marketing of a new product. When products are created, a certain amount of capital must be committed to their production before it is known whether or not they will be successful. The manufacture of gestating products is therefore expensive: because failure cannot be predicted, it is necessary to treat all as if they were expected to succeed. When, in the event, one (or more) of a group of gestating products shows clear signs of exploding, while others are judged to have failed, the flow of capital and other resources can be diverted appropriately, and even some of the committed capital adapted. But for reasons we have already examined, there is bound to be an element of inertia; the taking and carrying out of diversion decisions cannot be achieved instantaneously. Time, as ever, is necessary: time to observe the signs of criticality, time to transmit the observations from periphery to centre, time for the centre to evaluate the information, discuss it, and make up its collective mind. Time is then needed for the decision to be translated into operational form, and for the operational decisions to be carried out — for new equipment to be ordered and orders delivered. The more products there are to watch, relatively to the number of efficient managers, the less efficiently, beyond a certain point, will each be controlled, and the more capital will be wasted, locked up in products which have failed to explode, or be lost irrevocably through tardy diversion.

Such failures will of course affect the average productivity of all factors of production, but are particularly likely to affect capital. There are several reasons for this. In the first place, fixed capital, at least in principle, takes longer to install (and longer to divert) than other factors; therefore its overall productivity is particularly sensitive to lags in decision-taking. In the second place, fixed capital is, as its name implies, fixed, i.e. is an overhead. When the demand for a particular product fluctuates, the inputs of labour and raw materials can be made to respond fairly quickly, if not in strict proportion; but the input of capital is determined by the quantity originally installed. True, in the modern multi-product firm, equipment is less specific than is sometimes assumed — most new products are to some extent joint products with old — but this only emphasises the importance of nimble decisions concerning diversions. Therefore we may reasonably assert that the effect of over-strain in high-level decision-taking will be notably manifested in a tendency for the overall capital-output ratio to rise: while the demand for some products is insufficient adequately to utilise the capital currently allocated to them, the output of others will be restricted by lack of capacity. Hence the 'Penrose effect' may be well represented in a relationship between the diversification rate and the capital-output ratio. In the present model this will be assumed to be direct and monotonic. In the second model, for reasons given in Chapter 3 (p. 116), it is assumed to be at first indirect, becoming direct only after a moderate diversification rate is passed.

We associate the effect specifically with the diversification rate, because gestating and exploding products must require more attention than others, and in the case of the gestating ones this is true whether they are ultimately destined to fail or to succeed. Indeed, products which eventually fail may well tax high management as much as or more than those which succeed, if only because they create the necessity for an important and agonising decision as to whether and when they should be withdrawn. (In a 'no-failures' demand model this point disappears, but in such a model the internal restraint is most conveniently represented as a continuous increase in the relative cost of the 'quantity' of management required to maintain 100-per-cent success). Of course, we recognise that other costs than capital costs will also be affected, but since all such effects are qualitatively similar, and since the effect on capital costs is so prominent, we may, we believe, concentrate attention on this particular aspect without loss of generality. If this is accepted, we are ready to proceed.

Model 1: Complete Specification

If we combine all the assumptions suggested above, together with the assumptions of the finance-supply model of Chapter 5, we obtain the following assembly:

$$D^{\bullet} = D(d, m) \tag{6.1}$$

$$C^{\bullet} = r \cdot p' + N^{\bullet}v \tag{6.2}$$

$$p' = \left(\frac{m}{c} - ig\right)\Big/(1-g) \tag{6.3}$$

$$c = c(d) \tag{6.4}$$

$$v = (1-r)\Big/\left(\frac{k}{p'} - r\right) \tag{6.5}$$

$$k = \alpha_1 + \alpha_2 \cdot N^{\bullet} + \alpha_3 \cdot r^2 \tag{6.6}$$

$$v \geqslant \bar{v} \qquad (6.7)$$

$$g \leqslant \bar{g} \qquad (6.8)$$

$$C^{\cdot} = D^{\cdot} \qquad (6.9)$$

Equation (6.1) states that the growth rate of the firm's total demand (saleable output) is a function of the rate of diversification and the profit margin, the latter representing the effect of decisions relating to price policy and development and marketing expenditures. Equation (6.2) states that the growth rate of assets can be expressed as the product of the retention ratio and the net rate of internal return, plus the product of the new-issue rate and the valuation ratio. (This relationship assumes, it will be remembered, that the gearing ratio is steady so that the growth rates of gross and net assets are identical.) Equation (6.3) defines the net rate of internal return in terms of profit margin, interest rate, gearing ratio and capital-output ratio. Equation (6.4) states that the capital-output ratio is a function of the diversification rate (for reasons, see above); equations (6.5) and (6.6) show how stock-market behaviour is assumed to determine the valuation ratio; equations (6.7) and (6.8) indicate the constraints on the gearing ratio and valuation ratio respectively, while equation (6.9) represents the balance equation The system thus contains seven equalities, two inequalities or constraints, and twelve variables. Of the latter, one — the interest rate — is fully exogenous in the sense of being both beyond the influence of policy and independent of all other variables, five are 'policy variables' in the strict Tinbergen sense[8] — they are independent but subject to choice — and the rest are exogenous. The policy variables are the diversification rate, the profit margin, the retention ratio, the new-issue rate and the gearing ratio; the endogenous variables are the growth rates of demand and of capacity, the rate of return, the valuation ratio, the capital-output ratio and the discount rate. In the absence of constraints, this would represent a system of seven equations and eleven unknowns, so that determination of any four of the policy variables would be sufficient to determine the whole. As there are altogether five policy variables, there would be only four degrees of freedom among them; given any four choices, the fifth variable would have to be set consistently or the balance equation violated. There are, however, constraints, and the object of the exercise is to maximise one particular endogenous variable (growth rate of demand or capacity), subject to constraints on two others and to the condition that a third (the alternative growth rate) meet the balance condition, i.e. that the two growth rates must be equal. If it happened that in optimum conditions both constraints had to be effective, two of the endogenous variables would become 'known' (i.e. fixed at their constrained values, which are exogenous) and two degrees of freedom lost: the maximising problem would then appear to boil down to a free choice of only two policy variables. This conclusion, however, is fallacious, because when the constraint on v is effective, the two financial policy variables are unique functions of each other: given r, the value of N^* is given independently of the rest of the model; alternatively, given N^*, the same applies to r. Hence equations (6.5) and (6.6) may be eliminated from the mechanism of determination, and (6.2) may be thought of as representing C^* as a unique function of r and p'. This rationalisation eliminates two equations and one policy variable (N^*), leaving a system of five equations and seven 'unknowns', of which three, the diversification rate, d, the profit margin, m, and the retention ratio, r, are policy variables. In choosing them, there are still two degrees of freedom, although their number has been reduced by one. Thus the problem becomes that of choosing a pair from d, m and r, or alternatively, from d, m and N^*, but in general, of these two alternatives, we shall only present the former.

In Chapter 5 we saw how the growth rate C^* could be maximised for any given p (gross internal return), subject to the constraints on g and v, and that in these conditions both constraints must in fact always be effective. It is then possible to show that this subsidiary maximum is also a condition for the general maximum. (If, for example, C^* were below C^{**}, v would exceed $\bar{v}$, and it would be possible to raise r or N^* without violating the security constraint. Such adjustment would permit C^* to rise without raising either m or c, i.e. without lowering p'. Hence, if growth had previously been balanced, it would now be unbalanced, and balance could be restored by a secondary (downward) adjustment of m, causing D^*

to rise and $C^{\cdot}$ to fall until the two variables were again equalised at a level which, from the functional structure assumed, would necessarily be higher than the previous level.) Thus balanced growth cannot be *maximum* balanced growth unless both constraints are effective, and optimum values of retention ratio and new-issue rate are actually adopted.

In Chapter 5, (p. 219) we saw that given the gearing constraint (value of $\bar{g}$), and the valuation constraint (value of $\bar{v}$), and given the stock-market conditions, $C^{*\cdot}$ could be represented as approximately linear in the *gross* rate of return, p, and the constrained valuation ratio, $\bar{v}$. Hence, repeating (5.22) we again write,

$$C^{*\cdot} = \alpha \cdot p - \beta \bar{v} \qquad (6.10)$$

α and β representing partly the effect of the chosen $\bar{g}$ and partly the stock-market conditions (as applied to the assumptions of the finance model, see Chapter 5).

We thus eliminate a further 'unknown', the retention ratio, and are left with a finally reduced model of four equations and five unknowns, as follows:

$$D^{\cdot} = D(d, m) \qquad (6.11)$$

$$C^{*\cdot} = \alpha \frac{m}{c} - \beta \bar{v} \qquad (6.12)$$

$$c = c(d) \qquad (6.13)$$

$$C^{*\cdot} = D^{\cdot} \qquad (6.14)$$

Two of the 'unknowns', m and d, are policy variables, and a single choice of either is sufficient to determine the system. The problem thus finally reduces to that of choosing *either* the diversification rate *or* the profit margin in such a way as to maximise $C^{*\cdot}$ at some value which we may call $C^{**\cdot}$. If, having chosen the profit margin, the diversification rate is not set consistently, or the other way about, growth will be 'unbalanced', i.e. violate (6.14), i.e. be non-sustainable. But there is a continuous range of sustainable values of either diversification rate or profit margin, and the object is to attempt to find a unique such value consistent with $C^{**\cdot}$. Inasmuch as the profit margin is a proxy for other policies, it is convenient to imagine the ultimate choice, in fact, as that of diversification rate. Then the policies associated with the profit margin become contingent.

Model 1: Diagrammatic Analysis

Evidently the existence and nature of a solution depends on the character of the ingredient functions. Let us, therefore, reconsider these. Diagram (6.1) below represents the form of equation (6.11), the demand-growth function, as expressed in the manner suggested above. Diagram 6.2 suggests a form for equation (6.13), the capital-output (internal efficiency) function: it is based on the assumption that the internal restraint has the property that eventually, if the diversification is raised high enough, inefficiency becomes infinite — a way of saying that further acceleration is impossible under any circumstances. By combining equations (6.12) and (6.13) we obtain the relationship

$$C^{*\cdot} = C(d, m) \qquad (6.15)$$

which necessarily takes a form such as illustrated in Diagram 6.3. Hence the model further reduces to

$$C(d, m) = D(d, m) \qquad (6.16)$$

or, as already suggested,

$$C^{*\cdot} = f(d) \qquad (6.17)$$

We then search for $d^*_{(C\cdot)}$, the value of d required to maximise $f(d)$. That is to say, we search for that rate of diversification or attempted growth which maximises the growth rate actually achieved. For convenience, in what follows, we omit the suffix, hence d^* is to be read as $d^*_{(C\cdot)}$.

The possibility of a definite result is demonstrated in Diagram 6.4, which represents equation (6.16). In effect this diagram combines the curves of Diagram 6.2 with those of Diagram 6.3. Then equation (6.16) is satisfied only where the demand-growth curve for a given profit margin intersects a finance-supply curve for the same margin; if the coding of the margins is assumed the same for both families, these positions are indicated by the points of

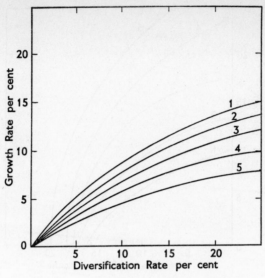

DIAGRAM 6.1. Family of Demand-Growth Curves
N.B. Numbers indicate profit margins

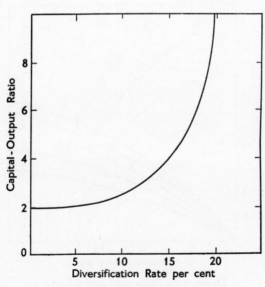

DIAGRAM 6.2. Internal Efficiency Relation

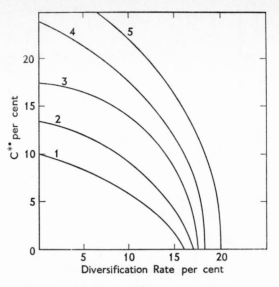

DIAGRAM 6.3. Family of Finance-Supply Curves
N.B. Numbers indicate profit margins
(for definition see text p. 238)

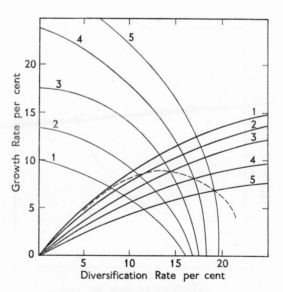

DIAGRAM 6.4. Balanced-Growth Curve
(for explanation, see text p. 238)

intersection of identically numbered curves. The set of such points, indicated by the broken line, represents the curve of equation (6.17), and, given the assumptions, has a maximum C^{**} obtained with a diversification rate d^* and a profit margin lying between nos. 2 and 3. This profit margin is then the growth-maximising profit margin, representing the price and marketing policies required for maximum growth.

Associated with the growth-maximising, or optimum-profit margin, which we may call $m^*_{(C')}$, there is also, of course, a growth-maximising, or optimum rate of return, which we call $p^*_{(C)}$. This is the ratio of $m^*_{(C')}$ to the capital-output ratio given by equation 6.13 when d^* is substituted for d. Thus in this model, although growth rather than profitability is being maximised, profitability remains of considerable importance. But rather than a maximum rate of return, we speak of an optimum rate of return, that is, the profit rate associated with and necessary for the policies required to maximise safe and sustainable growth. As in the case of d^*, from now on we omit the suffixes to m^* and p^*.

Model 1: A Mathematical Version

The character of the problem is such that diagrams are more easily employed than algebra. But suppose we endow the demand-growth function with a form such as

$$D = (1 - m) . f_D(d) \tag{6.18}$$

where f_D represents a function of the same general shape as the demand-growth curves suggested in the diagram: we thus arbitrarily assume that the effect of the profit-margin variable is linear and homogeneous. Then the finance-supply function might be represented by

$$C^{*'} = \alpha_S . m . f_C(d) - \beta_S . \bar{v} \tag{6.19}$$

where α_S and β_S correspond to the coefficients α and β in equation (6.12), and f_C is the reciprocal of the capital-output ratio, itself a function of d. For completion we may then add the balance equation $(C^{*'} = D')$, and attempt to maximise $C^{*'}$.

It is not difficult to show that when $C^{**} = C^{***}$,

$$C^{**} = \left(\frac{f_C}{f_D} \cdot \frac{\delta D^{\cdot}}{\delta C^{**}}\right) \div \left(1 + \frac{\delta D^{\cdot}}{\delta C^{**}}\right) \qquad (6.20)$$

and,

$$\frac{\delta D^{\cdot}}{\delta C^{**}} = \frac{\delta D^{\cdot}}{\delta d} \cdot \frac{\delta d}{\delta C^{**}} \qquad (6.21)$$

$$= \frac{(1 - m) \cdot f'_D}{m \cdot f'_C}$$

The derivatives, however, are not only not constant but vary with d in opposite directions, hence the ratio between them, and also the ratio f_C/f_D, are highly sensitive functions of d; equation (6.21) therefore represents an *ex post* equilibrium condition only and is of no great assistance for qualitative analysis. From the nature of the problem, if we want results we must attempt a more specific formulation. Suppose we assume

$$f_D = \frac{\alpha_D \cdot d}{1 + \beta_D \cdot d} \qquad (6.22)$$

and

$$f_C = \frac{1}{c_0}\left(1 - \alpha_C \cdot d^{\beta_C}\right) \qquad (6.23)$$

Where α_D, β_D, α_S, α_C and β_C are adjustable parameters: α_D and β_D control the slope and curvature of the demand-growth function, α_S represents the slope of the supply-growth function (i.e. corresponds to α in equation (6.10), reflecting, *inter alia*, the severity of the security constraint), while α_C and β_C represent the *non-linear* effect of the association between diversification and average capital-output ratio (c_0 is the capital-output ratio under conditions of zero diversification).

It can be shown that if we define F_d, a function of d, such that

$$F_d \equiv d \Big/ \left(1 - \alpha_C \cdot d^{\beta_C}\right)^2 \qquad (6.24)$$

Then in the maximum-growth conditions

$$F_d \simeq \left(\frac{\alpha_S}{\alpha_C \cdot \alpha_D \cdot \beta_C \cdot c_0}\right)^{\left(\frac{1}{1+\beta_C}\right)} \qquad (6.25)$$

This approximation ignores the effect of the term $(\beta_S \cdot \bar{v})$ from equation (6.10), which is assumed small enough to be ignored for determining the approximate value of d^*, although not, of course (see below), for determining the value of C^{**}. Then an approximate optimum diversification rate is a value of d satisfying (6.25).

Since the first derivative of F_a with respect to d is necessarily positive and independent of α_D, α_S and c_0, the result can be made to yield precise qualitative predictions concerning d^*, which may then be used (rather less precisely) to help make statements about C^{**}. Evidently, d^* must vary directly with α_S and indirectly with α_D and c_0. A reduction in the severity of the security constraint encourages faster diversification; a rise in c_0, implying (in the absence of a compensating fall in labour costs) an all-round decline in efficiency, has the opposite effect. A less obvious result is the effect of α_D: it can, however, be intuitively explained by noting that a rise in the coefficient implies an improved success-failure ratio for all given profit margins, hence it is no longer necessary to diversify as fast as before in order to achieve a given growth rate. α_C and β_C enter both sides of equation (6.25), and β_C is included in both the exponent and denominator of the right-hand side. It can be shown, however, that, as might be expected, d^* must vary indirectly with α_C.

Table 6.1 below suggests characteristic magnitudes.

TABLE 6.1. *Characteristic Magnitudes of Coefficients in Mathematical Version of Model* 1

Coefficient	Magnitude about
c_0	2·00
α_D	1·00
β_D	0·50
α_S	2·00
β_S	0·10
α_C	20·00
$\bar{v}$	1·0

If β_C is 2·0, it will be noted that the right-hand side of (6.25) varies only as the cube root of its base, and the optimum diversification rate is not very sensitive to the coefficients α_D, α_S and c_0. This is of very considerable assistance to qualitative analysis of the maximum growth rate, for, evidently,

$$C^{**\cdot} = \frac{1}{\dfrac{1}{\alpha_S \cdot f_C^*} + \dfrac{1}{f_D^*}} - \frac{\beta_S \, \bar{v}}{1 + \alpha_S \cdot \dfrac{f_C^*}{f_D}} \tag{6.26}$$

where

$$f_D^* \equiv \frac{\alpha_D \cdot d^*}{1 + \beta_D \cdot d^*}$$

and

$$f_C^* \equiv \frac{1}{c_0}\left(1 - \alpha_C \cdot d^{*\beta_C}\right)$$

Thus the coefficients, c_0, α_S, α_D not only influence the optimum diversification rate, through equation (6.25), but also enter the determination of the maximum growth rate directly, through their additional roles in equation (6.26). And because the former effect is insensitive, it will be found that qualitative analysis of equation (6.26) will generally be accurate even if d^* is treated as a constant. It then becomes clear that, as might be expected, $C^{**\cdot}$ varies directly with α_S and α_D — coefficients representing 'favourable' qualities in the supply and demand curves respectively — and indirectly with c_0, α_C, β_D, and β_S — coefficients representing the corresponding unfavourable qualities. In addition, if the security constraint is variable, the maximum growth rate varies indirectly with it, i.e. varies indirectly with $\bar{v}$: as would intuitively be expected, the greater the desire for security as represented by the choice of minimum valuation ratio, the slower, other things being equal, is the maximum growth rate.

From the basic equations it is also apparent that the rate of return associated with the maximum growth rate, a ratio which may loosely be referred to as the 'optimum profit rate', is given by

$$p^* = \frac{1}{\alpha_S}(C^{**\cdot} - \beta_S \, \bar{v}) \tag{6.27}$$

Substituting for $C^{**\cdot}$, we obtain

$$p^* = \left[1 \Big/ \left(\frac{1}{f_C} + \frac{\alpha_S}{f_D}\right)\right] + \left(\beta_S \cdot \bar{v} \Big/ \alpha_S \cdot \frac{f_D}{f_C}\right) \tag{6.28}$$

Thus the qualitative effect of the coefficients α_S and β_S, together with that of $\bar{v}$, are here reversed. Stock-market conditions favouring growth (such as high α_S) apparently have the opposite effect on profitability, and although the maximum growth rate varies indirectly with the minimum valuation ratio, the optimum profit rate does not, a point the significance of which is extensively discussed below. In the meantime let us summarise the qualitative conclusions as follows:

TABLE 6.2. *Summary of Qualitative Relationships in Model* 1
(+ indicates relationship is direct, − indirect)

Effect on variable: of coefficient:	$C^{**\cdot}$	p^*
α_D	+	+
β_D	−	−
c_0	−	−
α_S	+	−
β_S	+	−
$\bar{v}$	+	−

These theorems may be confirmed by experiment with Diagram 6.4.

Typical quantitative results may be obtained by inserting the magnitudes suggested in Table 6.1, and solving equation (6.25) by some suitably approximate method (a graphic solution is usually adequate). Such results are presented in Table 6.3:

TABLE 6.3. *Typical Results in Model* 1

Variable	Symbol	Approximate Value per cent
Optimum diversification rate	d^*	$12\frac{1}{2}$
Optimum profit rate	p^*	$9\frac{1}{4}$
Maximum growth rate	$C^{**\cdot}$	$8\frac{1}{2}$

The 'failure rate' in diversification is thus implicitly assumed to be about 30 per cent $(C^{**\cdot} - d^*)/d^*$ — a little high, perhaps, but considerably higher figures have been not infrequently reported empirically. The capital-output ratio, it will be found, works out at about two-fifths higher than c_0, i.e. it is implicitly assumed that, under the maximum growth conditions, there is sufficient organisational strain to cause capital to be used on average 15 per cent less efficiently than would be the case if the diversification rate were zero.

Model 1: Economic Implications

Most of the coefficients of the model, therefore, are easily interpretable and have similar qualitative effects. A firm with relatively favourable values of one or more of them will be able to grow faster and earn higher rates of return than less successful firms. For example, suppose a population of firms were alike in all respects except the value of c_0, which, as we have seen, can be taken as a general indicator of productive efficiency. Suppose all attempted (with success) to find their maximum growth rate position exactly in accordance with our hypotheses. In their optimum positions, the firms with the more favourable values of the coefficient would display above-average growth rates and above-average profit rates. Financial policies would be so adjusted that the supply of capital to the faster-growing firms was correspondingly above-average, although all valuation ratios were equal. Thus, in effect, the market would reward the more successful firms by permitting them faster growth rates without reduced valuation ratios. The situation would continue until something happened to disturb it.

We are not suggesting that such conditions would ever be observed in the real world, because, evidently, disequilibrium states are as likely in such a system as any other; but we do suggest that the picture represents a valid analogy to post-classical static equilibrium. In particular, the feature that all valuation ratios are the same reflects a condition of investor contentment with the postulated pattern of capital flow rates (as between firms), given the pattern of rates of return. In a classical system, such a condition would presumably be regarded as temporary, because, in the Marshallian long run, the differential growth rates would generate compensating forces tending to bring them (the growth rates) ultimately into equality. In our view, this conception of the long run, if it has any meaning at all, is so remote as to be academic. When demand growth is *created* by the individual firms, there is no reason why it should not continue among them at differential rates indefinitely. Similarly, when internal efficiency, as measured by c_0, varies between firms, the less efficient may continue in business for a very long time indeed. Alternatively, one can conceive of the process as the generator of the long-run size distribution among firms, damped, in all probability, by a tendency for the laggards to take in organisational slack while the leaders become complacent. Similar ideas have been present in most contemporary theories concerning the size distribution of firms, as well as in more explicit satisficing models (see below): they were first given an economic application in the highly original theory presented by J. Downie.[9] We are not wedded to a particular interpretation of our own model. We shall be content if we have succeeded in contributing a more comprehensive account of the type of basic micro-theory required to support this class of models in general.

So far we have been generally assuming that all firms are success-fully optimising. The model can also be employed to investigate the implications of other behaviour. A firm may maintain sustainable but non-maximum growth by various means, one of the most interesting of which is by deliberately setting an above optimum retention ratio. This arbitrary value could then be treated as if it were fixed, i.e. as if it were the optimum, and the maximising procedure described in the present and previous sections repeated. The 'maximum' sustainable growth rate would be lower, and the valuation ratio higher. In other words, the variation has the effect of an objective change in $\bar{v}$, and if, in addition to, or as an alternative to raising the retention ratio, the new-issue rate and leverage ratio are also similarly varied, this conclusion becomes general.

Alternatively we may consider these variations as, in effect, equivalent to variations in the level of the security constraint. Thus, unlike the other coefficients, $\bar{v}$ may be thought of as representing in part the result of deliberate financial policy, and is thus more in the nature of a decision variable than a constant. It is the outcome of choices among three true decision variables in the financial area, i.e. retention ratio, new-issue rate and gearing ratio.

This then is the moment to stop treating security as only a constraint, and to consider the possibility of a continuous trade-off between it and growth. In so doing, we remind the reader that by security we refer not only to a sense of freedom from fear of take-over, but also to any other satisfactions or dissatisfactions obtained from doing well or badly by stockholders.

The feature that $\bar{v}$ has inverse effects on the growth rate but direct effects on the rate of return is now seen to be of crucial importance. It may be explained intuitively as follows. If, starting for the sake of argument from some position of balanced growth ($D^{\cdot}=C^{\cdot}$), the retention ratio is lowered, the growth rate of capital must decline without any change in rate of return or growth rate of demand. Balance is therefore lost. For balance to be regained, the growth rate of demand must be lowered, and the growth rate of capital raised, a result which may be achieved by policy decisions implying increased profit margins: but as in any scissors-type relationship, unless one or other function is perfectly elastic, the new level at which balance is achieved must be lower than the old. Thus variation of $\bar{v}$ generates a continuous transformation between growth rate and security, on the basis of which, trade-offs, if desired, could be achieved in the usual manner.

With the present model, however, the implied shape of the resulting transformation function is not very convincing. For by our 'monotonic' assumptions, we have created a relationship between rate of return and growth rate which is inverse throughout: over all ranges of positive growth, the faster you grow the less you earn on your capital and the less your utility from security. It is time, therefore, to proceed to model 2. Before so doing, we underline a most important feature of model 1, whose significance, if not apparent immediately, will become clear later. *Given* any value of $\bar{v}$, decisions designed to improve the sustainable growth rate also enhance the profit rate, i.e. the relation is no longer inverse. Given $\bar{v}$, growth rate and rate of return are locked together by equation (6.27), and anything which favours the one must favour the other. For example, the balanced-growth curve in Diagram 6.4 implies the existence of a continuum of sustainable policies all yielding balanced growth with the given $\bar{v}$. In order to maximise the growth rate, it is necessary, we have seen, to choose a unique diversification rate and consistent profit margin such as will place the firm on the peak of this curve. But suppose, starting from the optimum position, the diversification rate is varied, i.e. the position is de-optimised. Assume that balance is maintained by a consistent adjustment of the profit margin. Then, if the variation is positive — a move in the diagram to the right along the balanced-growth curve — the growth rate is reduced but the profit margin is raised. But capital-output is also raised, and the net effect must be such as to lower the rate of return. Alternatively if the diversification rate is de-optimised leftwards, both growth rate and profit margin decline, the capital-output ratio is lowered, but the net effect is again a decline in the profit rate. Thus once $\bar{v}$ is fixed, any decision tending to raise the (balanced) growth rate also raises the profit rate, and all decisions may as well be taken on the one criterion as the other. This applies, for example, not only to decisions concerning techniques of production, but also to price, research and development policy, to the balance between imitative and differentiated expansion and, of course, to the choice of diversification rate. Both in terms of growth and in terms of profits it always pays to be efficient. This is why the criteria of profitability and volume (or growth) are so often used as synonyms in the relevant business literature. It may also explain why in the field of financial policy there is less consensus and more confusion: the choices here cannot be represented in terms of simple efficiency or maximising behaviour without a clear specification of objectives.

Model 2: Preliminary Account

Model 2, as already indicated, is destined to concentrate attention on the specific relation between profits and growth, and to eliminate the unrealities associated with our monotonic assumptions. The first step is to derive a composite relationship — representing the whole of the 'demand' side of the model — between growth of required capacity and profitability. One method of generating this curve is to postulate a 'no failures' demand model (see Chapter 4), and to assume that the curve is the correlate of continuous variation of the diversification rate. On the 'no failures' assumption the growth rate (of demand) and the diversification rate are identical, and the average rate of return is governed by the opposing forces of the effects of enhanced monopoly power on the one hand and of the increasing weight of the marketing expenses required to guarantee successes on the other. When the diversification rate is low, the first effect predominates, and the derived relationship between growth rate and profit rate is direct. But as the diversification rate is progressively raised, the second effect becomes increasingly severe and eventually overweighs the first, the relationship is reversed and the curve turns over.

A more sophisticated approach is to take the basic ideas of model 1 and appropriately modify them. We should then aim to generate a curve on which all relevant decisions (including the choice of diversification rate) were assumed to be so taken as to maximise the growth rate for all *given* rates of return, and this would by no means necessarily imply no failures in diversification. The curve could be thought of as an 'efficient' demand-growth curve, indicating the results of a condition in which, except for the decision concerning $\bar{v}$, all decisions were taken optimally (in the sense of providing maximum growth for given profitability or maximum profitability for given growth rate).

Such a curve may be constructed as follows. Consider a state of affairs where the coefficient α_S happened to be so small that both maximum growth rate and optimum diversification rate in model 1 were zero. Then postulate a small positive variation in the coefficient, after which the optimum diversification rate, profit margin and profit rate were again computed for maximum growth rate as in a normal application of model 1. We know from Table 6.2 that a rise in the coefficient α_S must raise both optimum diversification rate and maximum growth rate. But model 1 also requires certain contingent decisions leading to a fall in the profit margin; for example, marketing expenses must be increased to ensure that a sufficient proportion of the new products succeeds for balance to be maintained. Model 1 also implies that the capital-output ratio would rise; hence the rate of return associated with balance must decline. But suppose we now assume that, as a result of the increase in the growth rate, the effect of rising marketing expense associated with the optimum success ratio is more than offset by the additional profits earned through temporary monopoly in the new products which do succeed (or by the effect of the corresponding phenomenon in imitative cases). Consequently, the profit margin, when averaged over commercial operations as a whole, rises, instead of falling; at the same time, because decision-taking efficiency is positively stimulated rather than affected adversely by the departure from the humdrum conditions of zero diversification, the capital-output ratio falls, instead of rising. If the growth rate and optimum profit rates for the new α_S are computed on these modified assumptions, both will be higher than in the previous situation. Thus the relationship between growth rate and profit rate becomes direct. We may then repeat the argument, and create a curve between growth rate and profit rate which continues to rise until opposing forces take over in the manner already suggested: once the peak is passed, however, the picture is qualitatively identical to that which would be obtained by postulating similar variations in α_S in model 1.

The curve, which we shall loosely refer to as the 'demand curve', is shown in Diagram 6.5. As there presented, it postulates that a modest but positive profit rate would be obtained with a zero growth rate — the firm is obtaining modest but reliable returns from a constant catalogue of saturated products. If there were an autonomous trend in the demand for the saturated products, the next part of the curve should be virtually horizontal. But as soon as the indicated growth rate becomes large enough to require positive effort, i.e. diversification, the 'temporary monopoly' effect comes into play, and the profit rate rises linearly with the growth rate: the profit rate depends, *inter alia*, on the proportion of recently saturated items in the overall product-mix, and this, in long-run moving equilibrium, must be linearly determined by the growth rate itself.

In the example, however, we assume the trend in saturated demand to be zero. Subsequently, the 'opposition' forces may reasonably be represented as parabolic, increasing in intensity as the growth rate rises, turning the curve over at a growth rate of about 6 per cent, and then causing the profit rate to decline with

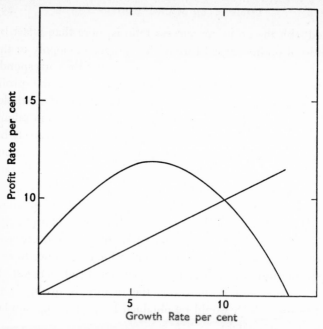

DIAGRAM 6.5. Demand Curve and Iso-Valuation Line or 'Supply Curve'

increasing rapidity until finally reaching the origin, at which point the model becomes inoperative. A reasonable approximation to the demand curve, with profit rate represented as dependent variable, would therefore be a simple parabola such as

$$p = \gamma_1 + \gamma_2\, C^{\cdot} - \gamma_3\, C^{\cdot 2} \qquad (6.29)$$

where γ_1, γ_2 and γ_3 are (positive) adjustable coefficients. If autonomous trend in saturated demand was to be included, a somewhat more complicated formulation would be required.

In Diagram 6.5 we also show a curve indicating the maximum permissible growth rate of capital on the assumption that the valuation ratio is still a constraint. Such a curve will from now on be loosely referred to as a 'supply curve'. It is, in fact, the curve, or line of equation (6.10) in model 1, with $\bar{v}$ set to unity. Variation in the magnitude of $\bar{v}$ thus shifts the supply curve bodily, and we may visualise such variation as generating a family of supply curves which are, in effect, iso-valuation-ratio lines. All combinations of growth rate and rate of return to the left of any given iso-valuation line, whether lying on the demand curve or not, must imply a stock-market situation in which the price of the stock, relative to the book value of the assets, is more favourable than with any combination on the line, and vice versa for combinations to the right of the line. Thus the maximum growth rate permitted by any given demand curve subject to any given valuation-ratio constraint may be found by setting up the iso-valuation line appropriate to the indicated constraint, and noting its furthest-right intersection with the demand curve. The area to the west of the intersection represents all those combinations, both on and below the demand curve, which are considered safe and could be made sustainable: the intersection itself represents the one among these where the growth rate is fastest. It is apparent that the optimum combination must then lie on the demand curve, which thus appears as an 'efficient' relationship between growth and profitability. Movement along the curve may be envisaged as resulting from deliberate varia-tion of $\bar{v}$, i.e. as by choice of alternative supply curves, but move-ment downwards and off the curve requires that one or more other decisions (such as choice of diversification rate) be taken non-opti-mally, in the sense of failing to maximise the growth rate for a given valuation ratio.

As the supply curve is shifted bodily upwards, without change of slope, the valuation ratio increases, while the maximum growth rate declines and the associated profit rate rises, thus confirming the corresponding theorem from model 1. The addition of a rising segment in the demand curve, however, now provides interesting qualifications. If the supply curve is moved far enough west, the most easterly intersection might eventually occur to the west of the peak of the demand curve, and the rate of return commences to decline. The firm is then in the paradoxical position that the con-straint, if it is a constraint, is causing not only growth, but also profitability to be inhibited: if diversification were accelerated, the rate of return would be expected to rise, but the financial adjust-ments necessary to maintain balance would cause such a rise in the market rate of discount that the effect of the rise in profitability would be more than offset, and the valuation ratio would decline. In this case, then, greater 'daring' (i.e. smaller $\bar{v}$) would increase not only the growth rate but also profitability, although the stock-market would nevertheless remain unapproving.

It is also worth noting that a *maximum* valuation ratio consistent with sustainable growth may be found by shifting the supply curve until it is at some point tangential to the demand curve. This position, which must lie to the left of the demand-curve peak, represents in effect the policy and growth rate required to maximise the market value of the business, and corresponds, therefore, to a 'neo-classical' solution. Evidently, it would be of some interest to find a method of presentation which could bring out these and related propositions more explicitly.

The Valuation Curve

In other words, it would be of interest to construct a curve in which the valuation ratio replaces the rate of return as the variable dependent on the growth rate. For any given demand-growth rate, the demand curve gives a rate of return. For any given rate of return, financial-policy choices are available to produce a growth rate of capital just equal to the indicated growth rate of demand. By inverting the argument of the last section of Chapter 5, it becomes apparent that the choices which there maximised the growth rate of capital for any given rate of return are also those which, for any given combination of (balanced) growth rate and rate of return, maximise the valuation ratio. Therefore, by inverting the equation representing the effect of a variable valuation ratio (5.22), it must be possible to generate a curve showing the best obtainable valuation ratio for any given point on the corresponding demand curve. This new curve, which we call the *valuation curve*, is then compounded of three basic elements: the equations of the share-valuation theory, the balance equation and the demand curve itself, i.e. as follows:

$$v = \frac{1}{\beta_S}(\alpha_S \cdot p - C^{\bullet}) \tag{6.30}$$

$$p = p(D^{\bullet}) = p(C^{\bullet}) \tag{6.31}$$

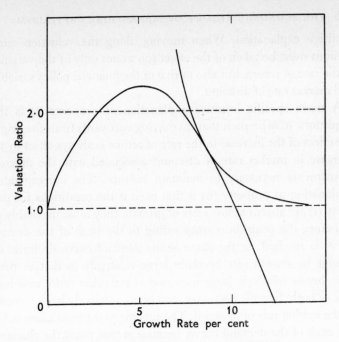

DIAGRAM 6.6. Valuation Curve and Managerial Indifference Curve

Hence,

$$v = \frac{1}{\beta_S}[\alpha_S \cdot p(C^*) - C^*] \qquad (6.32)$$

Diagram 6.6 suggests a typical valuation curve, i.e. curve of equation (6.32) above. It has the following interesting properties:

(i) It need have no positive maximum;

(ii) If it does have a maximum, this must always lie to the left of the peak of the demand curve;

(iii) Where the curve is declining, the negative slope will always be arithmetically greater than the negative slope at the corresponding value of C^* on the demand curve, and where, if anywhere, it is rising, the positive slope will always be smaller than the slope at the corresponding point on the curve.

These properties may easily be verified by differentiating v with respect to C^* in equation (6.32), and all have basically the same intuitive explanation. When moving along the valuation curve account must be taken of the effect (on v) not only of the variation of the rate of return, but also of that of the financial policy variables and market rate of discount.

A more specific intuitive explanation of property (i) is that conditions may be such that, in moving eastwards from the origin, the effect of the increase in the rate of return is always offset by the increase in market rate of discount associated with the financial adjustments necessary to maintain balance. The corresponding explanation of property (ii) is that even if the conditions for property (i) are absent at low rates of growth, they must inevitably set in before the position corresponding to the peak of the demand curve is reached: as the slope of the demand curve declines, the change in growth rate becomes large relatively to that in profit rate, hence relatively large increases in retention ratio, new-issue rate or both, become necessary, and hence relatively large increases in the market rate of discount. The turning point must come before the peak of the demand curve, because at that point the change in rate of return is zero and the valuation ratio already inevitably declining. Thus, in principle, a maximum valuation ratio can never be entirely consistent with maximum profitability!

If we provide the demand curve with the specific form (equation 6.29) suggested earlier, the specific form of the valuation curve becomes

$$v = \frac{1}{\beta_S}[C^* \cdot (\alpha_S \cdot \gamma_3 - 1) - C^{*2} \cdot \alpha_S \cdot \gamma_3 + \alpha_S \cdot \gamma_1] \qquad (6.33)$$

From which we may derive

$$C^{**}_{(v)} = \left(\gamma_2 - \frac{1}{\alpha_S}\right) \Big/ 2\gamma_3 \qquad (6.34)$$

$$C^{**}_{(p)} = \frac{\gamma_2}{2\gamma_3} \qquad (6.35)$$

where

$C^{**}_{(v)}$ = value of C^* for max. v,
$C^{**}_{(p)}$ = value of C^* for max. p,

Suppose $\gamma_1 = 0.05$, $\gamma_2 = 3$ and $\gamma_3 = 25$, while α_S and β_S continue to be set at 2·0 and 1·0 respectively. Then Table 6.4 below indicates the resulting values of the variables at the various positions of interest.

TABLE 6.4 *Values of Variables at Various Positions on Demand Curve and Valuation Curve*

Position:	Max. v	Max. p	$v = 1$
Variable:			
C^* (per cent)	5	6	10†
p (per cent)	13·75	14	10‡
v	2·25	2·2	1

† obtained by inverting equation (6.33)

‡ obtained by inverting equation (6.29)

Thus with realistic values of the coefficients, the leftward displacement of the peak of the valuation curve, as compared with that of the demand curve, appears likely to be comparatively small, a point which gains emphasis when the displacement is measured in terms of v itself or of p: it can be shown that this result obtains generally with any values of α_S and γ_2 consistent with a reasonable value of Max. p, the proportionate gap between the two growth rates being the reciprocal of the product of these coefficients. By contrast, the range of safe and sustainable growth rates lying between C^* (Max. p) and the maximum value of C^* consistent with $v = 1$, for example, is substantial. In the example, the maximum safe and sustainable growth rate for $\bar{v} = 1$ is over two-thirds greater than the maximum-profitability growth rate, and no less than twice the growth rate which would maximise the valuation ratio. For empirical and other practical purposes we shall therefore feel fairly safe in arguing as if the peaks of the two curves more or less coincided. But, we shall assume, the east ends of both curves may well have quite long tails, over which profit rates, valuation ratios and safe, sustainable growth rates can range widely.

The valuation curve incorporates the assumptions of all the previous chapters, together with the new assumptions introduced in the present chapter. It may therefore be thought of as summarising our whole micro-theory. Inasmuch as the dependent variable in the curve is presumably the main, if not the sole, element in shareholder welfare, and inasmuch as the curve appears to represent this variable and the growth rate as if in many circumstances competitive, it is important to re-emphasise that we are not in any sense implying shareholder indifference to the fruits of growth. Stockholders are assumed indifferent to the physical growth of the firm, as such, but by no means indifferent to the associated growth of dividends. A given position on the valuation curve represents a constellation of information and decisions which is supposed to continue indefinitely into the future in such a way as to create a specific expectation of a constantly growing stream of future dividends. The same set of facts also creates a specific market rate of discount at which this stream is to be capitalised. The indicated magnitude of the valuation ratio is the result of applying this discount rate to that expected annuity stream. Thus the indicated valuation ratio is the stock-market's reaction to all these aspects of the firm's situation which are relevant to investors. From our point of view, however, the curve's significance lies less in this feature than in its incorporating additional information of considerable significance for the welfare of managers.

Thus for the analysis of the general economic implications of model 2, the valuation curve has the advantage of presenting a relationship in which both variables are of a kind to enter the utility functions of either managers or shareholders quite directly, whereas the demand curve relationship involves one variable, namely the profit rate, in which the interest of both groups is inherently indirect. On the other hand, the valuation curve has some analytical limitations. For example, being based on the assumption that the firm is already on the demand curve, the valuation curve cannot be applied to non-optimal positions such as may result, for example, from satisficing behaviour (see Chapter 7 below). The valuation ratio of a firm which has taken up a position below its own demand curve cannot be found merely by dropping a perpendicular of proportionate length from the corresponding position on the valuation curve. For the analysis of such situations we still need the method of analysis based on demand curve and iso-valuation line. This method is also of value in empirical applications, there being at present considerably more data available which are appropriate for testing hypotheses framed in terms of C^* and p than in terms of C^* and v.

Model 2: Economic Interpretation

By means of the valuation curve, the model of maximising behaviour subject to minimum 'security' constraint can be made considerably more general. The most easterly intersection between the curve and any horizontal line representing a given v-value indicates the maximum growth rate permitted at that value. We then obtain the theorem that the lower the minimum v-value, the faster in all circumstances the maximum growth rate. When, however, the constrained v-level is higher than the level at which the curve cuts the axis, the firm faces a situation in which satisfactory security involves not only a maximum growth rate but also a minimum. This explains the often-reported executive who says his firm must grow in order to survive. If the minimum v-level, i.e. $\bar{v}$, is the one at which not only subjective but also objective risks of take-over become high, firms failing to meet the condition will tend not to be empirically observed. It is likely that failure to grow fast enough is in real life responsible for the largest proportion of actually successful take-over raids, as against mere threats or fears of raids. The firm threatened with take-over as a result of attempting to grow too fast is much more easily able to defend its position by convincing the market that it can rectify the situation than the firm whose proper defence requires a convincing promise of acceleration. The first firm has merely moved too far along the efficient demand curve, the second is in all likelihood right off the curve, and to boot unwilling, or unable, to get on it. The first firm has merely to lower the diversification rate, raise prices and/or reduce marketing expenditures; the second must become more efficient. Nevertheless, it is by no means unknown for a firm to be taken over as a result of attempting to diversify too fast, and not infrequently the new management initiates a policy of negative diversification, i.e. reduces the absolute length of the catalogue, this being probably the most efficient first step in a process of adjustment towards a lower long-run diversification rate.

Another case of some interest is the one where the relation

between the position of the valuation curve and the level of $\bar{v}$ is such that there is no intersection at all. This may be interpreted as a situation where the management would rather put the firm into voluntary liquidation than face the lowest risk of take-over consistent with remaining in business.

Maximising Managerial Utility

At last we are ready to consider a model in which security and growth may be traded off continuously. Let us presume a managerial utility function

$$U = U(C^{*}, v) \tag{6.36}$$

continuously differentiable and endowed with the usual properties. C^{*} and v then stand respectively as representatives of the manifold satisfactions associated with power, prestige and salary, on the one hand, and security from take-over, plus stock-market approval, on the other. As these variables are representing more fundamental utilities, the form of the function is determined not only by the underlying psychological preference system, but also by the factors determining the relationships between the variables and fundamental utility. For example, the utility associated with any given growth rate depends not only on the strength of the preference for growth of salary, power and prestige, but also on the factors determining the relationship between the growth rate of the firm and the rate at which enhanced 'quantities' of these satisfactions accrue to the management (an example of such a factor would be the Beta coefficient in the salary model in Chapter 2, p. 95). Of more immediate importance are the factors determining the relationship between a given valuation ratio and the strength of the associated sense of security or insecurity as the case may be. Here we might imagine that the factor lying behind v was some measure of the probability of being taken over if a given level of v were maintained. It would then follow that the utility of any given level of v would depend not only on the management's taste for security as such, but on the prevalence of take-over raiders and on the actual valuation ratios of comparable other firms. Thus the utility function, as we have defined it, depends not only on the idiosyncrasies of the management concerned, but also on the nature of the environment in general and the behaviour of other managers in particular.

The position of maximum managerial utility is found at the tangent between an indifference curve derived from the utility function and the relevant transformation curve, which is, of course, the valuation curve. In Diagram 6.6 we sketch in such a position, and show that on reasonable assumptions a utility-maximising management might choose to grow almost twice as fast and serve the shareholders a third less well than a valuation-maximising, or 'neo-classical', management. The valuation curve, it will be remembered, is more or less consistent with the quantitative assumptions suggested above (p. 245), and the shape and position of the indifference curve is consistent with the arguments below. Evidently, in economic terms the difference between 'managerial' and 'neo-classical' behaviour may be considerable.

The indifference curves will be convex to the origin in the usual fashion, the valuation curve is concave, and the tangency solution will occur at a point on the valuation curve which is either at the peak or to the right of it. It is impossible for the position to occur to the left of the peak, and if it occurs precisely at the peak, the tangential indifference curve must at that point be horizontal. We then obtain the following theorems:

(i) Only if the indifference curves are all horizontal throughout their entire length is the case where maximum utility occurs at the peak of the valuation curve inevitable: this would be a case where the management attached no direct utility to growth in any circumstances;

(ii) If all the curves are convex throughout their entire extent, managerial utility maximisation must always involve a faster growth rate and, in general, a lower profit rate than would shareholder utility maximisation

Case (i) represents that of a 'traditional' or in some sense classical utility function. Whoever or whatever controls the firm, they are motivated only to maximise the value of the stock. Case (ii) represents the more general one where some degree of 'managerial' motivation not only exists but is also effective decision-wise.

It is, however, by no means unlikely that the indifference curves of the managerial utility function would have a feature that is not usually found in, for example, the utility function of a consumer; the feature is that at some objectively ascertainable v-level the function might well become discontinuous. For managers are assumed to include valuation ratio in their utility functions for two reasons, to avoid pain from fear of take-over and to gain pleasure from stock-market approval. As the ratio is reduced, the first element is likely to become increasingly important. At some point, one would have thought, the danger of take-over must become so great that not even an infinite increase in the growth rate would compensate for a further increase in risk. If so, the indifference curves would all join in a common horizontal segment at the v-level in question. In effect, any combination of growth rate and valuation ratio lying below this line would yield zero utility; above the line the form of the curves would be 'normal'. They would branch out, convex to the origin and upwards from successive points along the horizontal minimum line, the west-east ordering representing ordinal utility. (A useful interpretation of the horizontal minimum line is that it represents the valuation ratio at which the probability of take-over becomes unity.)*

From this form of utility function, there would be at least three significant implications. First, we should expect to find empirically that observations of firms displaying very low valuation ratios were rare: in terms of the demand-curve diagram, if, as we should expect, observations were scattered both by variations in the positions of the curves and by non-maximising behaviour, the density of observations would decline (and with increasing rapidity) as we moved through the diagram diagonally and downwards, i.e. south-easterly. Second, if the curves were so placed that tangency between valuation curve and indifference curve occurred elsewhere than on the latter's horizontal segment, any favourable shift in the valuation curve, whether towards north, north-east or even east, would inevitably displace the utility-maximising position in such a way that in the new position, as compared with the old, not only the chosen growth rate would be higher, but so also both rate of

---

* Since the foregoing was set in print, the author's attention has been drawn to the possibility that the argument might more effectively be interpreted in terms of a lexicographic utility function, a concept of which he was previously totally ignorant.

return and valuation ratio: the increase in managerial 'real income' would be taken out partly in faster growth, partly in enhanced security. Hence the firms in what are loosely known as 'growth' industries — i.e. industries in which the demand curve of the representative firm is unusually favourably placed in any of the above senses — should display not only above-average growth rates but also above-average profit rates and valuation ratios.

Third, it is not impossible that the relative positions of indifference curves and valuation curves would be such that the tangency position occurred on the horizontal segment of the indifference curve and hence at the peak of the valuation curve. The maximum possible and minimum tolerable valuation ratios would then be identical. This is evidently a more sophisticated way of arriving at a classical type of result. If take-over raiders were cheap and elastic in supply in the sense originally described in Chapter 1 (p. 39), *their* rate of discount would be as low or lower than the maximum obtainable rate of return, hence the probability of take-over would become virtually certain at any valuation ratio less than the maximum. The picture becomes complete if we assume that by some competitive process the demand curves of all firms become identical; then the minimum v-level is unambiguously defined as that associated with the maximum profit rate, and firms could remain free of take-over only by choosing a position yielding a higher ratio. Since, as we have seen, the range of such positions is typically small (they are those lying between the peak of the demand curve and a point slightly to the left of the peak of the valuation curve), maximum utility would imply much the same policy combination for every firm; no firm failing to keep on the demand curve could survive, a result which has evident analogies with the long-run equilibrium in post-classical theories of imperfect competition. In the absence of these unrealistic conditions, however, a position of managerial utility maximisation well to the east of the peaks of both demand curve and valuation curve may be entirely sustainable, except in the sense that, in the very long run, if growth rates vary one firm must swallow the economy. The same result is obtained even when the positions are subject to stochastic disturbance, and theories about the size distribution of business firms [10]

usually postulate some damping factor, such as satisficing behaviour, in order to explain the evident fact that in the real world
concentration never reaches this level. It is nevertheless convenient to postulate a situation in which, although take-over raiders
are scarce, the demand curves and indifference curves of every
firm in the economy are the same. If take-over raiders are scarce,
the common indifference curve will be placed low relatively to the
common demand curve, and maximum utility is likely to occur to
the right of the peak of the valuation curve in the non-horizontal
segment of an indifference curve. This position could be maintained
throughout the economy indefinitely. It represents the paradigm
of managerial capitalism. The common demand curve by no means
implies the existence of perfect or pure competition, but merely
that the financial dynamics of imperfect competition are the same
for all. Partial monopolies are ever being created, ever exploited
and ever eaten away by new competition, while the average relationship between growth rate and profit rate is everywhere the
same. These constantly renewed monopoly profits are never as
high as they might be, because the process requires manufacturers
to devote considerable resources to sustaining it. The common
growth rate and common profit rate actually chosen might then be
thought of as representing the corresponding ratios for the economy as a whole. Evidently, whether any particular combination
was actually possible would depend on macro-economic factors
which have yet to be considered.

Once the assumption of identical demand curves and indifference
curves is dropped — firms being permitted to grow at differential
rates for as long as is reasonable without manifest absurdity — the
system has no particular rationality in terms of resource allocation
theory, except in the down-to-earth sense that it does tend to ensure that capital flows faster to the firms most able to use it. Firms
which — perhaps on account of good luck or good guidance in
discovering latent needs — face favourably placed demand curves
will be able to grow faster than others, provided only that they
display no offsetting tendency to be above-average in their tastes
for security. Here again, however, this is in no sense a macro-
optimum. The restraints on individual firms imposed by the desire

for security mainly enforce a degree of conformity of practice as between managerial organisations only: there is no reason to suppose they necessarily require the representative firm to behave in some manner which is optimal from the point of view of the community. In the absence of 'classical' take-over conditions, the position of the horizontal segment of the indifference curve of the individual firm is conditioned partly by that management's individual tastes and partly by the prevailing practices of other individual firms, the latter, in effect, determining the amount of security obtainable with a given valuation ratio. Therefore the dynamic allocation mechanism implied in the system functions in a relative sense only: it does not in any obvious way determine the capital flow into the corporate sector as a whole, but does ensure that the lion's share of the total is directed towards those firms with relatively high 'growth opportunities'. Given the average yield offered, investors as a whole might prefer the average growth rate of corporations to be different from what it is, but their power to express such preference is limited by the difficulty of finding comparable alternative outlets for funds. The corporations have a partial monopoly of commercial efficiency, and a partial monopoly of high-earning, inflation-protected, easily marketable securities. Consequently the investors' influence is inevitably marginal rather than absolute, and it is by no means unlikely that not only is the average corporate retention ratio to some extent collectively determined by managerial choices, but that by this means the corporations powerfully influence the national propensity to save: there is little evidence that either cyclical or secular changes in the average retention ratio tend to be offset by opposing changes in the personal propensity to save out of dividends. In order to 'rectify' this situation, investors would need to bring about far-reaching institutional changes — of which stock-option schemes provide only one example — tending to tip the managerial utility function in favour of v and away from C^*. To date, as we have seen, such changes on these lines as have occurred have not gone far. Consequently, what determinacy the system possesses must be macro-economic rather than micro-economic in origin. That discussion is reserved for Chapter 8.

CHAPTER SEVEN

BEHAVIOUR AND EVIDENCE

BEFORE finally turning to the question of 'macro' implications, we now, as promised in the Introduction, relate the micro theory to existing statistical evidence. This is also the most convenient moment to keep another promise, namely to consider the possible effects of satisficing behaviour (see p. 109). For, whatever his position in the debate between the behaviourists and the rationalists, one cannot deny that the behaviourist arguments are of crucial relevance in any empirical application. First, therefore, we state our general view about behaviourism in economics, then the application to our theory; then we attempt to satisplice the discussion to the empirical data.

Satisficing and All That

There is one proposition which, so far as the author is aware, not even the most ardent behaviourist would deny, namely that no person or organisation can satisfice at a utility level higher than would be theoretically obtainable from the maximising position: a maximum is after all a maximum. (We admit this begs the question of the psychological reality of a preference system.) On the contrary, the drive of satisficing theory derives from the possibility that in many cases the maximising solution may be so remote as to be of academic interest only. The author, however, believes that these cases are in practice rare. He also believes that if the behaviouristic approach were carried too far, attention could well be excessively diverted from fundamental problems towards the no doubt influential but essentially petty dynamics of the multiplicity of processes leading to sub-optimal stability in particular cases. Thus in several extant satisficing models, there is no way of telling whether the dynamic relationships postulated are consistent with the requirements of the underlying structure of the problem under investigation. If, for example, one wishes to postulate a relationship between the time rate of change of reward and the corresponding rate of change of effort, one must also specify the static structure from which these frictional relationships are derived (for example, the static transformation curve between effort and result). To put the point another way, Professor Simon once drew an analogy[1] with a man searching for a needle in a haystack which contained not one needle but many, all varying in sharpness. Rather than continuing until he believed he had found the sharpest needle in the whole stack, he would stop when he found one 'sharp enough' for his immediate purpose. But the economic interpretation of this is ambiguous. How do we know there is not a continuous relationship between the sharpness of the needle and the efficiency of the subsequent activity? Suppose the man were partnering his wife in a competition with a number of other couples to see who could find a needle and carry out a specified sewing task in the shortest total time: how would 'sharp enough' then be defined?

In rejoinder, the behaviourist would no doubt point out that even if the husbands in the example knew the relationship between time spent in search and the most probable sharpness of the best needle found (which characteristically they would not), and that even supposing they knew the relationship between sharpness and sewing speed not only for their own wives but for all the other competitors' wives also, they would still be faced with a horribly difficult optimising problem which might well prove amenable only to some application of game theory. The optimum strategy in extended form might have to specify how much longer the player should continue to search after any given discovery at any given stage of the search for all given previous sequences of discoveries. What more likely than that most players would instead decide to stop searching when they had found a needle of some arbitrary minimum sharpness? Satisficing theory would then begin to bite were it able to show that, if such a game were played repeatedly, the arbitrary cut-off level would be likely to be subject to a stable adjustment process based on experience. In a maximising theory, the adjustments would eventually result in the discovery of the strategy which maximised the expectation of a win. In a satisficing theory, by contrast, the result is not necessarily optimal, and the subject is supposed never to discover that by behaving otherwise he might improve his expectations. But the point we wish to emphasise is that, whether one believes the subject will satisfice or maximise, the basic structure of the problem must be specified first in order to begin any analysis: we must know the rules of the game, and, if unable to catch our haystack, at least must find our husband. Whether the players believe it or not, the result of the game will depend on this structure, as much when they satisfice as when they maximise.

And in many cases a realistic formulation of the satisficing model implies an unstable solution, in which case it is more than likely that the system will 'explode' to the maximum. To us, therefore, the main significance of satisficing theory, in relation to long-run problems of the type with which this book has been concerned, is essentially empirical. Having ascertained the nature of optimal (i.e. managerial utility-maximising) behaviour, we shall expect empirically to observe a great deal of scatter due not only to inter-firm differences in the positions of functions, but also to sub-optimal satisficing. The nature and direction of displacement, however, can only be suggested by specific assumptions. At present, there exists no general theory of satisficing. There are only examples.

Another difficulty is that since its invention, the word itself has come to be used in a wide variety of senses, and one suspects indeed, that its inventor cunningly intended just this to happen. There is one particular use which seems to us particularly confusing, if not plain wrong. This is the sense in which any form of behaviour which we would describe as 'managerial' is called satisficing behaviour.[2] The usage seems implicitly to assume that once the objective of maximising stockholder welfare is relaxed and managerial utility permitted to count, only a satisficing theory is appropriate: management, it is assumed, cannot of its nature possess any kind of clearly defined utility function on which it might be possible to maximise. It is then usually stated that management is likely to set up satisficing levels on a wide variety of dimensions — leverage, retentions, valuation ratio, rate of return, size, growth and many others. It is rarely indicated, however, whether this behaviour is supposed to result from the existence of discontinuities in a utility function or from what the present author would define as true satisficing behaviour (i.e. behaviour arising from various forms of ignorance as to how maximum utility might be achieved). Nor is the rationality of including so many variables adequately explained. Myron Gordon, for example, says,

'. . . Management has also (in addition to leverage) a satisfactory dividend, share of market, return on investment, price of its stock, etc.[3]'

But what happens when, as in both Professor Gordon's own stock-market theory and ours, dividend policy, rate of return and rate of growth combine together to determine the price of the stock, and so make such a system manifestly overdetermined? And surely it is inadequate merely to assert that management cares about the price of the stock without first carefully considering why this should be so? For only when we have a rational account of the basic motivation can we specify an appropriate utility function, or, if programming language is preferred, appropriate objective functions. And only when the relevant functions are adequately specified are we likely to be able to derive strong axioms of preference and behaviour. Dare we suggest that, because of contemporary prevalence in Certain Places of neo-classical ideology, 'satisficing' is deliberately being degraded to mean almost any form of behaviour which is, in the economic sense, non-normative? If so, we do not think this very helpful.

None of these remarks should be taken as implying a belief that the behaviouristic approach has no application to a well-specified problem such as we have attempted to develop in this book. Far from it. We have already made considerable use of implicit satisficing concepts in the constrained levels of leverage, valuation ratio and security in general, which were deployed at various stages of the earlier analysis. Until we adopted the continuous utility function, we assumed, in effect, that security was satisficed while growth was attemptedly maximised. We could as well perhaps have assumed these roles to have been reversed. It is also possible for satisficing to occur on both dimensions simultaneously: satisficing levels of both growth rate and valuation ratio might be established, outside which, if either was violated, the firm would behave as if utility had become zero; inside the constraints, on the other hand, any combination meeting both would be as good as any other. Then satisfactory utility would arise anywhere along some rather arbitrarily determined segment of the valuation curve. Here, rather than some internal adjustment process, the most likely determinants of the limits would in fact be external: the firm would be increasingly likely to decide that a given valuation-ratio and growth-rate combination was unsatisfactory the further it deviated from the observed centre of gravity of an external population of comparable competitors. In other words, so long as we considered only firms who were at least on (rather than somewhere below) their own demand curves, we should expect to find them scattered along their corresponding valuation curves in a distribution which had a well-defined mode but might well be skew: for example, it is not unlikely that the stimulus to attempt to pull back towards the centre would increase with the magnitude of the deviation more rapidly in the case of valuation ratio than in the case of growth rate; hence we should expect more spreading of the deviations on the growth rate side than on the 'security' side. Empirical observation would then probably be unable to discriminate between this situation and the predictions of the more orthodox hypothesis where all firms were assumed to be maximising, but the optimum positions were disturbed by differences in data. And since we have already admitted that the utility function is necessarily conditioned by the environment, the theoretical contribution of the introduction of satisficing assumptions is here relatively slight.

As soon, however, as we let firms wander off their demand curves, the picture becomes rather different. Such firms are experiencing organisational slack. They will grow more slowly for given security, experience less security for given growth rates, or, more likely, experience low security and slow growth together. In a 'bad' case, the firm would be growing slowly, be earning a poor rate of return, be compelled to adopt a relatively high retention ratio in order to finance even this modest growth rate, and hence be displaying a low valuation ratio and be in considerable danger of take-over. But if things became bad enough, according to the satisficing theory, the unpleasantness of the situation would eventually stimulate the taking-in of slack and some actual improvement. Oscillations would thus occur around a centre which was significantly sub-optimal, and if all firms were subject to the same type of hiccoughs, there is no reason why the collective mean should not be sub-optimal also. No one who has worked in an administrative organisation can fail to recognise the realism of the picture.

There are, however, good reasons for believing that the chances of finding the behaviouristic norm in any given position diminish with the distance of this position from the optimum position. In the case of model 2, satisficing deviations can only occur within the area enclosed by the demand curve, because, by definition, the demand curve represents all the possibilities permitted when slack is minimal. Then, we argue, if the optimum position is some point on the demand curve, the greater the spatial distance of any given point within the curve from the optimum point, the less likely is a satisficing centre of gravity to be found there. For over a wide range of quantitative assumptions concerning the values of adjustment coefficients, satisficing models tend to be rather un-damped, and it is likely, therefore, that in the course of oscillation the 'ceiling' represented by the demand curve will frequently be hit. But the firm must be presumed not fully to understand this cause of the apparent failure of its efforts to do better, and the reaction is therefore likely to be softened, i.e. the reverse swing of the pendulum (reappearance of slack) will be less marked than if no ceiling had been present. We shall therefore empirically expect to observe firms in various stages of the process, scattered in a diagram such as Diagram 6.5, with the means of measured growth rate and rate of return intersecting at a point which bears at least some relation to the theoretical optimum, and with the density of observations two-dimensionally skewed around this centre, in the sense that more observations would be expected to lie between the centre and the optimum position (or between the centre and the demand curve) than in the opposite direction. We may also expect additional bias from the fact that the stimulus to take in slack may be more effective in relation to one variable than the other. For

K

example, because the consequences of being taken over are much more unpleasant than the consequences of growing slowly, a given downward deviation in the valuation ratio may be more effective than a corresponding deviation in the growth rate. Therefore, in a demand curve diagram such as 6.5, we should expect observations not only to thin out as we moved south-westerly, but also as we moved south-easterly. For example, if firms were setting minimum satisfactory levels of the valuation ratio ($\bar{v}$ in our earlier discussions), they would tend to take in slack in order to avoid crossing the iso-valuation lines corresponding to those levels. The iso-valuation line, it will be remembered, is a rising diagonal running north-easterly through the diagram from a point near the origin; therefore this form of behaviour would produce a scatter pattern in which not only would observations become generally less dense as we moved in any downward direction from the centre of the distribution, but also in which the average size of 'vertical' deviations (negative deviations of the valuation ratio from its own mean) would notably diminish as we moved from west to east. This implies, as already indicated, that observations thin out both south-westerly and south-easterly, with corresponding consequences for measured regression patterns. Such a prediction should be testable.

So far, however, we have done no more than attempt to apply satisficing assumptions of the type characteristic in the literature, assumptions which were mainly developed for application to situations in which, however 'behaviouristic' the behaviour of the managers, the 'higher' objectives of the organisation remained essentially orthodox. We now attempt to develop a satisficing model more specifically designed for the problems discussed in this book.

In our view, the essence of satisficing is human reaction to having to take decisions in ignorance of their probable outcomes. Our theory not only presents subjects with a difficult maximising problem, but also with the considerable problem of merely maintaining decision consistency. Apart from the question of how the growth rate should be maximised, there is the more elemental but by no means easy question of how growth is to be made sustainable, of how, that is, the firm is to ensure that decisions will be consistent with balance between growth rate of demand and growth rate of capacity. Although we have denied the possibility of a persistent trend in the degree of capacity-utilisation in the long run, no one can deny that short-run utilisation fluctuations are not only possible, but belong to everyday experience of all business firms. Furthermore the level of utilisation is particularly likely to play the role of stimulus in satisficing behaviour, and, indeed, a wide variety of behaviouristic models have been based on this.[4]

Such models frequently make use of the idea of adjustable aspirations.[5] The subject, faced with a problem involving effort in order to obtain reward, is supposed to set up some initial, rather arbitrarily chosen, target or 'aspiration level'. The initial aspiration level is the actual reward with which at that time he believes he would be satisfied. He then makes an effort and achieves a reward. If the result is less than the aspiration ('negative goal discrepancy'), at the next round effort is stepped up and aspiration reduced, and conversely if the first-round discrepancy is positive. If the process continues it may in some circumstances lead ultimately to a stable solution in which effort, reward and goal-discrepancy remain constant at a level which has no particular relation to the optimum; in other cases, stability is impossible until a maximum is reached.[6] Although the psychological literature on which such ideas as the above are based now seems rather dated,[7] their possible applications to the balanced-growth problem are evident. For example, imagine a management attempting to maximise growth subject to a minimum security constraint as in the original version of model 1. But suppose they have only a most incomplete picture of the nature of the problem; not only are they ignorant of the values of the parameters, they do not really understand the structure. They set an aspiration level of balanced growth, not necessarily the maximum. There exists a vector of policy decisions which would at least provide the aspired result, but even this they do not know how to find. Instead they choose any set of apparently reasonable policies in the vague hope that these will prove satisfactory. In the event the decisions prove inconsistent, growth is unbalanced and at least one of the relevant rates, say the growth rate of demand, fails to satisfy — the firm has permitted too high a profit margin for the diversification rate. As likely as not, however, the cause of the failure will continue to be misunderstood, 'demand' will appear to have been constraining growth and the supply of finance to have become excessive. If then, rather than adjusting the profit-margin variables and diversification rate, this management, following the behaviour pattern described above, instead reduces the *aspiration* level (believing perhaps that they had been aspiring to the impossible), they would probably decide to reduce the growth rate of capacity in order to bring it into line with the arbitrarily arrived-at growth rate of demand. This could be done by means of financial decisions having the effect of raising the valuation ratio to a level higher than that which was originally felt to represent the safe minimum. They would then satisfice at a growth rate which was in every sense sub-optimal. A similar application could be made in the case where the utility function was continuous.

A firm which had reached this kind of position would inform investigators that it was not troubled by shortage of finance, meaning that it could increase the growth rate of capacity without taking risks considered likely to be excessive (or without visiting 'unreasonable' consequences on shareholders). However, had it so happened that the initial decisions had led the growth rate of demand to exceed that of capacity, although the adjustment process would have still produced a sub-optimal growth rate, it would not have produced the sensation of financial plenty. On the contrary, the firm would have pulled down the demand growth rate to match the finance supply, and would tend to report that it would be possible to grow faster if only capital were more plentiful. This may explain why even among large corporations much of the evidence on the subject of capital supply is conflicting, and also why there are such notable oscillations in the financial atmosphere within individual firms. It may also explain why senior executives seem to feel that, at any given time, they are usually faced with some one dominant problem: sometimes it is 'finance', sometimes 'demand', sometimes 'production'.[8]

The result is a solution entirely consistent with the dynamical outlook of the leading satisficing theorists. The problem we have posed is that of ensuring that the profits earned in period 1 are sufficient to attract or provide the necessary capital for capacity expansion in period 2; in terms of classical dynamics, the rate of change of profits must be in balance with the rate of change of demand. By postulating a certain pattern of reactions to dynamic discrepancies, we have shown how a solution may be found which is as much the result of the methods and accidents of the decision process as of a rational evaluation of optima. The statistical implications would be a tendency for companies to spread along demand and valuation curves in a manner which had no particular relation to the utility maximum, and was not necessarily concentrated round that position. Unless there are other (satisficing) constraints on v or C^* the distribution would not necessarily be skew, and might well be spatially rectangular. Here we assume that the result is at least on the demand curve. But the behaviour could also incorporate organisational slack, in which case a similar equilibrium would occur on a plane somewhere within the demand curve. In reality, of course, we shall expect to observe many examples of these various causes of scatter simultaneously.

The presence of the behaviour would also be consistent with another familiar observation, namely that a substantial proportion of large corporations control investment decisions by means of a 'target rate of return'.[9] One of the problems in sustaining balanced growth in a programme of diversification is that not only are the results of decisions uncertain, but, particularly in the case of new products, many must be taken both consistently and *sequentially*. If the firm does not know the shape of the demand-growth function (and, since the curve relates to events many of which are unique, there is a sense in which such knowledge is impossible), even if it well understands the finance-supply relationship, it will find particular difficulty in ensuring that the profits earned by new products launched today will be sufficient to support the capacity expansion required if and when today's new products succeed. In face of this problem, an excellent method of ensuring that growth will at least be balanced is to lay down a rule that no new product should be launched unless an unbiassed estimate of its prospects suggests a minimum probability of success and a minimum contribution to the firm's overall profitability position. The diversification rate actually arrived at then appears as an indirect consequence of the rules; provided the latter are well chosen and forecasts unbiased, at least growth in the long run will be balanced whatever the outcome. The 'target rate of return' thus appears as essentially a device for maintaining consistency. Many observers have confirmed this. Professor Baumol,[10] for example, gave almost precisely such an explanation for his observation that many of the firms who consulted him appeared to be attempting to maximise turnover subject to a minimum profit constraint: the profitability minimum represented, he thought, an estimate of what was required for consistency with long-run growth.

Our model provides that for every long-run growth rate there is a consistent rate of return. Therefore, every target rate of return, if actually maintained, is consistent with some balanced long-run growth rate. The latter may or may not be the maximum. There is no reason why, by a learning process, the firm should not find the target return associated with a maximum growth rate, provided (and the proviso is admittedly serious) that the optimum conditions are in the long run reasonably constant. If, as is more likely, the optimum conditions are always changing, the target rate of return and associated growth rate may well come to be settled by a satisficing procedure.

Thus 'target return' behaviour is consistent with both maximising and satisficing in a basically managerial model. It is also apparently consistent with neo-classical behaviour — the target rate would be the exogenous 'normal rate of profit', or 'cost of capital'. The acid distinction between our own and the neo-classical explanation is this. The neo-classical philosopher simply asserts that investment is not to be undertaken for expected returns below the target rate, because to do so would be both 'non-economic', and (probably) non-optimal for shareholders. We on the contrary assert that investment below the target rate is not undertaken because to do so would lead to inconsistencies and be probably non-optimal for managers. There is no evidence whatsoever that the rates employed are calculated by reference to stock-market indications of the true cost of capital, whatever that may be. Such exceptions as there are test the rule well: they are found mainly in replies given by managers who are still in business school!

In contrast with inability to rationalise the target in classical terms, managers are often able to give reasonable accounts of why it is necessary to set targets at all. Most of these relate in one sense or another to the problem of consistency, and not a few specifically mention the need for sustainable growth. Only a very few mention stockholders. Support for a satisficing type of interpretation is given by the fact that many respondents merely argue that something vaguely unpleasant would happen to both the firm and to themselves if profits were unduly low: profits, it is so often said, are necessary both for survival and growth, and growth is often necessary for survival (see model 2). Inter-firm variation in target rates of return is therefore quite consistent with either maximising or satisficing in our model, following the many variations in the conditions controlling individual situations. We believe these arguments to be conclusive, and with them conclude the section.

Econometric Support

We have repeatedly indicated that orthodox econometric measurements may not easily discriminate between our models and potential rivals, or between alternative interpretations of our models as such: in truth, despite appearances, the theory of the individual firm presents the statistician with a surprisingly acute identification problem. We have also indicated that we nevertheless plan a substantial programme of econometric research intended to test the ideas developed in this book and to contribute to knowledge in the area generally. There already exist, however, two excellent American econometric studies designed to test a wide variety of hypotheses in the theory of the firm, both of which deal in variables which play major roles in our own models. The types of hypotheses both studies were intended to test were, of course, different from ours, and it is of some interest, therefore, to set the findings against our comparable predictions.

The two studies to which we refer are those of Meyer and Kuh on the one hand and Myron Gordon on the other, the first published in 1956 and the second in 1962.[11] Meyer and Kuh provided, among many other things, simple correlation coefficients between retention ratio and growth rate of gross assets for a large sample of

U.S. firms by 17 industries and for five separate years, 1946–1950.[12] They also provided (Table 13) partial correlation coefficients between growth rate and rate of return — with certain other variables held constant — on an otherwise similar basis, except that three industries were in this case omitted. In what follows, all our references are to the 70 observations relating to the 14 industries which were common to both sets of data. The sample size varied between industries, but for no one industry was it less than thirty.

Myron Gordon employed two samples of just under 50 firms each, one drawn from the Machinery group, and other from Food Manufacturing. His time-period was 1954–58, but, for the results with which we are concerned, the appropriate data were presented on the basis of annual averages, rather than, as in Meyer and Kuh, moving cross-sections. A wide variety of simple correlations is available, from which we select for examination those between growth rate and rate of return, growth rate and retention ratio and retention ratio and rate of return: because the data are averaged, there are only two measurements of each coefficient.

What predictions would our own theory imply for these observations? We first note that as the observations do not include the valuation ratio, we must work mainly with the demand curve diagram, always bearing in mind that the valuation ratio is an important influence in the model, and being prepared, therefore, to posit the possible effects of security restraints where appropriate. Secondly, we note that if we were to attempt to take account of the possibilities inherent in the rather limited range of conditions in which firms might be positioned to the left of the peak of the demand curve, we should create considerable confusion without, in all probability, adding much to the argument: we therefore assume that all firms which are on the demand curve at all are always either at or to the right of the peak. Hence we state the 'ideal' hypothesis, which is that all firms should be found at their utility-maximising positions on, but somewhere to the right of, the peak of the curve. This position is theoretically determined by the tangency solution on the valuation curve. We then consider the various forms of disturbance to the ideal position which may be expected to produce scatter in cross-section data.

One source of scatter would be that resulting from inter-firm variations in the position of the demand curve and/or from satisficing deviations due to organisational slack. Such disturbances may alternatively be defined as those which would be observed even if all firms had the same utility function. We call them type A. Another form of scatter is that attributable to inter-firm variations in the proximate utility function and/or to satisficing behaviour in respect of the relation between security and growth, leading firms to take up scattered and somewhat arbitrarily determined positions *along* the demand curve. We call these type B.

We shall assume that these two types of disturbance cover all the analytically important forms of scatter, and shall expect both to be present simultaneously. We therefore predict a bi-variate frequency distribution of growth rate and rate of return, which will also determine the corresponding cross-correlations between these two variables and the retention ratio. In effect, the relevant variables form a tri-variate distribution, whose internal structure is expected to be influenced in particular ways to be predicted by the theory. For example, suppose a group of firms was scattered in the demand-curve diagram in such a way as to set up a rather flat regression line between profit rate and growth rate: then our theory predicts that among these firms there will also be found a positive correlation between growth rate and retention ratio, the reason being that we know that the increase in growth rate along the regression line is large relatively to that in profit rate, and we expect that the major burden of the additional finance will therefore have to be carried by increased retentions. Conversely, if the regression slope is positive and steep, we may expect the correlation between growth rate and retention ratio to be negative. In both these cases there is a positive correlation between growth rate and profit rate, however (although in the second the regression coefficient is higher), and the theoretical cross-correlation between profit rate and retention ratio is determined accordingly: in the first case this must be positive, in the second negative.

Type B disturbances, because they occur along the downward-sloping segment of the demand curve, must evidently imply a negative regression of profit rate on growth rate. This must mean a positive correlation between growth rate and retention ratio, hence a negative correlation between retention ratio and profit rate. It also means a negative correlation between growth rate and valuation ratio. The effect of type-A disturbances is less clear, because at least at first it would seem that organisational slack might take a firm anywhere. We can, however, make the distinction, suggested in the previous paragraph, between those cases in which the positive regression of profit rate on growth rate is small and those in which it is large, together with the associated predictions for the other correlations as described. We will call the former case type A(1) and the latter, type A(2). An A(1) disturbance typically represents the position of a firm whose organisational slack takes the form of failing to grow as fast as the observed rate of return would permit, while in an A(2) deviation we might say the firm was failing to earn the profits that the growth rate would permit. Remembering that iso-valuation lines are diagonals in the demand-curve diagram, it can also be inferred that a type A(1) disturbance, when considered as a movement westward, is likely to carry the firm onto a higher iso-valuation line, while an A(2) disturbance, considered as a movement southward, is likely to do the opposite: consequently, A(1) disturbances set up negative correlation between growth rate and valuation ratio, and hence negative correlation between valuation ratio and profit rate; A(2) disturbances set up positive correlation on both counts.

Let us signify the *correlation* coefficient between any pair of variables x and y by x, y, and summarise to this point as follows:

TABLE 7.1 *Summary of Predictions for Various Disturbance Types*

Sign of Correlation Coefficient:	$C^{\cdot}, p$	$C^{\cdot}, r$	p, r	$C^{\cdot}, v$	p, v
Type of Disturbance: A_1	+	+	+	−	−
A_2	+	−	−	+	+
B	−	+	−	−	+

The last two columns of Table 7.1 cannot be applied because we do not have appropriate data, but are of some analytical and practical interest nevertheless. From the practical point of view, they well illustrate the complexities and dangers involved in translating theories of the firm into statistical predictions: for example, it would be perfectly possible, the table shows, to observe a negative correlation between rate of return and valuation ratio. From the analytical point of view the significance of the columns lies in demonstrating the valuation-ratio changes contingent on a firm's permitting itself to be disturbed in certain ways. For example, bearing in mind that actual disturbances are constrained to occur within the demand curve, and that in both of the A-types the effect of slack must be to reduce growth rate or profit rate and in general both, we note that severe slack of type A(2) must seriously depress the valuation ratio (profit rate is reduced, valuation is positively correlated, therefore valuation declines). If then we believe that, for the reasons discussed earlier, satisficing behaviour is more likely to be sensitive to depressions of valuation ratio than to depressions of growth rate, A(2) disturbances are likely to be inhibited. A firm finding itself in a severe A(2) depression is particularly likely to take in slack before the effects have time to get into the data. This tendency, however, would be expected to be weaker the higher the level of valuation from which the disturbance occurred, because the higher this level, the further the permissible decline before fear of unpleasant consequences is likely to become serious. And since the upper level will tend (other things being equal) to be higher the higher the vertical positioning of the valuation curve, we should expect the inhibition of A(2) disturbances to be weaker in industries with more favourably placed curves than in others. If, as we earlier suggested, a favourably placed valuation curve is regarded as characteristic of a 'growth' industry, we may then say that, other things being equal, the relative prevalence of A(2) disturbances may tend to be greater in such industries than in others.

Otherwise, it is not easy to suggest presumptions as to the relative likelihood of the various disturbances and hence as to the regression patterns our theory (and for that matter most other theories) would actually predict. We must expect all the disturbances to occur simultaneously, and the regression pattern in any given cross-section to be the result of the accidents determining which types happened to predominate in the particular sample. We may well find that particular patterns are associated with particular external characteristics, and in some cases our theory may be able to explain this, in others not; many such associations will be the accidental result of subtle statistical interactions which could prove rather difficult to disentangle.

Nevertheless, a number of by no means trivial predictions remain possible. In the first place, since we expect the various forms of scatter to occur simultaneously, we predict that correlation coefficients in this area will tend to be small, and more often than not insignificant by orthodox tests. But although the coefficients should be small, we should nevertheless expect that in multiple observations such as those of Meyer and Kuh a definite pattern would emerge — a pattern of small, mostly individually insignificant coefficients, whose total effect was somehow definitely suggestive. We call this Prediction I. It is not trivial, because other theories would predict these coefficients to be large and significant, especially when, as in the Meyer and Kuh type of calculation, some possible sources of short-run disturbance have been eliminated by holding certain relevant variables constant.

In the second place (Prediction II) we should expect the signs of the coefficients to fluctuate both over time and between industries, according to the ups and downs of the battle between the various disturbance types. And we should expect data of the Meyer and Kuh kind to give the impression that, although no individual coefficient was necessarily significantly different from zero, if such fluctuations were observed they should somehow give the impression of having a meaning.

Finally, we can say that we require that the regressions and correlation patterns actually observed should at least be capable of reasonable rationalisation in terms of our theory: for example, we should not be surprised and should probably be pleased if we found patterns consistent with A(1) prevalence more common than those consistent with A(2), and both, on the whole, should be more common than those consistent with prevalence of B. Conversely, we do not want to discover many examples of patterns which cannot be explained by any of these methods. We call this group of suggestions Hindsight I. Then we may add, as Hindsight II, that we should like to find that the appearance of particular cases is convincingly associated with appropriate industrial or historical characteristics: for example, we should like to find that the A(2) case is, in fact, commonly associated with growth industries.

There is little difficulty about Prediction I. In both Meyer and Kuh and Gordon the coefficients are indeed generally small, yet in both books the authors felt the results had a meaning. Prediction II is also confirmed; the coefficients do indeed fluctuate: Meyer and Kuh, for example, found that almost a quarter of their partial correlations between profit rate and growth rate (C^*, p) were negative, and although these were on average smaller and less orthodoxly significant than the positive cases, they remain difficult to explain in classical terms. Meyer and Kuh also found that a third of the correlations between growth rate and retention ratio went one way, the rest the other (we discuss this further below).

The story as regards Hindsight I is as follows:

TABLE 7.2 *Meyer and Kuh Correlation Patterns*

Type of Result	Percentage of Observations
Consistent with A(1) prevalence	54
Consistent with A(2) prevalence	22
Consistent with B prevalence	13
No explanation	11

N.B. These results relate to 70 observations on 14 industries for five years. They are obtained by bringing together the signs of the coefficients reproduced in Tables 13 and 27 of Meyer and Kuh (omitting the three industries which were excluded from Table 13), according to the principles of Table 7.1 above. Thus a type A(1) case is one where, for a given industry in a given year, both C^*, p in Table 13 and C^*, r in Table 27 are positive, and so on. Note, however, that Meyer and Kuh use the pay-out ratio, i.e. $1 - r$, so all the signs in Table 13 must for our purposes be reversed. Note also that for C^*, p they give a partial correlation coefficient with certain factors, such as capacity utilisation and short-term liquidity, held constant. The period is 1946–50.

There are evident identification problems involved in the analysis of the above results, but because we have postulated (on p. 280 above) specific identifying restrictions with respect to the signs of the correlation coefficients expected to be associated with different kinds of errors, we believe we are not going too far afield in offering the interpretation which follows.

If the reader will refer back to the description of Hindsight I, he will see that here again the result is not bad, although the not insignificant proportion of 'no explanation' cases is somewhat unhealthy. We must, however, remember that although we *predict* the coefficient should be small, we still face a problem of inference.

Gordon's results were as follows:

TABLE 7.3 *Signs and Magnitudes of Correlation Coefficients in Myron Gordon Data*

	$C^{\bullet}, p$	$C^{\bullet}, r$	p, r
Food Sample	+0·3	−0·1	−0·3
Machinery Sample	0	0	−0·3

N.B. These results summarise Table 15·1 in Gordon, op. cit. They relate to data averaged over five years 1954–58, the two samples containing 48 firms. The reader should note that Gordon uses the symbol r where we use p, the symbol b where we use r and the symbol zeta for the investment rate. The coefficients are simple correlations.

The Food result is consistent with an A(2) disturbance. Machinery is more intriguing. From a statistical point of view the discovery of a relatively strong negative cross-correlation between a pair of variables which are negligibly correlated with a third variable can only be explained by the existence of negative covariance between deviations of some variables and error terms in others. This is precisely what one might expect to happen if, given the basic causal relationships of our model, an industry was experiencing a rather close mixture of two types of disturbance, for example, a close mixture of A(2) and B. This mongrel might produce a scatter diagram in which there was virtually no measured correlation between $C^{\bullet}$, p and $C^{\bullet}$, r; yet, as a result of non-accidental

co-variance in error terms, the correlation p, r could be both negative and quite strong; negative deviations in profit rate would be
associated with positive errors in growth rate (type B disturbance),
and positive deviations in growth rate associated with positive
errors in the retention ratio, because the latter co-variance works
negatively on the co-variance of p and r, while the former works
positively, both causes working in the explanatorily desired direction. Our theory, which implies that perturbations on one dimension must tend to cause deviations on another, explains results of
this type better than other theories, which might have to treat them
as accidents. But the result could also, of course, be regarded as an
attenuated manifestation of A(2).

As regards Hindsight II, Meyer and Kuh did find evidence
(Table 28) of a probably significant association between the A(2)
cases and 'growth industry' characteristics, although there is no
evidence either way in connection with the Gordon samples. On
the whole, it would probably have been more convincing from our
point of view if the latter samples had been more consistent with
A(1), for, although they are single measurements, they do in fact
represent an averaging of twenty cross-section observations over
the five years, and one would have preferred them to have followed
the pattern which on the Meyer and Kuh data emerged as typical:
the Food industry was not covered by Meyer and Kuh; the Machinery industry, however, did show A(2) results for two out of the
five years. (No Meyer and Kuh industry displayed more than two
A(2) results, but there were six, including Machinery, which reached
this maximum.) The explanation given by Meyer and Kuh of their
own results in this area is consistent with our theory, although a
little more complex. They argued that in expanding industries the
faster-growing firms would be particularly likely to experience
stock-market conditions of a kind in which a firm desiring to
maximise the supply of finance would find it better to lower the
retention ratio, raise the valuation ratio and so create conditions
favourable to new issues. In other words, framed in our language,
the supposition here is that in these industries the optimum
retention ratio would tend to be lower, and the optimum new-issue
rate higher, in the faster-growing firms than in the slower. Our

explanation is not necessarily more convincing: both are based on a growth-maximising hypothesis modulated by satisficing.

The reader is asked to believe that the relative success of the above predictions — if that is a fair interpretation — frankly surprised the present author himself, and that the theory developed in the foregoing pages was not originally designed to provide possible alternative explanations of the works of the three distinguished writers we have been discussing. It is now necessary, therefore, to consider to what extent, if any, the above 'tests' discriminate other, more classical, or more orthodox, hypotheses.

Classical-type hypotheses usually assume that the firm is striving only to maximise the welfare of the stockholders, i.e. to place itself always as near as possible to the peak of the valuation curve. They also imply that if a positive return discrepancy (excess of internal rate of return over 'cost of capital') does arise, the retention ratio should be set high until the discrepancy is eliminated. But in no circumstances should a high retention ratio be maintained if the return discrepancy is temporarily negative, because this would mean causing the shareholders to receive lower total returns than could be obtained by investing elsewhere: indeed, on extreme neo-classical assumptions, retentions should be virtually zero if the return discrepancy is negative.

Classical-type hypotheses must therefore regard the B-type regression phenomenon as pathological, because firms have no business to be wandering along the valuation curve to the right of the peak: if some firms are put into this situation by disturbance, there should be an equal number of cases disturbed in the opposite direction, and a negative regression between growth rate and profit rate should not, therefore, be observed. Not many B-type cases, we saw, in fact occurred in the Meyer and Kuh data: we at least are able to explain them, but as there were almost as many cases which neither we nor the classicals would be able to explain at all (see Table 7.2 above) the conclusions here are ambiguous.

They are much less so in the case of both the A-type results. If we appropriately modify the classical hypothesis to allow for organisational slack, we expect firms to be scattered inside the demand curve in the neighbourhood of the peak. But surely we should also expect that where this scatter is such as to set up a positive regression between growth rate and profit rate (as by definition occurs in all A-type cases), the regression line should *not* be relatively flat, i.e. surely we should not get the A(1) result? For this would mean that firms which, through inefficiency, had permitted themselves below-average profit rates were adding to the injury of stockholders by pushing out growth rates and depressing the valuation ratio further (see our Table 7.1). The behaviour might be consistent with some second-best response to the managerial utility function, but is very hard to reconcile with the ordinarily understood concept of utility. From the classical point of view, however, A(2) phenomena are little better. Although satisfactorily explicable in terms of the scatter pattern likely to be produced around the valuation-maximising position by organisational slack, they violate the classical presumption that above-average profit rates should always be associated with above-average retention ratios. (In A(2) cases, the opposite occurs.) We have already seen that nearly a quarter of the Meyer and Kuh cases were of this type, and negative correlation between profit rate and retention ratio was the only one of the six results reproduced in the summary of the Gordon data (Table 7.3 above) which was strongly consistent in the two samples. The consistency considerably increases the significance, a point which is reinforced when it is remembered that the Gordon data relate to five-year averages. It does seem, therefore, that the result must be very damaging for anyone who wants to believe that firms actually behave neoclassically.

Professor Gordon does not so believe, and the purpose of his book (to which, in concentrating only on the material presented in one of fifteen chapters, we have far from done justice) was essentially normative. We are not implying destructive criticism of either his work or the equally important work of Meyer and Kuh. Economic science owes a considerable debt to all three authors for their very large-scale contributions to knowledge and understanding in the field. We are merely, impertinently perhaps, offering alternative non-normative explanations. Professor Gordon, commenting on his own surprise (and distress) at finding negative correlation between profit rate and retention ratio, concluded, 'It is possible that the influence of other objectives subordinates the influence of maximisation of the stock value in corporate financing policy.'[13] With due humility we should like to claim that in this book we have provided an account of what these objectives might be and of how they could operate.

CHAPTER EIGHT

POSSIBLE MACRO IMPLICATIONS

IT was explained in the Introduction that the aims of this book lay mainly in the field of micro-theory. We wished to investigate the nature of the managerial enterprise, non-normatively, in a spirit of unrestricted intellectual curiosity; we did not want to be committed to producing a model which would necessarily be helpful in the conventional ways, such as informing bases for theories of price or income determination. But we naturally hoped that the results might also be of wider interest, and we have already indicated some possible implications of departing from partial-equilibrium analysis while retaining the basic theory. We also originally believed that the theory might have significant macro-implications, yet were not relying on this: we were genuinely uncertain as to what would be found when the stone had been lifted, and would have been by no means distressed had the discoveries tended merely to confirm existing orthodoxy in the area (if any such can be said to exist). However, now that the main work is complete, it does seem tempting to add, as it were by way of postscript, some speculations as to the possible macro-implications of a 'managerial' micro-theory. Of course, the economic macrocosm is much less managerial than the manufacturing sector: in agriculture, services and many branches of finance, traditional capitalism remains prevalent. In the government sector there is much managerialism but no managerial capitalism. Nevertheless, in most Western countries a very considerable proportion of national output, measured from the production side, is due to organisations to which our theory applies. Almost by definition managerial firms are above-average in size, and therefore contribute disproportionately to total production. Certainly it is far less inaccurate to treat the economy as if it were entirely managerial than is the common practice of treating it as if it were entirely traditional. In this final chapter we therefore briefly consider the macro-implications of a system which is in effect overwhelmingly managerial, but in which there remains a sufficient number of traditional capitalists to be capable of significantly influencing the managers' behaviour. We believe that this is, as a matter of fact, a fair description of typical mid-twentieth-century capitalism.

Working Assumptions

It seems best to continue with a system in which the demand, supply and valuation curves of all firms are at all times and throughout the economy identical, not only as to shape but also as to position. The object of the assumption is to clear away analytical difficulties associated with differential growth rates. We well understand, of course, that we may thus be suppressing the signal with the noise. It is possible that ever-present differences between individual firms represent an essential feature of the process by which the macro-economy attempts to find dynamic equilibrium. But if so, we shall be no worse placed than many other macro-theorists, and, specifically, we assume that:

(i) every firm in the economy is at all times growing at the same rate, earning the same rate of return and displaying the same valuation ratio; the common micro growth rate is also the macro or 'national' rate;

(ii) the common growth rate is equivalent to the growth rate of output of real total demand and of the capital stock measured in book value at constant prices — technical progress if any is always neutral;

(iii) all firms are identically motivated — whether the utility functions are 'traditional', managerial or mixed, they are the same in all firms as to character, form and quantitative specification;

(iv) there exists some mechanism (e.g. otherwise neutral government fiscal policy) for guaranteeing the maintenance at all times of 'Keynesian' full employment: the average utilisation of capacity is always high and stable, i.e. never afflicted by demand deficiency.

We then define the following analytical tools:

(i) the *partial demand curve* — the common demand-growth curve of the individual firm, based on the assumption that if the firm's policy were changed, the policies of all other firms would remain constant; associated with the partial demand curve we define a corresponding *partial valuation curve*;

(ii) the *partial utility function* — the firm's utility function as between valuation ratio and growth, rate based on the assumption that the policies and behaviour of all other firms would remain constant;

(iii) the *general demand curve* — a demand-growth curve for an individual firm, drawn up on the assumption that policy changes designed to move the firm along the partial demand curve would, in fact, be precisely copied by all other firms; with this is associated a corresponding *general valuation curve*;

(iv) the *general utility function* — a utility function based on the assumption that any change in growth rate or valuation ratio occurring in the individual firm would lead to identical changes by other firms.

The assumptions then imply that all the above curves are at all times the same for all firms. The 'general' curves are purely analytical conceptions, and will not generally be known or appreciated by individual firms; they are, however, from the analyst's point of view both objective and in principle ascertainable. The experiment required to ascertain the total valuation curve would be that of inducing all firms to vary diversification rate, profit-margin variables and financial-policy variables simultaneously and equally, in such a way as would have been expected to produce the same balanced movements along the corresponding partial demand curves. Then, after allowing due time for the disturbance to subside, the observed change in the common valuation ratio would indicate the total valuation curve.

The shape and position of the curves is clearly affected by familiar macro-factors. A rise in the general level of prices relatively to that of wages will raise both general and partial demand curves even though the micro-relationships which generated this curve remained unaffected. (If all prices rose relatively to wages, a higher profit margin could be maintained for a given diversification rate and success ratio.) And provided the change did not in some way affect financial conditions (which of course it well might), the valuation curve would be affected correspondingly. But the valuation curve could also be shifted independently of the demand curve by some general change in financial conditions, or for that matter by a change in the supply price of take-over raiders.

It should also be noted that some movements *along* the general demand curve may also imply changes in distributive shares, more particularly changes in the ratio of profits to national income. As we move along the demand curve we vary both the rate of return and the capital-output ratio, and these changes in turn imply a definite variation of the average profit margin, which is, of course, the share of profits after netting out transactions in intermediate goods. For example, the position of zero growth on the demand curve is virtually the position in post-classical, long-run equilibrium — i.e. the position where 'normal' profits are being earned by every firm in every industry, 'super' profits having been universally eliminated. Positions further to the right, such as for example the position at the peak of the demand curve, are comparable to post-classical, short-run equilibrium, generalised from the single industry to the economy at large; the short-run conditions, however, have become permanent. Profits are always abnormal, because under conditions of growth, there are always some products which are sufficiently new that 'normal' conditions have not yet in their cases been reached. In other words, at the peak of the demand curve the 'degree of monopoly' is higher than at all positions to the left, and prices generally higher relatively to wages. We seem, therefore, required to distinguish between this kind of change and the kind implied in a bodily movement of the curve. But as the problem only arises to the left of the peak (to the right, the profit rate declines because capital and other costs rise while the margin remains largely unchanged), we shall more or less ignore it. We shall generally assume that a given 'position' of the general demand curve implies the same macro-distributive situation (share of profits in the national income) wherever the firms are located on the curve, provided, of course, that they are not located to the left of the peak (see above).

The Aggregate Retention Ratio

We have already hinted that the general assumptions surrounding the micro-model seem to imply that the corporate leaders, acting collectively (but not collusively), may have considerable freedom to vary the aggregate retention ratio without running into serious restraints. In other words, it is possible that if all corporate retention ratios were to rise together, the effect on market rates of discount would be very considerably less than in the case where one ratio rises in isolation. Similarly, if all valuation ratios happened to decline together, the *ex post* decline in utility would be considerably less than where such a change occurred in isolation, because, of course, the associated increase in average individual probability of take-over would then be considerably damped. In other words, it is likely that the negative slope of the general valuation curve is considerably smaller, arithmetically, than that of the corresponding partial curve, and that the shape of the general utility function is considerably more biassed towards growth than that of the partial function. But although both will thus probably be positioned more favourably to growth than the partial curves, only if the firms had some means of colluding could they necessarily take advantage of the fact.

We would also argue that, if a change in the aggregate retention ratio does for some reason occur, there will be a definite and permanent effect on the national propensity to save. This is more controversial. It means that, in the event of a rise, for example, in the ratio, any offsetting variation in the propensity to save out of *personal* income (distributed profits plus non-profit incomes) will be insufficient to offset the national effect. Looked at in this light, the propensity to save out of profits takes on some rather new colours. It is now considerably influenced by decisions of individuals who are not thereby choosing between present and future consumption in the ordinary sense. The point is of such importance as to deserve further argument.

What we are saying, in effect, is that *given* the overall distribution of income between wages and profits, the particular legal and institutional arrangements of the corporate constitution do have a definite effect on overall savings. For example, suppose a law were passed requiring corporations to distribute all profits annually, but at the same time permitting them to make automatic 'rights' issues, designed to bring in any sum up to the full amount of the dividend, on terms such that any shares not taken up were cancelled rather than reissued to the public at large. To subscribe, however, shareholders would be required to undertake annually all the transactions involved in subscribing to any new issue: they would not be permitted to make any arrangement whereby their dividend was automatically reinvested.

Evidently, investors' reactions to such a change would be varied. Some would suscribe to all their rights, some to part. Of those who did not subscribe in full, some would reinvest the difference between their receipts under the new system and the old in other securities; some would increase their consumption. (It is important to note that reactions must be different from those to typical new issues under present conditions: under present conditions, 'rights' issues raise only a small proportion of total corporate finance, and tend to be confined to situations where valuation ratios are unusually favourable.) Few would deny that a considerable redirection of funds might occur, but many would argue that the national propensity to save would remain unaffected: consumption, it would be argued, would not increase because the savings withdrawn from the one outlet would merely be sent elsewhere, and if some individuals did increase their personal consumption, others would reduce it. The debate is important, because unless the national propensity to save is flexible, the corporations cannot, in fact, influence the growth rate through their influence on the retention ratio, except indirectly via changes in the share of profit in the national income.

If, on the other hand, the power to influence retention ratios does give direct influence over the propensity to save (we use the word direct in the sense of implying that the propensity could be affected even if distributive shares were fixed), then, when the retention ratio is collectively varied (a movement along the total valuation curve), the macro-warranted-growth conditions must be affected. The importance of this conclusion lies in the fact that, in previous growth models employing a 'capitalist propensity to save' such as Kaldor's, [1] the concept was thought of as representing (capitalists') consumption decisions which were quite independent of investment decisions. When these decisions are made by managers who are themselves major investment-decision-takers, their significance is drastically changed. The position becomes more similar to that implied in the neo-Marxist type of model, such as Mrs. Robinson's, [2] where no consumption from profits is admitted at all. We believe our own view to be the most realistic, because we believe that, in the imaginary institutional situation formulated above, some families would definitely increase their consumption, and while others would not, it is difficult to see good reason for expecting any of these actually to save more. By generalisation, we therefore presume that under the actual circumstances of both today and yesterday, long-run variations in the retention ratio must cause long-run variations in the national propensity to save (in the same direction, of course, but smaller in magnitude), even when distributive shares are held constant. But as the presumption is controversial we shall also analyse the anti-hypothesis, implying in effect that although the general demand curve is 'normal', the general valuation curve is cut off sharply at a point which depends on the macro-distributive situation. At this point, the corporations are taking savings from the economy at a rate such that any attempt to accelerate expansion by further raising the retention ratio would inevitably be frustrated in one way or another: to pass the limit it would be necessary to raise retentions to 100 per cent, whereupon, of course, all valuation ratios would become zero.

The alternative case, (the one in which we believe) we shall call only 'partly restricted', because, of course, we are not proposing to assume that if technical conditions permitted the managers could have any growth rate they wanted. We shall assume that the power collectively to influence the national propensity to save is a limited one, and that the total valuation curve is not, therefore, without downward curvature. But in absolute contrast to the 'fully restricted' case, for reasons given above (p. 293) its downward curvature is less steep than that of the corresponding partial curve. In both cases, of course, the total valuation curves are based on 'given' total and partial demand curves, which means, *inter alia*, that they are based on a given share of profits in the national income. In the fully restricted case, the firm cannot move past the cut-off point in any circumstances, hence growth cannot be increased without a change of distributive shares. In the 'partly restricted' case, the corporate sector has some freedom to vary the growth rate (subject to technical conditions), provided it is prepared to accept associated variations in the general level of the valuation ratio.

Natural and Quasi-Natural Rates of Growth

Since the original work of Harrod and Domar,[3] most contemporary growth models have been based on some development of the idea of a 'natural' growth rate. This is the maximum growth rate permitted the economy by technical and social conditions, or, more precisely, by the sum of the growth rates of population and of output per head. In the original conception these factors were essentially exogenous: the growth rate of productivity, for example, was not affected by variables within the model, such as the distribution of income, nor was population growth governed by any kind of Malthusian relationship with the growth rate of consumption. As Harrod and Domar saw the problem, an economy need not grow at its natural rate, but cannot grow faster, and problems of considerable analytical interest arose from possible instabilities associated with conflicts between the natural growth rate and the rate consistent with a moving Keynesian equilibrium (i.e., in Harrod's language, the 'warranted' rate). Subsequent writers have shown how such conflicts might be resolved by variations in the share of profits in the national income, which would lead in turn to variations in the national propensity to save, and thus to adjustments of the warranted rate itself.

Most contemporary writers, however, accept some form of exogenous growth rate, albeit with considerable modifications. In the Harrod-Domar models, as usually set out, technical progress is associated with capital accumulation in such a way that the growth rate of capital required to support the 'natural' growth rate of output per head happens to be equal to that of output, so that the capital-output ratio remains constant over time and the progress is said to be 'neutral'. Consequently, the conditions of Keynesian equilibrium also remain conveniently constant. One way of rationalising this type of model is to imagine that at any instant of time only a single technique of production is known for each and every commodity, but that all are being continuously improved in a manner implying neutral changes in the factor ratios. Mrs. Robinson, and Professors Meade, Solow and Swan,[4] provided more comprehensive arrangements in which there were always production functions — i.e. ranges of alternative techniques; these, however, could shift bodily over time as a result of the development of knowledge. At any given moment of time the economy was to choose a position *on* the function in such a way that the rate of return was maximised at the micro-level. It was then possible to show that, provided the function and its movement took restricted forms, the system could be got into moving equilibrium in which growth rates of output and capital stock were equal and constant, and so also the rate of return. Thus the apparent conditions of 'neutral' growth would be observed, but only as the coincidental result of a special condition on the trend. Disliking this feature, Kaldor[5] introduced a 'technical progress' function, to be contrasted with a production function, in which the neutrality or otherwise of progress became endogenous to the model. If the 'attempted' growth rate of the capital stock was rapid, relatively to that of the population, labour would tend to become scarce, and the inventions actually adopted would tend to be capital-using (i.e. to involve a rising capital-output ratio), and vice versa. There was, however, one growth rate at which neutrality was possible, and since this was the only one consistent with a stable moving equilibrium, Kaldor set out to investigate how the economy might find and maintain it. For the purpose he made use of more complex thriftiness assumptions, but the 'neutral' rate remained exogenous, and the system was thus basically similar to its predecessors.

If the dynamic technical conditions are in one way or another exogenous, the analyst already knows that one growth rate only is consistent with dynamic equilibrium. He is then left with two types of questions to consider: what are the other conditions, such as distribution of income, necessary to sustain the equilibrium; what are its stability characteristics? Most writers have to some extent attempted to answer both types of questions simultaneously, but Dr. L. Pasinetti[6] has recently shown that it is often fruitful to keep them separate: he has thus been able to show that if 'workers' make savings and receive interest thereon, the conditions of dynamic equilibrium involve not only the distribution of income but also that of property, a conclusion whose further theoretical implications appear to be considerable. We shall adopt the same approach here, and shall concentrate, in fact, entirely on the first type of question, making no attempt to contribute to the discussion of stability.

Few of the previous writers were entirely satisfied with the various forms of exogenous progress with which they had been compelled to endow their models, for none really believed it.[7] As the reader is aware, we have in this book almost ignored the topic, because, at the micro-level, if progress is occurring, the dynamic conditions for the individual firm do not change unless the wage-profit relationship changes: provided real wages are rising with productivity at the macro-level, the micro-conditions are constant. We also deliberately evaded the very considerable problem of defining progress in face of a constantly changing product-list. Most readers must have realised by now that these evasions are permissible only if the rate of progress (assuming it to be capable of a definition of some kind) experienced by the individual firm is independent of all the other micro-variables, and, in particular, independent of the diversification rate. In reality this is most unlikely. When new products are created, the firm must partly invent a new production function, and if no diversification occurs, no new functions will be invented. (In the case of imitative products, the technology may also be imitated, but improvements may occur nevertheless.) It follows that in moving along a total demand curve, the associated changes in the average rate of diversification and of new product creation (these are not identical, because much diversification is imitative, and therefore self-cancelling) are likely to be *causally* connected with variations in technical progress at the macro-level. It is, in fact, widely accepted that there is a close connection between innovation on the production side of the economic system and innovation on the consumption side: the desire to satisfy newly discovered latent needs not infrequently stimulates technical inventions, and technical inventions themselves not infrequently suggest new products and hence, ultimately, foster new wants. Let us, therefore, consider the possibility that the overall rate of diversification, which, it will be remembered, is the aggregated form of a genuine micro-decision variable, causes changes in the rate of technical progress. For convenience, let us do without a production or technical progress function, and assume that, whatever progress does occur, it is always neutral. But this neutral, natural rate is now endogenous to the diversification rate.

The diversification rate, however, has yet other implications of macro-importance. When we move along the partial demand curve, the overall diversification rate is increasing, but, as we have seen, the corresponding movement along the total demand curve is the result of successful differentiated diversification only, because much diversification is imitative. In other words, as soon as we move any distance along the total demand curve away from the origin, the implied process of macro-growth is essentially the result of new product creation, of the first satisfaction of new wants, rather than of increased satisfaction of old wants. We are therefore postulating a definite macro-pattern of consumer behaviour. We are saying that, whatever the growth rate of their purchasing power, families will not accelerate the growth of their consumption expenditure beyond a certain point unless tempted by suitable new products. In the absence of temptation, the consumption function would drift downwards, and in an extreme case we might imagine that the marginal propensity to save would become unity. The economic and social reasons for this were classically described by James Duesenberry,[8] and are also implicit, of course, in the modified theory of demand developed above in Chapter 4. The implication is not so much that the diversification rate causally determines the propensity to save, but rather that, for any given growth rate of total demand, a particular diversification rate is required for *any* long-run stability in the consumption function. The level of the function (as given by the propensities to save out of the various forms of personal income and the distribution of income between them) may be otherwise determined, but if the level is to be free of drift it must be associated with a given diversification rate. If the diversification rate were too low, the function would drift in favour of savings, if too high, in favour of consumption. The extreme case, where demand can grow only if new products are created (i.e. the demand for old products is always so saturated that no increase in real income can affect it at all), is, as we saw in Chapter 3 (p. 125), by no means fantastic. We call the overall diversification rate necessary to maintain stability of personal consumption functions (i.e. stability in the national propensity to save for any given distribution of income), the 'required' diversification rate: it is a function of the desired growth rate, and can be conceived in macro-terms only.

The required diversification rate is thus a function of the desired growth rate, with slope increasing in the general fashion of inverted micro-demand-growth curves: as growth is accelerated the public's palate becomes increasingly unresponsive, and an increasing proportion of new products fails. Eventually, we should assume, as the micro-demand-growth curves flattened, so a point would come at the macro-level where the indicated growth rate had become so rapid that no amount of innovatory effort would be capable of preventing the growth of demand from lagging behind. The effects of this non-linearity are displayed in the declining profit rate on the total demand curve, as increasing proportions of real resources are devoted to the maintenance of the optimum success rate; but this variation, we have seen, is independent of the share of profit in the national income, because on that segment of the curve distributive shares are not affected by movements along it.

The diversification rate is ultimately the result of managerial micro-choices. In a sense it measures the strength of the managerial effort to grow, and must be micro-economically consistent with the managerial utility function. We might even go as far as to say that it reflects the managers' 'animal spirits'. Is it, however, actually free at the macro-level? When managers choose their diversification rates to maximise their utility functions, are they or are they not merely choosing a position which had to be found anyway, because macro-equilibrium required the various general curves (and here associated partial curves) to find certain positions? Clearly, where a natural growth rate is exogeneous this must, in equilibrium, be the case. There is only one equilibrium growth rate, therefore there is only one sustainable position on the general demand curve, therefore if macro-equilibrium is to be maintained, either this curve or the utility function or both must somehow be adjusted to ensure that the partial equilibria of the individual firms actually occur at this growth rate. What then is the position when technical progress is endogenous?

The answer is that we now know that steady growth requires the diversification rate and associated growth rate to satisfy two conditions: the growth rate of real output and hence purchasing power must be equal to the natural rate, which is in turn *determined* by the diversification rate, but every growth rate also 'requires' a certain diversification rate in order to maintain stability in the consumption function. Therefore the growth rate and diversification rate must be such that the diversification rate is equal to the rate 're-quired' by the growth rate, and the growth rate is, in turn, the result of technical progress at the rate consistent with the diversification rate. We call such a growth rate a *quasi-natural* rate, and the associated diversification rate a quasi-natural diversification rate. We do not ask how an economy may find such a rate, but do insist that it is a valid requirement of equilibrium growth. Its reality may be seen in recent economic history in the United States, where there is considerable evidence that because the condition either has not been or cannot be met, consumers are increasingly reluctant to maintain consumption demand at the level required by the productive rate of progress.

It is thus perfectly possible that an economy may reach a situation where, until some major industrial or socio-economic revolution occurs, no quasi-natural rate exists. Disequilibrium states will then become chronic. This is one way, in fact, of explaining the post-Keynesian condition of 'secular stagnation'. But it also seems possible that, under other circumstances, there may exist within limits a continuous range of growth rates, all of which are quasi-natural. Within the range, small changes in the diversification rate would always generate changes in the rate of technical progress which were precisely consistent with the change in growth rate of demand for which the new diversification rate was the required rate. Productive innovations would have the qualitative character-istics necessary for consumers always to want to exploit them in full. The condition might be no accident, but due rather to a natural balance or lack of dichotomy in the two processes, productive innovations occurring because goods were wanted, goods becoming wanted as a result of becoming available. We think it unlikely, however, that this could be true over an indefinite range of growth rates. For example, at very low rates of diversification, it would seem that the rate of technical progress should become insensitive to variations, while the demand-consistent growth rate should not. At the other extreme, at high rates of diversification it seems un-likely that the demand-consistent and technical growth rates would begin to become insensitive together, although it is not easy to think of reasons for expecting one or the other relationship to flatten first. Provided, however, either one or the other became insensitive eventually, we should again face a definite upper limit on the growth rate, but this, we shall see, would be only partly analogous to the orthodox natural rate.

Three conditions may therefore be distinguished. There may be no quasi-natural rate. There may be one quasi-natural rate. There may be, within limits, a continuous range of such rates. In the first case, which is pathological, the economy is unable to find any kind of dynamic equilibrium until the position is somehow rectified. In the second, provided the one rate can somehow be found and the surrounding conditions are not unduly unstable, the equilibrium requirements are similar to those required in the case of an exo-genous natural rate; either case may loosely be described as one in which the macro-growth rate is inflexible. Although the partial demand curves may be generally formed in accordance with the micro-theory, on the total demand curve only one position is possible.

In the third case, which we may describe as one where the growth rate is flexible, there remains an upper limit which might at first sight appear to have similar properties to those of the single rate in the inflexible case. This would represent a half truth only. The natural rate in post-Keynesian dynamics is more than a maximum. It is also the minimum rate at which the economy must grow if it is to remain healthy. In Mrs. Robinson's evocative phrase,[9] an economy failing to grow at this rate is failing to meet the conditions for a 'Golden Age': only if total output is growing at a rate equal to the sum of the growth rates of productivity and population is the demand for labour growing as fast as the population; hence, if the condition is not met, employment is being offered to a continuously declining proportion of the people. Not so in an economy growing less rapidly than at its maximum quasi-natural rate. Consider, for example, a downward variation from this position. The diversification rate is reduced, so also the consistent growth rate of demand and so also, in precise balance, the growth rate of output per worker. Therefore the growth rate of employment remains unchanged. We are saying, in other words, that there may exist a range of growth rates all of which, provided other equilibrium conditions are satisfied, can well be 'Golden'. Furthermore, since movement among these rates is associated with variations in the overall diversification rate, which is in turn derived from a micro-decision-variable, it is possible that managers, in maximising utility, may influence the magnitude of the actual growth rate associated with macro-equilibrium.

In mildly taxonomic fashion, we therefore consider four possibilities: the case of the inflexible growth rate combined with that of 'fully restricted' thriftiness assumptions; the inflexible growth rate combined with only partly restricted savings assumptions; and the two alternative thriftiness cases combined with the flexible growth-rate assumption. We take them in order.

Inflexible Growth Rate and Fully Restricted Thrift

We must first be a little more specific both about the institutional conditions and the effects on the various curves. We assume that equity shares are widely held, but the distribution of total portfolios among the population at large is nevertheless very unequal and closely associated with a corresponding inequality of personal incomes. Personal savings functions are associated with personal position in the income-and-wealth hierarchy, but shareholders, however, behave as if their functions related to a total 'income' consisting of their dividends, their equity in undistributed profits and their personally-earned non-profit incomes: any variation in the average corporate retention ratio is always precisely offset by a corresponding variation in savings from personal income. Consequently, the total savings of this class cannot be varied by the retention ratio. Then if, as we shall assume, the ratio of their personally-earned incomes to the national income is exogenous, the ratio of their savings to the national income can be endogenous only through endogenous variations in the ratio of total profits to national income, i.e. only through variations in the wage-price relationship.

We have already indicated the general way in which this type of situation affects the general demand and valuation curves: the valuation curve must be so shaped as to make growth at faster than a certain rate impossible with any positive valuation ratio. With a given wage-price relationship this rate is equivalent to the Harrodian warranted rate. The general demand curve is shaped similarly to the corresponding partial curve, but the associated general valuation curve is at some point cut off sharply. When the macro-wage-price relation varies in favour of prices, profit margin associated with all given micro-demand-growth curves increases, the general demand curve rises bodily and there is a corresponding effect on the general valuation curve. But, because the share of profits in the national income has also varied, so has the national savings ratio, and this leads to a secondary effect on the relation between general valuation curve and total demand curve, consequently, as already indicated, the vertical segment of the general valuation curve moves eastward. But, and it is an important but, we know that no valuation curve can ever cut the horizontal axis to the right of the corresponding demand curve, because it is impossible to have a positive valuation ratio without a positive rate of return. Therefore this sideways movement of the valuation curve is restricted by the position of the demand curve. The latter, however, cannot move sideways unless we drop our original micro-assumption that the internal administrative restraint on growth at some rate becomes absolute. If we accept the absolute administrative restraint as a valid macro-phenomenon (in effect it is the maximum rate at which qualified persons can effectively be absorbed into the system of organisations), then there is an absolute limit to the extent to which the valuation curve can be pushed eastward: as such a movement develops, increasingly large distributive changes are required to produce a given displacement, because, although the profit margin is rising, increasing managerial inefficiency is causing the capital-output ratio to rise (and with increasing severity) also. We call this limit the maximum administrative growth rate.

The problem of dynamic equilibrium, then, is to get the vertical segment of the valuation curve to correspond to the inflexible growth rate. If this can be achieved by distributive changes, well and good. If not, chronic disequilibrium, or at least failure of Golden Age conditions, is inevitable. Following Kaldor, [10] we do not investigate the possible mechanism of distributive adjustment in detail, but merely assert that the existence of some such mechanism is required. It is also worth noting that Golden Age conditions are impossible if the quasi-natural rate exceeds the maximum administrative rate, and although our theory is not of course intended for application to the problems of under-developed countries, there is here a clear analogy to the case of a country where unemployment is rising because 'entrepreneurial' expansion cannot keep pace with the rising population of workers. Otherwise, we merely reach the familiar equilibrium conditions: there is an equilibrium 'position' of the valuation curve, implying an equilibrium share of profits in the national income; and the latter will be higher, the higher the inflexible growth rate and/or the lower the propensities to save of the several classes.

When a transformation curve is cut off sharply in the manner assumed, it is generally likely that maximum utility will be found at this point or some point rather close to the corner. If so, the managerial utility function provides few additional complications. But if managers were very strongly security-conscious, this conclusion might not hold: rather flat indifference curves would find tangency on a partial valuation curve at a point corresponding to a more westerly position on the total curve. The case then merges into the one where savings are only partly restricted, which we now discuss.

Inflexible Growth Rate, Thriftiness Partly Restricted

Consider a situation where the general demand and valuation curves are shaped more or less like the corresponding partial curves, subject only to the usual modifications of slopes caused by all firms moving together. The managerial utility function is 'normal', and, whether or not there is any effective horizontal segment in the partial indifference curves, there is no such limit on the corresponding total curves: provided all go together, there is no minimum valuation ratio which the managerial class would not be prepared to pass at a price. This does not mean that the 'traditional' raiders whom we have presumed to remain lurking in the economy are not feared at all, but merely that at no point on the general valuation curve would fear of them become infinitely intense.

Then suppose that the general and associated partial curves happen to be anywhere. Each firm, in maximising utility, will find a tangency solution in the micro-diagram, and as all the positions are on our assumptions the same, this implies a unique situation on the general curves. There is a unique growth rate, profit rate, profit margin and capital-output ratio. But this 'desired' rate of growth may not of course be equal to the quasi-natural rate. In order to find equilibrium, we must again invoke some macro-distributive adjustment leading the general demand and valuation curves to set up partial curves in such a situation that the tangency solution does, in fact, produce growth at the quasi-natural rate and no other.

Assuming that such an equilibrium can in fact be found, the conditions do then imply several rather suggestive theorems, for example:

(1) It remains true that the faster the quasi-natural rate, the greater, other things being equal, is the equilibrium share of profits in the national income;

(2) But one of the 'other things' is now clearly the character of the managerial utility function, as represented in the relative strength of the desires for growth and 'security' respectively — the greater the managerial preference for growth (steep indifference curves), the lower the share of profits required to sustain any given, inflexible, quasi-natural rate and vice versa;

(3) As a corollary, 'classical' behaviour, i.e. a utility function containing only the valuation ratio (indifference curves all horizontal), must always require an equilibrium share of profits greater than that required by any form of 'managerial' behaviour.

These results may be further explained as follows. When managers move eastwards through the diagram, they partly create the savings necessary for acceleration by appropriate variations of retention ratio and other similar adjustments to financial policy. But in aggregating the stock-market equations in order to generate the general valuation curve, we have not assumed that these additional savings can be obtained costlessly: they are achieved, in effect, at the cost of a rise in the 'macro' rate of interest. In effect, the 'national' propensity to save is 'determined' by the basic thriftiness attitudes, by the distribution of income and by the interest rate, and these set up a contingent relationship between warranted growth rate and general valuation ratio. But as the result of the existence of a managerial utility function, there are restrictions on the combinations of growth rate and valuation ratio which can be consistent with individual partial equilibrium. If these are not respected, macro-equilibrium will be violated by the attempts of the individual firms to adjust their partial positions, thus moving the system along the general curve. To meet the restrictions consistently with any one (quasi-natural) growth rate, the system's degrees of freedom are exhausted, and the share of profits in the national income is therefore determined.

This explains (1) above. If, however, managers have relatively strong preferences for growth, they mind less the consequences of a high interest rate and low general valuation ratios, hence more of the adjustment to equilibrium can be carried by increased retentions, and less needs to be carried by macro-distribution variation. The less the managers fear or respect stockholders, the more the equilibrium distribution of income is likely to favour those sections of society whose equity holdings are below average. This explains (2).

We then see that in shifting towards the classical case, the implied gain in shareholder welfare is intimately associated with an increase in the distributive share of the *rentier* class. Any given natural or quasi-natural growth-path generates various time-paths of absolute consumption for the various classes in society, according to their distributive shares. If the shareholding class can persuade managers to pay more attention to its interests, it can induce them to take actions which imply an equilibrium macro-distribution more favourable to itself: it then expresses the improvement in stock-market terms by placing a higher market value on any given collection of physical assets. In this sense, then, it is true that the managerial revolution favours the 'workers'. More precisely, the workers are favoured provided the share of executive compensation in the national income is not increased to an offsetting extent. Managerial utility associated with growth is derived from prospective gains in financial compensation, from power, from prestige and from the satisfactions of professional competence. Provided therefore the relative weight of the non-financial elements is significant, and provided the initial share of executive salaries in the national income is modest, it seems likely that institutional changes favouring the expression of more 'managerial' utility functions would be likely to yield at least some net gain for the majority of the population, i.e. for the class who are neither substantial property owners nor managers. There is here, perhaps, an element of harmony of interest between workers and managers which may at least partly qualify their more apparent social and political conflicts. *Rentiers* depend on workers for their *rentes*, managers for their livelihood. In a capitalist system, managers also depend partly on *rentiers* for capital supplies, but, as we have seen, ways have been found of greatly reducing the effectiveness of this dependence. Perhaps the managers' success in this respect reflects the knowledge that their services would be required even in a collectivist system, while those of shareholders would not.

A Flexible-Growth Model

The main effect of a flexible-growth rate, within the limits over which it applies, is the addition of a degree of freedom. The implications are not greatly different as between the two alternative thriftiness assumptions so we concentrate the discussion on the second. What, then, is implied by partially restricted thriftiness and flexible growth?

The answer is extremely simple. If one degree of freedom is gained, the macro-income distribution need no longer be endogenous. If the macro-distribution is exogenous, as was generally assumed by Keynesians until around 1955, the system is over-determined unless the growth rate is flexible: indeed this is one way of characterising Harrodian instability. But the escape from over-determination via the assumption of the existence of a macro-distributive adjustment mechanism has never been entirely easy because there is so much evidence, at least in the post-1918 world, [11] that the wage-price relation is not easily changed. Monopolistic and oligopolistic behaviour on the part of both employers and workers may well lead to a carve-up of the national cake which has no particular rationality and is yet remarkably rigid. Thus, while determining the share of profits in the national income as an equilibrium condition associated with growth remains an idea of considerable charm, we can by no means be sure that it represents the solution of the mystery. (It is significant that Kaldor, for example, in some 50,000 words in all he has published on the subject, has devoted less than 5000 to his account of the *modus operandi* of the distributive mechanism: in effect, he relies on the argument that in a system which is inherently unstable, the historical observation of long periods of Keynesian near-full employment proves the existence of a stabilising factor and that this can only be the wage-price mechanism — an argument, it should be noted, which is not without force. [12])

But we are not interested here in Keynesian under-employment (i.e. under-utilisation of a given capital stock). We are interested in the possibility that the system might have a dynamic equilibrium at some quasi-natural rate less than the maximum. Suppose that the wage-price relation is, in fact, rigid, and that the share of profits in the national income is thus from our point of view exogenous. Then the micro-utility function will determine a unique or 'desired' position on the total valuation curve (which is now itself exogenous), and, provided this is within the range of quasi-natural rates, such an equilibrium is perfectly sustainable. We are then back to earlier days in the history of economic thought, when distribution was thought to determine growth rather than the other way about. Alternatively, we do not have to assume that the macro-distribution is totally incapable of endogenous adjustment; we may merely assume that it is somewhat 'sticky', and then let it settle down at an arbitrary level and see what happens. Provided the level is consistent with a possible quasi-natural rate, nothing happens. All the conditions for a Robinsonian Golden Age are present, and no forces exist to cause disequilibrium. There is therefore no reason to suppose that the wage-price relation will be affected by macro-pressures, nor is there any special reason to expect the system to be driven to the quasi-natural maximum.

The significance of the result is that the rate of growth is then in a genuine causal sense determined not only by the distribution of income, but also by the growth propensities of the people who manage industry. This is a conclusion which would be acceptable to informed laymen, but has proved surprisingly difficult to rationalise in terms of economic theory. In both Keynesian and neo-classical models, capitalist micro-behaviour has an important implicit role, but, in almost all the extant examples, the underlying properties of the system are such that equilibrium can only be found at a growth rate which is ultimately exogenous. The role of behaviour is largely confined to influencing the stability characteristics of the system, and any influence over actual growth rates then derives from the fact that unless behaviour is stabilising, growth rates below the exogenous maximum may well become chronic. We do not claim very much for the development suggested above. It amounts to saying little more than if the growth rate is flexible, it is flexible. But perhaps we have managed to add just a little something.

NOTES

N.B. Owing to the diversity of the fields involved, a formal bibliography would be inappropriate. For the convenience of the reader a list of all authors and titles cited is given at the end of the notes on p. 325 below.

Notes to Chapter 1: The Institutional Framework

1. A. A. Berle, and G. Means, *The Modern Corporation and Private Property*, N.Y., 1932, p. 285.
2. We refer to the writings of Thorstein Veblen, A. A. Berle, Gardner Means, Chester Barnard, R. A. Gordon, George Hurff, Sargent Florence, Carl Kaysen, J. K. Galbraith, Mrs. Edith Penrose (listed in approximate historical order of publication). For a good general survey the reader is referred to *The Corporation in Modern Society*, Cambridge, Mass., 1960, edited by E. Mason, the notes to which may be used as a bibliography.
3. See Holman Hunt, *The Development of the Business Corporation in England*, Harvard, 1960, Chapter 6.
4. See for example, *The Economist*, Jan. 27, 1855, pp. 84–5.
5. See R. A. Gordon, *Business Leadership in the Large Corporation*, Washington, D.C., 1945 (and paperback, Berkeley, 1961), p. 14, and P. Sargent Florence, *The Logic of British and American Industry*, London, 1953, p. 170.
6. In the quest for empirical measures of the relation between ownership and control, a good deal of research on voting distributions has been undertaken and published on both sides of the Atlantic, the main sources being Berle and Means, *op. cit.*, Book 1; Gordon, *op. cit.*, Chapter 5, pp. 30–45; *The Distribution of Ownership in the 200 Largest Non-Financial Corporations*, TNEC, Washington, D.C., Monograph No. 29; P. Sargent Florence, *The Logic of British and American Industry*, London, 1953, pp. 186–203, and *Ownership, Control and Success of Large Companies*, London, 1961, pp. 68–69. A selection from these is given in Tables A and B below.

TABLE A

Proportions of Companies with Different Degrees of Vote Concentration, U.S. and U.K., 1936 and 1951

	Largest single holding exceeds half the votes		Largest single holding has less than half the votes but largest twenty holdings have more than half		Others		Total	
	1936 %	1951 %	1936 %	1951 %	1936 %	1951 %	1936 %	1951 %
U.K. Large Companies	10	7	18	5	72	88	100	100
U.K. Medium Companies	—	¼	—	8	—	91	100	100
U.S. 126 largest industrials	—	—	—	—	75	—	100	—

Sources: P. Sargent Florence, *op. cit.* (1961), pp. 68–9, and (1953), p. 189.

N.B. A large U.K. company is one whose nominal issued share capital exceeded £3 millions ($9 millions at 1960 exchange rate) in 1951, a 'medium' company is one whose capital lay between £2 and £3 millions in 1951. The sample therefore relates to the same list of companies in both years. The U.K. sampling fraction was 100 per cent for all companies with capital exceeding £1 millions and for all brewery companies; for all other companies it was 37½ per cent. Wholly owned subsidiaries are excluded throughout. The U.S. figure refers to 1937.

TABLE B

Median Percentage of Votes Held by 20 Largest Holders, U.K. and U.S.
1936 and 1951

	1936	1951
U.K. Large companies	35	22
U.K. Medium companies	—	28
U.S. 126 largest	28	—

Sources: Same as Table A.

7. For a discussion of Satisficing theory see p. 107 *et seq.*, and p. 266 *et seq.*, below.
8. We refer to the theories of Downie and Baumol. See J. Downie, *The Competitive Process*, London, 1958, and William Baumol, *Business Behaviour, Value and Growth*, N.Y., 1959.
9. For a discussion of the relation between organisation theory and economic theory, see Chapter 3, p. 111 *et seq.*
10. The private limited company, or closed corporation, provides an apparent exception, but is essentially a form of traditional capitalism of which it can be said that risk avoided by the owners is largely thrown onto creditors. See L. C. B. Gower, *Modern English Company Law*, London, 1957, p. 65.
11. He may of course be able to protect himself partly by a service contract providing for compensation in event of dismissal. See p. 17.
12. See the discussion of executive compensation in Chapter 2.
13. R. H. Tawney, *Religion and the Rise of Capitalism*, London, 1926.
14. Max Weber, *The Protestant Ethic and the Spirit of Capitalism*, translated by Talcot Parsons, London and N.Y., 1930.
15. Weber, *op. cit.*, p. 162.
16. Weber, *op. cit.*, p. 171.
17. See Paul Samuelson, *Economics*, N.Y., 1948, p. 131.
18. See Gower, *op. cit.*, p. 319, *et seq.*
19. See P. J. Wiles, *Price, Cost and Output*, Oxford, 1961 edition, p. 186.
20. James Burnham, *The Managerial Revolution*, N.Y., 1941.
21. Thorstein Veblen, *Absentee Ownership*, London, 1923.
22. Berle and Means, *op. cit.*
23. Gordon, *op. cit.* See also Earl Latham in Mason, *op. cit.*, pp. 228–31.
24. See Gower, *op. cit.*, pp. 471–2; W. G. Katz, 'The Philosophy of Mid-Twentieth Century Corporation Statutes', *Law and Contemporary Problems*, 1958, pp. 172 *et seq*; George Hurff, *Social Aspects of Enterprise in Large Corporations*, Philadelphia, 1950, p. 113.

25. See Gordon, *op. cit.*, Chapter 6.
26. Gordon, *op. cit.*, p. 119.
27. Gordon, *op. cit.*, Chapter 5.
28. See Chester Barnard, *The Functions of the Executive*, Harvard, 1938.
29. See *The Economics of Welfare*, by A. C. Pigou, London, 1920.
30. See Edith Penrose, *The Theory of the Growth of the Firm*, Oxford, 1959, p. 46.
31. Berle and Means, *op. cit.*, Table XIV.
32. See Gower, *op. cit.*, pp. 124–7.
33. See note 6 above.
34. According to Gordon, *op. cit.*, p. 27, the median proportion of votes held by officer directors in large U.S. companies in 1939 was one per cent, by other directors, $2\frac{1}{2}$ per cent, and by all directors, $3\frac{1}{2}$ per cent. Florence, *op. cit.* (1961), p. 104, gives the corresponding U.K. figures for all directors as 3 per cent in 1936 and $1\frac{1}{2}$ per cent in 1951. Pre-war, in only 27 per cent of the U.S. companies did all directors hold less than one per cent, and in only 33 per cent did they hold more than 10 per cent; the corresponding figures for the U.K. were 31 per cent of companies and 23 per cent of companies. (There was in the U.K. a significant relative decline in directorial holdings between 1936 and 1951.) The U.S. sample relates to 115 large manufacturing corporations, the U.K. sample to 102 industrial and commercial corporations with nominal issued capital exceeding £3 millions in 1951, and, on account of nationalisation, contains no railroads or utilities. Figures given by Villarejo in *New University Thought*, U.S., 1961, show that the position today in the U.S. is still very similar to that of 1939.
35. See for example, 'How Executives Invest their Money', *Fortune*, Feb. 1957, p. 133 *et seq.*
36. For an analysis of differences in market prices as between voting and non-voting (but otherwise equal) shares in the same company, see *The Economist*, London, July 27, 1957, p. 328.
37. The following is a selection of material on the subject of take-over raids: 'How Managements get Tipped Over', *Fortune*, May 1959; 'Pirates by Proxy', *The Management Review*, Dec. 1957; 'How Well-Bred Investors Overthrow a Management', *Fortune*, May 1959; *Bid for Power*, by George Bull and Anthony Vice, London, 1958; articles by Roy Jenkins (concerning attempted take-over of Courtaulds Ltd. by I.C.I. Ltd.) in the London *Observer*, March 18, 25, 1962; for the legal position in U.K., Gower, *op. cit.*, p. 490–5; for data on take-overs in the U.K., 1948–62, an article in *Economic Trends*, HMSO, London, April, 1963. The present author has a research grant from the Bank of England to study the financial implications of take-over; results expected to be published in 1965.
38. See Chapter 5, below.
39. See Berle and Means, *op. cit.*
40. For example, Florence, *op. cit.* (1953), noted two English companies, Dunlop Rubber and Harrods Stores, as presenting outstanding ex-

amples of dispersed shareholding, the largest holder in neither having more than one half of one per cent of the stock. Holdings dispersed in this degree imply 'managerial control', but also facilitate the task of the raider. Harrods, as the name implies, are not manufacturers but a large West End department store, world famous for both the variety and costliness of their wares. In 1960, against violent opposition from the existing management, the business was successfully raided by a traditional capitalist from Scotland. By contrast, not only are Dunlops, at the time of writing, inviolate, but several other attempted raids on manufacturing concerns have recently failed, the most notable case of course being that on Courtaulds, mentioned in n. 37 above.

41. See Oscar Lange, *Review of Economic Studies*, Vol. IV, No. 2, 1937, p. 127.
42. Joseph Schumpeter, *Capitalism, Socialism and Democracy*, 1942.
43. Downie, *op. cit.*

Notes to Chapter 2: Motives and Morals

1. P. J. Wiles, *Price, Cost and Output*, Oxford 1956 edition, p. 179. See also Preface and Chapter 11 of 1961 edition.
2. See, for example, W. Lloyd Warner and J. C. Abegglen, *Big Business Leaders in America*, N.Y., 1955. A partial exception to the remarks in the text is found in *The Managers*, by R. Lewis and Rosemary Stewart, N.Y., 1961. For a bibliography, see *Social Science Research on Business*, by R. A. Dahl, Mason Haire and P. Lazarsfeld, N.Y., 1959, pp. 151–2. The notes to Lloyd Warner's contribution in Mason, *op. cit.*, are also helpful.
3. See Herbert Simon, 'Decision Making in Economics', *AER*, June 1959. This article gives a good general bibliography, including Professor Simon's earlier works, of which the most immediately relevant are *Models of Man*, N.Y., 1957 (esp. Chapter 14) and *Organisations* (with J. G. March), N.Y., 1958.
4. William E. Henry, 'The Big Business Executive', *Am. Journ. Soc.*, Jan. 1949.
5. George Katona, *Psychological Analysis of Economic Behaviour*, N.Y., 1951, Chapter 9.
6. Baumol, *op. cit.*
7. Kenn Rogers, *Managers — Personality and Performance*, London (Tavistock Publications), 1963. See also discussion of this work in T. Barna, *Investment and Growth Policies in British Firms*, Cambridge, 1962, p. 54 *et seq.*
8. W. H. Whyte, *The Organisation Man*, N.Y., 1957.
9. C. Wright Mills, *The Power Elite*, N.Y., 1957.
10. Whyte, *op. cit.*, Chapter 11.
11. David Riesman, *The Lonely Crowd*, Yale, 1950.
12. J. H. Goldthorpe, in an unpublished lecture given to undergraduates in Cambridge, May 1962.

13. Goldthorpe, *op. cit.*
14. The author is here indebted to conversations with R. F. Kahn.
15. See James Duesenberry, *Income, Saving and the Theory of Consumer Demand*, Harvard, 1949.
16. See for example the account of the celebrated Bank Wiring Observation Room Study reported in *Management and the Worker*, by F. J. Roethlisberger and W. J. Dickson, Harvard, 1939.
17. See Barnard, *op. cit.*, pp. 142 *et seq.*
18. R. A. Gordon, *op. cit.* The references are to the 1945 edition but the passages quoted were repeated unchanged in the 1961 edition. The latter, however, had a new Preface in which the author indicated that he had found little evidence that his earlier conclusions needed modifying in the light of developments during the intervening period.
19. R. A. Gordon, *op. cit.*, p. 305.
20. R. A. Gordon, *op. cit.*, p. 305–6.
21. R. A. Gordon, *op. cit.*, p. 311.
22. For further information on the subject of of call girls see Sara Harris. *They Sell Sex, A Devastating Portrait of the Pimp in the Grey Flannel Suit*, N.Y., 1960. (Front cover states, 'A noted sociologist's documented inside story of how some of the nation's biggest industries and corporations use . . . high-priced prostitutes . . .'.)
23. See Downie, *op. cit.*, Chapter 7.
24. R. F. Henderson and Brian Tew, *Studies in Company Finance*, Cambridge, 1959, p. 298.
25. See Myron Gordon, *The Investment, Financing and Valuation of the Corporation*, Homewood, 1962, Table 15.1. The figures quoted in the text are adjusted to take account of differences in definition, Gordon's leverage ratio being that of Debt to Net Assets.
26. See R. A. Gordon, *op. cit.*, Chapter 12.
27. To the best of the author's knowledge the following bibliography is for practical purposes virtually complete (only articles whose results were subsequently incorporated in books listed being excluded):

      F. W. Taussig and W. S. Barker, 'American Corporations and their Executives', *QJE*, Nov. 1925; J. C. Baker, 'The Compensation of Executives', *Harv. Bus. Rev*, Spring 1935; J. C. Baker, *Executive Salaries and Bonus Plans*, N.Y., 1938; H. A. Simon, 'The Compensation of Executives', *Sociometry*, March 1957; David R. Roberts, *Executive Compensation*, Glencoe, 1959; A. Patton, *Men, Money and Motivation*, N.Y., 1961; J. W. McGuire and others, 'Executive Income, Sales and Profits', *AER*, Sept. 1962.

      The work of Roberts, *op. cit.*, is based on cross-section regression analysis of a sample of 77 U.S. corporations, averaged data, 1948–1950, the source being SEC. Patton and MacGuire use other sources, typically data available in *Fortune* and *Business Week*. MacGuire and associates use a sample of 45 firms on which to base moving cross-section regression analyses, 1953–9. They test a variety of hypotheses, including several involving lagged relationships, and the results generally confirm the conclusions of Roberts (see text below;

unfortunately the paper appeared too late for inclusion in our main argument). By contrast, the unconvincing hypothesis of Patton — that high salaries cause executives to 'work harder' thus leading to high profits — comes out very badly. (See MacGuire, *op. cit.*, p. 758.) Another interesting feature of the MacGuire material lies in the inclusion of imputed stock-option profits in the definition of compensation; that the results still show no significant partial correlation with profits tends to support our argument (text, above, p. 77) concerning the motivational significance of stock-option plans.

30. From Roberts, *op. cit.*, p. 54, and other sources.

31. These figures are based partly on Roberts, *op. cit.*, pp. 29–31, and partly on information in current periodicals (see, e.g., articles in *Harv. Bus. Rev.*, Jul–Aug. 1959, pp. 66–74, and in *Don's Review*, March 1958.

32. See *Management Record*, Sept. 1959, p. 270.

33. Roberts, *op. cit.*, Ch. 4.

34. The following regression was fitted to data relating to the firms in the Roberts sample, averages, 1948–50:

$$\log Y = a + b \cdot \log X$$

where,

Y = average number of corporate officers,

X = value of sales,

with the results:

$$a = -0.75 \qquad R = 0.6$$
$$b = 0.23 \mp 0.04$$

35. To the author's knowledge, the first writer to draw attention to this aspect of bonus incentive was N. S. Buchanan in 'Theory and Practice of Dividend Distribution', *QJE*, 1938, p. 64(n).

36. See ruling of Federal judge C. J. McNamee, reported in *Business Week*, May 31, 1958.

37. Roberts, *op. cit.*, p. 94.

38. See Penrose, *op. cit.*, p. 28(n).

39. Sources quoted in note 34, Chapter 1 above.

40. See note 39 above.

41. Gordon suggests that in the case of chief executives the figure is frequently decided by the incumbent himself, *op. cit.*, p. 277.

42. The measures of capital readily available are usually net rather than gross, inadequately adjusted for inflation and generally noisy, whereas turnover, by contrast is a relatively 'hard' variable.

43. In the available data capital is measured by 'tangible net worth', and differs from book value of capital and productive capacity by virtue of both leverage and other factors. The rate of return is measured by the ratio of net profits to net worth, and is also disturbed by leverage, but, we can show, to a smaller extent. As mentioned in the text, if the ratio of profits to turnover is substituted as the measure of profitability, none of the results are significantly affected. There is still the difficulty, however, that profits are taken net of interest charges, and will tend to be distorted by the scale effects of leverage. We do not think the trouble is likely to be serious, as, leverage ratios not being very dis-

persed, inter-firm differences in size are not much associated with leverage; indeed, as far as can be seen, the two variables are virtually independent.

44. The coefficient quoted is the ratio of the mean cubed deviations of observed from predicted values divided by the cube of their standard deviation. The reference is to equation 2.10.

45. See Simon, 1957, *op. cit.*, n. 27 above.

46. See *From Max Weber: Essays in Sociology*, ed. H. H. Gerth and C. Wright Mills, N.Y., 1946, p. 196.

47. See note 45 above.

48. See note 39 above.

49. Observation based on residuals from equation 2.10.

50. The most likely explanation of the apparent discrepancy between Roberts' and Whyte's conclusions in the matter of executive mobility is that the former is mainly concerned with mobility at high level, the latter at middle and low level. The Organisation Man changes his firm in order to establish his organisational standing; the status of the top executive is already established. The difference of emphasis is reflected in the authors' choice of data, and the reader will note that even Roberts' data show considerably greater mobility among the men who had not yet become corporate officers. Roberts, *op. cit.*, Chapter 4.

51. For example, Barnard, *op. cit.*, p. 145; Buchanan, *loc. cit.* (note 35 above); William Whyte in *Fortune*, Jan. 1954; J. K. Galbraith as quoted below; Downie, *op. cit.*, pp. 63-4; Penrose, *op. cit.*, p. 28; R. A. Gordon as quoted p. 63 above; George Hurff, *op. cit.*, p. 90; H. F. Lydall in the *Oxford Institute Bulletin* May 1959, reporting an enquiry of growth-aspirations in a sample of British manufacturing firms — only a third of the respondents did not envisage further growth in the immediate future, and at least half the chief executives hoped to double turnover within the foreseeable future. There is also considerable evidence of a value system based on growth in the periodical literature. For example, see 'One or Many Lines? Harder for Business to Base Growth on a Single Product', *Barron's*, 8th July, 1940; 'Diversification Quickens Growth', *Barron's*, 4th June, 1956; 'National Lead: A Study in Growth', *Magazine of Wall Street*, 4th Aug. 1956; 'Diversification: Is It Always the Answer [for companies planning growth]?' *The Iron Age*, 3rd Oct. 1957; 'How Diversification Pays', *Steel*, 24th Feb. 1958; 'What New Products Mean to Companies: Growth, Longer Life, Bigger Profits', *Printer's Ink*, 13th June, 1958; 'New Products Are Key to Future Growth', *Steel*, 8th June, 1959; 'Flintkote's Approach: A Definite Formula For Growth', *Industrial Development*, June 1959; 'The Importance of Financial Planning To a Growing Corporation', *The Commercial and Financial Chronicle*, 6th June, 1957; 'Financial Implications of Growth', *The Controller*, March 1958; 'Enterprises Whose Growth Has Been Achieved Without Major Outside Financing' *Magazine of Wall Street*, 20th Dec., 1958.

52. Robert Dorfman, 'Operations Research', *AER*, Sept. 1960, p. 608.
53. J. K. Galbraith, *American Capitalism*, Boston, 1952, p. 29.
54. Dale Jorgensen, in the presence of witnesses, in the Berkeley Faculty Club on a day in the Summer of 1961: the debate, needless to say, concerned the relative merits of neo-classical mathematics and the methods favoured by the writer.
55. See R. M. Cyert and J. G. March, 'Organisational Factors in the Theory of Oligopoly', (Section III) *QJE*, Feb. 1956.
56. Cyert and March, *op. cit.*

Notes to Chapter 3: Concepts and Methods

1. For some pertinent observations on the 'Marshallian' conception of the firm, see H. G. Johnson, *AER*, June, 1961.
2. Downie, *op. cit.*
3. Baumol, *op. cit.*
4. We refer particularly to the writings of the Oxford school, best surveyed in *Oxford Studies in the Price Mechanism*, edited by T. Wilson and P.W.S. Andrews, Oxford, 1951.
5. See for example the classic discussion of the problems of an imaginary organisation set up for the simple task of cutting wood, in Barnard, *op. cit.*, p. 246 *et seq.*
6. See J. Marshak, 'Elements for a Theory of Teams', *Management Science*, Jan., 1955.
7. In Cyert and March, *op. cit.*, firms are stimulated to take in slack by either low capacity utilisation or high prime costs. The effect is successful sales effort leading to increased utilisation. The *rationale* of the mechanism is apparently that low utilisation and high prime costs imply a relatively low ratio of quasi-rent to capital installed, i.e. relatively low short-run rate of return, this being the ultimate cause of the reaction. The result, however, is action on one dimension only, no mention being made of action to reduce prime costs. The present writer is at a loss to understand why the model was not more consistently formulated, for example with low profitability leading to various actions to raise profits (of which one, of course, would be sales effort), or low volume leading to actions to raise volume (of which one, of course, might be cost-price reducing improvements). The position is further complicated by the fact that although the stimulus on the utilisation dimension is represented by a static variable — the initial utilisation ratio — the stimulus on the other is represented by a rate of change, more precisely the change in unit prime costs relatively to that in other firms during the period of observation. Cyert and March would no doubt retort that their model nevertheless proved predictively successful. Predictive success, however (in the social sciences, at least), must always be judged relatively, and the authors made comparison only with the predictions of a very crude alternative

indeed. As a matter of fact it is easy to demonstrate that the data are as well or better explained by the more orthodox hypothesis that the observed changes in capacity utilisation were due to some unknown set of causes acting stochastically, and that the prime cost changes were then dependent on these (e.g. because the firms had rising static cost curves, or because the fast output changes induced fast factor supply-price increases). The significance of this will be better appreciated when it is realised that without the debatable prime-cost relationship the Cyert and March model virtually collapses, there being no significant association, direct or indirect, between the initial utilisation ratio and subsequent changes in utilisation.

The author is indebted to Professor S. Reiter for advice on this topic, but the latter cannot be held responsible for any errors in the argument as here presented.

8. Penrose, *op. cit.* For a further account of the present author's views on this work, see Marris, *EJ*, March 1961.

9. Harvey Leibenstein, *Economic Theory and Organisational Analysis*, N.Y., 1960.

10. Quoting C. Northcote Parkinson has now been adjudged unfashionable by a London glossy magazine, but academics remain compelled to recognise a horrid truth in many of his observations. The fundamental point is that the tendency for an organisation to expand is liable to become pathological if its activities lack operationality, i.e. if there is no recognised or recognisable relationship between administrative input (measured in heads) and whatever might be thought to be the appropriate concept of output. Parkinson's organisations grew by gross distortion of the input-output ratio; business organisations, in our conception, grow by causing output and input to expand in balance.   This is probably the most distinctive contribution of capitalism to human efficiency. (*Parkinson's Law* was first published in London in 1958 and has, of course, since been re-issued in many forms.)

11. Parkinson, *op. cit.*, Chapter 1.

12. See Penrose, *op. cit.*, p. 47 and Marris, *QJE*, May, 1963.

14. Mason Haire, *Modern Organisation Theory*, N.Y., 1959, p. 283.

15. Penrose, *op. cit.*, p. 29 and Marris, *op. cit.*, *EJ.*, 1961.

16. Baumol, *op. cit.*

17. See note 51, Chapter 2 above. A study of indexes shows that the frequency with which the word 'diversification' appears in titles to articles in business periodicals has displayed a consistent upward trend since the middle thirties.

18. See Penrose, *op. cit.*, 212–14. For a neo-classical treatment of diversification see M. R. Fisher, 'Towards a Theory of Diversification', *OEP*, Oct. 1961.

19. See for example R. A. Gordon, *op. cit.*, pp. 88–9; A. D. H. Kaplan, J. B. Dirlam and R. Lanzillotti, *Pricing in Big Business*, Menasha, 1958, Chap. 3, and 'How New Products are Planned and Why', *Printer's Ink*, 16 Oct. 1959, p. 72.

20. Penrose, *op. cit.*, Chapter 8.
21. See for example Ruth Cohen and Lesley Cook, *The Effects of Mergers*, London, 1958.
22. See Penrose, *op. cit.*, p. 22.
23. 'It follows from the comparison of the processes of internal and external growth that except under special circumstances, a greater rate of expansion is made possible by merger. . . . There is, however, no conclusive reason for thinking that (firms) tomorrow would not reach the position through internal growth that they have obtained today with the help of merger'. Penrose, *op. cit.*, p. 195.
24. See Penrose, *op. cit.*, p. 128.
25. See J. A. Schumpeter, *Business Cycles*, 1939.

Notes to Chapter 4: 'Demand'

1. For a study on the econometric measurement of static demand curves with residual trend, see J. R. N. Stone, *Consumer's Expenditure and Behaviour*, Cambridge, 1953.
2. Duesenberry, *op. cit.*
3. The author is here indebted to conversations with Mr. Gordon Pask.
4. Apart from Duesenberry, background reading for the following arguments includes S. Katz and P. Lazarsfeld, *Personal Influence*, N.Y., 1960, esp. Part I, Section 2; Riesman, *op. cit.*, Chapter 4, and Whyte, *op. cit.*, Chapter 26.
5. See Katz and Lazarsfeld, *op. cit.*, 1960, Part II, Section 2, Chapter V.
6. Cf. Duesenberry's classic account of the Demonstration Effect, *op. cit.*, pp. 26–8. The reader familiar with the passage will detect in our theory a difference of emphasis which will become increasingly apparent as the argument develops.
7. The author is indebted to P. E. Hart for this suggestion.
8. See Kaplan, Dirlam and Lanzillotti, *op. cit.*, pp. 59–60.
9. See Kaplan, Dirlam and Lanzillotti, *op. cit.*, p. 60.
10. See Katz and Lazarsfeld, *op. cit.*, p. 219 *et seq.*
11. See Katz and Lazarsfeld, *op. cit.*, p. 236.
12. See Whyte, *op. cit.*, p. 313.
13. Whyte, *op. cit.*, p. 314.
14. Katz and Lazarsfeld, *loc. cit.*
15. At a 'Tupperware Party' the sales representative has persuaded a suburbanite to invite her friends to coffee for the purpose of being persuaded to buy Tupperware. Advocates of this method of selling particularly emphasise the advantage that the parties tend to snowball, in other words set up a chain reaction. In our language, the trick is in finding a ready-made primary group. For a sociological account, see *New Society*, London, No. 8, 1962.
16. Whyte, *loc. cit.*

17. See James C. Early, *Pricing for Profit and Growth*, N.Y., 1962, esp. chapter entitled, 'Introducing and Pricing New Products'.
18. See note 4, Chapter 4 above.
19. See Kaplan, Dirlam and Lanzillotti, *op. cit.*, pp. 59–60.
20. See Joe S. Bain, *Barriers to New Competition*, Harvard, 1956, Chap. 3.
21. See *Printer's Ink*, August 2, 1957, p. 20. According to the figures given, the average failure rate in a sample of 200 U.S. firms, 1953–5, was about 20 per cent.
22. J. Von Neuman and O. Morgenstern, *The Theory of Games and Economic Behaviour*, Princeton, 1944.
23. Martin Shubik, *Strategy and Market Structure*, N.Y., 1960.
24. Joe Bain, *op. cit.*, Chap. 4.
25. Katz and Lazarsfeld, *op. cit.*
26. Bain, *op. cit.*, p. 25.
27. See R. Luce and H. Raiffa, *Games and Decisions*, N.Y., 1958, p. 483.
28. Shubik, *op. cit.*, pp. 214 *et seq.*
29. See Braithwaite, *The Theory of Games as a Tool for the Moral Philosopher*, Cambridge, 1955.
30. Duesenberry, *op. cit.*, Chapter 6.
31. Andrew Bain, Cambridge University Department of Applied Economics, Monograph, in process of publication, (Summer, 1963).

Notes to Chapter 5: 'Supply'

1. Modigliani, *AER*, Sept. 1959, p. 658.
2. See F. Modigliani and M. Miller, 'The Cost of Capital, Corporation Finance and the Theory of Investment', *AER*, June 1958, pp. 261–97, 'A Reply', *AER*, Sept. 1959, pp. 655–69, and 'Leverage, Dividend Policy and the Cost of Capital', paper read to Econometric Society, St. Louis, 1960; David Durand, 'Costs of Debt and Equity Funds for Business', Conf. on Res. in Bus. Finance, *NBER*, 1952 and 'The Cost of Capital, Corporation Finance and the Theory of Investment: a Comment', *AER*, Sept. 1959, pp. 639–55; John Lintner, 'A New Model of the Cost of Capital', paper read to Econometric Society, St. Louis, 1960; and Myron Gordon, *op. cit.*, Chapter 8 and 12 and pp. 189–93.
3. This is virtually Downie's position, although he does provide a couple of paragraphs of argument. Downie, *op. cit.*, p. 68.
4. See Modigliani and Miller, 1958, *op. cit.*
5. See Myron Gordon, *op. cit.*, p. 108.
6. See Myron Gordon, *op. cit.*, Chapter 5.
7. See R. Luce and H. Raiffa, *op. cit.*, Ch. 2.
8. A. D. Roy, 'Safety First and the Holding of Assets', *Econometrica*, July 1952.

9. Roy, *op. cit.*

10. For confirmation, see Myron Gordon, *op. cit.*, Table 15.1.

11. Myron Gordon, *op. cit.*, p. 65.

12. Myron Gordon concluded with a formulation in which the discount rate depended on the growth rate of the dividend as a whole, that is, in our notation, on rp, rather than on r alone. As the greater part of the present MS was complete at the time when Gordon's book (*op. cit.*) was first published (although see Chapter 7, below), we did not have time to investigate in detail the possible implications of this apparently more valid, and certainly more elegant formulation. The relevant conclusions of the two models are, however, evidently similar. In effect, Gordon's correction introduces what amounts to an additional non-linearity, but one working in the opposite direction to another non-linearity discovered, and assumed away, above. (We find the second derivative of max-safe growth rate with respect to profit rate to be small but positive, and treat it as if it were zero; Gordon's correction imports a negative tendency in this derivative and thus helps us.)

13. In a classic paper, Lintner found that the hypothesis that firms' dividend policies were governed by a long-run or 'target' pay-out ratio — towards which they attempted to move by a dynamic adjustment process — explained short-run fluctuations well. He did not attempt a precise formulation of the determinants of the target ratio itself, but indicated that his inquiries showed it to be generally influenced by the conflicting motives of growth on the one hand and normative treatment of shareholders on the other. See J. Lintner, 'Distribution of Incomes of Corporations among Dividends, Retained Earnings and Taxes', *AER*, May 1956, pp. 97–113.

14. In addition to the works cited in note 3 above, see also, Norman Buchanan, *op. cit.*, Oscar Harkavy 'The Relation between Retained Earnings and Common Stock Prices for Large Listed Corporations', *Journ. Fin.*, 1953; S. P. Dobrovolsky, *Corporate Income Retentions, 1915–43*, *NBER*, N.Y., 1951; Sargent Florence, 'Factors in Dividend Policy', *JRSS*, Series A, Part I, 1959, pp. 77–98; Henderson and Tew, *op. cit.*; G. R. Fisher, 'Some Factors Influencing Share Prices', *EJ*, March, 1961, and 'The Influence of Transitory Factors on Stock Exchange Prices', (unpublished MS, 1963).

15. 'Bodenhorn, Modigliani and Miller, and others have constructed elaborate models for the purpose of demonstrating that a share's price is independent of the expected future dividend without appearing to recognise that they are assuming away the fundamental problem.' Myron Gordon, *op. cit.*, p. 61.

16. See note 12 above, also (for statistical evidence) Myron Gordon, *op. cit.*, Chapter 12.

17. Modigliani and Miller, 1960, *op. cit.* (note 3 above).

18. See Fisher, 1963, note 14 above.

Notes to Chapter 6: Completed Micro-Models

1. At a seminar at Princeton, Dec. 1960.
2. See Kaplan and associates, *op. cit.*, pp. 130–161.
3. See Kenneth Arrow and Marc Nerlove, 'Optimal Advertising Policy under Dynamic Conditions', *Economica*, May 1962.
4. The following is a selection only: R. L. Hall and C. J. Hitch, 'Price Theory and Business Behaviour', *OEP*, no. 2, 1939, p. 12; F. Machlup, 'Marginal Analysis and Empirical Research', *AER*, Sept. 1946; R. A. Gordon, 'Short-Period Price Determination in Theory and Practice', *AER*, June 1948, p. 265; P. W. S. Andrews, *Manufacturing Business*, London, 1949; Richard Heflebower, 'Full Costs, Cost Changes, and Prices', in *Business Concentration and Price Policy*, Princeton, 1955; I. F. Pearce, 'A Study in Price Policy', *Economica*, May 1956, Peter Wiles, *op. cit.*
5. See references in note 19 Chapter 3 above.
6. See note 12, Chapter 3 above.
7. See Marris, *QJE*, May, 1963.
8. See J. Tinbergen, *The Theory of Economic Policy*, Amsterdam, 1955.
9. Downie, *op. cit.*, Chapter 7.
10. For a survey of theories of size distribution see H. Simon and C. Bonini, 'The Size Distribution of Business Firms', *AER*, Sept., 1958, and for a more recent stochastic model, P. E. Hart, 'The Size and Growth of Firms', *Economica*, Feb. 1962.

Notes to Chapter 7: Behaviour and Evidence

1. J. C. March and H. A. Simon, *Organisations*, NY, 1958, p. 141.
2. See, for example, Myron Gordon, *op. cit.*, p. 34.
3. Myron Gordon, *op. cit.*, p. 35.
4. See especially, Cyert and March, *op. cit.*
5. For an account of aspiration models, see Julius Margolis, 'The Analysis of the Firm: Rationalism, Conventionalism and Behaviourism', *Journ. of Bus. of the Univ. of Chicago*, July 1958.
6. See Marris, *QJE*, May, 1963.
7. See, for example, K. Lewin, 'Levels of Aspiration', in McV. Hunt, *Personality and the Behaviour Disorders*, NY, 1944.
8. See Katona, *op. cit.*, Chapter 9.
9. See Kaplan and associates, *op. cit.*, p. 149.
10. Baumol, *op. cit.*, p. 53.
11. Myron Gordon, *op. cit.*, John Meyer and Edwin Kuh, *The Investment Decision*, Harvard, 1957.
12. Meyer and Kuh, *op. cit.*, p. 157.
13. Gordon, *op. cit.*, p. 234.

Notes to Chapter 8: Possible Macro Implications

1. For a bibliography of the successive developments of the 'Kaldor model' see note 12 below.
2. Joan Robinson, *The Accumulation of Capital*, London, 1956.
3. R. F. Harrod, *Towards a Dynamic Economics*, London, 1948; Evesey Domar, *Essays in the Theory of Economic Growth*, Oxford, 1957.
4. Joan Robinson, *op. cit.*; James Meade, *A Neo-Classical Model of Growth*, London, 1961; Robert Solow, *Quarterly Journal of Economics*, 1956; Trevor Swan, *Economic Record*, 1956.
5. See note 12 below.
6. L. Pasinetti, *Review of Economic Studies* 1964, No. 2.
7. See Joan Robinson, *op. cit.*, p. 100.
8. Duesenberry, *op. cit.*
9. Joan Robinson, *op. cit.*, p. 99.
10. See note 12 below.
11. See R. G. Lipsey, *Economica*, 1960, p. 1.
12. This statement is based on an analysis of the following: Kaldor, *Essays on Value and Distribution*, pp. 228–36, *Essays on Economic Stability and Growth*, pp. 256–300, and in *The Theory of Capital*, Macmillan, London, 1961, pp. 177–220; also Kaldor and Mirrlees, *Review of Economic Studies*, June 1962.

LIST OF REFERENCES

ABEGGLEN, J. C., and WARNER, W., *Big Business Leaders in America*, New York, 1955

ANDREWS, P. W. S., and WILSON, T., *Oxford Studies in Price Mechanism* Oxford, 1951

—— *Manufacturing Business*, London, 1949

ARROW, K., and NERLOVE, M., 'Optimal Advertising Policy under Dynamic Conditions', *Economica*, May, 1962

BAIN, J. S., *Barriers to New Competition*, Harvard, 1956

BAKER, J. C., *Executive Salaries and Bonus Plans*, New York, 1938

—— 'The Compensation of Executives', *Harvard Business Review*, Spring, 1935

BARKER, W. S., and TAUSSIG, F. W., 'American Corporations and their Executives', *Quarterly Journal of Economics*, November, 1925

BARNA, T., *Investment and Growth Policies in British Firms*, Cambridge, 1962

BARNARD, C., *The Functions of the Executive*, Harvard, 1938

BAUMOL, W., *Business Behaviour, Value and Growth*, New York, 1959

BERLE, A. A., and MEANS, G., *The Modern Corporation and Private Property*, New York, 1932

BONINI, C., and SIMON, H., 'The Size Distribution of Business Firms', *American Economic Review*, September, 1958

BRAITHWAITE, R. B., *The Theory of Games as a Tool for the Moral Philosopher*, Cambridge, 1955

BUCHANAN, N. S., 'Theory and Practice of Dividend Distribution', *Quarterly Journal of Economics*, November, 1938

BULL, G., and VICE, A., *Bid for Power*, London, 1958

BURNHAM, J., *The Managerial Revolution*, New York, 1941

COHEN, R., and COOK, P. L., *The Effects of Mergers*, London, 1958

CYERT, R. M., and MARCH, J. G., 'Organisational Factors in the Theory of Oligopoly', (Section III), *Quarterly Journal of Economics*, February, 1956

DAHL, R. A., HAIRE, M., and LAZARSFELD, P., *Social Science Research on Business*, New York, 1959

DICKSON, W. J., and ROETHLISBERGER, F. J., *Management and the Worker*, Harvard, 1939

DIRLAM, J. B., LANZILLOTTI, R., and KAPLAN, A. D. H., *Pricing in Big Business*, Menasha, 1958

DOBROVOLSKY, S. P., *Corporate Income Retentions, 1915–43*, New York, 1951

DOMAR, E., *Essays in the Theory of Economic Growth*, Oxford, 1957

DORFMAN, R., 'Operations Research', *American Economic Review*, September, 1960

DOWNIE, J., *The Competitive Process*, London, 1958

DUESENBERRY, J., *Income, Saving and the Theory of Consumer Demand*, Harvard, 1949

DURAND, D., 'Costs of Debt and Equity Funds for Business: Trends and Problems of Measurement', In: *Conference on Research in Business Finance*, New York, 1952

EARLY, J. C., *Pricing for Profit and Growth*, New York, 1962

FISHER, G. R., 'Some Factors Influencing Share Prices', *Economic Journal*, March, 1961

FISHER, M. R., 'Towards a Theory of Diversification', *Oxford Economic Papers*, October, 1961

FLORENCE, P. S., *Ownership, Control and Success of Large Companies*, London, 1961

—— 'Factors in Dividend Policy', *Journal of Royal Statistical Society*, Series A., Part 1, 1959

—— *The Logic of British and American Industry*, London, 1953

GALBRAITH, J. K., *American Capitalism*, Boston, 1952

GERTH, H. H., and MILLS, C. W., eds., *From Max Weber: Essays in Sociology*, New York, 1946

GORDON, M., *The Investment, Financing and Valuation of the Corporation*, Homewood, 1962

GORDON, R. A., 'Short-Period Price Determination in Theory and Practice', *American Economic Review*, June, 1948

—— *Business Leadership in the Large Corporation*, Washington, D.C., 1945 (and paperback, Berkeley, 1961)

GOWER, L. C. B., *Modern English Company Law*, London, 1957

HAIRE, M., *Modern Organisation Theory*, 1959

—— DAHL, R. A., and LAZARSFELD, P., *Social Science Research on Business*, New York, 1959

HALL, R. L., and HITCH, C. J., 'Price Theory and Business Behaviour', *Oxford Economic Papers*, No. 2, 1939

HARKAVY, D., 'The Relation between Retained Earnings and Common Stock Prices for Large Listed Corporations', *Journal of Finance*, 1953

HARRIS, S., *They call it Sex, A Devastating Portrait of the Pimp in the Grey Flannel Suit*, New York, 1960

HARROD, R. F., *Towards a Dynamic Economics*, London, 1948

HART, P. E., 'The Size and Growth of Firms', *Economica*, February, 1962

HEFLEBOWER, R., 'Full Costs, Cost Changes and Prices', In: *Business Concentration and Price Policy*, Princeton, 1955

HENDERSON, R. F., and TEW, B., *Studies in Company Finance*, Cambridge, 1959

HENRY, W. E., 'The Big Business Executive', *American Journal of Sociology*, January, 1949

HITCH, C. J., and HALL, R. L., 'Price Theory and Business Behaviour', *Oxford Economic Papers*, No. 2, 1939

HUNT, H., *The Development of the Business Corporation in England*, Harvard, 1960

HURFF, G., *Social Aspects of Enterprise in Large Corporations*, Philadelphia, 1950

JENKINS, R., 'The Untold Story of how ICI became the Thwarted Giant', *The Observer*, March 18th and 25th, 1962

JOHNSON, H. G., 'The *General Theory* after Twenty-five Years', *American Economic Review*, June, 1961

KALDOR, N., and MIRRLEES, J. A., 'A New Model of Economic Growth', *Review of Economic Studies*, June, 1962

KALDOR, N., 'Capital Accumulation and Economic Growth', in F. Lutz, *The Theory of Capital*, London, 1961

—— *Essays on Value and Distribution*, London, 1960

—— *Essays on Economic Stability and Growth*, London, 1960

KAPLAN, A. D. H., DIRLAM, J. B., and LANZILLOTTI, R., *Pricing in Big Business*, Menasha, 1958

KATONA, G., *Psychological Analysis of Economic Behaviour*, New York, 1951

KATZ, S., and LAZARSFELD, P., *Personal Influence*, New York, 1960

KATZ, W. G., 'The Philosophy of Mid-Twentieth Century Corporation Statutes', *Law and Contemporary Problems*, Spring, 1958

KUH, E., and MEYER, J., *The Investment Decision*, Harvard, 1957

LANGE, O., 'On the Economic Theory of Socialism', *Review of Economic Studies*, Vol. IV 1937

LANZILLOTTI, R., KAPLAN, A. D. H., and DIRLAM, J. B. *Pricing in Big Business*, Menasha, 1958

LAZARSFELD, P., and KATZ, S., *Personal Influence*, New York, 1960

—— HAIRE, M., and DAHL, R. A., *Social Science Research on Business*, New York, 1959

LEIBENSTEIN, H., *Economic Theory and Organisational Analysis*, New York, 1960

LEWIN, K., 'Levels of Aspiration', In: McV. Hunt, *Personality and the Behaviour Disorders*, New York, 1944

LEWIS, R., and STEWART, R., *The Managers*, New York, 1961

LINTNER, J., 'A New Model of the Cost of Capital', paper read to Econometric Society, St. Louis, 1960

—— 'Distribution of Incomes of Corporations among Dividends, Retained Earnings and Taxes', *American Economic Review*, May, 1956

LIPSEY, R. G., 'The Relation between Unemployment and the Rate of Change of Money Wage Rates in the United Kingdom, 1862–1957: a Further Analysis', *Economica*, 1960

LUCE, R., and RAIFFA, H., *Games and Decisions*, New York, 1958

LYDALL, H. F., 'The Growth of Manufacturing Firms', *Bulletin of the Oxford University Institute of Statistics*, May, 1959

McGUIRE, J. W., *and others*, 'Executive Income, Sales and Profits', *American Economic Review*, September, 1962

MACHLUP, F., 'Marginal Analysis and Empirical Research', *American Economic Review*, September, 1946

MARCH, J. G., and SIMON, H. A., *Organisations*, New York, 1958

—— and CYERT, R. M., 'Organisational Factors in the Theory of Oligopoly', (Section III), *Quarterly Journal of Economics*, February, 1956

MARGOLIS, J., 'The Analysis of the Firm: Rationalism, Conventionalism and Behaviourism', *Journal of Business of the University of Chicago*, July, 1958

MARRIS, R. L., 'A Model of the "Managerial" Enterprise', *Quarterly Journal of Economics*, May, 1963

—— Review of E. T. Penrose: *Theory of the Growth of the Firm*, *Economic Journal*, March, 1961

MARSHAK, J., 'Elements for a Theory of Teams', *Management Science*, January, 1955

MASON, E., ed., *The Corporation in Modern Society*, Cambridge, Mass., 1960

MEADE, J. E., *A Neo-Classical Model of Growth*, London, 1961

MEANS, G., and BERLE, A. A., *The Modern Corporation and Private Property*, New York, 1932

MEYER, J., and KUH, E., *The Investment Decision*, Harvard, 1957

MILLER, M., and MODIGLIANI, F., 'The Cost of Capital, Corporation Finance and the Theory of Investment', *American Economic Review*, June, 1958

MILLS, C. W., *The Power Elite*, New York, 1957

—— and GERTH, H. H., eds., *From Max Weber: Essays in Sociology*, New York, 1946

MIRRLEES, J. A., and KALDOR, N., 'A New Model of Economic Growth', *Review of Economic Studies*, June, 1962

MODIGLIANI, F., 'The Cost of Capital, Corporation Finance, and the Theory of Investment: reply', *American Economic Review*, September, 1959

—— and MILLER, M., 'The Cost of Capital, Corporation Finance and the Theory of Investment', *American Economic Review*, June, 1958

MORGENSTERN, O., and VON NEUMAN, J., *The Theory of Games and Economic Behaviour*, Princeton, 1944

NERLOVE, M., and ARROW, K., 'Optimal Advertising Policy under Dynamic Conditions', *Economica*, May, 1962

PARKINSON, C. N., *Parkinson's Law*, London, 1958

PASINETTI, L. L., 'Rate of Profit and Income Distribution in Relation to the Rate of Economic Growth', *Review of Economic Studies*, October, 1962

PATTON, A., *Men, Money and Motivation*, New York, 1961

PEARCE, I. F., 'A Study in Price Policy', *Economica*, May, 1956

PENROSE, E., *The Theory of the Growth of the Firm*, Oxford, 1959

PIGOU, A. C., *The Economics of Welfare*, London, 1920

RAIFFA, H., and LUCE, R., *Games and Decisions*, New York, 1958

RIESMAN, D., *The Lonely Crowd*, Yale, 1950

ROBERTS, D. R., *Executive Compensation*, Glencoe, 1959

ROBINSON, J., *The Accumulation of Capital*, London, 1956

ROETHLISBERGER, F. J., and DICKSON, W. J., *Management and the Worker*, Harvard, 1939

ROGERS, K., *Managers—Personality and Performance*, London, 1963

ROY, A. D., 'Safety First and the Holding of Assets', *Econometrica*, July, 1952

SAMUELSON, P., *Economics*, New York, 1948

SCHUMPETER, J. A., *Capitalism, Socialism and Democracy*, London, 1942

—— *Business Cycles*, New York, 1939

SHUBIK, M., *Strategy and Market Structure*, New York, 1960

SIMON, H. A., 'Decision Making in Economics', *American Economic Review*, June, 1959

—— and BONINI, C., 'The Size Distribution of Business Firms', *American Economic Review*, September, 1958

—— and MARCH, J. G., *Organisations*, New York, 1958

—— *Models of Man*, New York, 1957

—— 'The Compensation of Executives', *Sociometry*, March, 1957

SOLOW, R., 'A Contribution to the Theory of Economic Growth', *Quarterly Journal of Economics*, February, 1956

STEWART, R., and LEWIS, R., *The Managers*, New York, 1961

STONE, J. R. N., *Consumers' Expenditure and Behaviour*, Cambridge, 1953

SWAN, T., 'Economic Growth and Capital Accumulation', *Economic Record*, November, 1956

TAUSSIG, F. W., and BARKER, W. S., 'American Corporations and their Executives', *Quarterly Journal of Economics*, November, 1925

TAWNEY, R. H., *Religion and the Rise of Capitalism*, London, 1926

TEW, B., and HENDERSON, R. F., *Studies in Company Finance*, Cambridge, 1959

TINBERGEN, J., *The Theory of Economic Policy*, Amsterdam, 1955

VEBLEN, T., *Absentee Ownership*, London, 1923

VICE, A., and BULL, G., *Bid for Power*, London, 1958

VON NEUMAN, J., and MORGENSTERN, O., *The Theory of Games and Economic Behaviour*, Princeton, 1944

WARNER, W. L., and ABEGGLEN, J. C., *Big Business Leaders in America*, New York, 1955

WEBER, M., *The Protestant Ethic and the Spirit of Capitalism*, translated by Talcot Parsons, London and New York, 1930

WHYTE, W. H., *The Organisation Man*, New York, 1957

WILES, P. J., *Price, Cost and Output*, Oxford, 1956 and 1961

WILSON, T., and ANDREWS, P. W. S., eds., *Oxford Studies in the Price Mechanism*, Oxford, 1951

INDEX

'ability quotient', of teams of managers, 80–1, 85–6, 88, 89, 102
accounting conventions, xvii–xviii
accounting practices, 66
activation
  of consumers, 144, 145, 146, 149, 156, 166, 169, 174
  of managers, 159
activity analysis, 113
administration, difficulties of, as constraint on growth of firm, *see* constraints
advantages, net, theory of, 15–16, 81, 92
advertising, 136, 137, 138, 142, 193
  expenditure on, 119, 143, 170, 180, 186, 227, 230
'affluent society', 60, 134, 136
agriculture, 91, 289
ambition (aspiration) of managers, 50, 51, 108, 273, 274
analysis, economic, methods of, 126–30
  see also behaviouristic approach, dynamics, statics
artists, incomes of, 93
assets, defined xvii
  fixed, xvii, 13
  gross, 206, 207, 277; definition of size and growth by, 118–19, 130; growth rate of, 48, 107, 119, 206, 222, 235–8, 241, 277; ratio of debt to, 66; ratio of new capital to, 286
  liquid, 13, 131
  net, 206, 235; book value of, 8, 22, 28, 31, 35, 36, 37, 39, 131, 206, 207, 209, 212, 253
  productive and non-productive, 41
  theories of holding of, 16, 210–16
authority, levels of, 63, 91
  and income, 92, 93

Babycham, 140–1, 147
balance equation, 235, 236, 241, 248, 254
balanced growth, *see* growth rate
'bandwaggoning', 187–92

bars and barriers, to socio-economic contact, 155–8, 172–3
behaviouristic approach, to theories of motivation, 48, 107–9, 135, 266–288
Beta coefficient (rate of gradation of salaries), 94–100, 260
bonuses to managers, 66, 68–70, 78, 90
  as percentage of total remuneration, 67
borrowing, 7–8, 206–8
borrowing power, 19
bureaucratic environment in large corporations, 33, 59, 78, 90–1, 99
bureaucratic model of firm, 99–101
'bureconic' theory of salaries, 89–99
  policy implications of, 99–101
business schools, 111, 276

capacity (productive), defined xvii
  growth rate of, 118, 175–6, 179, 204, 205, 206, 224, 249; and growth rate of demand, 65, 118, 224, 272–3, 274; and profitability, 249; and rate of return, 118, 188, 204, 208, 220, 225, 226, 275
  managers' salaries and, 73, 96–7
  utilisation of, 118, 119, 273, 283, 309
capital, xvii
  corporate, 12, 13, 33
  growth rate of, 9, 43, 123, 130, 206, 248, 254, 283, 286, 287, 297; maximisation of, 206, 207–8, 216–20, 237, 241, 244, 245
  ratio of output to, 292, 297, 305, 306; in micro-models (1), 228, 230, 233, 235, 239, 241, 242, 246, 249; (2), 250, 251; in neo-classical model, 83
  supply of, 204–23, 224, 274, 308
  see also assets, capacity, dilution, new issues
capitalism, capitalists
  managerial, xi, 1, 2, 4–5, 32–3, 60, 90, 112, 264, 289–90
  neo-classical conception of, 73
  traditional, 1–11, 32, 40, 57, 59, 90, 104, 171, 261, 289–90

chain reaction in development of demand
for consumers' goods, 145–50, 154, 157, 170, 175, 189–90
for intermediate products (producers' goods), 158–60
class, social, 48, 51, 105, 146–7, 156, 172
see also status, middle classes, working classes
Cola drinks, 140
committees, in business organisation, 91
Communist countries, 21, 91, 93
companies (joint-stock, limited-liability), 1, 4, 11–18, 110, 112
compensation, *see* salary
competence, professional, 56–61, 308
competition, 5, 186–92, 264
and innovations, 159, 176–7, 183
conformism, in development of demand, 148–9, 166, 167, 168
conscience
corporate, 51
of managers towards shareholders and shares, 19, 54–5, 75, 207
constraints, xvi
to avoid take-over, 30, 40
on growth rate: financial, 4, 7, 8, 204–23; institutional, 45; managerial or administrative, 4, 7, 114–18, 123–4, 224, 225, 228, 305; policy, 208, 210; shareholders', 46
see also 'gearing', security, valuation ratio
consumers
activation of, 144, 145, 149, 166, 169, 174
appeal of products to, 122, 146, 182, 185, 200
behaviour of, 61, 173, 174, 299
brain of, 135–7, 142
compactness of, defined 161
gregariousness of, defined 160; 166, 168, 169
groups of (primary, secondary and linked), defined 160; 149–57, 164, 171, 201
income of, 106–7, 147, 156
loyalty of, to established products, 192
needs of, 59, 60

tastes of, 172, 173
utility for, 106, 262
consumption
decisions about, 137, 295; *see also* prices
diversification and, 299, 300
growth rate of, 296
Puritans and, 10
consumption function, 124, 300, 301
contact, socio-economic
between consumers, defined 160; 138–9, 146–54, 166, 201; bars and barriers to, 155–8, 172–3
between managers, 159
control
separation of ownership from, xi, 14, 18, 33
span of, 94–5, 96
co-ordination, function of management in, 85, 91, 231
corporate rich, 51, 54, 104
corporations
constitution of, 11–18, 294
pre-history of, 5–11
see also officers, corporate
cost curve, 14, 85
critical ratio, *see* pioneer consumers
criticality in development of demand, defined 146, 163; 168, 169, 185
costs of, 179–82

debt, defined xvii; 66, 206
decisions, 2, 3–4, 120, 201, 204, 249, 250, 275
consistency of, 272, 276
efficiency of, 116–17, 251
organisation and, 57, 103, 127
procedure in, 228–30
speed of, 3, 231–3
variables in, 225, 247
see also consumption, policy
delegation, in business organisation, 91
demand, defined, 130–1
development of, 133–203
elasticity of, 143, 144, 145, 176
growth rate of, defined 131; and diversification rate, *see* diversification; and growth rate of capacity, *see* capacity; and management policy, 119–20, 227; and profit rate, *see* profit rate; and profitability, *see* profitability

see also criticality, 'explosion', gestation, saturation

demand curves, 251–4
  for different firms, 258, 270, 271, 272, 278, 279, 281
  families of, 227, 228
  for pioneer and 'sheep-like' consumers, 143, 144, 145
  for 'saturated' product, 177, 178
  in earlier theory, 119, 120
  in micro-model (2), 263–4
  static, 121, 135
  total (general) and partial, defined 291; 296, 298, 299, 300–2, 304, 306

demand functions, 227
  pioneer's, defined 161
  'sheep-like', defined 161; 172–5, 176

demand growth curves, 44, 239, 241, 250

demand growth function, 44, 199, 238, 242, 275

democracy, 91–2

development and research, expenditure on, 133, 170, 180–1, 183, 186, 199, 225, 227, 228–9, 230, 235, 249

dilution of capital, 25, 26, 27, 32
  by stock options, 71

directors, boards of, 12, 13, 14
  share-holdings of, 18

discount
  investors' rate of, 24, 214
  managers' rate of, 69
  market rate of, 22–5, 31, 39, 44, 204, 209, 258; and rate of return, 23, 75, 76, 207, 210, 216, 217, 253, 256, 293; and retention ratio, 42, 77, 213, 215, 216, 221, 222
  take-over raiders' rate of, 33, 34, 35–6, 40

dishwashing machine, example of want creation, 138–9, 147

diversification, defined 131
  differentiated, 121, 134–5, 175, 231, 299; balance of, with imitative diversification, 229, 249
  growth by, 60–1, 119–22, 126; dynamics of, 133–200
  imitative, 121, 122, 134–5, 186–8, 199–200, 298
  management policy on, 120, 175, 184, 199, 201, 224, 300–1

negative, 259
rate of, defined 131; 178; and growth rate of demand, 120, 129, 180, 224, 225, 226–49 *passim*, 250, 253, 299–300, 302; and index of profitability, 183, 184; optimum, 243, 244, 245, 250; and probability of success, 230; and rate of return, 183, 184, 253; and technical progress, 124, 126, 298–9, 302; variation of, 249, 291, 303

dividends, 12, 13, 14
  bonus schemes and, 68, 69
  price of shares and, 21, 209, 221, 269
  retention ratio and, 75, 214, 215, 221
  saving out of, 265
  take-over danger and, 20
  valuation ratio and, 28, 222, 258

dynamics
  classical, 127, 128, 275
  comparative, 127, 128
  post-Keynesian, 303

earnings of firms, defined, xviii; 13, 22, 24, 25, 209, 221, 222
  retained, *see* retentions

earnings discrepancy, 24

efficiency of management, 17, 31, 243, 247
  capital-output ratio and, 238, 239, 246, 305
  corporations' partial monopoly of, 265
  growth rate and, 45, 70, 116–18, 123, 224–7
  maximisation of, 118
  take-over and, 44

electricity supply concerns, studies of, 222

employment, 59, 303, 309

entrepreneurs, 1–5, 14

equity structure, 212, 213

executives, *see* managers

'explosion' of demand, defined 163
  probability of, 163, 164, 168
  products showing, 175, 176, 184, 185, 187, 189, 228, 232
  rate of, 125, 188, 192

failure
  financial, 55, 64, 65, 66, 103, 206
  rate of, among new products, 180, 245

feed-back, in behaviour system, 127, 128

finance
control of, 232
managerial policy on, 128, 247, 254, 256
separation of organising from, 33, 78
supply of, and growth rate, 4, 7, 8, 204 et seq., 274; maximisation of, 285; and share prices, 19; and take-over, 20, 34
traditional capitalism in, 289
finance-supply curves, 238, 240
finance-supply function, 241

firm
characterisation of the, 110–14
growth of the, see growth
micro-theory of the, 127–8
theory of the, 277
flotation, of new company, 6–7
food manufacturing firms, studies of, 278–88

'gambler's ruin', as economic model, 194
'gearing' ('leverage'), defined 131
bonus schemes and, 69, 70
constraints on, 107, 206, 235, 237
extent of, in U.K. and U.S., 66
maximum, 8
negative, 131
satisficing and, 268, 269
valuation ratio and, 207–8, 222
gearing ratio, defined, xvii, 131–2; 9, 107, 128, 129, 206, 207, 208
maximum, 8, 9
in micro-models, 225, 235, 247
geography, and socio-economic contact, 150–2, 156
gestation of demand for new product, defined 163; 180, 181, 182, 184, 186, 228, 232, 234
Golden Age, Robinsonian, 303, 305, 310
gradation of salaries, 93
rate of (Beta coefficient), 94–100, 260
gregariousness, of consumers, see consumers
growth of firms
capacity for, 58, 85, 113, 114
managerial motives for, 50, 53, 60–1, 63, 65, 66, 69, 70, 100

managerial propensities to, 230, 277, 300, 307, 310
methods of: by borrowing, 8, 208; by diversification, 60–1, 119–22, 126, 133–200; by merger, 122–4; by new issues, 213, 216, 218, 285; by retentions, 69, 207, 213; by threat of 'war', 197–200
'growth industries', 263, 281, 283, 285

growth rate
balanced (sustainable), 40–2, 44, 75, 118–19, 129, 179, 237, 240, 247, 248, 254, 272–7; curve of, 240, 248, 249
balanced and safe, 42–4, 205, 219, 224, 253; maximisation of, 241, 257
constraints on, see constraints
efficiency and, see efficiency
flexible, 309–10
inflexible, 303–8
maximisation of, 47, 104, 179, 184, 200, 216, 224, 225, 226, 269; in micro-models (1), 226–46 passim, (2), 250, 251, 253, 259, 260–5
natural and quasi-natural, 296, 303
security and, see security
supply of finance and, see finance
take-over and, see take-over
valuation ratio and, 220, 270
see also growth rates under: assets (gross), capacity, capital, demand
growth rates, rate of change of, xvi

'hedging' by investors, 18, 211
hidden persuaders, 192
hierarchical compression, 96
hierarchies, in business organisation, 64, 91, 92, 103
hindsight, 283, 284

imitation, see diversification, imitative
incentive schemes, 62
incentives, for managers, 53, 90
income
consumers', 106–7, 147, 156
corporate, 13
distribution of, 173, 308, 310
intellectuals', 93
managers', 48, 66–8, 93, 105, 263, 308
national, ratio of profits to, 292, 293, 294, 296, 305, 306, 307, 309

status and, 92, 93, 106
see also salary
indifference curves (between growth
    rate and valuation ratio), 107, 261,
    262, 263, 264, 305, 307
'inhibition', in development of de-
    mand, 173, 174, 182
'inner-direction,' 51, 167
innovations
    in consumption, 299
    in manufacture, 158–60, 176–7, 299,
    302; and size of firm, 183
input-output system, 112–13
intellectuals, income of, 93
interest
    percentage of profits paid out as, 66
    rate of, 9, 207, 208, 235, 307
investment policies of managements,
    20, 23, 31, 33, 46, 128, 295
investors, 7, 20–1, 204–15
iso-valuation lines, 252, 253, 258, 272,
    280
    see also supply curves
issues of stock, *see* new issues

labour force, of a firm, 31, 112, 233, 297
    see also workers, manual
latent needs of consumers, *see*
    needs
'leverage', *see* 'gearing'
liquidation
    forced, 8, 13
    voluntary, 260
liquidity, 131, 283
liquidity ratio, 41
loyalty
    of consumers to established pro-
    ducts, 192, 193
    of managers: to group, 62; to
    organisation, 52; to propertied
    class, 54; to shareholders, 19

machinery firms, studies of, 278–88
management, 9, 15–18, 31–2, 85–9
managerialism, 289
managers, 6, 14, 19
    activation of, 159
    dismissal of, 16–17, 19, 20, 27, 29, 64
    growth propensities of, 230, 277,
    300, 307, 310
    middle, 51, 72
    middle and junior, 31, 67, 93, 102,
    103, 130

mobility of, 33, 67, 89, 101, 102, 103
motives and morals of, 46–109
promotion of, 64
self-identification of, with firm, 15,
    50, 104, 105
teams of, 16, 32, 54, 56–61, 80–1,
    89; filling of vacancies in, 99–100
    101, 103
training of, 115
    see also constraints, income, salaries,
    shareholders, shares, utility
marginal product, of management,
    88
market
    share of, conceded to competitor,
    190–1, 197, 198, 200
    static, 187, 188, 192–9
    stock-, *see* stock-market
market population, defined 145; 146,
    150, 155, 156, 157, 163, 175
    growth rate of, 296, 303
    rationalised, defined, 160; 150, 153,
    155, 156
    size of, 145, 168–9, 176, 181, 183
    stratification of, defined 160; 157,
    166, 167, 168, 169, 173; index of,
    defined 161; 157–8, 168
market research (consumer research),
    141, 185
market value, *see* stock-market value
marketing
    expenses of, 119, 133, 224, 225, 227,
    228, 229, 230, 235, 250, 259,
    critical, 180–1, 183, 185, 186
    optimum order of, 178–9
Marxists, 1
    neo-, 51, 54, 295
meat, high quality, as example of want
    creation, 139
mergers, 32, 122–4, 133
middle classes, 56, 92, 100
monopoly, monopolistic behaviour,
    prices, etc., 5, 123, 125, 177, 250,
    264, 265, 292, 309
motives of managers, 46–9, 85, 109
    economic: broad, 48, 61–6; narrow,
    66–85
    psychological, 48, 49–51
    sociological, 48, 51–61

needles-in-haystack analogy, 267
needs, latent, of consumers, 139, 141,
    142, 147, 182, 183, 264, 299

new-issue rate, 208–10, 215, 216–17; in micro-models (1), 225, 235–7, 247; (2), 256

new issues of stock, 19, 23–7, 65, 69, 215

   growth by, 213, 216, 218, 285

obsolescence, 121

officers, corporate

   number of, and size of firm, 69, 74, 80, 96

   remuneration of, 67, 74, 76

   shares held by, 72, 76

oligopoly, oligopolistic behaviour, etc., 5, 110, 125, 130, 177, 178, 187, 201, 309

opinion leaders, 144, 193

optimum values, xvi

organisation

   as function of managers, 14, 32, 57–8, 90, 112, 114, 230

   separation of finance from, 33, 78

Organisation Man, 51, 149

Organisation Theory, 111, 112

'organisational slack', 108, 247, 270, 271, 275, 279, 280, 281, 286, 287

'other-direction', 51, 166

output

   growth rate of, 297, 301, 303

   per head, see productivity

   ratio of, to capital, see capital

   see also volume

ownership, separation of, from control, xi, 14, 18, 33

Parkinson's Law, 114

paternalism, 59, 60

'peace' and 'war' (commercial), 190, 191, 197

peerage, 105

personnel officer, 60

pioneer consumers, 142–5, 180

   critical ratio of, defined 164; 165, 168, 169, 173, 175, 179, 180, 181–182, 183, 185, 186; economic significance of, 170–1

   ratio of, to ultimate consumers, 171

pioneer demand functions, defined 161; 176, 182

pioneer firms, 159

planning, economic, 232

policy

   decisions on, 56, 63–4, 120, 175, 273

problems of, 180

'safe' (from risk of take-over), 31, 36–9, 44, 45

see also management policy under: demand (growth rate of), diversification, finance, investment, prices, retentions

policy models

   (1), 226–49

   (2), 249–65

population

   growth of, 303, 305

   market, see market population

power, managerial, 48, 62–3, 64, 66, 93, 107, 260, 308

precedence, in U.K. and U.S., 105

predestination, doctrine of, 10

press, the financial, 215

prestige, managerial, 17, 18, 62, 48, 105, 106, 107, 260, 308

prices

   in consumption decisions, 119, 138, 143, 144, 145, 172, 173, 174

   'full-cost', 230

   general level of, 130; relative to wages, 126, 128, 291, 292, 304, 309, 310

   in gestation period, 182

   in imitative diversification, 189–92

   management policy on, 46, 133, 201, 202, 224, 225; in micro-model (1), 226–30, 235, 249

   in 'saturated' market, 175–8, 182, 188, 201

   of shares, see shares

   size of market and, 175

   take-over and, 259

production

   costs of, 200

   techniques of, 124, 224, 231, 249, 297

production functions, 82, 124, 126, 297, 298; revised, 85–9

productivity (output per head), 126, 128

   growth rate of, 296, 301, 303

   wages and, 298

products

   intermediate (producers'), 158–60, 193

   new, see diversification, success

   unsuccessful, 121, 180, 184, 199, 233, 234, 245

see also 'explosion', gestation, saturation

profession, management as a, 33, 51, 52

professional competence, a norm of, 56–61, 308

profit function, 82

profit margin, 50, 119, 273, 304, 306
average, 292
growth-maximising, 241
in micro-model (1), 235–8, 240–1, 248, 249

profit margin variables, 291

profit motive, in traditional capitalism, 90

profit rate
growth rate of demand and, 5, 41, 279, 281; in micro-model (2), 250, 251, 256, 263, 264
'optimum', 244, 245, 251
retention ratio and, 287, 288
utility functions and, 258, 261
see also profits, rate of return

profitability
bonus schemes and, 68–9
curve of, for a product, 184
growth rate of capacity and, 249
growth rate of demand and, 42, 175–86; in micro-models (1), 224, 226, 227; (2), 250, 253
index of, for new product, 181, 182, 183, 185
maximum, 256, 257
salaries and, 84, 86, 88,
other references, 109, 119, 126, 245, 253–4

profits, defined xvii
age of product and, 184
managers and, 16, 50, 277
maximisation of, 2, 5, 10, 72, 77, 88–89, 102, 104, 110, 114, 119, 170, 176
minimum, as constraint on turnover, 50, 276
percentage of, paid out interest, 66; in salaries, 67, 76
rate of change of, 275
ratio of, to national income, 292, 293, 294, 296, 305, 306, 307, 309; to output, 228, 229
supply of capital and, 223
volume and, 176, 177, 179
wages and, 294, 298

see also profit rate, etc., profitability, return (rate of)

Protestantism, and capitalism, 10

psychology
of biases for and against products, 60
of managers, 49–51, 60
of traditional capitalism, 11

Puritans, 10

pyramid, in administrative structure, 91–2, 93–4

regression analysis
in neo-classical model, 83–4, 98
in studies of: electricity supply concerns, 222; food and machinery firms, 277–88; managers' incomes, 67

rentiers, 13, 21, 308

research, *see* development and research, market research

responsibility, and income, 93–7, 100, 102

restraints, *see* constraints

retention ratio, defined xviii
aggregate, 293–6
growth rate and, 213, 278–86 *passim*
growth rate of gross assets and, 277
managers' remuneration and, 73–7
market rate of discount and, *see* discount
in micro-models (1), 225, 235–7, 247, 248; (2), 256, 265
profit rate and, 287, 288
rate of return and, 213, 278–86 *passim*
stock-market and, 20, 22–9, 208–10, 221, 222
supply of capital and, 213–8
take-over and, 31–43 *passim*
valuation ratio and, 295

retentions (retained earnings), defined xviii
growth by, 69, 207, 213
management policy on, 208, 216, 307

return, rate of
demand curve and, 254, 257, 292
development of demand and, 170, 180–4, 186, 188, 193, 196, 199
diversification rate and, 183, 184, 253

growth rate of capacity and, *see* capacity

growth rate of gross assets and, 278–88 *passim*

internal, defined xviii; 208, 209, 210, 218

managers' remuneration and, 68, 69, 70, 73, 75, 98

market rate of discount and, *see* discount

maximisation of, 70, 82, 178, 224

in micro-models (1), 227, 228, 230, 235, 236, 241; (2), 250, 253, 254, 257

optimum, 241

price of shares and, 221

retention ratio and, 213, 278–86 *passim*

satisficing and, 268, 269, 281

size of firm and, 50

stock-market and, 22–9

supply of capital and, 204, 205, 208, 209, 213, 217, 220, 221

take-over and, 31–43 *passim*

target, 275, 276, 277

return discrepancy, 24–7, 36–9, 42, 73, 75–7, 209–10, 215, 218, 286

return discrepancy ratio, 24, 75

revolution, managerial, 1, 51, 308

risk

carrying of, in traditional capitalism, 3–4

spreading of, 206

stock-market and, 22, 212, 214, 215

see also take-over (risk of)

salaries, of managers, 48, 64, 66, 70, 73, 78–87, 90, 260

'bureconic' theory of, 92–9; policy implications of, 99–101 in neo-classical model, 78–85; revised, 85–9

as percentage of profits, 67, 76

see also income

sanctions, 16, 55

satisficing, 5, 107–9, 111, 266–77

satisficing behaviour, 128, 211, 258, 264, 279, 281

satisficing models, 247

saturation of demand (of market), defined 163; 125, 164, 184, 185, 192, 226, 228, 251, 300

prices after, 175–8

saving

by firm, 128

marginal propensity to, 299

national propensity to, 265, 293, 294, 295, 299, 305, 307

personal, 107, 293, 298, 300, 304

scale

constraints on, in traditional capitalism, 4, 6

diseconomies of, 114, 117, 125, 180

economies of, 10, 117, 177, 183

returns to, 81, 86, 117

satisfactions associated with, 46

see also size of firm

scanning mechanism of brain, 137–8

security

as constraint on growth rate, 208, 226–34, 236, 242, 243, 244, 247, 259, 264–5, 269, 273, 278

and growth rate, 48, 107, 248, 260, 263, 279, 305

of managers, 47, 62–4, 103, 105, 306

selling, selective, 144, 164, 170

see also marketing

'sensitivity', in development of demand, 167, 168

services, traditional capitalism in, 289

shareholders (stockholders), 9, 12–18, 46, 112, 258, 276, 304

committee of, in neo-classical model of firm, 78–9, 87, 88, 102

managers and, 54–5, 68, 69, 72–3, 75, 77, 206, 207, 248, 277, 308

maximisation of welfare (utility) of, 5, 72, 78, 261, 268, 286

new issues and, 25–7

stock-options and, 71–2

take-over and, 30

voting rights of, 12, 20, 29, 45

shares (stocks), 12

held by managers, 18, 54, 72, 73–7

par value of, defined xviii; rate of growth of, *see* new issue rate

prices of, 18–30, 35, 54, 107, 177, 205–6, 207, 213, 221, 253, 269; *see also* stock market value, valuation ratio

restraints on information about, 210–11, 215

transferability of, 18

see also new issues

'sheep' consumers, 142–5, 147, 169, 174

'sheep-like' demand functions, defined 161; 172–5, 176

Simon ('bureconic') theory of salaries, 89–99

size of firm, defined 130; 28, 39, 113–114, 117–19
  bonus schemes and, 68–9
  capacity to innovate and, 183
  distribution of, 40, 247, 263–4
  limits of, 7, 9
  managers and, 63, 80, 104, 105, 176
  managers' salaries and, 74, 85–9, 96, 98
  'optimum', 85
  see also scale

socialism, 40
  managerial, 2

socio-economic contact between consumers, see contact

'stagnation, secular', 301

statics, comparative, 125, 127, 135

status, 66, 105, 156
  and income, 78, 92, 93, 106
  see also class, social

stockholders, stocks, see shareholders, shares

stock-market, 18–29, 46, 76, 276
  approval or disapproval of, 24, 254, 260, 262
  behaviour of, 66, 77, 235; equations of, 209, 216, 234, 235
  conditions on, 220, 237, 245, 285

(stock-)market value of a firm, defined xviii; 18, 22, 28, 29, 219–20, 254, 308
  maximisation of, 55, 79, 261, 288

stock-option schemes, 66, 67, 70–8, 265

stratification, see market population

success of new products, 131
  probability of, 186, 230
  ratio of, 129, 243, 251, 292, 300

supply of capital, 204–23, 224, 278, 308

supply curves, 204, 205, 220, 252, 253; see also iso-valuation lines

supply function, 35, 36, 39

supply-growth function, 242

take-over, 29–45, 55
  fear of, 54, 75, 103, 207, 248, 262, 306
  growth rate and, 65, 122, 259, 272

risk (probability) of, 17, 64, 66, 260, 262, 263, 270, 292, 293
  share prices and, 19–20

taxation, xvii, 10, 71

technical innovation, 141, 299

technical progress, 126, 128, 129, 296, 299, 302
  and chain reactions, 158, 159
  and diversification, 124, 126, 298–9, 302

technical progress function, 297

television sets, sale of, and grouping of customers, 201

'threat' (of commercial war), growth by, 197–200

threshold stimulus, in development of demand, 161, 162, 163, 165, 166, 167, 169, 173

thrift
  fully restricted, 303–6
  partly restricted, 306–8
  see also saving

'transfer mechanism', generalisation of, 45

transformation curve, 261, 267, 305

transformation function, 66, 248

turnover, maximisation of, 50, 119, 276

U.K. (United Kingdom)
  case histories, etc., from, 140–1, 147, 222
  dispersion of shareholdings in, 17–18
  'gearing' in, 66
  government economic policy in, 232
  laws of, 4, 17, 27
  status in, 54, 105
  taxation in, xvii

under-developed countries, 305

unemployment, 305

universities, departmental structure of, 91, 111

U.S. (United States)
  corporation officers in, 14, 76, 80, 97
  dispersion of shareholdings in, 17–18
  econometric studies from 277–88
  'gearing' in, 66
  growth rate of firms in, 121, 125, 301
  laws of, 17, 27, 70, 72

status in, 92, 105, 106
taxation in, xvii
U.S.S.R. (Soviet Union), 91, 93
utility, 5, 15
  consumers', 106, 262
  managers', 5, 19, 45, 47, 64–6, 105–
    107, 171, 176, 258, 308; maximi-
    sation of, 5, 118, 179, 260–5, 268,
    278, 303, 305, 306
  shareholders', maximisation of, 5,
    72, 78, 261, 268, 286
  in traditional capitalism, 5, 6, 7, 10,
    11, 171, 261
utility functions, 11, 15
  consumers', 262
  managers', xi, 18, 48, 54, 258, 262,
    265, 269, 270, 306, 310;
  maximisation of, 301
  shareholders', 211, 258
  total and partial, 291, 293
  in traditional capitalism, 261

valuation (stock-market), theory of,
  18–22, 208–10
valuation curves, 254–63, 270, 286,
  291, 292, 295, 296, 304, 306, 310
valuation ratio, defined xviii, 22
  constraint on, 44–5, 73, 205, 206,
    216, 217, 219–20, 237, 252, 253,
    259
  'gearing' and, 207–8, 222
  growth rate and, 220, 270
  managerial motives and, 48, 55, 65,
    77, 102, 107

maximisation of, 254, 256, 257, 261,
  287, 295, 296
  in micro-models (1), 226, 235–7,
    245, 246, 247; (2), 252, 253, 258,
    259, 260, 263
  minimum, 55, 77, 206, 243, 263,
    272, 274, 306
  retention ratio and, 295
  satisficing and, 269, 281
  stock-market and, 23–8
  supply of capital and, 207, 208, 210,
    213, 218, 227, 223
  take-over and, 30–8 *passim*, 44–5,
    293
value, see assets (net), book value of;
  stock-market value
volume (of sales), 118, 171, 176, 177,
  178, 179, 249
  maximisation of, 170
voting rights, of shareholders, 12, 20,
  29, 45

wages
  and general level of prices, 126, 128,
    291, 292, 304, 309, 310
  and profits, 294, 298
wants, creation of, 137–42, 299
washing powders, as example of static
  market, 193
work, satisfactions of, 61–3
workers, manual, 46, 60, 62
  and managerial revolution, 308, 309
  saving by, 298
working classes, 92, 100

LIST OF EQUATIONS

THE following list reproduces all equations except those in Chapter 4. They are printed in numerical order, together with an indication of the page where first stated.

CHAPTER I

(1.1) $C^{*\cdot}=p\left(1-\dfrac{i}{p}\cdot\bar{g}\right)\Big/(1-\bar{g})$ 9

(1.2) $k=y+z$ 21

(1.3) $y=k-r\cdot p'$ 22

(1.4) $y=\dfrac{p'}{v}(1-r)$ 22

(1.5) $p'\cdot\left(\dfrac{1-r}{v}+r\right)=k$ 22

(1.6) $v=(1-r)\Big/\left(\dfrac{k}{p'}-r\right)=\dfrac{1-r}{1-r+\pi}$ 23

(1.7) $\dfrac{\varDelta\$}{\$}=\dfrac{\varDelta C}{C}\left(\dfrac{\rho-k}{k}\right)$ 25

(1.8) $\mathrm{Max}\left[\dfrac{\varDelta C}{C}\right]=\dfrac{k}{k-\rho}$ 26

(1.9) $\lim v=\dfrac{1-r}{1-r+\pi}$ 28

(1.10) $k_{ij}=f_j(T_{ij})$ 35

(1.11) $v_{ij}=\dfrac{p_{ij}}{k_{ij}}$ 35

(1.12) $v_{ij}=\dfrac{T_{ij}}{C_i}$ 35

(1.13) $k_{ij}(0)=f_j(C_i)$ 36

(1.14) $v_{im}>v_{ij}$ 36

(1.15) $\quad v_{im} = \dfrac{1 - r_{ii}}{1 - r_{ii} + \pi_{ii}}.$

 36

(1.16) $\quad$ Max safe $r_{ii} = \dfrac{q_j - q_i}{q_j(1 - q_i)}$

 37

(1.17) $\quad D_{ii}^{\cdot} = D(p_{ii})$

 41

(1.18) $\quad C_{ii}^{\cdot} = r_{ii} \cdot p_{ii}$

 41

(1.19) $\quad C_{ii} = D_{ii}^{\cdot}$

 41

(1.20) $\quad r_{ii} = \dfrac{D(p_{ii})}{p_{ii}}$

 41

CHAPTER 2

(2.1) $\quad W_1 = \dfrac{C \cdot f \cdot (1 - r)}{1 - r + \pi}$

 74

(2.1a) $\quad S^{\cdot} = \beta C^{\cdot} = \beta \cdot r \cdot p$

 74

(2.2) $\quad W_2 = \dfrac{C \cdot s}{1 - \beta r + \pi}$

 74

(2.3) $\quad W = W_1 + W_2$

 75

(2.4) $\quad \dfrac{s}{f} < \dfrac{\beta}{\pi}$

 75

(2.5) $\quad P = \alpha \cdot S^{\kappa} \cdot C^{1-\kappa} - S$

 82

(2.6) $\quad S_{(p)}^{*} = C \cdot \sigma_1$

 82

(2.7) $\quad p^{*} = \sigma_1 \cdot \sigma_2$

 82

(2.8) $\quad S_{(p)}^{*} = \dfrac{C \cdot p^{*}}{\sigma_2}$, or, $\dfrac{S_{(p)}^{*}}{C \cdot p} = 1/\sigma_2$

 82

(2.9) $\quad \log S = a + b_1 \log C + b_2 \log p$

 83

(2.10) $\quad \log Y = a + b_1 \log X_1 + b_2 \log X_2$

 83

(2.11) $\quad P = \alpha \cdot C \cdot \mu - S$

 86

(2.12) $\quad \bar{S} = \gamma \cdot C^{\beta}$

 86

(2.13) $\quad p^{*} = \alpha - \gamma \cdot C^{\beta-1}$

 86

(2.14) $\quad \dfrac{\delta p^{*}}{\delta C} = \dfrac{\gamma}{C^2}$

 86

(2.15) $h_L \simeq x_L^\beta$ 95

(2.16) $Y_T = Y_0 \cdot E_0^\beta$ 95

(2.17) $Y_L = Y_0 \cdot R_L^\beta$ 95

CHAPTER 5

(5.1) $C^{\cdot} = r \cdot \dfrac{(p - i \cdot g)}{1 - g} + N^{\cdot} \cdot v$ 206

(5.2) $\bar{p} = \dfrac{p - i \cdot \bar{g}}{1 - \bar{g}}$ 208

(5.3) $C^{\cdot} = r\bar{p} + v \cdot N^{\cdot}$ 208

(5.4) $v = (1 - r) \Big/ \left(\dfrac{k}{\bar{p}} - r \right)$ 209

(5.5) $k = \alpha_1 + \alpha_2 \cdot N^{\cdot} + \alpha_3 \cdot r^2$ 216

(5.6) $k = \bar{p}$ 217

(5.7) $\alpha_1 + \alpha_2 \cdot N^{\cdot} + \alpha_3 \cdot r^2 = \bar{p}$ 217

(5.8) $C^{\cdot} = r \cdot \bar{p} + N^{\cdot}$ 217

(5.9) $r^{*}_{(C^{\cdot})} = \dfrac{\bar{p}}{2} \cdot \dfrac{\alpha_2}{\alpha_3}$ 217

(5.10) $N^{*\cdot}_{(C^{\cdot})} = \dfrac{\bar{p} - \alpha_1}{\alpha_2} - \dfrac{\bar{p}}{2} \cdot r^{*}_{(C^{\cdot})}$ 217

(5.11) $C^{*\cdot} = N^{*\cdot}_{(C^{\cdot})} + \bar{p} \cdot r^{*}_{(C^{\cdot})}$ 217

(5.12) $C^{*\cdot} = \dfrac{\bar{p} - \alpha_1}{\alpha_2} + \dfrac{\bar{p}^2}{4} \cdot \dfrac{\alpha_2}{\alpha_3}$ 218

(5.13) $C^{*\cdot} \simeq \dfrac{\bar{p} - \alpha_1}{\alpha_2}$ 218

(5.14) $C^{*\cdot} \simeq \dfrac{p - i \cdot \bar{g}}{\alpha_2 (1 - \bar{g})} - \dfrac{\alpha_1}{a_2}$ 218

(5.15) $C^{*\cdot} = \alpha \cdot p - \beta$ 219

(5.16) $\alpha \equiv \dfrac{1}{\alpha_2 \cdot (1 - \bar{g})}$ 219

(5.17) $\quad \beta \equiv \dfrac{1}{\alpha_2}\left(\dfrac{\bar{g}}{1-\bar{g}}+\alpha_1\right)$ 219

(5.18) $\quad C^{*\cdot}=\dfrac{\bar{p}-\alpha_1 \cdot \bar{v}}{\alpha_2}+\dfrac{\bar{p}^2}{4}\cdot\dfrac{\alpha_2}{\alpha_3}\cdot Q^2$ 219

(5.19) $\quad Q \equiv 1 + \dfrac{\bar{v}-1}{\alpha_2}$ 219

(5.20) $\quad Z=\dfrac{\bar{p}^2}{4}-\dfrac{\alpha_1}{\alpha_2}$ 220

(5.21) $\quad \bar{p}<2\cdot\surd(\alpha_1\cdot\alpha_2)$ 220

(5.22) $\quad C^{*\cdot}\simeq\alpha\cdot p-\beta\bar{v}$ 220

CHAPTER 6

(6.1) $\quad D^{\cdot}=D(d, m)$ 234

(6.2) $\quad C^{\cdot}=r\cdot p'+N^{\cdot}v$ 234

(6.3) $\quad p'=\left(\dfrac{m}{c}-ig\right)\Big/(1-g)$ 234

(6.4) $\quad c=c(d)$ 234

(6.5) $\quad v=(1-r)\Big/\left(\dfrac{k}{p'}-r\right)$ 234

(6.6) $\quad k=\alpha_1+\alpha_2\cdot N^{\cdot}+\alpha_3\cdot r^2$ 234

(6.7) $\quad v\geqslant\bar{v}$ 235

(6.8) $\quad g\leqslant\bar{g}$ 235

(6.9) $\quad C^{\cdot}=D^{\cdot}$ 235

(6.10) $\quad C^{*\cdot}=\alpha\cdot p-\beta v$ 237

(6.11) $\quad D^{\cdot}=D(d, m)$ 237

(6.12) $\quad C^{*\cdot}=\alpha\dfrac{m}{c}-\beta\bar{v}$ 237

(6.13) $\quad c=c(d)$ 237

(6.14) $\quad C^{*\cdot}=D^{\cdot}$ 237

(6.15) $\quad C^{*\cdot}=C^{\cdot}(d, m)$ 238

(6.16) $C(d, m) = D(d, m)$ 238

(6.17) $C^{**} = f(d)$ 238

(6.18) $D = (1 - m) \cdot f_D(d)$ 241

(6.19) $C^{**} = \alpha_S \cdot m \cdot f_C(d) - \beta_S \cdot \bar{v}$ 241

(6.20) $C^{**} = \left(\dfrac{f_C}{f_D} \cdot \dfrac{\delta D^{\cdot}}{\delta C^{**}} \right) \div \left(1 + \dfrac{\delta D^{\cdot}}{\delta C^{**}} \right)$ 242

(6.21) $\dfrac{\delta D^{\cdot}}{\delta C^{**}} = \dfrac{\delta D^{\cdot}}{\delta d} \cdot \dfrac{\delta d}{\delta C^{**}}$ 242

$= \dfrac{(1 - m) \cdot f_D'}{m \cdot f_C'}$

(6.22) $f_D = \dfrac{\alpha_D \cdot d}{1 + \beta_D \cdot d}$ 242

(6.23) $f_C = \dfrac{1}{c_0} \left(1 - \alpha_C \cdot d^{\beta_C} \right)$ 242

(6.24) $F_d \equiv d \Big/ \left(1 - \alpha_C \cdot d^{\beta_C} \right)^2$ 242

(6.25) $F_d \simeq \left(\dfrac{\alpha_S}{\alpha_C \cdot \alpha_D \cdot \beta_C \cdot c_0} \right)^{\left(\frac{1}{1 + \beta_C} \right)}$ 242

(6.26) $C^{***} = \dfrac{1}{\dfrac{1}{\alpha_S \cdot f_C^{*}} + \dfrac{1}{f_D^{*}}} - \dfrac{\beta_S \bar{v}}{1 + \alpha_S \cdot \dfrac{f_C^{*}}{f_D}}$ 244

(6.27) $p^{*} = \dfrac{1}{\alpha_S} (C^{***} - \beta_S \bar{v})$ 244

(6.28) $p^{*} = \left[1 \Big/ \left(\dfrac{1}{f_C} + \dfrac{\alpha_S}{f_D} \right) \right] + \left(\beta_S \cdot \bar{v} \Big/ \alpha_S \cdot \dfrac{f_D}{f_C} \right)$ 244

(6.29) $p = \gamma_1 + \gamma_2 C^{\cdot} - \gamma_3 C^{\cdot 2}$ 252

(6.30) $v = \dfrac{1}{\beta_S} (\alpha_S \cdot p - C^{\cdot})$ 254

(6.31) $p = p(D^{\cdot}) = p(C^{\cdot})$ 254

(6.32) $v = \dfrac{1}{\beta_S} [\alpha_S \cdot p(C^{\cdot}) - C^{\cdot}]$ 255

(6.33) $\quad v = \dfrac{1}{\beta_S}[C^{\bullet} \cdot (\alpha_S \cdot \gamma_3 - 1) - C^{\bullet 2} \cdot \alpha_S \cdot \gamma_3 + \alpha_S \cdot \gamma_1]$ 256

(6.34) $\quad C^{*\bullet}_{(v)} = \left(\gamma_2 - \dfrac{1}{\alpha_S}\right)\Big/ 2\gamma_3$ 256

(6.35) $\quad C^{*\bullet}_{(p)} = \dfrac{\gamma_2}{2\gamma_3}$ 256

(6.36) $\quad U = U(C^{\bullet}, v)$ 260

GLOSSARY OF FREQUENTLY
RECURRING SYMBOLS

Note: This glossary excludes symbols used in Chapter 4 (for these, see p. 202), symbols used only in proximity to page where first defined, and Greek-letter coefficients whose definition changes (see Note on Concepts and Definitions, p. xv).

Symbol	Short definition	Page first defined
c	capital-output ratio	228
C	gross capital	xvii
$C^{\bullet}$	growth rate of C	xvi
$D^{\bullet}$	growth rate of demand	119
g	gearing (leverage) ratio	xvii
$\bar{g}$	constrained max g	9
i	interest rate	9
k	rate of discount	21
k_{ij}	raider j's discount rate for firm i	35
m	profit margin	228
N	aggregate par value	xviii
$N^{\bullet}$	growth rate of N	xvi
p	rate of return	xviii
p'	net rate of return, $[=(p-ig)/(1-g)]$	xviii
$\bar{p}$	p' when $g=\bar{g}$,	208
π	$=(k-p')/p'$	23
r	retention ratio	xviii
v	valuation ratio	22
v'_{ij}	raider j's effective v for firm i	35
$\bar{v}$	constrained min v	219